# One Body in Christ

## *The History and Significance of the Evangelical Alliance*

Ian Randall
&
David Hilborn

First published in 2001 by Evangelical Alliance and Paternoster Press

07 06 05 04 03 02 01    7 6 5 4 3 2 1

Paternoster Press is an imprint of Paternoster Publishing,
PO Box 300, Carlisle, Cumbria, CA3 0QS, UK
and Paternoster Publishing USA
PO Box 1047, Waynesboro, GA 30830-2047, USA
Website: www.paternoster-publishing.com

**British Library Cataloguing in Publication Data**
A catalogue record for this book is available from the British Library

ISBN 1-84227-089-3

Cover design by Campsie, Glasgow
Typeset by WestKey Ltd., Falmouth, Cornwall
Printed in Great Britain by
Cox and Wyman, Cardiff Road, Reading

# Contents

# Preface

Despite growing scholarly interest in the history of evangelicalism, the formation and development of the Evangelical
Alliance has been remarkably little studied. As we make clear in
the following book, while some in recent times have sought to
establish the Alliance's significance through journal articles
and the occasional monograph, others have treated it as little
more than a footnote, not only to modern Western church
history in general, but to the history of evangelicalism in particular. While in some cases there may have been ideological
motives for this marginalisation, we suspect that the more
common reason has been lack of access to the Alliance's extensive archive of minutes, reports, papers and photographs. For
many years, these valuable primary sources have been kept in
storage, and have remained effectively outside the orbit of
scholarship. For this project, however, we have thoroughly
re-organised the relevant material and have made considerable
use of it. As we have done so, it has become clear that the development of the Alliance over the last 155 years represents a
fascinating and important indicator of wider theological,
ecclesiastical and cultural developments.

As we shall see, the founders of the Alliance conceived it as a
thoroughly international body, but soon found themselves
having to devolve a considerable degree of power and autonomy to national organisations. Our focus here is very clearly on

the British/UK Alliance, but we have tried to set this body within the contexts of European and worldwide evangelicalism, and have sought to relate its history to broader social and historical trends. As such, we trust that we have not only done justice to our subject, but have opened up fresh avenues for others to explore.

The composition of the book has been very much a shared enterprise. We each originally drafted particular sections alone, Ian Randall taking responsibility for Chapters 1, 2, 3, 6, 7, 8, 9, 10, 11 and 12, and David Hilborn for Chapters 4, 5, 13 and 14. We must emphasise, however, that we then reviewed what the other had written and, where appropriate, revised it. Taking account of comments made by other readers, we subsequently agreed the full text that appears here. As such, the two of us, and the two of us only, take joint responsibility for any errors that have remained.

There are several people who deserve thanks for helping to make this project possible. It will become clear that while we have expanded considerably upon them, the texts written on the Alliance by J.W. Ewing in 1946 and by J.B.A. Kessler in 1968 served as invaluable markers for our investigation. Subsequently, a great deal of painstaking analytical work on the earlier archive materials was conducted by Clive Calver when General Director of the Alliance in the 1990s. Although this research never developed into the thesis Clive had originally planned, it has not gone to waste: the clarity and orderliness of his notes have served us exceptionally well here, as has his generosity in giving us access to them. We are also grateful to Clive's PA at World Relief, Barbara Elwell, for organising the safe dispatch of these materials from Wheaton. Kenneth Hylson-Smith, Steve Brady and Peter Lewis also contributed very useful papers on the Alliance's history to the book *For Such a Time as This*, which was published in connection with the Alliance's 150th anniversary in 1996. Our debt to these papers will be clear, and has been acknowledged in the notes.

Various past and present Alliance leaders have offered their reflections and comments. Gilbert Kirby and Maurice Rowlandson supplied us with illuminating background material, and helped to clarify a number of uncertainties and ambiguities. Robert Amess, Colin Saunders and Mark Birchall supplied helpful advice on the more recent history. In addition, the following people performed the vital task of acting as readers for the book, and we are indebted to them for the constructive feedback they offered: David Bebbington, Mark Birchall, Steve Brady, Kenneth Hylson-Smith, Tony Lane, Peter Lewis, Rob Warner, John Wolffe and David Wright. Thanks are also due to the Steering Group of the Alliance Commission on Unity and Truth among Evangelicals, for their support and encouragement throughout the project. Keith Jones at the International Baptist Theological Seminary in Prague, and Nigel Wright and Judy Powles at Spurgeon's College offered valuable help. Carolyn Skinner, Maggie Harding, Phil Seager, Adam Sparks and John Smith at the Evangelical Alliance have all provided help and encouragement at crucial times. We are also very grateful that, despite a very busy schedule, Joel Edwards has written the Foreword. We offer this book as a positive contribution to Joel's and the Alliance's vision of becoming a movement for change. As ever, the staff at Paternoster have been most supportive – Mark Finnie, Peter Little and Jill Morris have shown real enthusiasm from the outset, while Tony Graham has served us admirably as editor.

Finally, we would like to thank our wives, Janice Randall and Mia Hilborn, and our families, for their continued support.

Material in chapter 9 previously appeared in Ian Randall's article 'Conservative Constructionist: The Early Influence of Billy Graham in Britain', published in *The Evangelical Quarterly*, Vol. 67, No. 4 (1995). We are grateful to the editor of *EQ*, Howard Marshall, for granting permission to use this. Certain sections of chapter 13 draw closely on material previously

published by ACUTE – the Alliance Commission on Unity
and Truth among Evangelicals.

**Ian Randall**,
Director of Baptist and Anabaptist Studies,
International Baptist Theological Seminary,
Prague
Lecturer in Church History,
Spurgeon's College,
London

**David Hilborn**,
Theological Adviser,
Evangelical Alliance (UK),
Associate Research Fellow,
London Bible College,
London,

July 2001

# Foreword

When the founders of the Evangelical Alliance met in 1846 it was a most unlikely event. For the first time in Britain, Established churchmen came together in visible, organisational union with Nonconformists. In one sense, it should not have happened. But there were some compelling factors that caused them to overcome their historic differences and antipathies. They crossed ecclesiastical and cultural boundaries to forge a new trans-denominational identity. In effect, they became the first ecumenical movement.

As they met they were only too aware that the Bible and its truth claims were coming under threat. Secularism was already taking its toll and new scientific discoveries were leading many to present formidable challenges to historic Christian faith. Rather than being content to remain an essentially symbolic, 'do-nothing' organisation, the Alliance resolved both to meet these challenges and to offer constructive ways forward. As this study shows, it committed itself in the first instance particularly to national prayer and the active defence of religious liberties. As far as its Victorian supporters were concerned, evangelicalism needed to offer more than a reaction to the world; it was meant to add value to it.

When members and friends of the Evangelical Alliance met in 1996 to celebrate 150 years of its history one thing became very clear. Throughout the ups and downs of its distinguished past, a consistent thread had remained evident: the Evangelical Alliance had always been at its best when actively involved in the world, as a movement for change.

This welcome history of the Evangelical Alliance comes to us at an opportune moment. In one sense little has changed. The battle for biblical truth is still very much with us – and is, if anything, fiercer now than our evangelical forebears might have anticipated. More than ever, twenty-first century evangelicalism is faced with the challenge of combining our faith in the apostolic gospel with a united effort to transform society.

Ian Randall's and David Hilborn's refreshing new study will remind today's evangelicals of where we have come from and the lessons which have been learned along the way. My prayer is that it will also guide us into the future as we continue to become a movement for change.

Joel Edwards
July 2001

1

# A Broadly Based Religious Force

*The Evangelical Alliance and Modern British Church History*

From its beginnings in 1846 the Evangelical Alliance had as its motto '*Unum Corpus Sumus in Christo*': 'We are One Body in Christ'. The concern for unity expressed in this motif has remained a hallmark of the Alliance's identity and purpose ever since. Five prominent representatives of the mainline Protestant denominations in Britain – Edward Bickersteth (Anglican), Jabez Bunting (Wesleyan Methodist), James Hamilton (Presbyterian), John Leifchild (Congregational) and Edward Steane (Baptist) – signed a letter dated 10 November 1845 that encouraged participation in a proposed alliance of evangelicals.[1] As this alliance took shape, another of its advocates, David King, the Scottish Presbyterian, observed a common concern that it should adopt an inclusive approach and thereby exhibit 'catholicity'.[2] As we shall see, this ideal has been strained from time to time as certain evangelicals have questioned whether the Alliance has sufficiently represented their own views. The achievement of the Alliance, however, has been to draw together so many who have differed on important issues, but who have nonetheless taken their shared evangelical convictions to be a positive basis for co-operation.

1 'Proposed Evangelical Alliance', 10 November 1845. This letter is held with the Minutes of the Provisional Committee meeting in London, 1845.
2 *The Congregational Magazine* 9 (1845), pp.775-6.

D.W. Bebbington's seminal 1989 work, *Evangelicalism in Modern Britain*, explores these convictions in detail. Bebbington concludes that evangelicalism is a Christian movement distinguished by its adherents' emphasis on four key points: the authority of the Bible, the centrality of the cross of Christ, personal conversion and Christian activism.[3] The study will examine how those holding to these convictions have sought to express them through the Evangelical Alliance, and how, in so doing, they have exemplified a distinctively evangelical vision of 'oneness in Christ'.

## The Alliance in Context

Like any religious movement, the Evangelical Alliance has been shaped by its context. During its formative period this context was Victorian Britain – a society that is generally accepted to have had religion at its heart. But what kind of religion was it that obtained popular acceptance during this period? In his 1966 book *The Victorian Church*, Owen Chadwick concluded that throughout the mid-Victorian era 'the evangelical movement was the strongest religious force in British life'.[4] Writing a decade later, Ian Bradley pointed out that historians were generally agreed that evangelicalism had been 'one of the most important forces at work in shaping the character of the Victorians'.[5] In 1994, John Wolffe, in *God and Greater Britain*, described the evangelical movement in the opening decades of Victoria's reign as 'a dynamic and broadly based religious force, combining spiritual energy, institutional diversity and cultural sensitivity'.[6] As we shall see, the challenge

---

3  D.W. Bebbington, *Evangelicalism in Modern Britain: A History from the 1730s to the 1980s* (London: Unwin Hyman, 1989), pp.2-17.

4  See O. Chadwick, *The Victorian Church*, Part 1 (London: A. & C. Black, 1966), p.5.

5  I. Bradley, *The Call to Seriousness* (London: Jonathan Cape, 1976), p.14.

6  J. Wolffe, *God and Greater Britain: Religion and National Life in Britain and Ireland 1843-1945* (London: Routledge, 1994), p.30.

to those who were committed to the success of an alliance of evangelicals was to achieve a significant degree of unity against a background of denominational diversity, and even of interdenominational hostility.

The most pressing challenge faced by the Alliance's founders was the achievement of co-operation between Anglicans and Dissenters. Anglicans feared the growing interest among nineteenth-century Dissenters in the possibility of the disestablishment of the Church of England. Owen Chadwick overstates the case when he talks about 'the stink of disestablishment' in Evangelical Alliance speeches,[7] but the Alliance's advocacy of interdenominational activity did appear as an unwelcome provocation to those who were committed to the ecclesiastical status quo. Certainly, the Evangelical Alliance was launched at a time when evangelicals were enjoying significant gains within the Church of England. Although the first evangelical bishop of the modern era was arguably not appointed until 1815 – when Henry Ryder became bishop of Gloucester – by 1848 the evangelical John Bird Sumner had been appointed Archbishop of Canterbury. From 1800 to mid-century the proportion of evangelical clergy in England grew significantly and with Sumner as primate a moderate Anglican evangelicalism came to occupy a central position in the life of the established church.[8] With their attention focused on ecclesiastical advance, many Anglican evangelicals were not so attracted by the possibilities of interdenominational evangelical co-operation.

The degree of support for the Evangelical Alliance was greater among English Dissenting denominations (increasingly known in the nineteenth century as the Nonconformists and in the twentieth as the Free Churches). It was also strong among Scottish Presbyterians who operated outside the Church of Scotland. Indeed, the early leaders of the

7  Chadwick, *Victorian Church*, p.441.

8  N. Scotland, *John Bird Sumner: Evangelical Archbishop* (Leominster: Gracewing, 1995), pp.105-7.

Alliance were largely Nonconformists.[9] However, this was a
period when Nonconformists and Anglicans were uniting in
philanthropic enterprises.[10] The significance of the pan–evangelical initiatives that began in the nineteenth century and
which have continued to bear influence up to the present is
well demonstrated by Donald Lewis. In *Lighten Their Darkness,* Lewis has contributed an outstanding study of evangelical mission to working-class London from 1828 to 1860.[11]
Another factor drawing evangelicals together, and indeed one
clear motive for the formation of the Alliance, was anti-Catholicism. It must be stressed, however, that the strength of
this motive was hardly unusual for the time. Evangelicals were
very much in tune with the wider suspicion of Rome that
prevailed in mid-century Protestant Victorian England – a
suspicion that had been given greater intensity by Catholic
emancipation of 1829.[12] This, as much as philanthropy, was
viewed by its proponents as expressing common concern for
the nation's social and religious well being, and, as we shall
see, it undoubtedly convinced many Nonconformists and
Anglicans that united action was both possible and worthwhile.

For all evangelicals in Britain, whether in the Established or
Free Churches, the twentieth century brought unexpected re-
versals. Indeed, Adrian Hastings suggests in his *History of English Christianity* that by the 1920s, whether in 'vigour of
leadership, intellectual capacity, or largeness of heart', evangelicals had never been weaker.[13] Hastings is thinking mainly of
the Church of England, but the Free Churches were hardly in
better shape. From a membership peak in 1906, the major Free

9 J.W. Massie, *The Evangelical Alliance: Its Origin and Development* (London, 1847),
p.88.
10 K. Heasman, *Evangelicals in Action* (London: Geoffrey Bles, 1961), pp.27-8.
11 D.M. Lewis, *Lighten Their Darkness: The Evangelical Mission to Working-Class
London, 1828-1860* (Carlisle: Paternoster Press, 2001).
12 J. Wolffe, *The Protestant Crusade in Britain, 1829-1860* (Oxford: Clarendon
Press, 1991).
13 A. Hastings, *A History of English Christianity, 1920-2000* (London: SCM, 2001),
p.200.

Church denominations saw steady decline through the remainder of the twentieth century.[14] Although secularism is often viewed as a phenomenon of the later twentieth century, Jeffrey Cox sees fit to describe the churches in Lambeth in the period 1870 to 1930 under the title *The English Churches in a Secular Society*.[15] There is little doubt that church attendance sharply decreased in many places during the first half of the twentieth century. The assessment offered by Stuart Mews in his survey of the period 1920-40 is that churchgoing slumped in the 1930s, leaving remaining churchgoers 'clinging grimly to selected Victorian beliefs and values, or waiting doggedly for a revival, usually conceived along essentially Victorian lines'.[16] There were those evangelicals who were more open to the future, but this in itself caused division.[17] It is therefore not surprising that in this period the Alliance lost some of the momentum it had enjoyed during the Victorian age.

Fresh energy came, however, after the Second World War. In the late 1960s analyses of new Anglican ordinands showed that the proportion of those trained in the evangelical Anglican colleges had risen from an estimated 10% in the 1950s to over 30%. Moreover, this would exceed 50% three decades later.[18] Yet, after an upturn in the late forties and early fifties, overall churchgoing began to fall markedly; by 2000 the number of younger people with any church connection was tiny in comparison with a hundred years before.[19] Even in 1960 24% of children in Britain attended a Sunday School. In 2000 the

14 R. Currie, A.D. Gilbert & L.S. Horsley, *Churches and Churchgoers: Patterns of Church Growth in the British Isles since 1700* (Oxford: Clarendon Press, 1977), p.34.

15 J. Cox, *The English Churches in a Secular Society: Lambeth, 1870-1930* (New York: Oxford University Press, 1977).

16 S. Mews, 'Religious Life between the Wars, 1920-1940', in S. Gilley & W.J. Sheils (eds), *A History of Religion in Britain* (Oxford: Blackwell, 1994), p.466.

17 I.M. Randall, *Evangelical Experiences: A Study in the Spirituality of English Evangelicalism, 1918-1939* (Carlisle: Paternoster Press, 1999).

18 M. Saward, *The Anglican Church Today: Evangelicals on the Move* (Oxford: Mowbray, 1987), pp.33-4.

19 For an analysis of this trend see C.G. Brown, *The Death of Christian Britain* (London: Routledge, 2001), pp.170-92.

figure was estimated to be just 4%.[20] Yet at the same time there were areas of progress. In many evangelical churches the charismatic movement, which began in the 1960s, was associated with growth. Bebbington speaks about how 'charismatic renewal, a new spirituality for a new age, brought about rejuvenating change'.[21] The renewal movement spurred many evangelicals to open up to other Christian traditions, including Roman Catholicism.[22] It was also in the latter part of the twentieth century that the Alliance was itself rejuvenated.

## The Alliance and Campaigning

From its earliest days the Evangelical Alliance has been a campaigning organisation. As we shall see, some were prompted to form the Alliance in reaction to what they took to be the dangerous resurgence of Roman Catholic influence in Britain. Certain key founders of the Alliance had first co-operated in 1844-45, in protest against government funding of a Catholic seminary in the Irish town of Maynooth. Several others explicitly cast the Alliance as a bulwark against the encroachment of the 'Oxford Movement' – latterly dubbed the 'Anglo-Catholic' movement and led by John Henry Newman and Edward Pusey.[23] Yet it would be wrong to see such anti-Romanism as definitive of the Alliance's ethos. Indeed, it is significant that the Protestant Alliance was formed in 1851, just five years after the birth of the Alliance, to represent those committed to a more outspoken critique of Rome. There were significant

20  P. Brierley (ed.), *UK Christian Handbook Religious Trends 2000-2001, No. 2* (Eltham/London: Christian Research/Harper Collins, 1999), pp.2, 15.

21  D.W. Bebbington, 'Evangelism and Spirituality in Twentieth-Century Protestant Nonconformity' (forthcoming), p.35.

22  D. Bloesch, *The Future of Evangelical Christianity: A Call for Unity Amid Diversity* (New York: Doubleday, 1983), pp.38-42.

23  J.A. James et al, *Essays on Christian Union* (London: Hamilton, Adams & Co., 1845), 151; E.R. Norman, *Anti-Catholicism in Victorian England* (London: George Allen & Unwin, 1968), p.27; J.B.A. Kessler, *A Study of the Evangelical Alliance in Great Britain* (Goes, Netherlands: Oosterbaan & Le Cointre, 1968), pp.15-6.

Evangelical Alliance voices in favour of a less strident attitude to Catholics. To take one example, at an Evangelical Alliance conference in London in 1851, Norman Macleod, an ardent supporter of the Alliance and a Church of Scotland minister, asked that Roman Catholics should be addressed 'in a spirit of kindness and love'.[24] Count Andreas von Bernstorff, a prominent Alliance figure in Germany in the later nineteenth century, took the view that individual Roman Catholics who wished to join the Alliance should be welcome to do so.[25] It is far from accurate, therefore, to see the Evangelical Alliance's first leaders as united by a common antipathy towards Roman Catholicism. Indeed, in the later nineteenth century it was the growth of Protestant 'infidelity' that would more urgently claim the attention of several Alliance figures – an indication that the organisation's concerns were far broader than anti-Romanism. As we shall see, bigotry was more muted than has often been suggested, and the Alliance was at times prepared robustly to defend the religious rights of Roman Catholics.

As the nineteenth century progressed, it was the effectiveness of evangelical Christian witness in Britain and abroad that became a more central issue for the Alliance. The Alliance sought to foster prayer and study focused on how evangelicals could co-operate to meet the challenge of home mission. From the beginning there was an emphasis on prayer, which led to the Alliance's Worldwide or Universal Week of Prayer, held during the first week of each year. This call to prayer stimulated Christians of many denominations to a deeper awareness of their united witness. Over a period of 60 years the British Alliance also organised annual conferences at which questions concerning the church and society were considered. Issues of social justice were discussed alongside matters of

24 R. Rouse, 'Voluntary Movements and the Changing Ecumenical Climate', in R. Rouse & S.C. Neill (eds), *A History of the Ecumenical Movement 1517-1948* (2nd edn; London: SPCK, 1967 [1954]), p.323.
25 'World Mission Notes', *Evangelical Christendom*, May-June 1934, p.109.

evangelistic strategy. There were also smaller open meetings for
study and debate called 'Conversaziones'. In 1868 a joint committee was set up, which included members of the Alliance
Council and representatives from the London City Mission,
the Open Air Mission, the Evangelisation Society and other
bodies, to consider action to counteract 'secularist errors'.
Members of the committee debated with 'secularist' lecturers
around London and 'united action for the maintenance and
defence of true Christianity' was urged on all branches of the
Alliance.[26]

World mission and international action on social justice featured especially on the agenda of the Alliance's international
conferences. In the nineteenth century, such conferences were
held in Paris (1855), Berlin (1857), Geneva (1861), Amsterdam
(1867), New York (1873), Basle (1879), Copenhagen (1884)
and Florence (1891). All were generously supported by the
British Organisation, which was continually referred to as the
parent body. The British Evangelical Alliance Organisation felt
that it held a position of world leadership by virtue, as was said
in 1886, of the British Empire's influence across the globe – an
influence which ensured that it had 'thousands of members
and its affiliated committees in all parts of the world'.[27] Indeed,
in 1912 the so-called 'Evangelical Alliance (British Organisation)' went so far as to change its name to 'World's Evangelical
Alliance (British Organisation)'. It was in this period that leaders of the British Alliance heard the proposals of Alexander
Duff, the pioneer of university-level Christian educational
work in India, for an International Missionary Conference.[28]
This vision would, however, be taken up by those committed
to the wider ecumenical movement. Alliance internationalism
would move in a different direction with the formation of the
World Evangelical Fellowship in 1951. For its part, the British
Alliance would revert to its original name in 1953.

26  Executive Council Minutes, 9 December 1868; 27 January 1869; 10 February
1869; 27 October 1869; *Evangelical Christendom*, 1868, pp.471-4.
27  Executive Council Minutes, 10 June 1886.
28  Rouse, 'Voluntary Movements', p.322.

Linked with the internationalism of the Alliance has been a concern to defend those facing persecution for their faith. Throughout its history, the Alliance has been committed to upholding the fundamental principles of religious liberty. Cases of religious oppression were often featured in the Alliance's highly informative journal, *Evangelical Christendom*. In 1855, as a direct outcome of resolutions passed at the Paris Conference, Sir Culling Eardley (formerly Sir Culling Eardley Smith), Chairman of several meetings associated with the founding of the Alliance, headed an international group in making representations to the Turkish Sultan appealing for religious freedom. Although spasmodic outbreaks of religious intolerance occurred in the Turkish Empire during subsequent years, a major concession was gained. In 1856 the Sultan declared freedom of religion for all his subjects. Recognising the importance of this issue the Alliance appointed a foreign secretary, Herman Schmettou, during the 1860s.[29] As we shall see in chapter 4, these were just some of the more notable features of a concerted programme of action that saw the Alliance's Executive Council draft memorials and send deputations to numerous governments, in order to secure religious freedom not only for evangelicals, but also for Roman Catholics, Nestorians, Jews and others. As chapter 4 will further make clear, these initiatives have been unduly overlooked by scholars inclined to paint the Alliance as a quietistic body disengaged from socio-political concerns.

At the heart of all these campaigns was the drive for unity. Indeed, so foundational was this concern to the birth and development of the Alliance that some have suggested that it effectively functioned as the first ecumenical body in Great Britain. We have already seen that it undoubtedly brought significant numbers of Anglicans and Nonconformists into a

29  C. Calver, 'The Rise and Fall of the Evangelical Alliance, 1835-1905', in S. Brady & H. Rowdon (eds), *For Such a Time as This: Perspectives on Evangelicalism Past, Present and Future* (London/Milton Keynes: Evangelical Alliance/Scripture Union, 1996), p.155.

deeper relationship with each other in the nineteenth century, and, as Normal Goodall notes, the word 'ecumenical' was actually used within the Alliance to denote its transcendence of national and denominational divisions.[30] An early honorary secretary of the Alliance, John Stoughton, Professor of Church History at the Congregational Hackney College, has been termed 'the prophet of ecumenism amongst Free churchmen'.[31] At the inaugural Alliance conference of 1846, Adolphe Monod of the French Reformed Church spoke of the *esprit vraiment oecumenique* – a comment that appears to have entailed the first recorded instance of the word 'ecumenical' to denote a positive 'attitude' towards the superseding of national and confessional differences.[32] Furthermore, the Alliance welcomed to international conferences observers who were not its own members, which helped to spread ecumenical awareness. In 1873 the Old Catholic Church (which had broken away from the Roman Catholic Church in protest at the decrees of the first Vatican Council in 1870) was invited to a conference and expressed pleasure at the invitation.[33]

Despite all these initiatives, however, J.B.A. Kessler demonstrates in his brief but valuable *Study of the Evangelical Alliance in Great Britain*, that the Alliance has evolved an approach to unity distinct from that which has been developed by the ecumenical movement of the twentieth century. The Alliance began by seeking to establish evangelical unity among individuals rather than church denominations. By contrast, the World Council of Churches (WCC), from its commencement in 1948, has pursued structural and institutional unity between the historic denominations. Yet there have always been those within the Alliance who have been concerned for such organisational

---

30  N. Goodall, *The Ecumenical Movement* (London: Oxford University Press, 1964), p.6.
31  H.R.T. Brandreth, 'Approaches of the Churches Towards Each Other in the Nineteenth Century', in R. Rouse & S.C. Neill (eds), *A History of the Ecumenical Movement*, p.284.
32  Appendix 1 of Rouse & Neill, *A History of the Ecumenical Movement*, p.738.
33  Brandreth, 'Approaches of the Churches', 269, pp.293-4.

unity. The Alliance was represented in Amsterdam when the WCC was formed in 1948. The January–March 1949 issue of *Evangelical Christendom* commented that the WCC appeared to have avoided the dangers of false union outside of the truth, reunion with Rome and any attempt to form a super-church. The Alliance Council stated that the right policy for evangelicals was to avoid opposition to the World Council, but 'carefully and prayerfully to foster that unity of the Spirit, which already exists between all true believers and is something infinitely deeper than the outward form of union which the World Council has brought into being'. The view taken at this time was that if evangelicals opposed the WCC or did not co-operate with it, 'the Modernists or the Ritualists' might capture it, whereas involvement by evangelicals could mean that they might become 'an instrument in the hand of God for reviving the churches'.[34]

## Tracing the History

Overall, this study of the Alliance will focus on themes rather than on personalities. As its history unfolds, it will become clear that the Alliance's fortunes have fluctuated, and that periods of relative strength and weakness have been due to much more than simply the character and ability of a particular leader. Indeed, our aim in this book is to set the development of the Alliance in a broader social and cultural context than has been considered in previous studies. Having said this, it should be acknowledged that the Alliance's pan-evangelicalism has led it to sit relatively light to institutionalised structures, and that this has allowed certain key figures to stamp their individual character and gifting on the organisation in a memorable way. Admittedly, this was not so apparent at the outset: the first official Secretary, Alexander Digby Campbell, made little impact, and although the respected Anglican Edward Bickersteth

---

34  'The Problem of Unity', *Evangelical Christendom*, January–March 1949, p.1.

and the renowned Wesleyan Jabez Bunting worked hard for
the new organisation, they died before it began to grow.[35]
Edward Steane, a Baptist minister, then served as Hon. Secretary, but the time he could give was limited. The Alliance did
make some headway, however, when James Davies was General
Secretary, from 1859 to 1878, and this accelerated while A.J.
Arnold and General Sir John Field held the secretariat. In 1879,
for example, it was reported that 300 new members had been
accepted into the Alliance in the previous year in London
alone and that overall there were more new members than in
any previous year.[36] Alliance annual conferences in Britain
attracted around 1,500 people. In that period the Alliance's
premises were at 7 Adam Street, London. T.D. Harford-
Battersby, the founder in 1875 of the highly influential Keswick Convention, was a member of the Council of the
Alliance. The Alliance summed up its own vision in this
period when in 1883 it commended Harford-Battersby's
'large-hearted, catholic spirit'.[37]

   This progress was halted towards the end of the century. By
1896 Arnold, who had done much to foster international Alliance links, was too old to continue. He died two years later.
The new Secretary was John Field's son Percy, but he could not
work with the Chairman of the Alliance, Lord Kinnaird. Field
was dismissed in 1903 and he subsequently sued the Council of
the Alliance. The matter was finally settled in 1905 when
Field's case was dismissed in the High Court.[38] Henry Martyn
Gooch, aged thirty, whose father, W. Fuller Gooch, was a member of the Alliance Council, took up the secretaryship of the
Alliance in 1904. In 1912, new offices at 19 Russell Square
were purchased. Gooch gave considerable attention to issues of
liberty of conscience. He also fostered the Week of Prayer and
other large prayer gatherings. As an Anglican layman, Gooch

35  Calver, 'Rise and Fall', p.152.
36  *Evangelical Christendom*, January 1879, p.25.
37  *Evangelical Christendom*, September 1883, p.288.
38  The Executive Council Minutes, 1903-5, contain the High Court proceedings.

was keen to draw leading Anglican clergy into the orbit of the Alliance. Stress on the European dimension was a feature of Gooch's period, with his travels taking him to Russia, Poland, Finland, Sweden, Norway, Denmark, Germany, Switzerland, Italy and Malta.[39] The weakness of Gooch's approach was that he often seemed to be working on his own rather than with a team. This was remedied when Roy Cattell became the General Secretary. Cattell, also an Anglican layman, gave the Alliance a significant boost during the years 1949-55. By then the offices were at 30 Bedford Place, a German flying bomb having wrecked 19 Russell Square.

In November 1956 Gilbert Kirby, a Congregational minister with wide links in evangelicalism, was appointed General Secretary. He extended the Alliance's activities further under the slogan 'Spiritual Unity in Action'. The Evangelical Missionary Alliance (EMA) was formed in November 1958 through the merger of the Alliance's Overseas Committee and the Committee of the Fellowship of Interdenominational Missionary Societies. At one stage, Kirby, who had an insatiable appetite for work, was secretary of the Evangelical Alliance, the EMA and the World Evangelical Fellowship, and took a keen interest in developments in Europe.[40] The stories of the EMA and the European Evangelical Alliance, formed in 1952, merit separate treatment and are not covered in this book. When Gilbert Kirby became the Principal of London Bible College in 1966, Morgan Derham, who was working for Scripture Union, succeeded him. Derham, however, remained only two years, and from 1969 to 1982 Gordon Landreth, who had worked for the Inter-Varsity Fellowship, was General Secretary. The period from 1966 to the early

---

39 J.W. Ewing, 'Dropping the Pilot', *Evangelical Christendom*, July–September 1949, pp.57-8.

40 S. Brady, 'Gilbert Kirby, An Evangelical Statesman: A Tribute and a Profile', in S. Brady & H. Rowdon (eds), *For Such a Time as This*, p.9. For the World Evangelical Fellowship see D.M. Howard, *The Dream That Would Not Die: The Birth and Growth of the World Evangelical Fellowship, 1846-96* (Wheaton/Exeter: World Evangelical Fellowship/Paternoster Press, 1986); W.H. Fuller, *People of the Mandate* (WEF; Grand Rapids/Carlisle: Baker Book House/Paternoster Press, 1996).

1980s was a difficult one for the Alliance because of evangelical divisions over attitudes to the ecumenical movement. Clive Calver, who became General Secretary in 1983, represented a younger generation that brought a fresh perspective, and the Alliance grew rapidly. Whitefield House in Kennington had begun to house the Alliance's offices shortly before Calver's arrival. Since 1997 the Alliance's strong position in British Christianity has been sustained under Calver's successor, Joel Edwards.

## Sources for the Book

Most of the primary sources for this project are held in the Alliance's archive. This is lodged at Whitefield House. Central to the work presented here have been the minute books of the Alliance's Provisional Committee, its Executive Council, its Committee of Council and what would become its Council of Management. Also of great value have been the notes of its various annual conferences, and of the international conferences attended by delegates of the Alliance's British Organisation. In some cases, these large gatherings were commemorated by the publication, in book form, of the papers presented at them. Several of these commemorative volumes, which are held at Whitefield House, have proved illuminating. Copies of them, and of other key volumes relating to the early history of the Alliance, are held in the British Library. From time to time, special sub-committees have been formed for particular purposes, and, where appropriate, we have consulted the minutes they have produced.

From 1847–1954 the Alliance issued a regular journal called *Evangelical Christendom*. A digest of news, comment, letters and more in-depth theological writing, this is a rich, extensive resource that has hitherto remained largely unexplored. It offers fascinating perspectives, not only on modern evangelicalism, but also on nineteenth- and twentieth-century church history as a whole. Indeed, it has far more to offer than we have possibly been able to present within the confines of this text and, like the rest of the archive, provides fertile ground for further investigation. *Evangelical Christendom* was succeeded by *The Evangelical Broadsheet*, which ran from 1954-78. A new magazine, *idea*, was then launched, and continues to this day. The evangelical periodical *Crusade* was not directly produced by the Alliance, but between 1955 and 1980 it featured many Alliance-related writers and articles, and offers substantial insight into the agenda and ethos of the organisation during this period.

The secondary sources that exist about the Alliance are limited. *Goodly Fellowship: A Centenary Tribute to the Life and Work of the World's Evangelical Alliance*, by the Baptist leader J.W. Ewing, was published for the centenary celebrations of the Alliance in 1946, but covered its whole international network rather than focusing specifically on its British expression. Kessler's *Study of the Evangelical Alliance in Great Britain* is essentially the dissertation from a taught doctorate, and presents a useful survey of how the Alliance has functioned as an instrument for evangelical unity. Yet just under one half of it deals with the Alliance's foundation and opening years. Also, Kessler concentrates on the theological and ecumenical character of the Evangelical Alliance, virtually to the exclusion of its other concerns. No doubt the theme of unity is important, and the stress that is to be found among Alliance speakers on 'catholicity' is certainly reflected in the present study. Even so, it would be wrong to assume that this was the *only* interest and activity in which the Alliance engaged. Furthermore, although Kessler draws on annual reports, on *Evangelical Christendom* and on *The Evangelical Broadsheet*, he makes no use of *Crusade* for his study of the post-Second World War period, and refers only sparingly to the Executive Council and Council minutes. Besides, his book was never made widely available. Moreover, as will become clear from the later chapters included here, the Alliance has undergone remarkable transformation and growth in the period since Kessler's work was published in 1968. An excellent article appeared in 1986

by John Wolffe, entitled 'The Evangelical Alliance in the
1840s: An Attempt to Institutionalise Christian Unity'.[41] The
volume edited by Steve Brady and Harold Rowdon in commemoration of the Alliance's 150th anniversary, *For Such a
Time as This: Perspectives on Evangelicalism Past, Present and Future*, also contains much useful material. With the Alliance
now looking to its development in the twenty-first century,
however, there is a need for a more detailed appraisal of its
history.

## Charting the Book

This book begins with the foundation of the Alliance in the
mid-nineteenth century. Chapter 2 looks at earlier moves towards unity that provided the impetus for the formation of the
Alliance, while chapter 3 records the formation itself. Chapter
4 examines the commitment of the Alliance to religious freedom, especially in the Victorian period. Chapter 5 analyses
some of the theological controversies that challenged the Alliance's unity during the same time span. Chapters 6 and 7 then
take up the international dimensions of the Alliance. As we
have mentioned, the first half of the twentieth century was a
problematic era for British evangelicals. Chapter 8 traces the
theological tensions that the Alliance faced during those decades. In chapter 9 the renewal of Alliance life, especially
through united mission in the 1950s, is explored. This renewal
was followed, as chapter 10 shows, by deep divisions over
ecumenism. In the 1960s and 1970s evangelicals found themselves in a further period of change, which is analysed in chapter 11. The remarkable period of Clive Calver's secretaryship
from 1983–97 is then recounted in chapter 12. More attention
was given to theological reflection towards the end of this time,

41 J. Wolffe, 'The Evangelical Alliance in the 1840s: An Attempt to Institutionalise Christian Unity', in W. Sheils and D. Wood (eds.), *Voluntary Religion, Studies in
Church History*, Vol. 23; Oxford: Blackwell, 1986), 333–46.

and developments on this front are examined in chapter 13. Finally, the role and agenda of the Alliance under its current General Director, Joel Edwards, is explored in chapter 14. It will become clear that the Alliance has developed increasingly through the later twentieth century as a broadly based religious force. Joel Edwards underlined this when he spoke in 1997 about knowing 'true biblical unity in our legitimate diversity'.[42] As we shall see, the original vision – the vision of a movement bold to proclaim 'We are One Body in Christ' – is still very much alive.

42  *idea*, June/July/August 1997, p.3.

# 2

# An Evangelical and Catholic Union

## The Origins of the Alliance

In the previous chapter we looked at the evangelicalism of the
Victorian era and the way that the Evangelical Alliance was
shaped by that context. The desire for pan-evangelical unity,
however, pre-dated the nineteenth century. In 1795 David
Bogue, a Congregational minister, preached a memorable
sermon on the occasion of the formation of the London
Missionary Society (LMS), an event which for him marked
'the funeral of bigotry'.[1] Initially, the LMS brought together
representatives from the Church of England and Dissenting
denominations, but such co-operation was not sustained.
Nonetheless, the formation of the Evangelical Alliance in 1846
was a result of forces that had been encouraging evangelical
unity over at least the preceding 50 years. Thus Edward
Bickersteth, an Anglican leader who was a central figure in the
founding of the Evangelical Alliance, was a secretary of the
LMS and also a director of the Religious Tract Society, a body
that gradually brought a number of Anglicans, Wesleyans and
Baptists into the realm of pan-evangelical endeavour. The
Sunday School movement was another important interdenominational influence. At the same time, there were deep

---

1  J. Bennett, *Memoirs of the Life of the Revd David Bogue, DD* (London, 1827); cf.
R.H. Martin, *Evangelicals United: Ecumenical Stirrings in Pre-Victorian Britain,*
*1795-1830* (Metuchen & London: The Scarecrow Press, 1983), p.43.

differences between the Church of England and Dissent (known increasingly as Nonconformity). Historic tensions over such issues as restrictions on political freedom for Dissenters and payment by Dissenters of the church rate were exacerbated by fears among clergy in the Church of England that to be associated with Dissenters was to risk being branded as revolutionary.[2] Yet, as we shall see in this chapter, the early part of the nineteenth century saw significant development towards the inauguration of a pan-denominational alliance of evangelicals.

## Evangelicals and Unity

The impact on British Protestantism of the eighteenth-century revival led by the Church of England clergymen John Wesley and George Whitefield has been thoroughly analysed by David Bebbington. He describes, in *Evangelicalism in Modern Britain*, how the decade beginning in 1734 'witnessed in the English-speaking world a more important development than any other, before or after, in the history of Protestant Christianity: the emergence of the movement that became evangelicalism'.[3] In 1735 Whitefield, then an Oxford undergraduate, experienced an evangelical conversion, and three years later John Wesley, in a meeting in Aldersgate Street in London, famously felt his heart 'strangely warmed'.[4] The influence of Whitefield and Wesley stretched widely. Dissenters, especially Baptists and Congregationalists, were affected. A new movement, Methodism, was developed on the model of Wesley's remarkable ministry. Evangelicals within these different

---

2 Lewis, *Lighten Their Darkness*, 11. The background was the French Revolution and the pro-Jacobin sentiments of some Dissenters.

3 Bebbington, *Evangelicalism in Modern Britain*, p.20.

4 For Whitefield see H.S. Stout, *The Divine Dramatist: George Whitefield and the Rise of Modern Evangelicalism* (Grand Rapids: Eerdmans, 1991). For John Wesley see H.D. Rack, *Reasonable Enthusiast: John Wesley and the Rise of Methodism* (London: Epworth, 1989).

streams, although they were aware of their denominational
distinctives, recognised their common convictions. Thus
Samuel Walker of Truro, a clergyman who was dramatically
transformed by the message preached during the evangelical
revival, urged that 'all friends of the gospel', although differing
denominationally, should 'unite in heart for the support of the
common cause'.[5]

At the Methodist Conference of 1757 John Wesley set out
his own hope that there might be 'a national union of evangelical clergy'. He saw this union as drawing together Methodist societies and the evangelicals in the Church of England.
There was little support for the scheme at the time. Even
clergymen who spoke of a common evangelical cause were
wary of any moves that would undermine the established
church. Wesley returned to the theme in a paper written
seven years later. He argued that what was needed was not a
union in opinions, expressions or outward order, but a unity
based on belief in original sin and justification by faith, and
characterised by holiness of life on the part of those who
joined this bond of union. In fact, it was difficult to achieve
unity even within Methodism. Whitefield and Wesley were
divided over the doctrine of predestination and over the
question of whether 'perfect love' towards God was (as Wesley believed) possible in this life. By 1769 Wesley had come to
the view that his efforts to achieve wider union had been
fruitless. He now saw the evangelicals whom he had hoped to
draw together as a 'rope of sand'.[6]

Nonetheless, there was an underlying evangelical sense of
shared purpose. Evangelicals were evidently united in their
commitment to active mission and to conversion. This
included evangelism at home and overseas. In looking at the
forces that made for unity it is important to recognise not

5 Cited by K. Hylson-Smith, *Evangelicals in the Church of England* (Edinburgh: T.
& T. Clark, 1988), p.23.

6 F. Baker, *John Wesley and the Church of England* (London: Epworth, 1970),
pp.183, 191, 196.

only the place of movements within Britain but also the impact of overseas mission. The end of the eighteenth century saw vigorous Protestant missionary activity that led to the formation of British missionary societies. Baptists were the first, in 1792, to form a denominational missionary society, largely due to the efforts of William Carey, a young Baptist pastor in Leicester, and the support of several Northamptonshire Baptists. Although this was a denominational enterprise, Carey and those associated with the venture had been affected by non-Baptists, notably by the outstanding American theologian Jonathan Edwards and his 1747 book entitled *An Humble Attempt to Promote Explicit Agreement and Visible Union of God's People in Extraordinary Prayer.*[7] The Northamptonshire Baptist Association issued its own 'Prayer Call' in 1784, and the idea of visible unity would soon extend beyond praying together to acting together. In 1806 Carey proposed to Andrew Fuller, the Secretary of the Baptist Missionary Society, the idea of a conference that would bring together Christians from all denominations and all parts of the world.[8]

Congregationalists and some Wesleyans were also active in moves towards unity. Philip Doddridge, a Congregationalist with expansive views, called for united prayer as early as 1742. The LMS provided an example of overseas missionary co-operation. It was a bold initiative, started by some Church of England, Congregational, Presbyterian and Wesleyan representatives. The intention was to channel mission to the South Seas. Increasingly the LMS became a Congregational society, with Baptists and evangelicals within the Church of England supporting their own societies. With the founding of the Church Missionary Society in 1799 and the Wesleyan Missionary Society in 1813 it might have seemed that evangelicals

7  B. Stanley, *The History of the Baptist Missionary Society, 1792-1992* (Edinburgh: T. & T. Clark, 1992), pp.4, 13.

8  E. Carey, *Memoir of William Carey, DD* (Hartford: Canfield & Robins, 1837), p.364.

were stuck in denominational grooves. It was very difficult for the barriers between the Church of England and Nonconformists to be transcended. Nonconformists were still, in terms of their legal status, second-class citizens. They could not play a full part in public life. Yet the idea of common participation in the wider evangelistic task had taken root and would continue to have an impact. John Newton emerged as an example of a bridge-building Church of England clergyman. The formation of the British and Foreign Bible Society in 1804 was a co-operative move that would have enduring effects.[9] It was to be cited by early Evangelical Alliance leaders as inspirational in its example.[10]

## Evangelical Tensions

During the early years of the nineteenth century the Established Church and the Dissenting denominations were often at loggerheads. Only relatively few well-known Church of England clergymen, such as Baptist Noel (who became an Evangelical Alliance leader and subsequently fulfilled his name by becoming a Baptist), were calling in the 1830s for understanding of Dissent.[11] Neither was there a great deal of sympathy flowing in the other direction. A body called the Anti-State Church Association (which in 1853 became the Liberation Society) brought together a number of 'political Dissenters', as Anglicans often called them, who waged a sustained campaign against the privileged position of the Church of England. There was a similar state of unrest in Scotland. Evangelicals in Scotland, who were to be significant in the founding of the Evangelical Alliance, were growing, with Presbyterian Dissenters in Edinburgh in 1835 comprising

9  Martin, *Evangelicals United*, especially pp.80-146.
10  Report of the Proceedings of the Conference held at Freemasons' Hall, London, From 19 August to 2 September Inclusive, 1846, p.63.
11  B.W. Noel, *The Unity of the Church, Another Tract for the Times, Addressed Particularly to Members of the Establishment* (London, 1837), p.9.

one-third of the churchgoers in the city.[12] Their numbers were
to be boosted considerably within a decade. The acknowledged leader of evangelicals still within the Church of Scotland
in the 1830s was Thomas Chalmers, a professor at Edinburgh
University who had also given an outstanding example of how
to rise to the urban challenge in Glasgow.[13] In 1843 Chalmers
would give a lead to many evangelicals who would leave their
parishes and form the Free Church of Scotland.

The tensions that existed were not only connected with the
place of the established churches. Edward Irving, a young and
flamboyant Scottish Presbyterian minister, was one of those
engaged in a sharp critique of existing evangelical thinking and
practice, whether among members of the established or Nonconformist bodies. Irving, who had assisted Thomas Chalmers
in Glasgow, enjoyed considerable fame in the 1820s as the minister of the Church of Scotland's congregation in Hatton Garden, London. Several of London's aristocrats came to hear his
dramatic preaching. But Irving succeeded in alienating many
evangelical leaders. In 1824, in a highly controversial sermon
preached before the LMS, Edward Irving argued that missionaries should not go out supported by missionary societies.
Rather, he said, they should renounce all human support. Later
his espousal of speaking in tongues meant that he found even
more of the evangelical establishment ranged against him.
Irving challenged the 'love of order, moderation, piety and
prudence' that characterised evangelicals in the Church of
England.[14]

There were also tensions over eschatology. Highly respected
evangelicals, such as Charles Simeon, whose ministry at Holy

---

12  C.G. Brown, *The Social History of Religion in Scotland Since 1730* (London:
Methuen, 1987), p.61. D.W Bebbington uses the figure of one third, noting that
Baptists and Congregationalists are wrongly classified by Brown as Presbyterian
Dissenters. See *Evangelicalism in Modern Britain,* pp.21, 284.

13  S.J. Brown, *Thomas Chalmers and the Godly Commonwealth in Scotland* (Oxford:
Oxford University Press, 1982), chapter 3.

14  J.F.C. Harrison, *The Second Coming: Popular Millenarianism, 1780-1850* (London: Routledge, 1979), p.7.

Trinity Church, Cambridge, had national significance, had no
interest in debates about a visible return of Christ. In this Simeon represented the mainstream thinking of Church of England evangelicals of the early nineteenth century.[15] But there
were increasing numbers of younger evangelicals who, like
Irving, were placing great emphasis on the personal return of
Christ, the advent hope. They believed that this would be followed by a thousand-year reign of Christ on earth – the belief
known as premillennialism.[16] Edward Bickersteth, who was
perhaps the best-known and most colourful evangelical in the
Church of England after Simeon, decided in the 1830s to
produce a book on the Second Advent and in the course
of writing it he changed his position and adopted
premillennialism.[17] In fact, Bickersteth would go on to reiterate his premillennial beliefs at the founding conference of
the Evangelical Alliance.[18] Among those influenced by
Bickersteth's premillennialism was Anthony Ashley-Cooper,
later the seventh Earl of Shaftesbury, who was a determined
campaigner for better working conditions in Britain and was
especially concerned about the exploitation of children.[19] For
others this adventist emphasis was a distraction. For all that it
transcended denominational boundaries, it did not appear to
contribute much to evangelical unity.

The rejection of the moderate and optimistic evangelicalism of Simeon by a younger group in the Church of England
was symbolised by the founding in 1828 of the periodical, *The
Record*. By 1838 this had the largest circulation of the religious

---

15  Bebbington, *Evangelicalism in Modern Britain*, pp.83–4.

16  See D.W. Bebbington, 'The Advent Hope in British Evangelicalism since
1800', *Scottish Journal of Religious Studies* 9.2 (1988), pp. 103–14; for America see
T.P. Weber, *Living in the Shadow of the Second Coming: American Premillennialism,
1875-1982*.

17  T.R. Birks, *Memoir of the Rev Edward Bickersteth*, Vol. 2 (2 Vols., London: Seeleys,
1850), pp.43–4.

18  Report of the Proceedings of the Conference held at Freemasons' Hall,
London, From August 19th to September 2nd Inclusive, 1846, p.234.

19  For Shaftesbury see G.B.A.M. Finlayson, *The Seventh Earl of Shaftesbury,
1801-1885* (London: Eyre Methuen, 1981).

papers. It fostered a climate of religious confrontation. Roman Catholics, broader evangelicals in the Church of England and Nonconformists were all attacked in uncompromising terms. But the opposition to Dissent was widespread among Anglican evangelicals of all shades of opinion. In the wake of the 1828 repeal of the Test and Corporation Acts, which had effectively excluded Nonconformists from public life, there was considerable fear that Dissenters would use their greater political freedom to help bring about the disestablishment of the Church of England.[20] Many within the Church of England, not least evangelicals, saw the established church as a bulwark of the nation. By contrast, for most Nonconformists this arrangement was a denial of the freedom of the church to order its own life and a denial of liberty of conscience. Disputes about the 'voluntary' nature of religion were to be revived in the 1840s, when they impinged significantly on the founding of the Evangelical Alliance. Indeed, attitudes adopted on this issue had a clear effect on the support that different evangelicals gave to the fledgling organisation.

Evangelicals within the Church of Scotland were involved in precipitating a major secession – the Disruption – in 1843. In fact, the leaders of the Free Church that was formed in Scotland as a result would go on to play a significant part in the founding of the Evangelical Alliance. A focus of their unhappiness, which led to the division, was the role of patrons. Although many who seceded – including, most notably, their leader Thomas Chalmers – were in favour of a national church, they argued that appointment of Church of Scotland ministers by patrons was inappropriate since it took away the freedom of the heads of families in each local congregation to choose their own minister. Over one-third of the Church of Scotland's ministers (451 out of 1,203) left their parishes.[21] An English Baptist minister, Edward Steane, later one of the honorary

---

20 Lewis, *Lighten Their Darkness*, pp.14–25.
21 See G.I.T Machin, *Politics and the Churches in Great Britain, 1832-1868* (Oxford: The Clarendon Press, 1977), pp.112, 141, 145.

secretaries of the Evangelical Alliance and the editor of its journal *Evangelical Christendom*, wrote of the way 'the voluntary controversy' in England and Scotland operated at 'fever heat'. He commented that 'the bitterness of the controversy caused much scandal and was the source of great weakness to the church, paralysing its efforts to reach the world'.[22] Certainly, this period saw major obstacles being placed in the way of evangelical unity.

## Uniting Against Common Enemies

Further challenges to evangelicalism came from the Anglo-Catholic Oxford Movement and the extension of Roman Catholicism in Britain and America. On 14 July 1833 John Keble, the Oxford Professor of Poetry and a priest of the Church of England, gave the Assize sermon (so called because it was preached before the Assize judges), which is often thought to mark an important stage in the emergence of the Oxford Movement. Keble asked for the church to be regarded as an instrument of the divine will and not as a national institution. Another leader of this movement was Edward Pusey, Regius Professor of Hebrew at Oxford. On 9 September 1833 the priest who would soon become the most prominent figure in this movement, John Henry Newman, published three tracts – hence the name Tractarian Movement – which were on the office of the ministry as properly constituted by 'apostolical descent', the 'catholic church', and the liturgy. The emphasis as the movement took off was on defence of tradition in the face of changes, the revival of piety and the priority of holiness, the importance of the sacraments, and a higher view of the ministry and ordination. Much of this was a direct challenge to prevailing evangelical priorities.[23]

---

22  *Evangelical Christendom*, June 1863, p.259.
23  S. Gilley, *Newman and his Age* (London: Darton, Longman & Todd, 1996), pp.116-9. See also P.B. Nockles, *The Oxford Movement in Context: Anglican High Churchmanship, 1760-1857* (Oxford: Clarendon Press, 1994).

Newman himself had experienced an evangelical conversion at the age of fifteen, towards the end of 1816. The influence of the Anglican evangelical Thomas Scott's book, *The Force of Truth*, had been important in this. In the 1820s, during his early years in Oxford, Newman was involved in the evangelical Church Missionary Society. But the study of the church fathers was moving him in a new direction. It is true, as some writers have indicated, that there was continuity between the doctrinal orthodoxy of Tractarianism and evangelicalism.[24] But the constant aim of the Oxford Movement's leaders was to show that evangelical theology was inadequate.[25] In 1841 the series of tracts came to an end when Newman sought to prove that the Church of England's doctrinal position was consistent with Roman Catholic teaching, and in 1845 Newman seceded to the Roman Catholic Church. Many other Tractarians, however, remained in the Church of England. The need for a more united evangelical front against Tractarian growth was part of the background to the formation of the Evangelical Alliance. In 1845 John Angell James, who was pressing hard for a united evangelical witness, wrote that 'Puseyism has effected a fearful schism, and the rent is growing wider and wider.'[26]

In the same period, the strengthening position of the Roman Catholic Church also provoked Protestant reaction. As we have already noted, some writers have placed emphasis on the 'anti-Romanism' that they consider to be an important factor in the birth of the Evangelical Alliance.[27] No doubt this was a significant influence, even if at times its extent has been overplayed. In 1844 Sir Robert Peel's government decided to increase the annual grant to the Roman Catholic seminary in Maynooth,

---

24 See, for example, D. Newsome, *The Parting of Friends* (London: John Murray, 1966).

25 D.W. Bebbington, *Holiness in Nineteenth-Century England* (Carlisle: Paternoster Press, 2000), p.11.

26 James, et al., *Essays on Christian Union*, p.151.

27 Goodall, *The Ecumenical Movement*, p.161. D.H. Yoder, 'Christian Unity in Nineteenth-Century America', in Rouse & Neill (eds), *A History of the Ecumenical Movement*, p.225. M. Hennell, *Sons of the Prophets* (London: SPCK, 1979), p.82.

near Dublin, from £8,000 to £25,000. It also proposed to make
the grant permanent, rather than subject to yearly review. This
struck a raw Protestant nerve. As a consequence, 1,039 delegates
from various parts of Britain and from different denominations,
held a conference in Exeter Hall, London, from 30 April to 3
May 1845 to get the measure overturned. Some present at the
London meeting opposed any kind of financial support from
the State for religious organisations. Included among these were
well-known Baptist ministers such as J.H. Hinton, then Secretary of the Baptist Union and someone who was to be at the
heart of early Evangelical Alliance life, J.P. Mursell of Leicester,
and Charles Stovel of East London. Another Baptist, William
Brock, later minister of the well-known Bloomsbury Baptist
Chapel, spoke at Yarmouth in the same year of the 'damnable
doctrines which are inculcated at Maynooth', and expressed
outrage that Maynooth should be 'provided with a princely income' from State funds.[28]

This kind of anti-Catholic rhetoric might have united evangelicals, but, in fact, Maynooth served to highlight internal
Protestant divisions. *The Record* was incensed at what it saw as
betrayal of the Protestant heritage by the Conservative government. In the light of the crisis, and despite the great differences
it maintained on secondary matters, *The Record* was prepared in
March 1845 to encourage working with Dissenters, since Anglican evangelicals were 'one with them in the fundamentals of
gospel truth'.[29] In December 1845 *The Record* disagreed with a
sermon delivered by Hugh M'Neile from Liverpool, a
doughty Protestant and defender of the Anglican establishment who argued that there could be 'no real bona fide co-
operation' between Anglicans and Dissenters; he had insisted
that far from the proposed Evangelical Alliance doing good,
the moves towards it were already creating mischief.[30] For

---

28  *The Endowment of Maynooth*, p.4, cited by Norman, *Anti-Catholicism in Victorian
England* (London: George Allen & Unwin, 1968), p.27.

29  *The Record*, 17 March 1845, p.4.

30  *The Record*, 18 December 1845, p.4; 22 December 1845, pp.2, 4. Cf. Wolffe,
*Protestant Crusade*, p.141.

some on both sides of the Anglican-Nonconformist divide, co-operation was certainly deemed to be impossible. J.H. Hinton and his fellow Baptist, Edward Steane, withdrew from the anti-Maynooth committee because, as Baptists, they were opposed to any state funding of religion, not only the funding of a Catholic seminary. But a mediating party led by Sir Culling Eardley Smith, a Congregationalist who was to play a pivotal role in the establishment of the Evangelical Alliance, survived. The Maynooth committee failed to influence the government, but the bulk of those meeting in London in 1844 agreed to plan for a Protestant body 'to embrace this country, the continent and the world', with the aim that Protestants 'may be prepared to meet a powerful and united foe'.[31] As such, it is clear that the 'anti-Maynooth' action ignited a desire for a more permanent vehicle for Protestant association.[32]

## Steps Towards 'Catholic Union'

More positive moves towards unity were also evident. As early as 1825 ministers from different denominations in Liverpool met to encourage united prayer. Three of these leaders – the Wesleyan minister, Jabez Bunting, and the Church of England evangelicals Edward Bickersteth (who was committed to evangelical action and who was for six years Secretary of the Church Missionary Society) and Josiah Pratt – were to emerge later as key figures in the formation of the Evangelical Alliance. Americans were similarly active in promoting the idea of better relations between denominations. In 1839 the US Society for the Promotion of Christian Union was created. The leader of this movement was Samuel Simon Schmucker, a central figure in the founding of the first ecumenical American Lutheran body. He was also a respected Professor of Theology at the Lutheran seminary in Gettysburg, Pennsylvania. In his

31  Massie, *The Evangelical Alliance*, p.103.
32  Machin, *Politics and the Churches*, p.176.

*Fraternal Appeal to the American Churches* (1838), Schmucker advocated full recognition of membership and ministries between different denominations. He wished, as his book's sub-title put it, for 'Catholic Union on Apostolic Principles'.[33] In Geneva, the Swiss theologian and historian Merle D'Aubigné also did much to promote Christian unity. A German leader, Dean Kniewel of Danzig, made a tour through England, France, Belgium, Switzerland and Germany in 1842 to forge closer links between leaders in different denominations.[34]

John Angell James, who from 1806 was minister of Carrs Lane Independent Chapel, a noted Congregational church in central Birmingham, was one of the first in Britain to suggest an evangelical alliance. In doing so, however, he paid tribute to a letter from William Patton, a Presbyterian leader in New York and a director of Union Theological Seminary, who had written to James urging that a 'General Protestant Convention' be called.[35] At a meeting of the Congregational Union in May 1842, James proposed that a union should be formed amongst churches holding the voluntary principle (i.e. Dissenting churches). This, he said, should have the objects of combating infidelity and also 'Popery, Puseyism and Plymouth Brethrenism'.[36] As we have seen, opposition to Roman Catholicism and the Oxford Movement was then standard fare among Protestants generally, even if a significant American Evangelical Alliance leader, Philip Schaff, would engage in long conversations with Edward Pusey.[37] As for James' opposition to the Plymouth Brethren, he spoke tartly of this lay-led

33 P.D. Jordan, *The Evangelical Alliance for the United States of America, 1847-1900: Ecumenism, Identity and the Religion of the Republic* (New York & Toronto: Edwin Mullen, 1982), pp.34-5.

34 N.M. Railton, *No North Sea: The Anglo-German Evangelical Network in the Middle of the Nineteenth Century* (Leiden: Brill, 2000), p.2.

35 Jordan, *Evangelical Alliance for the United States of America*, p.206; James, et al., *Essays on Christian Union*, pp.224-5.

36 Rouse & Neill (eds), *A History of the Ecumenical Movement*, p.318.

37 Railton, *No North Sea*, pp.183-4.

movement espousing 'the high-sounding but hopeless ambition of swallowing up all denominations in the endearing name of "Brethren", thus usurping that title, and designing to withhold it from others'.[38] In the event, however, Alliance opposition to the Brethren was soon dropped from its list of priorities.

Two months after his Congregational Union address, John Angell James extended his idea of unity. He wrote in a letter published by the *Congregational Magazine* about the possibility of embracing within a broader evangelical unity not only Dissenters in the United Kingdom, but also 'pious clergy of the Churches of England and Scotland'.[39] This represented a considerable step for James, who had commented previously that it seemed to be the policy of the Church of England to suppress Nonconformists. Certainly, many in the Established Church regarded Congregationalists as 'sectarians'.[40] A committee was formed to take James' idea forward and a rally was held in June 1843 at the Exeter Hall in the Strand, London – a building erected in the 1830s and owned by a group of wealthy evangelical laymen. A remarkable 11,000 people applied for tickets, a clear indication of the interest that the subject was now generating. However, the main hall could accommodate only about 4,000. Those who led this meeting were soon to play important roles in the formation of the Evangelical Alliance. At this stage, however, there was no pan-evangelical organisation, and the resolutions passed by the meeting were little more than statements of intent. In addition, although a few churchmen such as Baptist Noel attended, the supporters were almost entirely Nonconformists. This was a period marked by national ecclesiastical conflict over the education clauses of Sir James Graham's Factory Act, whose Anglican-dominated stipulations on religious instruction had alienated Dissenters.[41]

---

38 James et al, *Essays on Christian Union*, p.151.

39 *Congregational Magazine*, 1842, pp.458–62, cited by Wolffe, 'The Evangelical Alliance in the 1840s', pp.333–46.

40 Calver, 'Rise and Fall', p.149; Massie, *The Evangelical Alliance*, p.86.

41 Wolffe, 'The Evangelical Alliance in the 1840s', p.336.

The vision of William Patton for a convention had continuing influence on British evangelicals. Patton worked with other American Presbyterian leaders such as Samuel H. Cox and Thomas Skinner in Union Theological Seminary, then became editor of a weekly Presbyterian paper in New York and was finally appointed President of Howard University. Patton, Cox and Skinner saw the possibility of evangelical unity on a world scale and indeed encouraged a group seeking to set up an evangelical ecumenical movement in North America. In his letter to James, Patton suggested that evangelicals worldwide would respond to an international gathering if a call came from Britain, the leading Protestant power of the day.[42] Specifically, Patton urged James to 'Open a correspondence with Dr Chalmers, and Dr Wardlaw and others of Scotland; with prominent men among the Baptist, Methodist, Moravian and other denominations'.[43] He added, 'Sir Culling Eardley Smith will go heart and soul with you.' This was indeed the case. James published the letter by Patton as an appendix to an essay in an important book, *Essays in Christian Union*, which is referred to below. Specific steps towards unity came, therefore, from both sides of the Atlantic.

## Scottish Divines

Vital encouragement to foster unity came from a number of Scottish evangelicals.[44] There was a strong desire for some kind of drawing together of Scottish and English evangelicals following the events that led to the Disruption of 1843. Within a year of the Disruption the Free Church erected about five hundred churches, was supporting its own ministry and establishing its own colleges. In July 1843 a bicentenary celebration of the Westminster Assembly of Divines, held in Edinburgh, assumed the character of a demonstration in support of the

---

42  Jordan, *Evangelical Alliance for the United States of America*, p.33.
43  James, et al., *Essays on Christian Union*, p.224.
44  Kessler, *A Study of the Evangelical Alliance*, chapter 2.

Free Church.[45] One of the speakers, J.W. Massie, a Manchester Congregational minister who was a Scottish Presbyterian by background, spoke of how John Angell James was inviting 'Christians of every denomination to recognise Christian catholicity, in the formation and exhibition in practice of an evangelical and catholic union in England'. Robert Smith Candlish, a younger leader of the Free Church of Scotland who would later become Principal of New College, Edinburgh, said that he 'concurred most cordially' in the desire expressed by Massie for 'a Christian catholic union'. He added that he hoped – presumably in the Scottish context – this would not be limited to Presbyterians who followed the Westminster Confession.[46]

This emphasis on 'catholic union' was given greater weight by the contribution of the venerable Robert Balmer of Berwick-on-Tweed. A Professor of Theology for the United Secession Church, Balmer had not been scheduled to speak. Yet, when asked to do so from the Chair by Thomas Chalmers, he argued that the New Testament called for visible unity among Christians and that the 'principles of catholic union', as he put it, were distinctly recognised in the Westminster Confession. For him there should be 'no schism in [Christ's] mystical body'. If, Balmer urged, Christian believers have love towards one another as they ought to have, 'it will either compel us to put an end to our divisions, or our divisions will compel us to relinquish our love'. This point was met with shouts of 'hear, hear'. In a reference to Philippians 3:15-16, Balmer urged his audience to 'walk together in the things in which we are agreed'. He considered that the denominations were not yet ripe for 'incorporation' (by which he meant organic church union), but believed that if they were to co-operate in the things in which they were agreed 'our incorporation would be ripened and would come in due time'.[47] This was an explicit

---

45  Wolffe, 'The Evangelical Alliance in the 1840s', p.337.
46  Massie, *The Evangelical Alliance*, pp.93-4.
47  Ibid., pp.97-8.

articulation by a revered evangelical churchman of a hope for
future visible unity.

Robert Balmer's speech had a profound impact on his Edin-
burgh audience and was to be significant in the genesis of the
Evangelical Alliance. Among those present was John
Henderson from Glasgow, an elder of the United Secession
Church and an enterprising businessman. The Henderson
brothers, John and Robert, had directed a thriving East India
trading company, which they had begun and developed in
Glasgow, and to which they had subsequently added extensive
shipping and banking enterprises to create a business empire.
But tragedy had struck them. The two brothers, together with
their minister, David King (minister of the Greyfriars United
Secession Church in Glasgow), and a female domestic servant,
were involved in a boating accident on the river Clyde in
which Robert and the maid were drowned. This tragedy
deepened John's desire to use his wealth wisely. His donations
for religious and benevolent purposes reached thirty to forty
thousand pounds annually. During Balmer's address in Edinburgh, Henderson had the thought that essays on the subject of
Christian unity could be invited, with the best awarded a prize.
His minister, David King, suggested instead the production of a
volume of essays on the theme of union. As a consequence, *Essays on Christian Union,* a volume of 440 pages, was published in
1845.[48]

All except two of the contributors to this volume (John
Angell James and Ralph Wardlaw) were Scottish Presbyterians.
In the first of the essays, Thomas Chalmers emphasised the
value of co-operative efforts to reach out to others with the
Christian gospel. The second essay was by Balmer. He put the
case for acceptance of those from other denominations to the
Lord's Supper, suggesting that 'to exclude from the Supper of
the Lord those whom the Lord himself invites, seems mani-
festly repugnant'. He added that divines such as Richard
Baxter and Philip Doddridge had called for 'Catholic

---

48  Kessler, *A Study of the Evangelical Alliance,* pp.19–20.

Communion'.[49] Another essay, by Robert Candlish, looked at
Christ's prayer in John chapter 17. Candlish saw visible unity as
a necessary goal, but argued, in idealistic fashion, for 'a union,
not of man's contrivance, but of God's inspiration'.[50] John
Angell James asked: 'Can it be pleasing to our common Father
to see his children thus shutting themselves up in their separate
rooms in the great house of the holy catholic church, and never
coming into one common hall to own their relationship?'
Ralph Wardlaw, who was a Congregational minister in Glasgow and a supporter of the LMS, took up the same theme. His
essay was entitled 'A Catholic Spirit' and argued that intolerance and uncharitableness were 'the very opponents of catholicity'.[51] This concern for catholicity among the Alliance's
founders reflected a desire to rekindle a commitment that, as
W.R. Ward has shown, had been prominent among evangelicals in the 1790s, but which Balmer, Angell James, Wardlaw
and their colleagues thought had been largely lost in the interim. The participation of avowedly 'catholic' Moravians in
the genesis of the Alliance would serve as a reminder that some
had managed to sustain the spirit invoked by Wardlaw
throughout this period, but the formation of the Alliance offered genuine hope that it would once again enter mainstream
evangelical life and thought.[52]

Each of the essays had theological and practical elements.
However, David King who looked at local unity in Scotland,
and Gavin Struthers who examined sectarian aspects in
church life, had a less evidently theological purpose. Struthers
bemoaned the 'coldness, and distance, and repulsiveness' to be
found among Scottish churches. 'Their love', as he saw it, 'fills a
nut shell, while their party feuds fill the land.'[53] When consid-

49 James, et al., *Essays on Christian Union,* pp.57-8, 64.

50 Ibid., p.134.

51 Ibid., pp.193, 318.

52 W.R. Ward, *Religion and Society in England* (London: Batsford, 1972); C.J.
Podmore, *The Moravian Church in England, 1728-1760* (Oxford: Clarendon Press,
1998); Kessler, *A Study of the Evangelical Alliance,* p.22.

53 Ibid., p.405.

ering the practical expressions of visible unity, the authors took different positions. Some advocated the goal of ultimate union, while others did not want to go beyond changed attitudes that could issue in greater co-operation. Kessler suggests that Chalmers took an Arminian view and emphasised human responsibility for unity, whereas James held to a high Calvinistic view and argued that the church was already united. Balmer, he suggests, held a middle position.[54] But to see differences as based on soteriology is misleading. Chalmers was not Arminian in his beliefs and James was a moderate rather than a high Calvinist. Nor were the writers of the essays divided over the view that what should govern their thinking was the idea of the catholicity of the church. Rather, variations had more to do with how such catholicity might be expressed.

## The Keynote of 'LOVE'

There were continuing discussions between interested parties about the way forward for evangelical unity, with John Henderson, David King and John Angell James among those who were deeply involved. King's view was that a smaller meeting should be convened to draw up a doctrinal basis for a new co-operative 'alliance'. Although James agreed, he did not feel that evangelicals in England could take the initiative because of their divisions about the voluntary nature of the church over against a state church. He suggested instead that the first move must be made from Scotland.[55] The indefatigable David King then suggested to a number of other leaders in the Scottish denominations that a meeting might be held in the strategic port city of Liverpool. An invitation was issued on 5 August 1845 to attend a conference from 1–3 October 1845. Fifty-five ministers from Scotland, all but nine of whom were Presbyterian, signed it. None of these, however, were from the

54  Kessler, *A Study of the Evangelical Alliance,* pp.21-2.
55  R.W. Dale, *The Life and Letters of J.A. James* (London, 1861), p.412.

Church of Scotland. Five Congregationalists and four Baptists made up the non-Presbyterian element.[56] The lack of evangelicals from the established churches was a feature of this early period. Only fifteen of the 216 who attended were Church of England clergy. Edward Bickersteth was uncertain and went 'with many fears and anxieties'.[57] Nonetheless, *The Record* saw the objectives of the conference as worthy of support, offering hope both of evangelical harmony and of 'repelling the advances of Popery'.[58]

Again, however, it must be emphasised that opposition to Roman Catholicism was not the predominant note of the meeting. At the beginning of the conference, which was held at the Medical Hall in Liverpool, John Angell James was asked to occupy the chair. He duly took the opportunity to declare: 'In every chorus of human voices, the harmony depends on the "key-note" being rightly struck: that note I am now appointed to give and it is LOVE.' David King followed with a paper in which he stressed that Christian union, not doctrinal debate or controversy, would be the first object of the intended alliance. Unity, as Christ prayed for it, was to be visible so that the world might believe. Thus unity was, said King, an important end, but in another sense was simply a means, with the end being people coming to faith in Christ.[59] Yet the conference delegates, from twenty denominations, were by no means united themselves. For example, a statement by Scottish delegates was not approved because it wished the new movement 'to associate and concentrate the strength of an enlightened Protestantism against the encroachments of Popery and Pusey-

---

56 D. King, 'Historical Sketch of the Evangelical Alliance', in E. Steade (ed.), *The Religious Condition of Christendom: A Series of Papers Read at the fifth annual Conference Held at Freemasons' Hall, London August 20th to September 3rd 1851* (London: James Nisbet & Co., 1852), pp.39–40.

57 E. Bickersteth to the editor, 5 November 1845, *The Christian Observer*, December 1845, p.729.

58 *The Record*, 6 October 1845, p.4.

59 *Conference on Christian Union; Being a Narrative of the Proceedings of the Meeting held in Liverpool, October 1845*, p.6; Massie, *The Evangelical Alliance*, pp.115, 120.

ism' and because it mentioned the anti-Maynooth committee. The opposition to Puseyism was unacceptable to Anglicans, while the reference to Maynooth was deemed too political.[60]

The bulk of those who attended the Liverpool conference were evangelicals with pan-denominational sympathies who wished for a new body which would act as a positive force for unity, rather than being known for its opposition to the beliefs of others. Thus James Hamilton, a Free Church of Scotland minister at the Scotch Church, Regent Square, London, and a strong pan-denominationalist, said: 'I should regret to say that this were even chiefly, or principally an anti-papal movement, or even an anti-infidel movement, or that it took any mere *anti* form.'[61] Thomas Rawson (T.R.) Birks, the son-in-law and biographer of Edward Bickersteth and himself a leading Alliance figure, recalled in 1850 that what was taking place was a 'growing conviction, in the minds of sincere Christians … that their real union of heart and judgement [was] far greater than the outward appearance'.[62] This union did not draw its main power from oppositionalism. Granted, one of the objects of the Alliance was to resist 'the efforts of Popery', together with 'every form of superstition and infidelity'. Granted, too, the Alliance committed itself to promoting the 'Protestant faith in our own and other countries', several of which were predominantly Roman Catholic.[63] No doubt, also, as we shall see, the Alliance continued to attack Roman Catholicism in the coming decades. Yet, despite all this, it is also clear that from its beginnings it was a body that had a positive and broad vision of unity at its core. In this sense it represented a significant departure from the more confrontational stances to be found among many evangelicals at the time.

The Liverpool conference agreed to set up a provisional committee with four sub-divisions to plan for the formation,

---

60  Kessler, *A Study of the Evangelical Alliance*, p.24.
61  Massie, *The Evangelical Alliance*, p.117.
62  Birks, *Memoir of the Rev. Edward Bickersteth*, p.303.
63  King, 'Historical Sketch of the Evangelical Alliance', pp.45-6.

as soon as possible, of what would be known as the Evangelical Alliance. One division was to meet in London and was to concentrate its efforts on relationships with other countries, as well as having responsibility for the midland and southern counties of England. The second was to gather in Liverpool, with responsibility for the northern counties and Wales. The third was to convene in Glasgow and take responsibility for Scotland. The fourth was to meet in Dublin and to act for Ireland. The conference agreed that the membership of the Alliance that was to be created should be restricted to individuals. This had, from the perspective of the time, several advantages. It stressed existing spiritual unity, which could be a reality between individuals but was certainly not a reality between denominations. Second, it meant that there would not be a focus on contentious questions of ecclesiology. At the same time, the restriction of membership to individuals did not hinder the taking of organisational initiatives. Many of those present at Liverpool who had come as official delegates of their churches may have been over-ambitious in pressing for a commitment to a more visible union of different ecclesiastical bodies. But at least the conference as a whole was not prepared to content itself with a mere affirmation of spiritual unity: concrete steps to express that unity were also being taken.

## A Doctrinal Proclamation

A meeting of evangelicals such as that which took place at Liverpool was bound to generate different opinions about the place and content of a doctrinal basis. Some felt that it would be possible for evangelicals to set out agreed foundational truths that could properly be described as evangelical. Algernon Wells, the secretary of the Congregational Union and a participant at Liverpool, referred to the predominantly Lutheran Confession of Augsburg of 1530, the Presbyterian Westminster Confession of 1649 and the Thirty-Nine Articles of the Church of England. He wanted to take hold of the word 'catholic' and wondered if evangelicals could unite around six or seven cardinal points contained in each of these Reformation Confessions. The beliefs mentioned by Wells were 'the sole authority and sufficiency of Holy Scripture, the Trinity and the Unity of the Godhead, the fall of man, the redemption by Christ, justification by faith, regeneration by the Spirit and so on'. Edward Steane, a leader among the Baptists present, saw the Baptist tradition as one that refused to impose creeds. He was therefore prepared to do without a doctrinal formula. His proposal was to 'fix upon Christian character, the elements of vital and experimental godliness, as, at once, the only, and the necessary, pre-requisites to the fellowship we desire to realise'.[64]

Those in favour of a doctrinal basis were in the majority, however, and a sub-committee was appointed to formulate a short evangelical statement of belief. It seemed as if this committee would fail in its task, but at the last minute unanimous approval among committee members was achieved on the following eight points, which were read out to conference members by Robert Candlish:

1   The divine inspiration, authority and sufficiency of Holy Scripture.
2   The unity of the Godhead, and the Trinity of persons therein.
3   The utter depravity of human nature in consequence of the Fall.
4   The incarnation of the Son of God and his work of atonement for sinners of mankind.
5   The justification of the sinner by faith alone.
6   The work of the Holy Spirit in the regeneration and sanctification of the sinner.
7   The right and duty of private judgement in the interpretation of Holy Scripture.

---

64  Massie, *The Evangelical Alliance*, pp.160-61, 177.

8 The divine institution of the Christian ministry and the authority and perpetuity of the ordinances of Baptism and the Lord's Supper.[65]

(*See also Appendix 1*)

Candlish explained that the sub-committee had considered the view that the words of the older confessions of faith should be used, but its members had come to the unanimous conclusion that the basis should be 'framed anew, to suit the exigencies of modern times'. He added that this was not meant to be a creed to which all would have to concur (a very important *caveat*), but rather a 'general statement, which could not be mistaken by parties who acted in good faith and which should indicate with sufficient clearness what sort of persons ought to be entitled to compose this Union'. J.H. Hinton noted that the article on the Christian ministry and the ordinances of baptism and the Lord's Supper would probably exclude the Quakers. Candlish replied that in their deliberations the committee had been aware of this problem, but they had felt that since the Alliance would be called upon, as a Protestant body, to enter into debates about Roman Catholic doctrine, a clear statement on the ministry and on the sacraments was essential.[66]

Discussion was to continue on this issue, since it was clear that it introduced the question of ecclesiological distinctives. One of the points made several times in discussions was that the Alliance meetings had been, and would continue to be, opened with audible prayer. This, it was pointed out, would in itself be likely to exclude Quakers, with their practice of silent waiting and little audible prayer. Thus the issue was not simply a doctrinal one. The position of the Brethren was also a factor, since the Brethren rejected ordained ministry. On the other hand, Brethren assemblies held that every believer was a priest, they practised baptism and the Lord's Supper, and they also appointed recognised preachers. Indeed, Charles Hargrove, a

---

65 *Conference on Christian Union*, p.33.
66 Ibid, pp.33-4.

former Anglican clergyman who had joined the Brethren, saw the Alliance as embodying Brethren principles.[67] It is evident that there could have been no Anglican affirmation of the Alliance if the Christian ministry and the sacraments of the church had not been included in the basis of faith. The only change that the Liverpool conference made to the doctrinal statement produced by the sub-committee was that the word 'regeneration' was changed to 'conversion' in the sixth article of the statement. This Basis of Faith would prove to be an important foundation for the formation of the Evangelical Alliance ten months later, in August 1846.

In order to further the work done at Liverpool and to prepare for the 1846 meeting, planned for London, the members of the provisional committee met on a number of occasions. At a provisional committee meeting on 4 November 1845 it was agreed to publish 5,000 copies of the Liverpool proceedings. Letters were sent out on 10 November, and later the committee decided to double the number of copies of the proceedings from Liverpool.[68] Resolutions passed at Liverpool were advertised in Christian newspapers such as *The Record* and *The Patriot*. It was hoped to establish a network of 500 corresponding Alliance members across the denominations. As the work increased, and in order to ensure efficient preparation for the August 1846 conference, offices were rented in Exeter Hall, London, which facilitated contact with the many evangelical groups that used the Hall. Contacts were further developed with evangelical leaders in France and Germany who might come to the London meetings. On 9 December 1845 it was

---

67 T.C.F Stunt, *From Awakening to Secession* (Edinburgh: T. & T. Clark, 2000), p.292. The Churches of Christ would have been in a similar position to the Brethren, having also rejected ordained ministry while maintaining the sacraments – but there is no mention of them in the relevant Alliance minutes from this period.

68  Minutes of the Provisional Committee, 4 November 1845; p.25. The letter of 10 November 1845, signed by Edward Bickersteth, Jabez Bunting, James Hamilton, John Leifchild, Edward Steane and Alexander Digby Campbell is held with the Minute book of the London Provisional Committee.

reported to the provisional committee that at a meeting in Geneva, 130 European ministers had indicated their desire to be part of the proposed Alliance after reading the Liverpool document.[69] J.W. Massie was happy to report that invitations had been sent everywhere, 'so far as Christian catholicity seemed to promise them a reception'.[70] The groundwork for the formation of an 'evangelical and catholic union' was being carefully undertaken.

## Conclusion

There were various motives that moved evangelicals, from the eighteenth century onwards, into closer co-operation. Evangelicals were, however, often divided among themselves. Some of the forces making for unity were negative, such as the existence of perceived common enemies – the 'monster', as it has been described, with the names of popery and Puseyism.[71] However, as the vision of an evangelical alliance became clearer, the arguments in favour of such a body became more constructive. The Liverpool conference of 1845 showed that there was sufficient common ground among disparate evangelicals to put in place a new body, with a basic doctrinal framework, which was committed to the promotion of a broadly based unity. It was in the final session at Liverpool, after three days of serious debate, that those present approved the name of 'Evangelical Alliance' for the body that, they hoped would be formed. Here, too, they agreed that steps would be taken to convene an international assembly in London. At this stage, it appeared that a strong momentum had been created, and this sense of purpose was carried forward into the provisional committee. The meetings in London in 1846, however, would prove to be more protracted and difficult than those in

---

69  Minutes of the Provisional Committee, 9 December 1845.

70  Massie, *The Evangelical Alliance*, p.207.

71  E.R. Sandeen, 'The Distinctiveness of American Denominationalism: A Case Study of the 1846 Evangelical Alliance', *Church History* 45.2 (1976), p.223.

Liverpool. Although Robert Candlish's dream was of 'a union not of man's contrivance' – suggesting that divine shaping was taking place and that catholicity would be a major theme – many obstacles remained in the path of those committed to seeking such evangelical unity.

3

# Across the Partition Wall

*The Formation of the Alliance*

Although the lead-up to the inauguration of the Evangelical
Alliance was promising, its actual launch in August 1846
proved to be more complicated. This was not apparent when
the 1846 Conference began. The approximately 800 or so
people who gathered on 19 August 1846 in the Freemasons'
Hall, Great Queen Street, London met in a somewhat incon-
gruous setting for evangelicals, with the signs of the zodiac
decorating the walls. There they heard Sir Culling Eardley
Smith, who had been elected Chairman, assert rather extrava-
gantly that the conference was 'the first experiment' that had
been made to combine the interest of truth and love.[1] As
early as the second day of the conference those present unanimously resolved to proceed 'to form a confederation under
the name of 'THE EVANGELICAL ALLIANCE'. Enthusiasm about unity crested early.[2] The remainder of the conference's time was to a large extent spent dealing
with differences of opinion over evangelical doctrine and
over the issue of slavery. Given that there were representatives from nine major English and Welsh denominations, six
Scottish denominations and three Irish denominations, plus

1 *Report of the Proceedings of the Conference held at Freemasons' Hall, London, From
August 19th to September 2nd Inclusive, 1846*, p.5.
2 Sandeen, 'The Distinctiveness of American Denominationalism', p.224.

members representing ten denominations in America, and
members from five countries of continental Europe, difficulties might have been anticipated.

The more serious of the two problems that emerged was the
issue of the owning of slaves by evangelicals, a practice that was
then common in the southern states of America. The fact that
the question of slave holding received such attention shows
that evangelical unity could not be confined to the spiritual
realm. An alliance of evangelicals had to examine the connection between evangelical faith and life in society. British evangelicals, such as William Wilberforce, had exemplified this
process of engagement in the long campaign against the slave
trade. If American evangelicals had tried to form their own
Evangelical Alliance it is almost certain that the attempt would
have foundered over slave holding. As it was, the Americans
present in London in August 1846 hoped that an international
gathering would enable them to transcend their internal di-
lemmas. They could show that they were able to act together –
in Britain.[3] But the fact that most British evangelicals had
strongly backed the anti-slavery campaign would impinge
powerfully on thinking about unity. David King, from Glasgow, hoped that the Alliance could achieve substantial unity,
and used a vivid metaphor: 'We meet to shake hands', he said,
'across the partition wall and the agreement is that the partition
wall is not to be disturbed, but when we shake hands, what if
the partition wall will not bear the shaking?'[4] As it turned out,
however, the wall would prove remarkably resilient.

## Preparatory Thinking

As the provisional arrangements were made for the conference
in August 1846 to set up the Evangelical Alliance, there was a
concentration on practical, socio-ethical matters. In April

---

3  Ibid., p.226.
4  *Report of the Proceedings ... 1846*, p.205.

1846, as planning for the August conference took on a sharper focus, a meeting of the provisional committee held in Birmingham put forward a number of practical recommendations. It was agreed that the proposed Alliance should obtain information on the growth of the Roman Catholic Church; the situation regarding religion in Britain generally and especially the degree of irreligion; the public observance of Sunday; and the existing state of Christian education. These items indicate the way in which the Alliance was seeking to address concrete societal issues, even if at this point the international concerns that were to become important later were markedly absent. There was a reaffirmation that 'the grand object' was 'manifesting and promoting the unity of Christ's disciples'. The task of the Alliance was, above all, to encourage the expression of the spiritual unity that already existed.[5] Edward Bickersteth, as a former secretary of the Church Missionary Society, had an internationalist perspective, but he and others knew that it was unwise for the Alliance to take over what was being done by missionary and other bodies.[6] Bickersteth and the inner circle accepted that there was 'a vagueness resting, like a mist, on the objects of the Alliance', a situation that was seen as inevitable until it became clearer how far members of different bodies were ready for union.[7]

The idea of united action attracted increasing attention in the lead-up to the formation of the Alliance. At a meeting in the Free Trade Hall in Manchester a capacity crowd of 5,000 people heard addresses by, among others, Baptist Noel, Bickersteth and Culling Eardley Smith. It was reckoned that clergy and ministers were present from the Episcopal churches in England and Ireland, the various branches of Presbyterianism, the Methodist denominations, Congregationalism, the Baptists and the Moravians. The perspective offered was international as well as interdenominational.

---

5  King, 'Historical Sketch of the Evangelical Alliance', pp.47-8.

6  Wolffe, 'The Evangelical Alliance in the 1840s', pp.342-5.

7  Massie, *The Evangelical Alliance*, p.210.

Eardley Smith referred to the anticipated presence at the August conference of friends from America and said that the Alliance might 'even tell upon the slavery of the United States'.[8] Thomas Chalmers, writing in 1846 before the inaugural meeting, applauded the practical resolutions being put to the conference.[9] He had been worried that practicalities would be played down and that the proposed Alliance might turn out to be 'a do-nothing society'.[10] He was later quoted as having feared that the Alliance would be 'union without work', and as having added that such a union would 'not constitute an alliance worth preserving'. The Christian spirit, he said, 'must live by working'.[11]

Although there was sympathy for Chalmers' championing of evangelical activism, his suggestion that the Alliance should abandon a declaration of faith and should operate as a broader 'Protestant Alliance' was not accepted.[12] Indeed, a Basis of Faith was increasingly seen as something that would save the Alliance from becoming merely a political crusade against Catholicism.[13] In the discussion that continued to take place about the doctrinal basis, however, there were, understandably, those who were concerned over the relegation of certain beliefs (about the nature of the church, for example) to the realm of non-essential convictions. Bickersteth addressed these concerns on a number of occasions, arguing that as a churchman he did not abandon his convictions by associating with those who differed from him. As the most widely respected evangelical Anglican of the time, Bickersteth was making an important positional statement. He was equally clear that Dissenters should not abandon their opinions. For him there could be 'a unity of spirit within a diversity of

---

8  Ibid., pp.212, 242.

9  T. Chalmers, *On the Evangelical Alliance; its Design, its Difficulties, its Proceedings and its Prospects: with Practical Suggestions* (Edinburgh, 1846), p.40.

10  Dale, *The Life and Letters of J.A James*, p.412.

11  *Jubilee of the Evangelical Alliance*, p.497.

12  Chalmers, *On the Evangelical Alliance*, p.36.

13  Sandeen, 'The Distinctiveness of American Denominationalism', pp.224-5.

forms'.[14] The Episcopal system he saw as having been pre-
served in the Church of England through the goodness of
God, but for him it was not essential to the existence of the
Church. What was essential was profession of a true faith,
coupled with true preaching and the due administration of
the sacraments.[15] This seemed to offer a basis for unity.

Those who drafted the statement of faith did not intend it
to be a statement of all the fundamentals of the gospel.[16] J.W.
Massie referred to the basis as 'a selection and not a compen-
dium of scriptural truth', pointing out that 'no body of unin-
spired men possessed authority to declare what are important
or unimportant truths'. Rather, the basis highlighted the
prominent characteristics of the designation evangelical.[17]
The provisional committee accepted one suggestion for a
change to the Liverpool statement, which came from some
Scottish Presbyterian leaders. The fourth article in the Basis
of Faith concerned belief in the incarnation and the atonement, and to this was added belief in Christ's 'mediatorial intercession and reign' – that is, his unique provision of access to
God the Father, and the divine authority confirmed in his ascension to the Father's side (cf. 1 Tim. 2:5; Heb. 10:12-13).
There was much more extensive debate about the article on
the ministry and the sacraments, with very different views being put forward. Some of those from North America who
were involved in the preparatory work also, crucially, wished
to add a statement about life after death and the last things.
Hours of discussion took place about this in the provisional
committee. As a result the conference was asked to agree
that a ninth article of belief be added: 'The immortality of
the soul, the resurrection of the body, the judgement of
the world by our Lord Jesus Christ, with the eternal blessedness of the righteous and the eternal punishment of the

---

14 Massie, *The Evangelical Alliance*, pp.132-3.
15 E. Bickersteth, *The Promised Glory of the Church of Christ* (London, 1844),
Appendix 1, pp.393-6.
16 Kessler, *A Study of the Evangelical Alliance*, p.31.
17 Massie, *The Evangelical Alliance*, pp.355-7.

wicked.'[18] The Americans were prompted to call for this addition largely in response to the rise of Unitarianism in their own country. Until the mid-nineteenth century, the main challenge to the traditional view of death, judgement, heaven and hell presented in their proposed new clause had come from universalism – the view that everyone will eventually be saved. Now, however, increasing numbers of theologians and Christian leaders were seeking a 'middle way' between these two well-established positions. The most popular such course turned out to be annihilationism – the view that rather than being tortured forever, the unredeemed will be destroyed by God some time after they have been judged and punished. Unitarians took their name from their assertion of God's oneness over against the Trinity, but from their formation in the 1770s onwards they had also been known as advocates of this increasingly popular annihilationist eschatology. In time they would come overwhelmingly to embrace full-blown universalism, but in the 1840s their and others' promotion of eventual destruction was deemed sufficiently threatening by the US delegation to warrant clear censure in the Evangelical Alliance's Basis of Faith.[19]

## Potential for Conflict

It was recognised that a statement of this kind had the potential to create division, although the strength of feeling that was later generated over this issue seems to have been a surprise. Nor was the Alliance prepared for the conflict that ensued over slave holding. The provisional committee members agreed a resolution which stated that while they considered it 'unnecessary and inexpedient to enter into any question at present on the subject of slaveholding', they were 'of the opinion that

---

18  *Report of the Proceedings … 1846*, pp.79–81.
19  For more detail see G. Rowell, *Hell and the Victorians* (Oxford: Clarendon Press, 1974); also ACUTE (Evangelical Alliance Commission on Unity and Truth among Evangelicals), *The Nature of Hell*, pp.60-67.

invitations ought not to be sent to individuals, who whether by their own fault or otherwise, may be in the unhappy position of holding their fellowmen as slaves'.[20] Although there were suggestions later, when the matter became divisive, that the subject should never have been mentioned, it was such a major issue for transatlantic evangelicalism that ignoring it would have been inconceivable. The problem was that the question of slaveholders had not been debated at Liverpool and therefore it was left to the provisional committee to come to a decision about an important limitation in the invitations to the forth-coming 1846 conference. An additional problem was that the provisional committee had not studied the position of slave-holders in the United States. One American, Leonard Bacon, minister of the First Church of New Haven, Connecticut, and editor of two leading journals, The *New Englander* and the New York *Independent*, although progressive in his views, was outraged by the provisional committee's decision. We shall return to these issues below.[21]

There were other areas in which conflict was more immedi-ately apparent. *The Christian Observer*, a periodical that had been established by Wilberforce's so-called Clapham Sect to speak for moderate Anglican evangelicals, was fairly dismissive of the plans for an Alliance. Alliance supporters within the Church of England were dismayed by comments in 1845 sug-gesting that the Alliance was 'a scheme of sectaries to increase strife and confusion', and that it was 'a help and encourage-ment to Anabaptism'.[22] This was in line with the antipathy that, from time to time, the *Observer* showed towards Noncon-formity.[23] The references to sectaries and Anabaptism seem to have been directed towards Baptists and Scottish seceders in particular. Later, in 1845, after referring to the fact that two well-known Baptist leaders, J.H. Hinton and Edward Steane,

---

20 Massie, *The Evangelical Alliance*, p.357.
21 R. Baird, *Address on the History, Present State, and Prospects, of the Evangelical Alliance Cause in the United States* (London, 1851), p.51.
22 Massie, *The Evangelical Alliance*, p.250.
23 Lewis, *Lighten Their Darkness*, pp.10-14.

had been unwilling to co-operate with Anglicans in the
anti-Maynooth committee yet had taken a leading part in the
1845 Liverpool conference, the *Christian Observer* took thirty
pages to make its position quite clear. It asked whether it was
reasonable to think that these 'warm partisans' (for voluntary
rather than state support of religion) had now abandoned
'their evil will at our national Zion' (i.e. the Church of England). The Evangelical Alliance was dismissed as a 'new
anti-Church League and Covenant' led by 'Scottish sectaries'
and designed as an agency for destroying the established
church.[24]

From the Baptist side there were also, ironically, allegations
of sectarianism directed at the Evangelical Alliance. In May
1846 two articles, one for and the other against the Alliance,
appeared in *The Baptist Magazine*. There were obvious Baptist
concerns about how involvement in the Evangelical Alliance
could undermine fundamental Baptist convictions on believer's baptism, congregational church government and
church-state relationships. William Groser, editor of *The Baptist Magazine*, set out the reasons for not joining the Alliance.
He described it as 'essentially sectarian' since it excluded some
who it believed to be members of the body of Christ. The crucial problem for Grosner, and the reason why he was so confrontational, was because the Alliance had a 'creed'. He
challenged the Baptist members of the provisional committee
with these trenchant words: 'You have assented to the adoption
of a creed as the text of admission. The belief of that creed neither you nor I regard as justifying faith. The acknowledgment
of that creed is not, in your own judgment, any proof of vital
religion.' Grosner argued that 'since there are genuine Christians whom that creed will exclude ... Is it not just ... to say
that your union is not catholic, in the good sense of that term,
but sectarian?'[25]

24  *The Christian Observer*, December 1845, pp.731-61.
25  *The Baptist Magazine*, May 1846, cited by J.H.Y. Briggs, *The English Baptists of
the Nineteenth Century*, pp.232-3.

Other Nonconformist newspapers made similar points, showing the difficulties that the pro-Alliance leaders had to overcome in their search for 'an evangelical and catholic union'. There were strong criticisms in *The Nonconformist*, which was edited by Edward Miall, a Congregationalist, and was dedicated to achieving the separation of church and state, and in *The Christian Witness and Church Member's Magazine*. To join with Anglicans, they held, was to compromise the voluntary position. *The Nonconformist* also saw the attempt at 'compelling' people to subscribe to a particular statement of faith as 'unjust and unscriptural'.[26] In fact, joining the Alliance was voluntary, but 'compulsion' to assent to a Basis of Faith stirred up some Nonconformist feelings. John Campbell, a London based Scottish Congregationalist who edited *The Christian Witness*, was a powerful writer, and as the official organ of the Congregational Union his publication was influential, if unpopular with many Congregationalists.[27] Campbell claimed, in a letter to Bickersteth in January 1846, to yield to no man in his 'admiration of a Catholic spirit', but he expressed 'quenchless hostility to all Ecclesiastical Establishments'. His vision of unity was to bring together 'the entire sisterhood of Dissenting communities'.[28] Concrete actions by denominations to further Christian union would not be undertaken until much later, but the Alliance did confound its critics by pointing a way forward in ecumenical endeavour.

## Establishing an Alliance

On 19 August 1846 the conference that formally brought the Evangelical Alliance into being began in London. Of the 922 people who signed as attendees, 84% came from Great Britain, over 8% from the United States and over 7% from European

---

26  *The Nonconformist*, 28 January 1846, pp.43.

27  Lewis, *Lighten Their Darkness*, pp.179–80.

28  John Campbell to E. Bickersteth, 7 January 1846, *The Christian Witness*, 2 February 1846, pp.85–90.

continental countries, from Canada and from areas of the
world where western missionaries were serving. Indigenous
leaders from the non-western world were noticeably absent.
Although assessments of denominational affiliation at the
meeting vary somewhat, Clive Calver has calculated that the
largest group represented was Presbyterian in allegiance, with
the majority of these coming from Scotland, and a further 27
from the United States. In addition, there were 187 Methodists,
and 182 Congregationalists, thirteen of whom had come from
the USA. The strong representation of these three groups
reflected the well-established ecumenical commitment which
had been demonstrated in their formation and development of
the London Missionary Society in the preceding decades.[29]
Anglicans and Episcopalians together numbered 172, and
there were some 80 Baptists. Among the Americans, the Presbyterian group comprised an especially distinguished party of
advocates for unity, most of whom had left for Europe almost
immediately after they received an invitation to the conference.[30] The first few hours of the conference were largely
taken up in reading and discussing a report, which David King
had been asked to compile, that outlined the steps leading to
that point.

Ralph Wardlaw, the Congregational minister from Glasgow
who had written a paper entitled 'A Catholic Spirit' in *Essays
on Christian Union*, emphasised that the conference was being
held primarily to 'confess' Christian union and that there were
representatives from more than twenty evangelical Christian
denominations present who were involved in this process. The
conference was not there to bring union into being, he
stressed, but to recognise a union which already in fact existed.
It was Wardlaw who presented the first resolution to the conference. It read:

29  R. Lovett, *The History of the London Missionary Society, 1795-1895*.
30  Calver, 'Rise and Fall' p.150; Massie, *The Evangelical Alliance*, p.286. Compare
the somewhat divergent statistics in Jordan, *The Evangelical Alliance for the United
States of America*, p.36.

That this Conference, composed of professing Christians of many different Denominations, all exercising the right of private judgment, and, through common infirmity, differing in the views they severally entertain on some points, both of Christian doctrine and ecclesiastical Polity, and gathered together from many and remote parts of the World, for the purpose of promoting Christian Union, rejoice in making their unanimous avowal of the glorious truth, that the Church of the living God, while it admits of growth, is one Church, never having lost, and being incapable of losing its essential unity. Not, therefore, to create that unity, but to confess it, is the design of their assembling together. One in reality, they desire also, as far as they may be able to attain it, to be visibly one; and thus, both to realize in themselves, and to exhibit to others, that a living and everlasting union binds all true believers together in the fellowship of the Church of Christ.[31]

A number of elements in this resolution are important. In the first place, in its affirmation of 'the right of private judgment' it is a clearly Protestant document, with a leaning towards Nonconformist thinking. Secondly, differences between Christians are seen as arising 'through common infirmity'. Something important is seen as being lost because of denominational divisions. Yet, at the same time, the church is 'one church'. Essential unity, in fact, remains. One reading of this might suggest that the issues dividing the churches are relatively unimportant, although this is not what is said. Rather, overarching unity is seen as incapable of being destroyed, despite the serious ecclesiastical divisions that exist. Finally, the resolution affirms the goal of being 'visibly one'. Although the subsequent history of the Alliance has not usually been linked with attempts to achieve visible unity, and although some have even seen it as opposed to such a goal, the idea of visible unity is undoubtedly here.

There were those at the conference who were outspoken in their anti-denominational statements. Stephen Olin, President of the American Wesleyan University (and a minister of the Methodist Episcopal Church), while welcoming the resolution, suggested that 'our Denominational names and peculiarities are the hay and stubble', and spoke of a 'visible

---

31 *Report of the Proceedings ... 1846,* p.44.

church' that was emerging which he saw as transcending denominationalism. He said that he had offered up his 'sectarian bigotry' on the altar of his Saviour.[32] There was also hope of overcoming racial barriers. A black minister, M.M. Clark, from the African Methodist Episcopal Church in Washington, spoke on behalf of African Americans and was enthusiastically received. Some of the conference members present from mainland Europe also spoke in strongly pan-denominational and pan-national vein. Those from France, such as George Fisch from an independent church in Lyons, explained that the major argument of the Roman Catholic Church against the credibility of Protestant churches was that Protestantism was hopelessly divided. The French, despite having only thirteen members at the conference, constituted a significant European presence.[33] Eduard Kuntze from Germany talked about the way a meeting in Germany organised by a group of rationalists had stimulated evangelicals to realise the need to come together with others, from Germany and elsewhere, in a deeper unity.

The 'one church' that was affirmed in the resolution certainly indicated a unity that brought together not only different denominations but also different countries. A British Member of Parliament who was present, J.P. Plumptre, highlighted the international character of the conference. Yet it was different national perspectives that were to prove so problematic. It was because of a desire for freedom for evangelicals to deal with their national contexts that the British would have preferred to give each country authority to set up its own Evangelical Alliance organisation. British leaders, in discussions that took place before the conference, generally saw anything beyond that as too ambitious. In these discussions, however, representatives from the United States, led in particular by Samuel Schmucker, argued that such a loose affiliation was inadequate. World-scale thinking, as we have seen, had

---

32  Ibid., pp.47-9.
33  Railton, *No North Sea*, chapter 1.

already been present in the United States before British plans for an Alliance took shape. It was this concept of international co-operation that would cause problems in defining the statement of faith. It would also ultimately steer the delegates towards a rock on which the very existence of the Alliance almost foundered.

Although the commitment to 'one church' was a noble sentiment, it was recognised that in many places, not least in Britain, denominational allegiance was held quite tenaciously. F.A. Cox, a British Baptist who wrote a favourable review in 1845 of *Essays in Christian Union* and who deplored denominational 'walls of separation', nevertheless realised the limits of what could be achieved. In his frustration with the status quo concerning denominational unity, he caricatured Bible Society supporters as meeting at society anniversaries and leaving 'generally with undiminished prejudices, jealousies and dislike – with scarcely a shake of the hand'.[34] On the other hand, Cox brought forward a resolution to the conference designed to allay fears that the Alliance might seek to destroy denominations. He asked that the Alliance should be considered an alliance of individuals. Cox himself was hopeful that 'at some distant period' there might be wider union. An individual joining the Alliance 'does not abandon his denomination; he only moves out for a moment into this vast fraternity and brotherhood'. There was to be no 'new ecclesiastical organization', no union of 'systems'. This seemed to play down the Alliance's contribution to unity, although the conference did affirm that 'on the basis of great evangelical principles' the Alliance would give opportunity for united action.[35]

It was the predominant view of the delegates throughout the discussions at the inaugural Alliance conference that it was important to seek to reach out across the divisions that existed

---

34 'Christian Union', *The Eclectic Review,* June 1845, p.670; cf. J.H.Y. Briggs, 'F.A. Cox of Hackney: Nineteenth-Century Baptist Theologian, Historian, Controversialist and Apologist', *The Baptist Quarterly* 38.8 (2000), p.393.
35 *Report of the Proceedings ... 1846*, pp.178-9, 202.

within the church as a whole, but that it was not realistic at that point to seek to remove the divisions themselves. This was Cox's position. Nonetheless, there were those who saw the possibility that the Alliance would bring into being a new era in the history of the church.[36] Hopes were high when, on the second day of the conference, Robert Buchanan a Free Church of Scotland minister in Glasgow, seconded by a Rev Dr De Witt of the Dutch Reformed Church in New York, formally proposed the formation of the Evangelical Alliance. De Witt stressed that this marked a stage in a spiritual journey. 'It is good for us to be here', he acknowledged, but echoing the experience of Jesus with his disciples on the 'mountain of transfiguration', he urged that the conference members should 'build no tabernacles', in the sense of feeling that this was the place where they should settle. Rather, they should carry the message of eternal life to the world. The proposal to form the Alliance was put to the conference and after a period of silent prayer it was passed unanimously, delegates singing the doxology and shaking hands with one another.[37]

## Defining and Re-defining

The third morning of the conference saw the commencement of discussion of the doctrinal statement. Debates about this, which were intense, continued until the end of the fifth day. In his speech presenting the basis, Edward Bickersteth stressed that although the doctrines in the statement kept some people out of the Alliance, this was not to be taken as suggesting that they were outside the church. He did, however, see the basis as setting out the essential elements – 'the most vital truths' – of evangelical Protestantism, and embracing most, though admittedly not all, 'real Christians'. There was certainly an inference here that those who did not hold to the basis were not holding

---

36  Massie *The Evangelical Alliance*, p.112; cf. C. Calver, 'Rise and Fall', p.150.
37  *Report of the Proceedings … 1846*, pp.65-70.

to fundamental evangelical beliefs. It was not the intention to admit Roman Catholics to the Alliance, said Bickersteth, 'though some of them might be real Christians' (others said that 'many' Roman Catholics were to be counted as such), since the Alliance was designed to link those who could act together in unity. Bickersteth later emphasised the 'private judgment' as set out in the Basis of Faith, and contrasted this with the way in which the Roman Catholic Church had recently denied the reading of Scriptures to the laity.[38] The right of private judgement, in Protestant thinking, meant that there was room for fresh interpretations of Scripture and thus it followed that no basis of faith was ultimately binding.

Unsurprisingly, most of the articles of faith provoked virtually no debate. All the delegates affirmed that the reality of human sinfulness and justification by faith alone were central evangelical doctrines, and they were not prepared to argue about wording. The Trinity was central: the American delegation in particular insisted that a strong position must be taken on this and that there must be no truck with Unitarianism. As we have seen, the Americans were also insistent on the inclusion of an article concerning the immortality of the soul, the eternal blessedness of the righteous, and the eternal punishment of the wicked. Indeed, so concerned were they at the erosion of these doctrines by Unitarians, annihilationists and others that William Patton implied in one of his statements that the Americans would form their own separate Alliance — 'which would truly hold to a biblical position' — if the clause on life after death was not included.[39] Theologically, these Americans represented the middle ground rather than the conservative pole of American evangelical thinking. Ultra-conservatives, those on the more liberal wing of American Protestantism, and those of

---

38 *Report of the Proceedings … 1846*, pp.77-8; 94-5; 116-19; 137-8; see commentary by Jordan, *Evangelical Alliance for the United States of America*, pp.45-6; *The Nonconformist*, 26 August 1846, p.575 — W.W Ewbank, from St George's, Everton, spoke of many Roman Catholics who were real Christians.
39 *Report of the Proceedings … 1846*, pp.111-4.

high-church persuasion did not attend the conference. In-deed, only one of the Episcopalians present at the conference was from the USA.

A number of British delegates were unhappy about the in-clusion of the statement about eternal punishment. One of the most outspoken was J.H. Hinton, secretary of the Baptist Union. He agreed with the truths contained in the article but did not see the need for it. Having himself faced censure in the Baptist Union for his unusual views on the work of the Holy Spirit in conversion, Hinton was worried about 'a grand inquisitorial court' investigating members' beliefs on this issue.[40] It was only Unitarians and those who were 'avow-edly Infidel', Hinton believed, who denied the doctrine of eternal rewards and punishments. Hinton even threatened to resign over the issue and at one point alleged that the Alliance would be seen as a new denomination – the 'eternal tormentists'. Other British participants, however, regarded this as an extreme reaction. John Angell James argued for the additional article, suggesting that it was an article of belief that Congregationalists, while appearing divided on it, did affirm. This was not, however, the view of another Congregational-ist, Thomas Binney, who said that 'many good men' whom he knew did not believe in eternal punishment. Ralph Wardlaw was a Scottish supporter of the article, pointing out that it was the only part of the Basis of Faith that mentioned the future. It was clear that the tide of opinion had moved to the point where this additional article would be accepted. The existing article on the sacraments was retained, in line with Anglican wishes. Thus the final version of the basis was proposed to the conference on 24 August. Hinton and four others abstained in the vote, but both doctrinally and politically the formula of belief seemed to satisfy the vast majority of those present (for the full text see Appendix 2).[41]

---

40 *The Nonconformist*, 26 August 1846, p.575. On Hinton's pneumatology see Bebbington, *Evangelicalism in Modern Britain*, p.8.

41 *Report of the Proceedings ... 1846*, pp.101–7; 112–15; *The Nonconformist*, 26 Au-gust 1846, p.575. For background see Rowell, *Hell and the Victorians*.

The days immediately before and after the acceptance of the doctrinal statement appeared to indicate that the conference was destined to end on a harmonious note. On Sunday 23 August delegates preached in eighty-one London churches of various denominations. Holy Communion was celebrated in Baptist Noel's remarkably ecumenical Anglican church, St John's Chapel, Bedford Row, at 8am on that Sunday, with 150 people from a number of countries and denominations participating. From 25 to 27 August there was discussion by the conference of propositions urging practical co-operation. Uncharitable judgements about other evangelicals were deprecated. These 'practical resolutions' were to prove a continuing theme of Alliance life (see Appendix 4). The prominent Anglican T.R. Birks, then the incumbent at Kelshall, Hertfordshire, would later find himself at the centre of doctrinal controversy on the nature of hell. Here, however, he proposed that 'the great object of the Evangelical Alliance be to aid in manifesting as far as practicable the unity which exists among the true disciples of Christ; to promote their union by fraternal and devotional intercourse; to discourage all envyings, strifes and divisions'.[42] Johann Oncken, the German Baptist leader, encouraged steps that would broaden the worldview of British Christians, especially relating to Europe, where their knowledge was 'sadly deficient'.[43] The vision of Baptist Noel was that gatherings of Christians of different denominations throughout the world would hold 'the banner of unity'.[44]

## Deep Divisions

A group chaired by Samuel Schmucker had worked out the details of the proposed organisation of the Alliance, and he put

---

42  Ibid., pp.229-31.
43  Ibid., p.242.
44  *The Record*, 27 August 1846, p.3.

these to the conference on 29 August. The plan, which reflected American thinking, envisaged a world Evangelical Alliance divided into five regional organisations – Britain, the USA, France, Germany and Switzerland – to be linked by international conferences held every seven years or oftener. Schmucker's idea was that there should be genuine universality and that there should not be a concentration of power in the hands of leaders from any one country. By now, on the ninth day of the conference, many delegates were tired and wished to return to their pastoral duties rather than discuss organisational matters. J.H. Hinton, however, insisted that there had to be clarity over whether the proposal meant independent Alliances or a worldwide organisation. If what was to be implemented was the latter, then Hinton asserted that slaveholders must be explicitly excluded from membership. Hinton was committed to the British anti-slavery movement and was one of those who had pledged not to have any fellowship with slaveholders. If regional Alliances were to be independent, Hinton accepted that the issue of membership for slaveholders was a regional matter. American leaders had managed to preserve unity in the 1830s within evangelical organisations by ruling out discussion of slavery. In the 1840s, however, both Methodist and Baptist denominations split into two over the issue. Given this background, Americans resented what they saw as Hinton's interference.[45]

How important was this debate? For many decades after the Alliance was founded, the divisions that were exposed over the issue of slavery continued to have an impact, and – in the light of this – those who attempted to write official versions of the history of the Alliance were faced with a dilemma. One possibility was to deal with the subject of this 'partition wall' openly. The other, which was usually the preferred way, was to pass over the topic. Kessler notes that when he wrote his history he

---

45  *Report of the Proceedings … 1846*, p.290; see T.L. Smith, *Revivalism and Social Reform: American Protestants on the Eve of the Civil War* (New York: Harper & Row, 1965).

found that in the only copy of the report of the Evangelical Alliance's Manchester conference (which followed the 1846 London conference) that was available the pages of the section dealing with slavery had not been cut open. All the other pages had been cut and were well marked.[46] This reluctance to talk about the pain that Alliance members felt is seen in the fact that J.W. Ewing, in his book *Goodly Fellowship*, published in 1946, devoted only two paragraphs to the question.[47] Even Kessler does not mention that there was a contribution to the 1846 conference from a Jamaican perspective, with a 'gentleman of colour' (as the conference report put it), a minister from the Methodist Church in Jamaica, arguing for Christian unity as the means of fighting the slave trade.[48] As it was, the debate on whether slaveholders could be members of the Alliance took up four days of the conference.

Although the Americans were not completely united in their position – J.V. Himes from Boston, for instance, supported Hinton – William Patton of New York and several other American delegates stated that they had not come to join an Anti-Slavery Society. If slavery was to be dealt with and condemned, they argued, so should intemperance, child labour, exploitation in factories and other social problems that existed in Britain. For the Americans, slavery was a political as well as a moral issue with roots in the War of Independence, in the same way as the existence of the links in Britain between the state and the Church of England was a political issue with roots in the very formation of the nation. Patton declared that the American delegates had travelled to London not to see a British child born, and to be godfathers of such a child, but to found a world Alliance. If the slave-holding issue was introduced, then there could be only a British Organisation and the hopes of world unity would be

---

46 Kessler, *A Study of the Evangelical Alliance*, p.43.
47 J.W. Ewing, *Goodly Fellowship: A Centenary Tribute to the Life and Work of the World's Evangelical Alliance* (London/Edinburgh: Marshall, Morgan & Scott, 1946), pp.18f.
48 *Report of the Proceedings … 1846*, pp.217-8.

dashed.[49] There were some British voices that were conciliatory to the American consciences, such as W.W. Ewbank, an
Anglican vicar from Everton. A proposal was put forward that
condemned slavery but did not exclude slaveholders from Alliance membership. Professor Emory, of the Methodist Episcopal Church in the United States, was in sympathy with this
approach. He said that his denomination had taken a stand on
slavery and had lost 400,000 members as a result. Even so, he
argued that slavery was not a theological question. Adolph
Monod, professor in the theology faculty at Montauban University, France, took a similar line.[50]

F.A. Cox then proposed a motion, which Edward
Bickersteth seconded and Hinton supported, that an ad hoc
group should be convened to seek to resolve this problem. Ac-
cordingly, an Anglo-American sub-committee of forty-seven
people was set up and engaged in protracted deliberations.
Eventually the group's members, who included the influential
American Presbyterian educationalist and theologian, Robert
Baird, proposed that there might be a way forward if a resolution were accepted by the conference that strongly condemned 'slavery and every form of oppression'. The evils of
intemperance, duelling and profaning Sunday would thus be
linked with slavery. From the American point of view the spotlight would be taken off America; evils that were present
throughout the nations linked through the Alliance would be
included in a general condemnation. Alliances in the regions
were to be given the responsibility of addressing the situations
that pertained in their context. This was a way of recognising
evangelical diversity. Confidence was expressed that no branch
of the Alliance would admit into membership slaveholders
who continued in that position out of self-interest and willingly.[51] British members hoped that this would save the Alliance. Despite continued American expressions of unease, the

---

49  Ibid., pp.311–16.
50  Ibid., pp.317–38.
51  Ibid., pp.371.

motion was carried by a large majority on the Saturday evening of the second week of the conference, and this again raised hopes of success.

These hopes were to be dashed. On the Monday morning the Americans reported that subsequent to Saturday evening's apparent agreement they had met for their own discussions and had reconsidered their position. In their more open internal discussions it had become clear that out of over twenty Americans who had been on the sub-committee only five had supported 'with entire goodwill' the resolution that had been put on Saturday evening. One delegate summed up the problem, stating baldly that they would be regarded as having violated American patriotism. It was suggested that three-quarters of American Christians would not support an Alliance set up in the way proposed. Robert Baird, who had helped to formulate the resolution on Saturday, now withdrew his support. [52] Two years later, as he reflected on his thinking at that stage, Baird told an Evangelical Alliance audience in London that in his view the Alliance between church and state had done a hundred times more to corrupt sound doctrine, blend the church and the world and prevent people entering heaven than all the slavery that had ever existed. [53] Bitterness had been generated that would not readily be dispersed.

The debate on the issue of slavery continued for two more days, with the conference appointing a fresh sub-committee, but agreement could not be reached. J.W. Massie, who was close to the Presbyterian contingent, said that the Scots had made the maximum concessions possible to the Americans. [54] The resolutions and plans that had been agreed were, with considerable reluctance, ultimately rescinded. Baird believed that the 'great evil' of slavery would be abolished, but he was not prepared to be told by the British when and how this

52  H.M. Baird, *The Life of the Rev Robert Baird* (New York: A.D.F. Randolph, 1866), pp.233-5.
53  Baird, *Address on the History*, p.42.
54  *Report of the Proceedings...1846*, p.397.

should be done. 'We will do it', he said later to the British Alliance, 'but not in consequence of your bidding'.[55] The idea of the international Alliance envisaged by Schmucker was dropped. Instead, it was recognised that the British suggestion, to have loosely linked national organisations that could operate with a degree of independence over some issues, was the only workable solution. This would mean that the British would not be drawn into fellowship with slaveholders and each Alliance body could rightly say that it was not responsible for actions taken in another region. Partition walls divided nations. In the final resolutions of the conference, however, there was no mention of slavery. Although there had been deep divisions, *The Record* noted what it considered to be the 'Christian and Catholic SPIRIT' of the conference.[56]

## A British Alliance

Given nineteenth-century British world power, it was inevitable that the British Alliance would take the lead from this point onwards. The attempt to establish a world body had failed. Founding membership of the Evangelical Alliance, it was decided, would be limited to those who were at the London conference, of whom none were slaveholders; these members would set up seven regional organisations. The countries in which there were to be organisations were Great Britain, the United States of America, Belgium, France and French Switzerland, North Germany, South Germany and German Switzerland, Canada and the West Indies. These regional organisations would not be responsible for the policies and activities of other regions. Members of the regional organisations could only become members of the Evangelical Alliance as originally founded with the consent of all the regions, or by a general conference decision – this was designed

55  Baird, *Address on the History*, p.46.
56  *The Record*, 7 September 1846, p.4.

to ensure that slaveholders could not be members of an Evangelical Alliance in which British evangelicals participated. British members were to return to the strong line that had been challenged by the Americans.

The British members of the Evangelical Alliance met again in November 1846 at a conference in Manchester to set up the British Organisation. The work that had been done to produce the doctrinal basis for the August conference, to outline the aims of the movement and to present practical resolutions on Christian behaviour, was taken as foundational. But slavery was still touching raw nerves. J.H. Hinton said that he had heard that a slaveholder was within the Alliance movement, to which the conference Chairman, Sir Culling Eardley Smith, replied that there was an Alliance member connected with a Brazilian mining company that employed slaves. Apparently, however, the person in question had withdrawn from the Alliance. This was greeted with applause.[57] Discussion then moved to the issue of whether somebody owning shares in a company that held slaves should be admitted to the Alliance. Lord Kinnaird, a respected figure in the British evangelical community, later indicated to the conference that he – like many others – was connected with a brokerage firm that dealt in the shares of slaveholding companies. He asked the meeting to leave the issue and the matter was dropped.[58] Nonetheless, the conference confirmed that slaveholders were banned from any connection with the British Alliance.

The Manchester conference also dealt with procedural issues. The structure of the British Alliance, as it was outlined by Edward Steane – who did a great deal to shape the early constitution and who was to serve for a long period as an Alliance honorary secretary – was that Britain was divided into seven regions, each with a committee. These committees, comprising not more than 100 members, would meet every three months; they would all meet to-

---

57 *Proceedings of the Conference of British Members held at Manchester from November 4th-9th* (London, 1847), p.43.

58 Ibid., pp.76-7.

gether once a year. It was agreed that new members must assent to
the Basis of Faith and should also show the effects of their faith in
their conduct. Two existing members of the regional committee in
their area would recommend such members. In 1846 there were
about 3,000 members of the Alliance and by 1859 the figure was
6,000. At first, in common with the patriarchal structure of many
other church organisations at the time, women played no part in
the Alliance, but the annual report of 1850 stated that 'a considerable number of Christian females' were now in membership. While
none of these women are mentioned by name, the executive of the
Council did resolve in April 1850 to seek to form ladies' committees.[59] It was local initiative rather than national policy that broad-
ened the membership in this way. If these early attempts to include
women appear modest only by the standards of today's post-femi-
nist culture, it must be acknowledged that even in more recent
times, the Alliance has appeared somewhat reluctant to assign key
leadership roles to women. For example, while its current Direc-
torate now includes two female managers, the Senior Management
Group remains exclusively male, which it has always been. No
doubt this reflects the fact that even in the twenty-first century
many British evangelical churches maintain a traditional view of
women's roles. Granted, a 1998 poll of 848 Alliance member
churches showed 81% in favour of women's ordination; two years
later, however, a pastoral care survey on a similar sample established
that only 5% of affiliated congregations actually had a female pastor.
(By comparison, at the same point female clergy representation in
the Church of England had risen to over 10%).[60]

Another important step for the Alliance was the launch in
1847 of *Evangelical Christendom*, the Alliance's magazine. John
Henderson was the magazine's owner and financial backer, and

---

59  Executive Council Minutes, 17 April 1850.
60  Evangelical Alliance, 'EA Member Churches: 1998 Opinion Survey', Question 11, p.7; L.J. Francis, M. Robbins & W.K. Kay, 'Pastoral Care: Practice, Problems
and Priorities in Churches Today: An Interim Report from the Major Survey
Conducted for CWR and the Evangelical Alliance by the Centre for Ministry
Studies, University of Wales, Bangor'; P. Brierley (ed.), *Religious Trends 2000/2001
No.2*, p.54.

Edward Steane was its moving force as editor. It was published monthly up to 1898 and bimonthly or quarterly until 1954. The magazine was informative and thorough. It carried news from different parts of the world about evangelical activity and especially about mission. It also included theological papers by leading evangelicals. The theme of Christian unity received considerable coverage. As we shall see in the next chapter, the Alliance was committed to helping persecuted minorities in other countries – an issue that was given prominence in the magazine. The magazine also highlighted united prayer meetings. From its commencement the Alliance designated the first week in January as a period of united prayer and this week was observed in many parts of the world. It was through drawing evangelicals together with a sense of common identity that the Alliance exercised its greatest influence. The Alliance provided a framework that linked diverse sectors of evangelicalism and promoted concerted activity.[61]

## Conclusion

The period of planning for the inauguration of the Evangelical Alliance was one in which there was an optimistic outlook and what was often termed a 'catholic' spirit. It seemed that traditional divisions between evangelicals could be overcome. To a remarkable extent this was achieved, for example through the acceptance of a common statement of faith. But national ethical perspectives proved to be much more problematic. British evangelicals were not prepared to relegate what they saw as a massive social evil, slavery, to a position of relative unimportance. American evangelicals refused to accept the British position, seeing it as arising from ignorance of their situation. Hence the vision for a worldwide Alliance was not fulfilled. Practical actions did ensue, however, and the Alliance's leaders worked hard to encourage co-operation

---

61  Calver, 'Rise and Fall', p.152.

between evangelicals with diverse denominational views. Partition walls undoubtedly remained, but more proactive figures within the Alliance did manage to point the way to a wider, and even to an international, unity. As the next chapter shows, they did this substantially by reaching beyond their own boundaries to champion the cause of religious freedom in many parts of the world.

# 4

# Some Common Action

*Religious Liberty and the Search for a Social Agenda*[1]

## The Proper Basis of Unity

The division on slaveholding at the 1846 inaugural conference inevitably bred caution about further socio-political moves within the British Organisation of the Alliance. For all Thomas Chalmers' initial concerns that the new body might be a 'do nothing society',[2] many now feared the opposite – namely, that by attempting to do *too much* in the civic realm it might jeopardise the very unity on which, and for which, it had been founded. Indeed, just a fortnight after the London conference, even so active an evangelical social reformer as Anthony Ashley-Cooper, the seventh Earl of Shaftesbury, could write that while the Alliance had become, like the Anti-Corn Law League, 'a great fact', it now seemed 'unlikely' that it would 'have practical results in the same proportion'. For the foreseeable future, he added, its 'chief result' would be its sheer formation – the wonder 'that such a meeting could have been collected and conducted on such principles and in such a manner'.[3] Shortly afterwards, David King and J.W. Massie

---

1 In addition to the published sources formally cited here, we are indebted to the extremely helpful notes made from the Alliance archive on this issue by Clive Calver.

2 In Dale, *The Life and Letters of J.A. James,* p.412.

3 Lord Shaftesbury's Diary, 16 September 1846.

would take a similar view, disavowing any attempt to make the Alliance a 'political organization', and warning that it should avoid duplicating the social projects developed by other Christian bodies.[4]

Despite the slavery debate, these viewpoints were not new. They reflected a strain of thinking which had been present from the earliest, embryonic phase of the Alliance's life. In 1845 Gavin Struthers' contribution to the King-edited *Essays on Christian Union* had argued strongly that past church divisions had too often been caused by so-called 'non-theological factors', among which he included disputes over social action.[5] Likewise, although the Alliance had been substantially conceived amidst protests against government funding of the Roman Catholic seminary at Maynooth, by the time of the Preparatory Conference in Liverpool in October 1845, mention of the anti-Maynooth committee had been sidelined – despite the presence among the 216 delegates of its Chairman, Sir Culling Eardley Smith. As Kessler puts it, at this delicate stage most founders of the Alliance had 'wished to avoid involvement in issues which had become politically coloured'.[6] Indeed, as we saw in chapter 2, for many the keynote to be struck from Liverpool onwards would be neither an oppositionalist nor a controversialist one but rather the keynote of 'Love' – where 'Love' implied fellowship between evangelicals, as against concerted, high profile agitation.[7] Somewhat later, Adolphe Monod, the leading French evangelical, an energetic figure who had helped to found the Alliance at its inaugural 1846 London conference, would quote an anonymous Church of England bishop on the same point. Considering whether the Alliance should develop from being an essentially relational network to becoming a force for social transformation, the bishop told Monod bluntly that the new

---

4  King, 'Historical Sketch of the Evangelical Alliance', pp.15-6; Massie, *The Evangelical Alliance*, p.176.

5  James, et al., *Essays on Christian*

6  Kessler, *A Study of the Evangelical Alliance*, p.24.

7  Massie, *The Evangelical Alliance*, p.115.

body would be overreaching itself if it pursued the latter course:

> He said to me in his turn, 'An Evangelical Alliance, with any common co-op-eration, is an impossibility. I am ready to acknowledge as my brother any and every man who acknowledges Jesus Christ as his Saviour. I could even ac-knowledge him for my brother, though he should refuse to acknowledge me as his; nay, should he regard me as a child of the devil. But other conditions would be necessary before I could unite myself with him in any common enterprise. How, for instance, could I, who believe that I ought to uphold and serve the es-tablished church, act permanently with a brother who thinks that he ought to attack and destroy it? Suppress every common action, or your Alliance will perish.'[8]

Most church historians have emphasised this non-interventionist current in early Alliance thought, and have gone on to present the whole organisation as a disappointingly static entity committed to little more than the resolution of internal evangelical disputes. Thus, comparing the achievements of the Alliance with those of George Williams' YMCA, founded in 1844, Clyde Binfield suggests that Lord Shaftesbury's immediate verdict was justified: 'The Alliance', concludes Binfield, 'did not possess the vital influence to be expected from the nineteenth century evangelical revival's only ecumenical movement.'[9] Likewise, other commentators have portrayed an introspective, pietistic Alliance at odds with more radical Protestant groups formed during this period – not least militant Nonconformist bodies like the Anti-State Church Association and the Liberation Society. Hence Michael Watts proposes that the evangelical Nonconformists who comprised the majority of the Alliance's founder members were wedded to an 'escapist' spirituality, which paled beside the steps taken by left-wing Congregation-alists and Baptists towards constitutional and social change.[10]

---

8 A. Monod, 'Intervention of the Evangelical Alliance on Behalf of Persecuted Brethren', *Evangelical Christendom,* Vol. V (1851), p.430.

9 C. Binfield, *George Williams and the YMCA: A Study in Victorian Social Attitudes* (London: Heinemann, 1973), p.158.

10 M. Watts, *The Dissenters: Volume II: The Expansion of Evangelical Nonconformity, 1791-1859* (Oxford: Clarendon Press, 1995), 510-11.

Less pejoratively, W.H. Mackinstosh casts those Nonconformists who helped form the Alliance as a comparatively 'more
peaceful' constituency.[11] So too, David M. Thompson maintains
that while some Dissenters were lobbying parliament and holding public demonstrations, 'others eschewed political action
altogether and formed the Evangelical Voluntary Church Association and were later involved in the Evangelical Alliance'.[12]
Even the generally sympathetic Kessler judges that an 'individualistic attitude' and an 'aloofness from the practical issues of life'
hindered the early witness of the Alliance and 'prevented many
who were associated with it from realizing that spiritual unity
was dependent not only on love and truth, but on the believer's
situation in this world'.[13]

While such observations reflect a genuine aspect of the Alliance's identity, the full picture is more complex. First, the obvious point needs to be emphasised that once it had resolved to
unite evangelical Nonconformists with Anglican churchmen,
the Alliance per se had effectively to distance itself from its
strong voluntaryist and disestablishment roots. Despite what
Thompson implies, however, this does not mean that individual members of the Alliance abandoned such commitments. In
fact, as Timothy Larsen has pointed out, F.A. Cox (a militant
Dissenter), Ralph Wardlaw (the Scottish Voluntary) and Robert Eckett (the leading Methodist radical) all saw fit to operate
as founding members of the Anti-State Church Association
while maintaining strong support for the Evangelical Alliance.[14] Indeed, this was possible precisely because the Alliance
had decided to work to new agenda – an agenda which would
stress what Anglican churchmen and evangelical Dissenters
had in common qua evangelicals, rather than those issues of

11  W.H. Mackintosh, *Disestablishment and Liberation* (London: Epworth, 1972),
pp.34–5.

12  D.M. Thompson, 'The Liberation Society, 1844–1868', in P. Hollis (ed.), *Pressure from Without* (London: Edward Arnold, 1974), p.213.

13  Kessler, *A Study of the Evangelical Alliance*, p.114.

14  T. Larsen, *Friends of Religious Equality: Nonconformist Politics in Mid-Victorian
England* (Woodbridge: The Boydell Press, 1999), p.258.

church polity and constitutional order on which their respective denominations differed. Again, the observations of Larsen are salutary here:

> the political philosophy of [the] mid-Victorian Dissenters was rooted in their theology. The specific principles which they wielded, however, were derived more from the distinctive theology within some of the Nonconformist denominations than from pan-evangelicalism ... Nonconformist politics was rooted in theology, but not in the soteriology of evangelicalism, but rather in the ecclesiology of Congregationalism. Baptists and Congregationalists shared in common both their political views and their ecclesiastical views, but they were not always able to gain the political co-operation of those groups which held a different pattern of church government, notably the Wesleyans and the Unitarians (let alone churchmen).[15]

Larsen's point is well illustrated by the fact that even leaving aside its Anglican members, the fledgling Alliance held together evangelicals who disagreed vigorously on political ideology and strategy. For example, while Robert Eckett pressed for radical constitutional reform, another Wesleyan, Jabez Bunting, resisted many of the measures he proposed. However, both worked alongside one another in the Alliance. Likewise, during its formative years the Executive Council contained both Culling Eardley Smith, who ran for Parliament as a Liberal candidate in favour of disestablishment, and Robert Grosvenor (Baron Ebury), a Tory Anglican, who upheld the church-state link in the House of Lords.

While it might be tempting to suggest that such co-operation was possible only because the Alliance's new agenda eschewed political issues altogether, this was not, in fact, the case. Rather, the Alliance set out to avoid undue controversy and fragmentation by limiting itself to the 'investigation' of relevant social concerns, then passing the fruits of such investigation to those in its membership who might be in a position to act upon them in other forums. Hence, from its foundation in January 1847, the Alliance's monthly journal, *Evangelical Christendom*, carried pages of 'intelligence' from home and abroad as

---

15 Ibid., p.253.

a means of alerting its readers to matters of public concern –
not least in regard to the perceived growth of Roman Catholic
power within governments and institutions. Clearly, this information was meant for more than prayer alone. Furthermore,
although it would still officially be decrying political activism
as inimical to its own character and ethos into the 1870s and
80s,[16] the Alliance nonetheless made sure that its Executive
Council was replete with key parliamentarians and figures of
influence. Indeed, at one point during this period it boasted six
peers and seven MPs, as well as the Lord Mayor of London, a
High Court judge and the Dean of Canterbury.[17]

Even beyond this relational, 'behind the scenes' approach
to public affairs, the Alliance found that in certain areas, it
could not ignore the need for more direct action. Nowhere did
this need become more apparent than in the arena of religious
liberty.

## From Investigation to Campaigning

By the end of the 1840s, the British Organisation of the Alliance was still seeking to clarify its purpose. Although it had
resolved to move on from the specific political protests that had
brought so many of its members together, it was realising that
merely convening for fellowship and exchanging information
would not be enough to sustain things in the long term. The
Alliance needed a signature cause, even if that cause would
have to be such as to maintain, rather than threaten, the delicate
balance and unity that had been achieved thus far. As we saw in

16 Minutes of Special Meeting of Executive Council, 16 November 1870, Vol. II.
17 Executive Council Minutes, 10 November 1880. The President at this time
was Right Hon. Lord Polworth; Vice Presidents included Right Hon. The Earl of
Chichester, Right Hon. Lords Ebury, Waveley and Wriothesley Russell, Right
Hon. William Brooke, Alderman McArthur MP (Lord Mayor of London), Right
Hon. Lord Justice Lush and The Very Rev Dean of Canterbury. Executive Council
members included W.S. Allen MP, Richard Davies MP, Alderman Fowler MP, A.
McArthur MP, Sir Thomas McClure MP and Sir Charles Reed MP.

the last chapter, together with their European neighbours, the British had stuck fast to their convictions on slave holding at the inaugural conference in 1846. But the Westminster Parliament had abolished slavery in 1833, and since Alliance national committees were now operating with a significant degree of autonomy, this would no longer function as a front-line campaigning issue. Even so, if freedom had been championed successfully in that area, there was another front on which it still required significant advocacy.

Prominent among the early 'foreign intelligence' published in *Evangelical Christendom* were stories of believers around the world who had been persecuted, oppressed or otherwise restricted in the exercise of their faith. As such intelligence mounted, it occurred to many that this issue might merit more concerted action. The cause of religious liberty had, in fact, already been acknowledged at the inaugural conference when Robert Baird had underlined that the 'right to preach the gospel everywhere ought to be recognised by a Christian government', and had prompted the passing of a motion to this effect.[18] The same cause had been reiterated by the inaugural conference of the Alliance's British Organisation, held in Manchester in November 1846. Indeed, this meeting had passed an even fuller resolution, which pledged to monitor 'the progress of vital religion in all parts of the world', but especially of 'those who may be engaged, amidst peculiar difficulties and opposition, in the cause of the gospel, in order to afford them all suitable encouragement and sympathy, and to diffuse an interest in their welfare'.[19] Of course, Britain at this time was developing an immensely powerful empire – one that helped it to operate at the forefront of the international missionary movement. As Brian Stanley has noted, these factors were significant in motivating British evangelical concern for religious

18 Evangelical Alliance, *Proceedings of the Conference Held at Freemasons' Hall*, (London, 1846), pp.231–40.
19 Evangelical Alliance, *Proceedings of the Conference of British Members Held at Manchester from November 4*[th]*-9*[th] (London, 1847), Part VI: Concluding Resolutions.

liberties: in the 1840s, they were central to a growing evangelical sense that 'providence had marked out for Britain a humanitarian and salvific role in the world'.[20]

By the time of the annual conference of the British Organisation held in Bristol during June 1848, these general convictions began to be more specifically applied. Delegates to the conference welcomed and prayed for efforts being made to counter legal restrictions imposed by the State Council in the Swiss Canton de Vaud on a fast-growing Free Church denomination.[21] Indeed, the Bristol conference went so far as to convene four special committees to act as 'watchdogs' on religious persecution in France, Italy and Germany, as well as in Switzerland.[22] At this point, such moves were qualified by the familiar caveat that overt political interference lay beyond the Alliance's remit. By the following year, however, this non-interventionist stance had become severely strained.

Having dismissed from office any public educator who declined to attend 'official' church services, the Canton de Vaud Council of State now moved to forbid all religious assemblies save those held by its own approved Protestant church. The Free Church consequently established a 'dissenting academy' and continued to grow as it met in private houses – but it had to do so in the face of police and army patrols.[23] At its October 1849 conference in Glasgow, the British Organisation duly crossed the line from 'investigation' to overt action as it adopted a memorial for direct transmission to the State Council, protesting its policies and urging it to uphold the rights of the Free Church. This more direct approach owed much to the influence of Baptist Noel, who had written a book about the Canton de Vaud problem, and whose recent transfer from

---

20 B. Stanley, 'British Evangelicals and Overseas Concerns: 1833-1970', in J. Wolffe (ed.), *Evangelical Faith and Public Zeal: Evangelicals and Society in Britain, 1780-1980* (London: SPCK, 1995), p.81.

21 Evangelical Alliance, Minutes of Annual Conferences, Bristol, 1848.

22 Ibid., ;Executive Council Minutes, Bristol, 17 June 1848.

23 Ewing, *Goodly Fellowship*, pp.58-9.

the Church of England to the Baptist Union had boosted his commitment to religious freedom'.[24] Although this move provoked little immediate response, a covert branch of the Alliance was formed in the canton and, in time, the Free Church was recognised.[25]

If the Canton de Vaud crisis had nudged the British Organisation towards a more proactive stance, another religious freedom issue arose around the same time that would cause it to redefine its approach even more markedly. While it might have diversified from its early preoccupation with 'popery' and 'Puseyism', the establishment of monitoring groups on Italy and France confirmed that Rome still loomed large in the suspicions of many British Alliance members. In particular, early contributions to *Evangelical Christendom* often castigated the 'double standard' whereby the Vatican would support widescale religious liberty in countries where its influence was relatively weak, while doing little on the issue in regions where Catholicism was dominant.[26] This concern came to a head in the case of Dr Achilli.

Achilli was a prominent Catholic priest, who became a Protestant, and began distributing the Bible in Rome. He was arrested and imprisoned in the Castle of St Angelo, and was set to be transferred to the prison of the Inquisition. When word of this reached London, the Executive Council of the Alliance's British Organisation sought to investigate the matter, and challenge charges that it assumed had been trumped up against Achilli. The same Glasgow conference that had undertaken to support the Canton de Vaud Free Church duly assigned a special deputation to deal with the matter. Those chosen to pursue the case were Sir Culling Eardley (who had

24 For more detail see D. W. Bebbington, 'The Life of Baptist Noel', *Baptist Quarterly* 24 (1972), pp.389–411.

25 Ewing, *Goodly Fellowship*, p.59.

26 For a typical instance, see A. Thomson, 'On the Extent to Which Religious Liberty is Enjoyed by Protestants or Denied to Them in Foreign Countries', *Evangelical Christendom*, 1851, pp.431ff.

by now inherited his mother's estates and dropped the paternal 'Smith' from his name), Baptist Noel, the Scottish MP Charles Cowan, the leading Baptist and editor of *Evangelical Christendom* Edward Steane,[27] and Lord Wriothesley Russell, the respected Anglican evangelical clergyman. The Alliance undertook to fund a three-point programme for this group. First, they would seek to find sympathetic advocates for Achilli at Westminster. Then they would proceed to Paris, where they would enjoin the French government to mediate on Achilli's behalf with Rome – a plan made necessary by the fact that France was at this time occupying Italy. Finally, if necessary, they would themselves proceed to Rome to plead Achilli's cause.[28] In the meantime, a 'Special Meeting for United Prayer' was called, which would seek God's protection for the deputation. This took place at Carrs Lane Chapel in Birmingham, where the chapel's minister, John Angell James, and the distinguished Methodist surgeon John Melson explained Achilli's plight.[29]

As it turned out, the Alliance found powerful allies in the then Liberal Foreign Secretary Lord Palmerston, and in Lord Normanby. They persuaded the renowned French Foreign Minister and political philosopher Alexis de Tocqueville to block Achilli's transfer to the inquisition. By March 1850, the converted priest had been freed altogether and the Executive Council of the British Organisation were making plans to honour him at a series of special receptions, where thanksgiving would be offered 'for his deliverance from the Roman Inquisition'.[30] Achilli subsequently visited Britain in August of the next year, addressing Alliance members at the Freemasons' Hall and elsewhere.[31]

---

27  Steane edited *Evangelical Christendom* from its inception in 1847 until 1864.
28  Executive Council Minutes: Meeting Held in Merchants Hall, Glasgow, Fourth Session, 11th October 1849; Meeting Held at 7 Adam Street, 5 March 1850.
29  Ewing, *Goodly Fellowship*, p.60.
30  Executive Council Minutes, 5 March 1850.
31  Executive Council Minutes, 23 August 1851.

## France, Britain and 'Common Co-operation'

As we shall see, Achilli would subsequently embarrass the Alliance, but in its immediate wake his case had a galvanising effect, not only on the British Organisation, but also on its French counterpart. Indeed, following de Tocqueville's intervention, the Committee of Paris was inspired at its April 1850 meeting to adopt a resolution which it hoped would gain international assent from the Alliance as a whole. This resolution proposed 'That the Alliance should, as far as lies in its power, undertake the defence of any brother, throughout the whole world, who may be persecuted for the Saviour's cause.' Significantly, it resolved to join forces with the 'Committee of London' in presenting this form of words – partly in recognition of the success that the British had achieved in the Achilli case, but also in acknowledgement of the growing power of the British Empire in the world.[32]

One of the most illuminating contemporary accounts of these developments is presented in an article for *Evangelical Christendom* by the French pastor and professor of theology, Adolphe Monod. As we have seen, Monod had been a delegate at the 1846 London inaugural conference, and had spent a considerable amount of time after that pressing for religious liberties concerns to be placed at the centre of the Alliance's work. Reflecting on the Paris Committee resolution, and his own part in persuading the British to co-sponsor it, Monod demonstrates a profound appreciation of the debates then surrounding evangelical social engagement in general, and the Alliance's approach to it in particular. He explicitly recognises that Achilli has provided the catalyst for the resolution, and praises the British Organisation, without whose 'interposition' he would 'still be in the prisons of Rome'. Even so, Monod bears out the continuing caution of the Alliance about such matters when he specifies that the resolution commits it 'to interfere only in favour of *brethren* – and brethren *persecuted*'. He explains this in the following terms:

---

32  Monod, 'Intervention', pp. 428-30.

> Every man who suffers for his sincere belief, whether true or false, be he
> Protestant, Papist, Jew, Mahometan, or even Pagan, has a right to our commis-
> eration and sympathy; but the Evangelical Alliance, as an Evangelical Alliance,
> is not called to take up any but those who have one common faith with it, and
> who suffer for that faith ... Personal or local sufferings, which our brethren
> have to endure for the faith, demand, in all cases, our warmest sympathy, but do
> not require the interference of the Alliance; a public evil only requiring a pub-
> lic remedy. Nor is even labour endured, and difficulty met with in preaching
> the gospel, sufficient to call for the interposition of the Alliance; its work being,
> not so much to emancipate, as to assist, and beginning only in case of real per-
> secution.[33]

The balance between models of the Alliance that would preserve it as an essentially static association, and those which
would cast it as an essentially single-issue pressure group, is
being sought here. In Monod's terms, the search for a clear
position between these two poles represents nothing less than
the definitive 'problem' of the Alliance's development. Moreover, as subsequent chapters in our study will confirm, his
exposition of this problem is relevant not only to the history of
the Alliance's work on religious liberties as such, but also to its
wider record of social and political involvement. It is, he says,
the problem of how exactly to work out 'one common
co-operation'. On the one hand, he writes, there are those who
conceive such co-operation in terms of direct, high-profile
engagement:

> The Evangelical Alliance, say some, must have *common action*. If it confines itself
> to the mere declaration of Christian union, where is the necessity of a perma-
> nent and organised existence? For the publication of a principle, nothing more
> is required but to meet once in order to prepare and issue a common declara-
> tion. If meetings are periodically to be held, merely to renew that declaration, a
> languid uniformity will inevitably ensue, which will make the Evangelical Al-
> liance more prejudicial than profitable to the sacred cause which it avows.
> Some kind of common action, which will embody the principles of the Evan-
> gelical Alliance in things visible, is absolutely required to give it an existence,
> *sui generis*, a real influence and a usefulness perceptible to everyone.[34]

33  Ibid., p.429.
34  Ibid.

By contrast, there are those who take a more purely 'spiritual' view:

> But others say – that the Evangelical Alliance cannot undertake any common action – that unity which exists between all true Christians, and which it is the object of the Evangelical Alliance to recognise and confess, is purely spiritual, and cannot be promoted by brethren belonging to different or opposite ecclesiastical parties, except on condition of scrupulously confining itself to the superior sphere of things invisible. The moment that any common action be attempted, we shall place ourselves in a position where divergent and contrary notions will arise to divide; so that what we have done in favour of union, will prove less to its promotion than to its injury. The Alliance can only become permanent by confining itself to those reunions which shall have for their sole object to recognise, proclaim, and encourage Christian union.[35]

These distinctions would be played out more starkly in the divergence of 'liberal' from 'conservative' evangelicalism in the early twentieth century, but would then to some extent be reconciled through the 'recovery' of evangelical social concern after the Second World War (see chapters 9 and 11). Back in the 1850s, Monod was unapologetic about siding with those committed to 'some common action', but insisted that this should be such as to enrich, rather than unduly strain, the intrinsic unity which was so precious to the quietists. The 'common action' in question would therefore be 'strongly organised', yet would 'belong to an order of things where secondary discrepancies of true Christians do not reach'. The religious freedom of fellow evangelicals would fit this requirement best, urged Monod, not least because it was a transparent, cardinal principle on which few would be likely to disagree:

> To interfere in favour of brethren persecuted for the faith will be doing a work of indisputable usefulness, which will require the most prompt and best-combined efforts, but at the same time, a work in which all true Christians can concur, because such an interference is so natural and necessary a consequence of fraternal love, that nothing is beyond that love made visible.[36]

---

35  Ibid., p.430.
36  Ibid.

As it was, although Monod made Achilli the cue for this 'natural and necessary' shift in the Alliance's focus, Achilli himself
would turn out to have been a less ideal precedent. After his
appearances on various pan-evangelical platforms in Europe,
he relocated to the United States, where he founded his own
heterodox, sectarian movement and was exposed as a woman-
iser.[37] By this point, however, the Alliance had already developed its campaigning on several other fronts, and had
effectively accepted Monod's argument. If anything, in fact, it
would prove to be more radical than he had envisaged, since it
would find itself compelled to defend a number of individuals
and groups who hardly fitted the description 'evangelical'.

By 1852, with the joint London–Paris resolution adopted,
the minutes of the British Organisation were already recording
that memorials and deputations had been sent on behalf of
persecuted evangelicals and Nonconformists to 'Turkey, the
Holy Land and Holland',[38] Germany[39] and Italy.[40] Many more
causes would be championed all over the world in the next few
decades; the details of these fill literally hundreds of pages of
*Evangelical Christendom*. The sheer weight of this documentary
evidence and its corroboration in the minutes of the Alliance's
Executive Council, bears out Ruth Rouse's observation that
the defence of religious liberty became the Alliance's 'one distinctive, strong and continuous practical activity' during the
Victorian era.[41] If Rouse is also justified in noting that the Alliance was 'prone, sometimes perhaps uncritically, to defend the
small body or sect against the national church',[42] it should be
realised that it was prepared consistently to support such un-
derdogs when others barely noticed them. No doubt, as with
Achilli, it made occasional misjudgements, but the vast bulk of

---

37 M. Trevor, *Newman: The Pillar of Cloud* (London: Macmillan, 1962),
pp.547-602. Calver, 'Rise and Fall', p.155.

38 Executive Council Minutes, 23 August 1851.

39 Executive Council Minutes, 6 May 1852.

40 Executive Council Minutes, 24 August 1852.

41 Rouse, 'Voluntary Movements', p.323.

42 Ibid.

its work in this area contributed positively to our modern understanding of 'freedom of religion'. Indeed, the sentiments expressed by this Executive Council resolution from May 1854 have a strong resonance with the religious liberties campaigning of our own day – even if the focus on continental Europe may now have shifted elsewhere:

> That in the present position of the continental nations, moreover and especially in view of the numerous and severe persecutions which so many of their fellow Christians are called to suffer, and which disgrace alike the age and the countries in which they are perpetrated, the Council feel themselves constrained to manifest their sympathy with those foreign brethren who for conscience towards God endure grief, suffering wrongfully, and to use their efforts in every legitimate method which Divine Providence may open to them for the removal of the restraints which are imposed upon the human conscience by many of the Governments of Europe, so that full Religious Liberty may be enjoyed by all their peaceful and loyal subjects.[43]

Shortly after this declaration, the Executive Council appointed a 'Foreign Secretary', Hermann Schmettou, specifically to develop its religious liberties work. While space does not permit an exhaustive analysis of this work as it expanded in the ensuing years, it is worth recalling key representative examples as they emerged within different geographical and confessional contexts, and as they established a pattern of worldwide campaigning which has continued into the present.

## Catholic Europe

While the Canton de Vaud case had shown that evangelicals could suffer at the hands of state church Protestants as well as Roman Catholics, the anti-Romanist sentiments stirred up by the Achilli episode continued to run deep.

---

43 Executive Council Minutes, 11 May 1854. Punctuation has been added here for clarity: the original minute eschews almost all punctuation in favour of a 'legal' style.

In 1851, the Duke of Tuscany signed a decree authorising his magistrates to jail anyone found in possession of a Bible. One prominent victim of this new measure was Count Guicciardini, a Florentine nobleman who had renounced Catholicism and who had begun to attend Protestant services. Seeking support from the Evangelical Alliance, Guiccardini made preparations to attend its international conference, which had been scheduled for London in August – to coincide with the Great Exhibition.[44] As we have seen, the liberated Achilli managed to speak at this gathering; the Count, however, was arrested before he could travel there, and was incarcerated. By the following year, when the conference convened in Dublin, the Alliance Council again called on the advocacy of Edward Steane, who formed a committee with C.M. Bissell and a Dr Kirkpatrick, so that a memorial could be presented to the Grand Duke of Tuscany, urging him to repeal the offending law.[45] At the same time, Steane informed the Council that a Protestant couple, Francesco and Rosa Madiai, had also recently been condemned with hard labour to the galleys of Florence, on suspicion of heresy.[46] The key charge against them had become familiar in the region: that they had read and distributed the Bible. At his trial, Franceso was apparently asked whether he had been born a Roman Catholic. In response, he said, 'Yes, but now I am a Christian according to the Gospel.'[47] As well as passing resolutions deploring their treatment, the Alliance Council managed to publicise the Madiais' plight in *The Times*. This in turn led to a protest meeting in Exeter Hall. Steane's committee then met the Foreign Secretary, Lord John Russell, after which a deputation went to Florence to negotiate with the Grand Duke. Initially, the Tuscan government resisted what it perceived to be bullying by northern Protestant powers. On 18 March 1853 however, Lord

---

44  Executive Council Minutes, 21 August –3 September 1851.
45  Executive Council Minutes, 24 August 1852.
46  Ibid., p.267.
47  Ewing, *Goodly Fellowship*, p.62.
48  Ibid.

Russell was able to tell the House of Commons that the Madiais had been freed.[48]

Another country in which Roman dominance went hand in hand with the oppression of evangelicals was Spain. In mid-1861, the various national organisations of the Alliance met for a world conference in Geneva. One of the sessions at this gathering was devoted to religious liberty, and was addressed by the French theologian Dr. de Pressensé. De Pressensé had already established himself at an earlier international conference, in Paris in 1855, as an eloquent promoter of religious freedom, and as an equally eloquent critic of the Vatican's record in this sphere.[49] At Geneva, he outlined the biblical basis of religious liberty and then turned more specifically to reports from Spain that some Protestants were currently languishing in jail there because of their faith.[50] After asking, 'Shall we do nothing, gentlemen, for these glorious and well-beloved captives?', de Pressensé persuaded the conference to adopt a resolution deploring the persecutions and committing their respective home organisations to take appropriate action. The British would prove especially diligent in pursuing this challenge.

From the autumn of 1861, both the Executive Council Minutes and the 'foreign intelligence' sections of *Evangelical Christendom* showed growing concern for what they called the 'Spanish persecution'. In a meeting held at 7 Adam Street on 19 November, the Executive considered a draft resolution on this issue.[51] Two days later, the wording of the resolution had been developed so as to focus more specifically on an individual whose plight would become a genuine *cause célèbre* during the next two years – a young evangelist from Malaga called Manuel Matamoros.[52] Matamoros had converted from Catholicism to Protestantism, and had moved swiftly into

---

49  Ibid., pp.85-6.
50  Ibid., p.67.
51  Executive Council Minutes, 19 November 1861.
52  Executive Council Minutes, 21 November 1861.

successful outreach across his home region. Soon, his influence extended much farther, to Seville, Granada and Barcelona. In Barcelona, however, he was arrested and called before the magistrates. As Ewing records it, when asked by them, 'Do you profess the Catholic Apostolic Roman faith, and if not, what religion do you profess?', he answered, 'My religion is that of Jesus Christ: my rule of faith is the Word of God, or Holy Bible ... The Roman Catholic and Apostolic Church not being based on these principles, I do not believe in her dogmas, still less do I obey her in practice.'[53] Matamoros was next ordered to appear at the Council of Granada, but the Paris and London committees of the Alliance heard of his case and managed to send money to defray his travelling expenses. When Matamoros had been jailed on his arrival, they then despatched a delegation and a joint memorial to the Madrid government on his behalf, and on behalf of other persecuted evangelicals in the country.[54] As it happened, Sir Robert Peel the Younger also visited Matamoros while on a visit to the Iberian Peninsula, and managed to negotiate an improvement in his conditions.[55]

When Matamoros' case was eventually heard, he was acquitted of political agitation, but was found guilty, along with several other Spanish Protestants, of apostasy. The sentence imposed was seven years' penal servitude – a term which was actually extended to nine years after appeals.[56] In response, the Alliance lobbied the Westminster Parliament on several occasions, with its Edinburgh, Glasgow, Liverpool and London committees each presenting petitions to Lord Palmerston, who had now become Prime Minister. In addition, a major rally was held at St James' Hall, where both Lord Shaftesbury and Sir Robert Peel spoke on behalf of the convicted Spaniards. Following this, the Alliance deputed its new Chairman, Major-General Alexander, to lead a delegation to put the prisoners' case to the Spanish

53 Ewing, *Goodly Fellowship*, p.65.
54 Executive Council Minutes, 21 November 1861.
55 Ewing, *Goodly Fellowship*, p.66.
56 Ibid., pp.66-7.

Prime Minister, the Duke of Tetuan.[57] When this and a subsequent visit by French evangelical women proved unsuccessful, the British Organisation convened a long and agonised meeting on 19 February 1863, after which it resolved to join forces with Alliance representatives from Austria, Bavaria, Denmark, France, Holland, Prussia, Sweden and Switzerland to petition Queen Isabella II. She commuted the prisoners' sentence from imprisonment to banishment, but refused to retract her earlier denunciation of them as heretics whose crimes ranked worse than those of common criminals.[58]

Matamoros continued to encourage Spanish Protestant evangelists and preachers from exile in Pau, Bayonne and then Lausanne. However, he died aged 32 in 1866. Indeed, there seemed little sign that progress had been made by the Spanish government when, two years later, the Alliance was led, through Lord Stanley, to protest once again at the imprisonment of a young evangelical – Julian Vargas of Malaga.[59] Despite some relaxation of constraints against Protestants after a change of regime later in 1868, *Evangelical Christendom* was still citing abuses of religious liberty in Spain well into the late nineteenth century.[60] Even in 1929 the London Executive was moved to back the Alliance's Spanish Committee financially when it supported Carmen Padin – a Spanish woman tried for declaring that Mary had borne other children besides Jesus.[61]

Elsewhere in Catholic Europe and its outposts, as 'common action' on religious liberty became the Alliance's hallmark, the British Organisation backed a whole range of further causes,

57 Executive Council Minutes, 17 October 1862; Ewing, *Goodly Fellowship*, pp.67–8.
58 Executive Council Minutes, 'Special Meeting "Exclusively to Consider and Decide Upon the Action of the Evangelical Alliance with Reference to the Spanish Prisoners"', 19 February 1893.
59 Executive Council Minutes, 7 May 1868; also 29 July 1868'.
60 A. Benoliel, 'Religious Liberty in Spain', *Evangelical Christendom,* September 1874, pp.287–8.
61 Ewing, *Goodly Fellowship*, pp.76–7.

from calls for Protestant chaplains in the French army,[62] through defence of persecuted evangelicals in Barletta, Italy[63], and of gagged missionaries in the French Colonies,[64] to campaigns on behalf of jailed evangelists and witnesses in Portugal.[65] No doubt, these initiatives were given impetus by the Alliance's general antagonism towards the Vatican. It would be wrong, however, to assume that religious liberty was a mere flag of convenience for anti-papist attack. Indeed, the record shows that even after the de Vaud episode, the Alliance as a whole, and the British Organisation in particular, devoted at least as much time to abuses of evangelicals by state Protestant churches.

## Protestant Europe: Established Churches Against Independent Evangelicals

As early in the life of the Alliance as September 1847, Sir Culling Eardley was warning the British Executive Council that many 'Lutheran brethren' in the German region of Bavaria were proving 'exclusive in their sentiments'.[66] Over the next few years this concern would extend across Germany, as the dominant Protestant state churches typically set themselves against the Alliance's efforts to secure the rights of independent evangelicals, and Baptists in particular.

62 I. Molenaar, 'European Intelligence: France – Protestant Chaplains to the Army', *Evangelical Christendom*, 1855, pp.39-49.
63 Executive Council Minutes, 3 May 1866.
64 Executive Council Minutes, 24 June 1868. See also Executive Council Minutes, p.29 December 1869.
65 The Alliance defrayed the legal expenses of two Portuguese Evangelicals sentenced to two years imprisonment for speaking against the state Catholic church – Executive Council Minutes, 29 July 1868. It also defended an English merchant, 'Mr. Cassels', who was deported from Oporto for convening Protestant services on a Sunday and for attempting to win converts from the Roman church for his own 'sect' – 23 December 1868, 2 June 1869.
66 Executive Council Minutes, 'Statement Laid on the Table by Sir Culling Eardley Respecting the Continent, 29 September 1847'.

One German state that especially repressed Baptists was Saxe Meningen. It prohibited the small Baptist community there from meeting together and from observing the Lord's Supper. It also barred their pastor from home visitation. This prompted the Alliance to appeal to the Minister of the Interior, and a degree of liberty was granted as a result.[67] Elsewhere, and not least in the Principality of Lippe-Schaumburg, Edward Steane told a May 1853 meeting of the British Executive Council that German Baptists continued to be imprisoned for their convictions. Steane went on to report that Arthur Fitzgerald Kinnaird and Samuel Morton Peto, the evangelical MPs, had called on the Foreign Minister, Lord Clarendon, to intervene.[68] Some progress had already been made in Prussia, and the same meeting suggested that the openness exhibited by Frederick William IV, the King of Prussia, might be presented as an example to harder-line areas. Indeed, the Executive Council worded a memorial to this effect, which is typical of the many they issued in this period:

the Council desire to express their thankfulness to God 'by whom kings reign and princes decree justice' for the favourable issue to which by this good providence their communications with the Prussian Government and those of other friends of Religious Liberty have been conducted. They place on record their deep sense of obligation to his Majesty the King of Prussia for the personal interest which he has manifested in the wrongs endured by his subjects who have suffered from the operation of intolerant laws, and the enlightened and liberal views by which he has guided the recent measures of his government in relation to this subject. They offer their Christian congratulations to their brethren of the Baptist denomination on the new liberty they have acquired in that kingdom; and finally they renew their protest against religious intolerance wherever it persists, their sorrow at learning that it is still so prevalent in Protestant Continental states, and their earnest hope that the other Governments of Germany, influenced by the example of Prussia, will in like manner proceed to recognise the right of their subjects to the free profession of their religious convictions, and the free exercise of their religious worship, without molestation or hindrance.[69]

---

67  Ewing, *Goodly Fellowship*, p.63.
68  Executive Council Minutes, 11 May 1853.
69  Ibid.

The German situation was publicised not only in *Evangelical Christendom,* but also in the *London Quarterly Review,* and by 1853 the Alliance had joined forces with the Protestant Alliance and the embryonic religious liberties pressure group, the Hombourg Conference, to lobby the state church assembly – the Kirchentag – on the matter.[70] Further petitioning of the Prussian King in 1855 led to a gradual liberalisation of attitudes in other states,[71] but Lippe–Schaumburg remained intransigent through the 1860s despite further deputations from London.[72] Furthermore, Episcopal Methodists had to appeal to the British Organisation in May 1869 to help them remove constitutional barriers to evangelism in Saxony.[73]

The other established Protestant church to which the Alliance paid special attention in the mid-1800s was the Lutheran church in Sweden. In 1851 *Evangelical Christendom* published a paper by the Swedish Baptist pioneer F.O. Nilsson, which reported that all Swedish subjects except the Jews were obliged to be members of the State church. Nilsson continued:

> No dissent is tolerated, upon penalty of the loss of property, and banishment for life from the country. By a law that, although obsolete, is not repealed, parents are subject to a heavy fine, if they neglect to have their infants baptised. At the age of fifteen or sixteen, every person must go through a course of catechising, previous to his confirmation. Then, after a man has been confirmed, he must, according to law, receive the sacrament at least once in twelve months, or else he will lose his privileges as a citizen.[74]

Nilsson went on to catalogue restrictions on independent meetings for worship and on evangelism, listing several cases of

---

70 'Religious Liberty in Germany', *Evangelical Christendom,* August 1855, pp.233ff;. See also Lord Shaftesbury's account of the convening of the Homburg Conference, and its subsequent transmutation into the Committee for the Vindication and Promotion of Religious Liberty in *Evangelical Christendom,* 1854, p.16.

71 Ewing, *Goodly Fellowship,* p.64.

72 Executive Council Minutes, 3 May 1866. 'European Intelligence: Germany', *Evangelical Christendom,* January 1856, pp.14–33.

73 Executive Council Minutes, 'Adjourned Meeting', 10 May 1869.

74 F.O. Nilsson, 'On Religious Liberty in Sweden', *Evangelical Christendom,* 1851, pp.426–7.

oppression by the state. At the same time, however, he pointed to more tolerant politicians and clergy who were inclined to see the offending conventicle law abolished.[75] By 1857 these liberal influences had managed, with support from the Alliance, to persuade the King to draft a new law granting a degree of religious freedom to non-established congregations. Although the Swedish Diet formally rejected this, new proposals were adopted which nonetheless eased the situation for the Dissenters.[76] Later, in April 1873, the Executive Council of the British Organisation were asked by the Alliance's Stockholm Committee to help them prepare a response to a new Bill of Religious Liberty for Dissenters, which had been tabled in the Swedish Parliament.[77] Although both groups raised objections to certain points in the legislation, the existence of the bill, and its subsequent adoption, bore testimony to the progress that had been made over the previous two decades.

## Russia: Orthodoxy and the Tsar

The Alliance's defence of German Baptists in the 1850s was extended to their Russian counterparts in the following decade. At the Dublin Rotunda in September 1863, J.H. Millard, a Secretary of the Baptist Union, addressed the Alliance's annual conference. He told delegates that Baptists were being severely oppressed by the Russian authorities in Poland; he asked the Conference to support the Baptist Union and the German Committee of the Alliance in their petitioning of those authorities. It was duly agreed that a deputation including Lord Frederick Calthorpe and Arthur Kinnaird MP should wait upon Russian ambassador.[78]

---

75 Ibid., pp.426-8.
76 G. Scott, 'Sweden: Question of Religious Liberty', *Evangelical Christendom,* January 1858, pp.25-7; 'Sweden and Finland: Proposed Law on Religious Liberty', *Evangelical Christendom,* December 1859, pp.482-4.
77 Executive Council Minutes, 2 April 1873.
78 Executive Council Minutes, 4 November 1863.

Russian suppression of evangelicals combined the formidable power of the Tsar with the antagonism of the Orthodox Church. These forces proved to be particularly severe in the Baltic States. In 1871, a multi-national deputation from the Alliance appealed to the Russian Court on behalf of evangelicals in this region, and urged the Tsar to recognise the solemn right of all to cherish, profess and propagate their religious convictions. The British Organisation was prominent in this action, having convened a strong committee specifically to address it. On behalf of the Tsar, the Chancellor, Prince Gortschakoff, emphasised that religious liberty was curtailed in Russia only insofar as people were not permitted to leave the Orthodox Church once baptised into it, and that the Tsar alone could repeal this restriction. Such repeal was not forthcoming, but the Alliance's efforts did result in some relaxation of the penalties imposed against converts to Protestantism.[79] Despite this, in May 1873 reports were still reaching the Executive Council of 'most harassing' acts of 'cruel persecution of Baptist Christians ... who had previously belonged to the Russian Greek Church [sic]'. The Council heard that in the southern states 'several brethren, rather than recant their faith, had now been a year in prison, nine others and a sister 6 months'. Again in co-operation with the German Alliance, it was resolved, subject to further investigation, to 'take up the case and act rigorously on behalf of our suffering brethren'.[80] By the following year, when the Tsar visited London, the British Organisation was able to congratulate him on his personal intervention in this and other such cases – even if it typically asked at the same time that 'further progress in religious liberty may be made throughout his majesty's empire'.[81]

As far as the Baltic States were concerned, the caveat would remain sadly necessary. In 1888, persecutions returned to a level which prompted a fresh appeal to the Tsar. On this

79 Executive Council Minutes, 28 December 1870; Ewing, *Goodly Fellowship*, pp. 70-1.

80 Executive Council Minutes, 12 May 1873.

81 Executive Council Minutes, 1 April 1874.

occasion, however, he appears to have left the matter in the hands of the Procurator of the Holy Synod of the Orthodox Church, M. Pobedonostzeff. His response characterised the attitude of most clergy in the region:

> You ask for all sects an equal and full liberty. Russia is convinced that nowhere in Europe do heterodox faiths, and even those which are not Christian, enjoy so full a liberty as in the bosom of the Russian people. But Europe does not know this. And why? Only because among you religious liberty comprises also an absolute right to unlimited propagandism, and so you exclaim against our laws against those who pervert the faithful from orthodoxy ... In Russia the Western faiths are always ready to attack the power and unity of the country. Never will she allow the Orthodox Church to be robbed of her children.[82]

Of course, the arrival of communism in the early twentieth century meant that the Russian Orthodox Church would go on to suffer its own share of persecution. Even then, however, it could be argued that the suppression of independent evangelical churches, and 'unregistered' evangelical churches in particular, was proportionally even greater than that meted out to the former state church. What is more, religious persecution of evangelicals by the Orthodox has returned as an issue in the post-Communist era, as the Russian Church has reasserted its national identity and priority. Hence, even now, evangelical associations and mission agencies concerned with religious liberty in Russia find themselves following the example and methods of their Alliance forbears.[83]

## The Muslim East: Turkey and Persia

From the mid-1850s onwards, abuses of religious freedom in the Muslim world occupied an increasing amount of the

---

82 Cit. Ewing, *Goodly Fellowship*, pp.72-3.
83 M. Bordeaux, *Protestant Opposition to Soviet Religious Policy* (Basingstoke: Macmillan, 1968); also *Gorbachev, Glasnost and the Gospel* (London: Hodder & Stoughton, 1990); Interserve/Middle East Media, *Turning Over a New Leaf: Protestant Missions and the Orthodox Churches of the Middle East* (London, Lynnwood, 1992).

Alliance's attention. Chief among its concerns on this front was the treatment of Christian converts in Turkey.

In 1855, the international Alliance conference in Paris approved a memorial from the Executive Council to the Turkish Sultan, asking him to halt the routine execution of those who turned from Islam to Christianity. Overseen by Lord Shaftesbury and transmitted by the French Ambassador Count Walewski, the memorial appealed for 'the establishment of real religious freedom' in the Turkish Empire and complained that it was 'still a capital offence for a Turk to make a profession of Christianity'. Then, in a confession of past errors that would resonate with many evangelicals today, the text continued:

> God forbid that Europe should oppose such an evil in the spirit of the crusaders upholding the cross in the East by exterminating the Crescent! ... In entreating your Majesty to adopt this course, we are unanimous in desiring that the whole of Europe should practise what the Allied Powers would enjoin on Turkey.[84]

To the Alliance's considerable surprise, on 21 February the following year the Sultan responded with a detailed edict which allowed 'all forms of religion' to be 'freely professed', and which insisted that 'no subject shall be hindered in the exercise of the religion that he professes, nor shall be in any way annoyed on this account'.[85] The edict specifically applied this new freedom to the building of churches, synagogues and temples, to employment policy, education, military service, legal processes, taxation, housing and municipal funding. Not surprisingly, Edward Steane and his fellow editors at *Evangelical Christendom* prefaced their publication of the Sultan's text by stating that it was an 'extraordinary' document, and a 'triumph' for the cause of religious liberty. It was now 'well understood by the Turks', they confirmed, 'that they may now become

---

84 'Memorial to the Emperor of the French on Religious Liberty in Turkey', *Evangelical Christendom*, September 1855, p.299.
85 'Religious Liberty in Turkey: Firman and Hati-Sherif by the Sultan, Relative to Privileges and Reforms in Turkey', *Evangelical Christendom,* April 1856, pp.117-21.

Christians without molestation'. Indeed, wrote the editors, 'It is no exaggeration to say that, regarded in almost any, but especially in a religious point of view, the nations of Europe have not read a State paper for centuries destined to effectuate such marvellous changes as this.'[86]

As with other such advances, there would be periodic setbacks in subsequent years. In September 1868 the Executive Council wrote to the press and the government Foreign Secretary, Lord Stanley, about 'the cruelties committed against Protestant Christians' in Mesopotamia by the Turkish Governor, Ismael Pasha, 'at the instigation of the Romish Patriarch, Pillibos.'[87] The following year the British Organisation appealed for its Turkish counterpart in Constantinople on behalf of Protestants suffering beatings and unjust taxation at Biblis.[88] Similarly, in January 1874, representation was made on behalf of three converts from Islam who had been forced to serve in the Turkish army and barred from attending church services.[89] This last case in fact engaged not only the British government, but also Queen Victoria, to whom the Countess of Gainsborough had given a copy of *Evangelical Christendom* bearing a report on the matter.[90] Although the Executive Council considered buying the men out of the army, a compromise was eventually reached whereby they were moved to Constantinople from their base in Damascus.[91] Although they received better treatment there, the Alliance still saw fit to send a deputation, led by Lord Francis Collingham, to visit the men and appeal on their behalf to the Grand Vizier.[92]

---

86 Ibid., p.117.

87 Executive Council Minutes, 30 September 1868.

88 Executive Council Minutes, 27 October 1869.

89 Executive Council Minutes, 7 January 1874. See subsequent developments at minutes for 4 February 1874, 1 April 1874, 6 May 1874, 17 June 1874.

90 Executive Council Minutes, 'Special Meeting', 24 August 1874.

91 Executive Council Minutes, 4 November 1874.

92 Executive Council minutes, 22 February 1875, 3 March 1875.

Dealing with Islamic governments did much to persuade the Alliance to extend its defence of 'evangelical brethren' to other persecuted Christian groups. After centuries of Muslim oppression, the Nestorian Christians of Persia saw in the Alliance an activist body that might use its influence to further their cause. In May 1861 two of them duly set out on foot from Oroomiah for London. In a journey that took six months, they travelled through Armenia, Russia, Poland and Germany, and then by sea to England. On arrival, their first question was 'Where is the Evangelical Alliance?' The Alliance then appealed on behalf of the Nestorians to the Shah, who granted them land on which to rebuild their systematically destroyed churches, and money with which to construct them. He also dismissed the official who had been responsible for the campaign of destruction.[93]

## Defending Catholics and Jews

If the imperatives of religious liberty moved the Alliance to work beyond its own natural constituency, it nevertheless exceeded the expectations of many when it moved to defend the rights of Roman Catholics in Japan in 1872. Along with Protestant converts, native Catholic Christians had come to face an increasing threat of desecration, legal oppression and exile.[94] At its meeting on 5 December 1872 the Executive Council resolved to lobby a visiting official from the Japanese court on behalf of both groups.[95] The following year, the Alliance's British, American, French and German Organisations co-ordinated an impressive campaign of lobbying,[96] and the Japanese government annulled key restrictions on Catholics and Protestants alike, releasing a number of jailed converts in the process.[97]

---

93  Ewing, *Goodly Fellowship*, pp.69–70.
94  Ibid., p.71.
95  Executive Council Minutes, 5 December 1872.
96  *Evangelical Christendom*, 1873, p.29; 1872, 125; 1873, 153.
97  *Evangelical Christendom*, 1872, 217; 1974, p.127. Minutes of Annual Conferences, Glasgow, October 1849.

Perhaps even more surprising still was the Alliance's defence of persecuted Jews. As we have seen, the Alliance essayed a delicate balance in socio-political matters between Anglican churchmen and higher Wesleyans on the one hand, and more radical Dissenters on the other. Whereas the former tended to be more conservative on the implications of religious equality for constitutional reform, the latter followed those implications through in a more thoroughgoing manner. The tension between these two groups was typified in the mid-Victorian era by their respective attitude toward the right of Jews to become members of the Westminster Parliament. As Larsen points out, evangelical churchmen in particular led the opposition to such Jewish representation, even as evangelical Dissenters strongly advocated it.[98] Indeed, it is salutary to note that for all his later veneration as an exemplar of evangelical social action, and despite his keen support of the Alliance's general policy on religious freedom, Lord Shaftesbury was set bitterly against his Nonconformist brethren on this issue:

> Some years ago they stood out for a Protestant Parliament. They were perfectly right in doing so, but they were beaten. They now stood out for a Christian Parliament. They would next have to stand out for a white Parliament; and perhaps they would have a final struggle for a male Parliament.[99]

Despite this background, atrocities committed against the Jews in Tsarist Russia in 1882 managed to unite the Executive Council in a common resolve to petition the court with a memorial expressing its 'horror and indignation' at what was taking place. As conveyed through the Liberal Foreign Secretary Earl Granville, the memorial noted the special relationship of Judaism to Christianity and underlined the repeated manifestation of God's 'displeasure' towards those who had 'oppressed and persecuted the Jews'.[100] In a letter of thanks, the Chief Rabbi, N. Adler, wrote: 'I fully and gratefully recognise

---

98 Larsen, *Friends of Religious Equality*, pp.126-7.
99 *Hansard*, XCV, 1278 (16 December 1847).
100 Executive Council Minutes, 19 January 1882.

the fact that the Council of the Evangelical Alliance gave the first note of that warm sympathy for the persecuted Jews of Russia which was so powerfully echoed throughout Great Britain.'[101]

## Conclusion: The Enduring Legacy of 'Common Action'

We have seen in earlier chapters that the first 'external' concerns of the Alliance as it was being formed were popery, infidelity, Sabbath observance and Christian education.[102] As has become clear, however, it also very quickly seized upon the issue of religious liberty, and this became its hallmark for the remainder of the nineteenth century. As it laboured in this area, the Alliance sometimes championed marginal groups which hardly reflected its own theological outlook, yet by promoting freedom of religion largely without fear or favour, it established a formidable reputation with governments and civic institutions as an 'honest broker' on behalf of the oppressed. Thanks to the power of the British Empire and the related, considerable presence of British missionaries around the world, the London-based Executive Council of the British Organisation was able to lead the way in this work. As it did so, it ensured that its membership comprised a remarkable number of active peers, MPs and civil servants.

As the new century dawned, *Evangelical Christendom* continued to carry a good deal of 'foreign intelligence' on the persecution of evangelicals, but the British Organisation itself became relatively less activist in this area. This was due to a number of factors. First, the rise of the ecumenical movement prompted the Alliance to concentrate rather more on the question of Christian unity, and under the long secretaryship

---

101  Executive Council Minutes, 9 March 1882.

102  These were the four key areas of social endeavour outlined at the Provisional Committee meeting in Birmingham, 1846: Kessler, *A Study of the Evangelical Alliance*, p.30.

of Henry Martyn Gooch (1904–1949, detailed in chapter 8), it responded by positioning itself as a broad Protestant movement over against the emergence of both theological Fundamentalism and liberalism.[103] Second, while the Alliance maintained its commitment to corporate prayer for international issues and pressed for a spiritual dimension to be recognised within the League of Nations, the rise of premillennialism within evangelical circles during the inter-war years blunted the edge of its social concern.[104] Gooch's father, Fuller Gooch, was a leading advocate of premillennial doctrines, while D.M. Panton captured an increasingly popular mood when he wrote in a 1924 edition of *Evangelical Christendom* that all international political reform was doomed because it was a denial of the imminence of the Second Coming.[105] Third, Gooch's determined stress on the Protestant nature of the Alliance meant that to some extent its anti-Roman Catholic identity, which had been mitigated by religious liberties work in the Victorian age, became more distinctive. This all reflected a more general playing down of socio-political involvement among evangelicals during this period – a trend which David Moberg has called 'the great reversal'.[106]

Although we shall see in chapter 8 that the British Alliance supported Karl Barth and the German Confessing Church in their struggle against the Nazis in the 1930s,[107] it would only be after the Second World War that its former international focus on religious liberties would be recovered. This would occur, however, not through the old model of a London-based Executive leading other international committees in the

---

103 I.M. Randall, 'Schism and Unity: 1905-1966', in Brady & Rowdon (eds), *For Such a Time as This*, p.164.

104 Ibid., p.168.

105 *Evangelical Christendom*, November-December 1924, p.178; Randall, 'Schism and Unity: 1905-1966', p.168.

106 D. Moberg, *The Great Reversal: Evangelism versus Social Concern* (London: Scripture Union, 1973).

107 See, for example, *Evangelical Christendom*, January-February 1930, p.35.

petitioning of various repressive regimes, but through a new global body – the World Evangelical Fellowship. The story of WEF as a whole has been told elsewhere[108] and will be dealt with at greater length in chapter 10. At this juncture, however, it is worth noting that when WEF was formed at Woudschoten, Holland in 1951, it immediately set itself to work on a religious liberties agenda.[109] By 1962, at an international meeting in Hong Kong, it had established a special Religious Liberty Commission, and it is significant for our story that the first convenor of that body was the then General Secretary of the British Alliance, Gilbert Kirby.[110] It was subsequently chaired by another prominent figure within the British organisation, John Langlois, and appointed a London-based Alliance staff member, Mike Morris, as its Research Associate in the late 1980s.[111] Today, the Commission is convened by a Finn, Johan Candelin, has an office at the United Nations, and is active in the many areas of the world which remain less than open in terms of religious freedom – from Iran and Pakistan to Nigeria, China and parts of post-Communist Eastern Europe.[112] The commitment made in London in 1846, and applied so effectively through the first fifty years of the Alliance's life, has regained its prominence.

---

108  Fuller, *People of the Mandate*, pp.114–5.
109  Howard, *The Dream That Would Not Die*.
110  Ibid.
111  Fuller, *People of the Mandate,* 105.
112  Ibid., pp.103–17.

# 5

# For the Maintenance of the Truth

*Nineteenth-Century Theological Controversies*

From its first days the Alliance functioned as an arena of theological debate. We have already described in chapters 2 and 3 the arguments on eschatology, sacraments and moral character that surrounded the drafting of the doctrinal basis in 1845-6. We have also seen that even as the inaugural London conference agreed the text of this basis of faith, delegates clashed and then divided on the ethics of slaveholding. Over the next few decades, however, further issues would arise which would test the Alliance's view not only of what it meant to be 'evangelical', but also of how it might deal with those in its ranks who appeared to diverge from that definition.

## Darwinism and Revivalism

In 1859 Charles Darwin's *Origin of Species* presented a radical challenge both to traditional evangelical understandings of creation and to established evangelical views of the relationship between 'fixed' and 'progressive' revelation. As the implications of Darwin's work became clear, some within the orbit of the Alliance took up this challenge and sought to reconcile his ideas on evolution and natural selection with an evangelical theological outlook; others, by contrast, viewed his theories as a severe threat in need of robust opposition. Either way, foundational concepts were at stake. In Kessler's terms, whereas until around 1860 most Christians had regarded divine truth as essentially static, eternal and transcendent, and had seen the imprint of that truth in nature, 'with Darwin and his contemporaries ... truth was no longer considered to be something static, but something which was developing dynamically as a result of the interplay of the various forces at work in human society'.[1] In fact, this 'progressive' view of truth owed as much to the longer-standing influence of Romanticism as to Darwin, and, as we shall see, was also implicit in the new critical approaches to sacred texts which had been developing on the continent since the late eighteenth century.[2]

In any case, it would be some considerable time before the Alliance moved seriously to address this paradigm shift: even as late as a decade after Darwin's epochal text was published, its records contain little or no discussion of evolution, or of new scientific approaches generally. Granted, various international Alliance conferences from 1873 onwards would address these concerns,[3] and by 1884 the report of one such meeting in Copenhagen would record 'great interest attached to the more apologetic discussions on science and revelation, especially in regard to evolution'.[4] Yet before this, the most that can be found in the British minute books, or in *Evangelical Christendom*, are more general expressions of concern about 'infidelity', 'rationalism', 'skepticism' and 'philosophical

1 Kessler, *A Study of the Evangelical Alliance,* pp.65–6.

2 On Romantic influences see B. Reardon, *Religion in the Age of Romanticism* (Cambridge: Cambridge University Press, 1985). On the development of biblical criticism during this period see G. Bray, *Biblical Interpretation, Past and Present* (Leicester: Apollos, 1996), pp.221–375 (cf. pp.255–6 on Romanticism). See also D.N. Livingstone, et al., *Evangelicals and Science in Historical Perspective* (Oxford: Oxford University Press, 1999).

3 D.N. Livingstone, *Darwin's Forgotten Defenders: The Encounter Between Evangelical Theology and Evolutionary Thought* (Grand Rapids/Edinburgh: Eerdmans/Scottish Academic Press, 1987), pp.78, 109–10.

4 *Report Presented to the Thirty-eighth Annual Conference of the Evangelical Alliance,* (Brighton, 1884), p.3.

forms, novel and peculiar to the present times'.[5] This entry, from 24 February 1869, is typical:

> Secretary read draft circular letter from this Council to the committees of the EA throughout the United Kingdom on the subject of the action already taken by this Alliance to counteract the rationalist and secularist opinions openly disseminated in the present day and suggesting methods by which this important work may be carried on in different cities and towns where branches of the Alliance exist.[6]

During this period, the London-based Executive actually went so far as to operate an 'Infidelity Committee' – but the work of this group appears to have been focused on long-standing heresies and anti-Sabbatarian attitudes, rather than on Darwinism per se.[7]

No doubt some who served the British Organisation of the Alliance did oppose evolutionism, *in an individual capacity*, as one of those 'novel and peculiar philosophical forms' that threatened the evangelical faith during the 1860s and 70s. Most prominent among these was T.R. Birks. An Anglican clergyman, Birks had served as curate to Edward Bickersteth in Watton during the 1830s, had married his daughter in 1844, and succeeded him as an Honorary Secretary of the Alliance in 1850.[8] As we shall see, Birks' relationship with the Alliance would end on a distinctly low note, but for the nineteen years during which he served it, he wrote extensively and influentially on a wide range of theological topics.[9] In particular, after

---

5 For a summary see Ewing, *Goodly Fellowship*, 85-7. See also *Report Presented to the Thirteenth Annual Conference*, (Belfast, 1859), p.15.

6 Executive Council Minutes, 24 February 1869.

7 Executive Council Minutes, 10 February 1869.

8 For biographical details see C.D. Hancock, 'Birks, Thomas Rawson', in D.M. Lewis (ed.), *Dictionary of Evangelical Biography*, Vol.1 (Oxford: Blackwell, 1995), pp.101-10; Hylson-Smith, *Evangelicals in the Church of England*, pp.74, 138-9, 143, 160; R. Bromham, 'A More Charitable Christian Eschatology: Attempts from the Victorian Era to the Present Day to Mitigate the Problem of Eternal Punishment, with Particular Attention to the Teaching of T.R. Birks and Its Influence' (M.Phil., University of Wales, 2000), pp.55-116.

9 E.g., *Horae Evangelicae* (1852); *Modern Rationalism* (1853); *The Inspiration of the Holy Scriptures* (1853); *The Bible and Modern Thought* (1861); *First Principles of Modern Science* (1873); *Modern Utilitarianism* (1874).

the *Origin of Species* emerged, he distinguished himself as one of Darwin's most eloquent detractors. Having first critiqued Darwinism in his book *The Bible and Modern Thought* in 1861, Birks continued to do so until, at Cambridge in 1876, he offered one of the most comprehensive rebuttals of it in a series of lectures entitled 'Modern Physical Fatalism and the Doctrine of Evolution'. Three years later, he would summarise his position in another volume, *Supernatural Revelation*: according to Darwin, wrote Birks, 'The universe will exhibit to us nothing but a Proteus without reason or intelligence, going through a series of endless changes, without conscious design, or any intelligible end or purpose in those changes.'[10] The extent to which Birks featured in this and other key debates of the period is borne out by the fact that in 1872 he was appointed to the prestigious Knightbridge Professorship in Moral Theology and Philosophy at Cambridge.

While it is hard to imagine that Birks' views on evolution would not have affected his fellow Executive Council members, it remains the case that on a formal level, Darwinian ideas were conspicuous by their absence from the British Alliance's agenda during his Honorary Secretaryship. Prompted by the independent evangelical leader E.J. Poole-Connor, Kessler suggests that a major reason for this was the impact of the so-called 'Second Evangelical Awakening' or 'Ulster Revival', which had spread from the United States to Northern Ireland, and which had also touched Wales, Scotland and parts of England in 1859 – the very same year in which the *Origin of Species* appeared.[11] Not only did the Alliance play a significant role in this revival through its extensive co-ordination of united prayer;[12] it is also reasonable to infer, as Kessler does, that the British Organisation assumed for some time after it had arrived that this fresh outpouring of spiritual life would provide a far

---

10  T.R. Birks, *Supernatural Revelation* (London 1879), p.136. Also J.R. Moore, *The Post-Darwinian Controversies* (Cambridge, 1979).

11  Kessler, *A Study of the Evangelical Alliance*, pp.70-71.

12  E. Orr, *The Second Evangelical Awakening* (London & Edinburgh: Marshall, Morgan & Scott, 1955); Kessler, *A Study of the Evangelical Alliance*, pp.60-61

better antidote to secular intellectual trends than any number of tracts, seminars or lecture tours.

Having said all this, it should be underlined that even if the Alliance *had* decided explicitly to attack evolution, it would not have been able to count on the support of all its members. Indeed, it is fascinating to note that the very academic whom the Alliance appointed to offer an apologetic for the 1859 revival turned out to be a leading advocate of rapprochement between evolutionary thought and Christian theology.

Professor James McCosh was hardly unique among Alliance supporters in his embrace of 'old earth' and evolutionary ideas. The great Thomas Chalmers, no less, had willingly interpolated long stretches of geological time into the creation narrative of Genesis chapters 1-3,[13] while the respected Swiss-born Professor of Physical Geography at Princeton University, Arnold Guyot, had begun to develop a 'biblical cosmogony' which was patient of evolution through natural causes.[14] As we have seen, Chalmers was one of the architects of the Alliance; the somewhat younger Guyot represented the American branch at the Alliance's international conference in Geneva in 1861, and he went on to speak at its sixth general congress in New York in 1873 on 'The Biblical Account of Creation in the Light of Modern Science'.[15] At the second of these meetings, he shared the platform with the president of McGill University and first president of the Royal Society of Canada, Sir John William Dawson. Like Guyot, William Dawson was hardly a straight Darwinian, but was at this time just beginning to develop a qualified form of theistic evolution.[16] It was even more significant, however, that McCosh should address this Sixth Congress.

By this stage in his career, McCosh had joined Guyot at Princeton, but he had earlier studied under Chalmers at Edinburgh University and, after a brief spell as a minister in the

---

13 Livingstone, *Darwin's Forgotten Defenders*, p.9.
14 Ibid., pp.22, 77-8.
15 Ibid., pp.78, 109.
16 Ibid., pp.80-85, 109.

Scottish Free Church, had assumed the chair of logic and metaphysics at Queen's College, Belfast. While there, he emerged as a keen supporter of the Alliance, and established his reputation with two books – *The Method of Divine Government* (1850) and *Typical Forms and Special Ends in Creation* (1855). Both volumes confirmed McCosh as a leading assimilator of natural theology with contemporary scientific ideas; in particular, they owed a debt to the French zoologist Jean Baptiste Lamarck, who had postulated that acquired characteristics can be inherited by future generations. It was little surprise, then, that McCosh took a keen interest in Darwin's theories soon after the *Origin of Species* appeared in November 1859. Just a few weeks before this, however, he found himself engaged by the Alliance on a somewhat different task.

The Alliance's close association with the 1859 revival had won it a good deal of support, but had also attracted criticism from those convinced that it had been driven by unbiblical emotionalism and manipulation.[17] In order to answer these opponents, the Executive Council recruited McCosh to write an article for the October edition of *Evangelical Christendom*. McCosh had himself been an enthusiastic participant in the revival and duly produced a paper entitled 'The Ulster Revival and Its Physiological Accidents'.[18] In it, he argued that the prostrations, trembling and other dramatic phenomena associated with the revival could function as legitimate marks of the Holy Spirit's work, even if they required authentication in the changed moral and spiritual character of those who experienced them. In taking this view, McCosh echoed the analysis that had been presented by the eighteenth-century theologian of revival, Jonathan Edwards, in his classic texts, *The Distinguishing Marks of a Work of the Spirit of God* (1741) and *The Religious Affections* (1746).[19] McCosh also anticipated the response

17  Kessler, *A Study of the Evangelical Alliance*, p.61.
18  *Evangelical Christendom,* October 1859, pp.368ff.; Livingstone, *Darwin's Forgotten Defenders,* p.106.
19  J. Edwards, *The Distinguishing Marks of the Spirit of God* (1741), in *Jonathan Edwards on Revival* (Edinburgh: Banner of Truth Trust, 1965); *The Religious Affections* (1746) (Edinburgh: Banner of Truth Trust, 1961).

which would be given by the Alliance a century and a half later, when challenged to pronounce on the validity of another putative 'revival', the so-called 'Toronto Blessing' of 1994-6 (see chapter 13).

McCosh moved from Belfast to Princeton in 1868.[20] It is a mark of the esteem in which the British Organisation held him that a special meeting of the Alliance's Executive Council was organised prior to his departure, to thank him for his work, to wish him well, and charge him with the task of forging closer relations with the American branch.[21] On arriving in the United States, McCosh embarked on a series of lectures eventually published in 1871 as *Christianity and Positivism*.[22] Here, he sought to work from Darwin's premise that life on earth had developed and diversified over aeons of time due to innumerable mutations and adaptations within and across species. Although McCosh departed from Darwin's scheme by maintaining a unique and distinct place for humankind – which, he argued, 'modifies Natural Selection by bringing things together which are separated in natural geography'[23] – he was nonetheless very keen to fuse Darwin's concept of organic progression for the rest of the natural world with the Christian doctrine of providence:

> every one trained in the great truths of science should see a contemplated purpose in the way in which the materials and forces and life of the universe are made to conspire, to secure a progress through indeterminate ages. The persistence of force may be one of the elements conspiring to this end; the law of Natural Selection may be another, or it may only be a modification of the same … [T]he law of the progression of all plants and animals … [implies] adjustment upon adjustment of all the elements and all the powers of nature towards the accomplishment of an evidently contemplated end, in which are displayed the highest wisdom and the most considerate goodness.[24]

20 The university at this point was still known as 'The College of New Jersey'.
21 Executive Council Minutes, 'Special Meeting of Members of Council … to Meet and Confer with Rev Dr McCosh Prior to His Departure for the United States', 8 July 1868.
22 J. McCosh, *Christianity and Positivism: A Series of Lectures to the Times on Natural Theology and Christian Apologetics* (London: Macmillan, 1871).
23 Ibid., pp.69-70.
24 Ibid., pp.90-92.

When McCosh appeared alongside Guyot and William Dawson in the philosophical section of the Alliance's New York Congress two years later, he summarised his ideas in a paper entitled 'Religious Aspects of the Doctrine of Development'— 'development' being his preferred theological gloss on 'evolution'. Having made his case for a rapprochement between theistic design and Darwin's 'natural law', McCosh added that it would now be pointless to tell younger naturalists that there were no grounds for the theory of evolution. Despite its problems, he said, 'they know that there is truth [in it], which is not to be set aside by denunciation'. Moreover, he suggested, 'Religious philosophers might be more profitably employed in showing them the religious aspects of the doctrine of development; and some would be grateful to any who would help them to keep their new faith in science.'[25]

McCosh would go on to explore these themes further in his 1887 Bedell lectures, which were subsequently published as *The Religious Aspect of Evolution*.[26] Granted, he continued to present a benevolent God intervening to mitigate the random-ness, profligacy and cruelty inherent in the Darwinian worldview. Granted, too, he extrapolated from natural selec-tion a 'spiritual progressivism' that would be increasingly chal-lenged by Darwinians.[27] Even so, his example, and that of Guyot, William Dawson and others, shows that despite its ini-tial caution, the Alliance moved on willingly to debate and ex-plore new scientific ideas. Indeed, as we shall see, it would never align itself as an organisation with the fundamentalist movement that, in the 1920s, would come to define anti-evolutionism as a *sine qua non* of evangelical orthodoxy. Hence, too, when the UK Alliance conducted a survey of theological views among its member churches in 1998, it

---

25  J. McCosh, 'Religious Aspects of the Doctrine of Development', in P. Schaff & S. Irenaeus Prime (eds), *History, Essays, Orations and Other Documents of the Sixth General Conference of the Evangelical Alliance* (New York: Harper & Brothers, 1874), pp. 264–71.

26  J. McCosh, *The Religious Aspect of Evolution* (New York: Scribner's, 1890).

27  For further discussion, see Livingstone, *Darwin's Forgotten Defenders*, pp. 106ff.

would find 37% affirming a 'young earth' or 'six day' creation, but 58% endorsing a more general form of theistic evolution.[28]

## Historical Criticism and Biblical Authority

Shortly after the publication of the *Origin of Species* debate was aroused among evangelicals by the appearance, in 1860, of the landmark volume, *Essays and Reviews*. Comprising seven papers by leading Anglican liberals, this book did much to introduce the then-emergent school of German 'higher criticism' to a more general readership. Pioneered by the 'Tübingen school' of F.C. Baur, Albrecht Ritschl and D.F. Strauss, the higher critical method subjected the Old and New Testaments to the sort of historical, contextual and scientific scrutiny which was becoming commonplace within textual studies as a whole. Its willingness to treat the Bible as a human canon redacted and compiled over many centuries for varied sociological purposes, and its related questioning of supernatural and miraculous elements within the narrative, were perceived by many as a challenge to established belief in the uniqueness, authority and inspiration of Scripture.[29] Indeed, as David Bebbington has noted, evangelicals were among the most prominent opponents of *Essays and Reviews*, with anyone leaning towards its sceptical approach being marked, by definition, as 'broad church'.[30]

Despite this initial resistance, however, by the late 1870s the influence of the new movement began to affect evangelicalism. William Robertson Smith, a gifted Old Testament scholar from the Free Church College in Aberdeen, contributed an article on 'The Bible' to the *Encyclopedia Britannica* that assumed higher critical principles. Although a close vote of the Free Church Assembly in 1880 allowed him to stay in his post, a

---

28  EA Member Churches: The 1998 Opinion Survey, 5, Question 2.

29  For a summary of the contents and impact of *Essays and Reviews*, see Bray, *Biblical Interpretation*, pp.287ff.

30  Bebbington, *Evangelicalism in Modern Britain*, p.184.

more radical article for the same publication saw him dismissed the next year.[31] This episode would prove significant for the Alliance, not least because of the Free Church's key role in its formation.

As with evolution, the 1859 revival appears to have diverted the British Organisation of the Alliance from an immediate, concerted response to the critical movement, even if certain of its individual members were moved to engage with it from an earlier point. A minute from 7 May 1868 records the Council's support for a campaign of the so-called Hackney Bible Defence Association to oppose 'the spread of infidelity both in London and the Provinces', but does not explicitly relate this to higher criticism.[32] Likewise, the Infidelity Committee, whose appointment we noted above, was reported in February 1869 to be 'meeting by various agents the infidel preachers and lecturers around London', with a view to prompting others to counteract 'the attacks made by secularists upon revealed truth', but, again, the only such attack mentioned directly is the neglect of the Sabbath.[33] Further notes in the 1870s make reference to the 'invidious attack' of 'rationalism' on the gospel,[34] and to the need to uphold 'doctrines which form the basis of society',[35] but these are passing references, and no thoroughgoing attempt appears to have been made by the British Organisation as a whole to relate these concerns to contemporary debates on biblical exegesis and interpretation. Rome, of course, continued to be monitored with suspicion – but hardly because of its embrace of German higher criticism![36]

Only in the late 1880s did British Alliance reports begin to allude more obviously to biblical critical controversies, as the

---

31  Ibid., pp.184–5.

32  Executive Council Minutes, 7 May 1868.

33  Executive Council Minutes, 10 February 1869.

34  Executive Council Minutes, 5 June 1872.

35  Executive Council Minutes, 4 February 1874.

36  See, for example, the Alliance's 'Manifesto' against Protestant participation in an ecumenical council summoned by the Pope – Executive Council Minutes, 3 December 1869.

Council aligned itself with those seeking 'to contend for the faith once delivered to the saints' in the face of others whom it took to be set on undermining God's word.[37] By March 1888 the Alliance raised its public profile considerably on this front by organising rallies in various cities to affirm 'the great central truths of faith in Christ', and to protest against 'the prevalence of erroneous teaching'. In doing so, it sought to engage speakers for these events who would bear 'faithful testimony to the cardinal truths of the Christian gospel', and who would 'possess the confidence of the Christian public' as they did so.[38] Significantly, one such speaker was the leading Baptist and 'prince of preachers', Charles Haddon Spurgeon.

Spurgeon's selection by the Alliance Executive to lead its first rallies in London was indicative of a more urgent concern about theological compromise – not least in relation to Scripture. In 1864, he had actually resigned from the Alliance over its unwillingness to take his side in the so-called 'Baptismal Regeneration Controversy' – a dispute about the Anglican theology of initiation in which Spurgeon had suggested that evangelical clergy in the Church of England perjured themselves by using the Book of Common Prayer, when they did not actually believe its teaching on the salvific effect of infant baptism.[39] Given its history of conciliating between evangelical Anglicans and Nonconformists, the British Alliance had been reluctant to exacerbate the division.[40] Spurgeon had subsequently been reconciled with the Alliance, but now he was appearing on its platform at a time when he had become embroiled in another dispute – one that was, if anything, even more clamorous than that which had led to his withdrawal from the Alliance twenty-four years earlier.

---

37 *Report Presented to the Forty-First Annual Conference*, Aberdeen 1887, pp.13ff.
38 Executive Council Minutes, Vol. IV, 14 July 1887, pp.142-3; 8 September 1887, pp.146-8; *Report Presented to the Forty-Second Annual Conference*, (Plymouth, 1888), p.8.
39 I.H. Murray, *The Forgotten Spurgeon* (Edinburgh: Banner of Truth Trust, 1973), p.146.
40 For more detail, see M.T.E. Hopkins, 'Spurgeon's Opponents in the Downgrade Controversy', *Baptist Quarterly* 32.6 (April 1988), pp.274-94.

The so-called 'Downgrade Controversy'[41] was initiated by a series of articles written in *The Sword and The Trowel* – the widely circulated bulletin of Spurgeon's large congregation at the Metropolitan Tabernacle, Kennington. The earliest of these articles were unsigned, but are thought most probably to have been penned by Robert Shindler of Addlestone.[42] In February 1887, under the heading 'The Down Grade', the first contribution argued, in line with the fears expressed by the Alliance Council in the preceding years, that 'rationalism' was threatening evangelical truth, and that as a result, evangelicals as well as liberals were in danger of 'going downhill at breakneck speed'.[43] However, whereas the Alliance had generally refrained from detailing the causes of this problem, the author quite explicitly laid the blame at the door of 'the Germans' – that is, the higher critics and the philosophers, such as Immanuel Kant, Gotthold Lessing and Georg Hegel, who had influenced them.[44] Further unsigned articles traced the spread of higher critical approaches through Holland to Andover Newton, a leading Congregationalist seminary in United States.[45] In particular, they appeared to implicate Baptist ministers such as William Landels, J.G. Greenhough and W.E. Blomfield, who had accepted higher critical methods and who had embraced some of their theological implications.[46] Then, in August, Spurgeon himself openly joined the fray, offering a sharp summary of the decline presented thus far:

---

41 For detailed accounts of the Downgrade Controversy, see Hopkins, 'Spurgeon's opponents in the Downgrade controversy', pp. 274–94; P.S. Kruppa, *Charles Haddon Spurgeon: A Preacher's Progress* (New York: Garland, 1982); E. Payne, *The Baptist Union: A Short History* (London: Baptist Union, 1958), pp. 127–43; E.W. Bacon, *Spurgeon: Heir of the Puritans – A Biography* (London: Allen & Unwin, 1967), pp. 128–46.

42 M. Nicholls, *C.H. Spurgeon: The Pastor Evangelist* (Didcot: Baptist Historical Society, 1992), pp. 131–45.

43 *The Sword and the Trowel*, February 1887, pp. 122–6.

44 R.M. Grant & D. Tracy, *A Short History of the Interpretation of the Bible* (London: SCM, 1984), pp. 110–18, 155–6.

45 *The Sword and the Trowel*, 1887, pp. 174–5, 274–9.

46 Nicholls, *C.H. Spurgeon*, pp. 136–41.

the atonement is scouted, the inspiration of Scripture is derided, the Holy Spirit is degraded into an influence, the punishment of sin is turned into fiction, the Resurrection into a myth, yet the enemies of our faith expect us to call them brethren and maintain a confederacy with them.[47]

More specifically, Spurgeon concluded, 'We cannot be expected to meet in any Union which comprehends those whose teaching is upon fundamental points exactly the reverse of what we hold dear.'[48] As a result, he withdrew from the Baptist Union on 28 October 1887.

Spurgeon's influence was such that the Baptist Union took his allegations and secession very seriously indeed. Its Council meeting, in December, demanded that he either substantiate or withdraw his allegations, and appointed a delegation to draw him back in. During the subsequent discussions, Spurgeon made it clear that the Baptist Union was susceptible to heretical influences – such as those associated by him with higher criticism – because it did not have a clear doctrinal basis. In this, he averred, it could learn from the Alliance, whose statement of faith defined exclusively those who were part of its fellowship.[49] Indeed, when forming his own Pastors' College Evangelical Association later in 1888, Spurgeon and his trustees would adopt the Evangelical Alliance Basis 'with certain alterations and additions' as 'a convenient summary of the faith'.[50] Taking the preacher's point to heart, both Union representatives and Spurgeonites drew up doctrinal declarations, and it was while a compromise between their respective drafts was being negotiated, in March 1888, that Spurgeon appeared at Exeter Hall and Mildmay Conference Hall in the capital to promote 'Fundamental Truth' on behalf of the Alliance.[51] As he did so, the 'Down Grade Controversy' was extending far

47 *The Sword and the Trowel,* 1887, p.379.
48 Ibid., pp.509-15.
49 Nicholls, *C.H. Spurgeon: The Pastor Evangelist*, pp.141-2.
50 L. Drummond, *Spurgeon, Prince of Preachers*, (Grand Rapids: Kregel, 1992), pp.706-7.
51 Kessler, *A Study of the Evangelical Alliance*, p.71; Executive Council Minutes, 12 April 1888.

beyond the confines of an internal denominational debate, and was attracting copious comment across the wider evangelical and Protestant community.[52] As things turned out, when it met at the City Temple on 23 April 1888, the Baptist Assembly went on to adopt a form of words more moderate than Spurgeon had hoped for, and he retreated, with a small number of followers and churches, into relative isolation.[53]

That the British Organisation should have seen fit to spotlight as controversial a figure as Spurgeon at so sensitive a time underlines the alarm which was then felt within the Executive Council at the implications of historical criticism. This alarm would remain for some while, but it would begin to abate as the new century approached. One early indication of this shift came with an address given at the Alliance's 1890 annual meeting in Manchester by Alfred Cave – an address entitled 'The Old Testament and Higher Criticism'.[54] Cave had been a fierce critic of William Robertson Smith,[55] but now he argued for an acceptance of critical methods insofar as they operated in constructive relation to the primacy of the Scriptures themselves. As Kessler comments, 'Up to this moment the Alliance had contented itself with modernized restatements of the old faith, but this was something new.'[56] Indeed, it was telling that Spurgeon quickly dissociated himself from Cave's apologetic, on the grounds that Cave had accepted the classic higher critical model of the 'documentary hypothesis' for Genesis. Spurgeon declared that this notion, which ascribed multiple sources to a text traditionally assumed to derive from one period and one community, had severely compromised the Bible's historicity and accuracy.[57] For Spurgeon and his supporters, higher criticism remained an unnecessary 'prop'

52  Payne, *The Baptist Union*, pp.131-43; Drummond, *Spurgeon*, pp.688-94.

53  Nicholls, *C.H. Spurgeon*, pp.141-5.

54  *Evangelical Christendom,* November 1890, pp.305ff.

55  Bebbington, *Evangelicalism in Modern Britain*, p.185.

56  Kessler, *A Study of the Evangelical Alliance*, p.71.

57  H.D. MacDonald, *Theories of Revelation* (London: George Allen & Unwin, 1963), p.271.

for faith in the Bible; by contrast, they contended, the Bible itself bore sufficient testimony to its own reliability as the word of God written.[58]

The Spurgeonic party would go on to define their understanding of biblical inspiration and authority in more detail in June 1891, as part of what they dubbed 'A Timely Manifesto':

> We, the undersigned, banded together in Fraternal Union, observing with growing pain and sorrow the loosening hold of many upon the Truths of Revelation, are constrained to avow our firmest belief in the Verbal Inspiration of all Holy Scripture as originally given. To us, the Bible does not merely *contain* the Word of God, but *is* the Word of God. From beginning to end, we accept it, believe it, and continue to preach it. To us, the Old Testament is not less inspired than the New. The Book is an organic whole. Reverence for the New Testament accompanied by scepticism as to the Old appears to us absurd. The two must stand together. We accept Christ's own verdict concerning 'Moses and all the prophets' in preference to any of the supposed discoveries of so-called higher criticism.[59]

While there are many in the Alliance today who would align themselves wholly with this definition, it undoubtedly goes beyond the essential 'inspiration, authority and sufficiency' of the Scriptures affirmed in the original 1846 Basis of Faith. As such, it positioned the Spurgeonites closer to what might now be termed a fundamentalist view of the Bible than the more general evangelical position represented by the Alliance per se. Indeed, the assertion here of 'the Verbal Inspiration of all Holy Scripture' reflects a growing divergence at this time between those content to affirm the overall supremacy of Scripture while applying historical critical study to its constituent parts, and those who rejected any such 'modern' interpretation in favour of more absolutist definitions of its 'infallibility' and 'inerrancy', and its 'plenary verbal' inspiration.

Now it must be admitted that if the drafters of the 1846 Basis of Faith saw no need to reinforce its assertion of biblical 'inspiration, authority and sufficiency' by adding that it was thereby 'infallible', most of those who first endorsed it would

---

58  *The Sword and the Trowel*, 1981, p.246.
59  *Word and Work*, 26 June 1891.

have believed the latter to have been *implied* by the former. Edward Bickersteth, who proposed the Basis of Faith to the inaugural London conference, had certainly taken the 'infallible' line that a God who is altogether trustworthy and true must have produced an utterly reliable written revelation.[60] In doing so, he had followed Henry Venn, who had earlier defended an 'infallible Word of God', the Countess of Huntingdon's Connexion, which had affirmed the 'infallible truth' of the Old and New Testaments, Robert Haldane, who had written influentially on the 'infallibility and inspiration' of Scripture, and many other Victorian evangelicals.[61] Having said this, even in the early nineteenth century there had been some evangelicals prepared to admit the possibility of errors in the Bible, while maintaining that this did not threaten its thoroughgoing inspiration. Charles Simeon and Henry Martyn, for example, had defended this view by placing emphasis on the inspired *sense* or *meaning* of biblical discourse, rather than on every individual word.[62] Certainly, from its earliest days, the Alliance had contained proponents of each viewpoint.

As these distinctions became more marked following the 'Downgrade Controversy' and Cave's address to the Manchester conference, the Alliance worked hard to maintain a balanced course. While continuing to repudiate liberal attacks on core Christian doctrine, it undoubtedly essayed a greater openness towards higher critical interpretation. Hence by 1906, in an address sponsored by the Alliance and delivered at King's Hall, Holborn, the Brethren evangelical Sir Robert Anderson told of how a friend had given an unsigned exposition of his to a prominent broad church vicar. When the vicar

---

60  E. Bickersteth, *A Scripture Help, Designed to Assist in Reading the Bible Profitably* (17th edn; London, 1838), p.2.

61  H. Venn, *The Complete Duty of Man* (3rd edn; London, 1779), p.51; 'The Fifteen Articles of the Countess of Huntingdon's Connexion', in E. Welch (ed.), *Two Calvinistic Methodist Chapels, 1743-1811* (Leicester: London Record Society, 1975). For further references see Bebbington, *Evangelicalism in Modern Britain,* pp.13-4.

62  For detail, see. D Tidball, *Who Are the Evangelicals?* (London: Marshall Pickering, 1994), p.87.

learned that Anderson had written the exposition, he replied, 'If I were from this pulpit to put out such statements as that, then you would call me a higher critic.' Anderson retorted by admitting that he was indeed a higher critic, but with the distinction that he still read the Bible as the word of God.[63]

We shall see in chapter 10 that tensions on the authority, inspiration and interpretation of Scripture would flare up again half a century later, as the international fabric of the Alliance was reconfigured at the founding of the World Evangelical Fellowship. Even here, however, while others would insist on the affirmation of 'infallibility', the British Alliance would again find itself brokering a leaner definition of biblical authority.[64] Then, as in the later nineteenth century, it would be characterised by a cautious but moderately progressive attitude to new theological thinking.

If the Alliance sought generally to adopt an eirenic approach to intra-evangelical doctrinal disputes, there is one episode from its Victorian period that stands out as an exception. Ironically, it involved the Alliance's leading anti-Darwinian, T.R. Birks.

## T.R. Birks: Hell and the Parameters of Alliance Doctrine

As we noted in chapter 3, there is little doubt that the majority Christian tradition up to the nineteenth century had taken hell to be a place of unending physical and psychological punishment. Moreover, with the possible exception of children who die in infancy and those who never hear the gospel, this majority tradition had assumed hell to be the fate of all who die without faith in Jesus Christ.[65] Hence, when it affirmed 'the

---

63  *Thy Word is Truth: A Report of the Meetings for the Testimony to the Integrity of God's Word, Held in King's Hall, Holborn*, p.112; Kessler, *A Study of the Evangelical Alliance*, p.72.

64  Kessler, *A Study of the Evangelical Alliance*, pp.95–101.

65  For accounts of the evangelical tradition on this subject see R.A. Peterson, *Hell on Trial: The Case for Eternal Punishment* (Phillipsburg: P&R Publishing, 1995),

immortality of the soul' and 'the eternal punishment of the
wicked', the Alliance's 1846 Basis of Faith was following a theology articulated by early church fathers like Tertullian, Jerome
and Augustine, by the medieval teaching of Thomas Aquinas,
and by the magisterial Protestant Reformers.[66]

As Geoffrey Rowell has shown, however, the period in
which the Alliance was formed was marked by a rise of interest
– among evangelicals as well as others – of alternative views on
hell and the afterlife.[67] From the days of Origen until Victorian
times the main challenge to the traditionalist doctrine of eternal punishment had come from universalism. Rather than
holding to the unending torment of the wicked, Origen proposed a theory of *apokatastasis* in which everything, perhaps
even Satan and his angels, would eventually be restored to God.
This 'restitution of all things' did not exclude the possibility of
hellfire and divine condemnation, but saw them as ultimately
remedial, rather than eternally penal. Universalism recurred in
several variations thereafter and came to hold sway in more liberal circles as the nineteenth century progressed. Insofar as it
proposed salvation for all regardless of faith, universalism never
significantly appealed to British evangelicals. On the other
hand, however, some were happy to interpret restitution not so
much as a *remission* of judgement, but as a *positive consequence* of
judgement – i.e. as something which must follow God's condemnation and destruction of wicked people and things at the
end of the age.

Latterly, this view would take its place within the mediating
positions known as 'conditional immortality' and 'annihilationism'. Conditional immortality argues that the concept
the 'immortal soul', as affirmed in the 1846 Alliance Basis of

---

65 (*continued*) pp.97-117; Rowell, *Hell and the Victorians*; D. Powys, 'The Nineteenth and Twentieth Century Debates about Hell and Universalism', in N.M. De
S. Cameron (ed.), *Universalism and the Doctrine of Hell* (Carlisle: Paternoster Press,
1992), pp.93-138.

66 For more detail on this tradition see R.J. Bauckham, 'Universalism: A Historical Survey', *Themelios* 4.2 (January 1979), p.48; Peterson, *Hell on Trial*, pp.97-138.

67 Rowell, *Hell and the Victorians*, 1974.

Faith, owes more to Greek neo-Platonic thought than to biblical teaching. Rather than accepting that unbelievers will forever be tortured by a wrathful God, conditionalists infer from Scripture that the unrighteous will ultimately be destroyed, or annihilated – either at the point of death, or after a period of punishment in a hell which will itself pass away once God has recreated the universe. They see this as more consistent with the actual vocabulary of the relevant texts, and God's grand plan of salvation: they also argue that it more adequately reflects his character as a God of love and mercy. For these reasons, conditional immortality is often identified as 'annihilationism', though in specific terms 'annihilation' is better understood as *following from* conditional immortality, rather than fully defining it.

As we have seen, American delegates to the Alliance's inaugural conference in 1846 were seeking to head off these very ideas when they proposed adding 'eternal punishment' to the Basis of Faith. Certainly, they seem to have anticipated that such ideas would make their mark on evangelicals, as well as on others. Indeed, a later *Evangelical Christendom* editorial would echo such concerns when it observed: 'there seems to have occurred a considerable amount of tampering, even in England, with this important doctrine; not merely by Unitarians, Universalists or sceptics, but by evangelical clergymen, ministers and others deemed to be, in other respects, evangelical Christians.'[68]

Partly in response to final wording of the 1846 Basis of Faith, F.D. Maurice, the former Unitarian-turned-Anglican, published a book of *Theological Essays* in which he argued that the phrase usually translated 'eternal punishment' in Matthew chapter 25 referred to the quality, rather than the duration, of God's retribution. In particular, he contended, it should be understood to denote 'the punishment of being without the knowledge of God', rather than a physical and everlasting torment in hellfire.[69] Maurice was dismissed from his Chair at

---

68 'The Evangelical Alliance and Eternal Punishment' *Evangelical Christendom*, February 1870, p.33.

69 F.D. Maurice, *Theological Essays*, (Cambridge/London, 1853) p.450.

King's College, London for expressing these views, but they were growing more popular – a fact evident not only in the backing given to them by the liberal authors of *Essays and Reviews*, but also in events which would soon shake the Alliance to its foundations.

As we have noted, T.R. Birks established a reputation as a distinguished commentator on a range of theological issues in the years after his appointment as Honorary Secretary of the Alliance in 1850. Thus it was hardly surprising that he should in time turn his attention to the growing debate on hell. What took the Alliance aback, however, was the unusual approach he adopted towards this now highly contentious subject. Its reaction to this approach, and the crisis which arose as a result, did much to point up the tensions inherent in the constitution of the Alliance. Although Kessler offers a useful summary of the 'Birks Controversy',[70] Raymond Bromham has presented a more recent and more thorough account of it. This, coupled with the minutes of the Executive Council and relevant copies of *Evangelical Christendom*, offers a telling insight into the theological and institutional dynamics of the Alliance in the third decade of its life.

In 1867 Birks published a book called *The Victory of Divine Goodness*.[71] In it, he took a broadly restitutionist line, going so far as to suggest that 'the lost' might develop in the afterlife to a point where they could eventually share some of the joy of God's re-made cosmos, if not its full blessings. Birks held that this was consistent with the Alliance's theology and, in a way, it was. His scheme *did* maintain unbelievers in an eternal realm rather than annihilating them, and this eternal realm *was* divided off from heaven. It was, however, palliative (if not exactly remedial), and this hardly reflected the intent of those Americans who had first inserted the 'hell' clause into the Basis of Faith. Neither did Birks' decidedly speculative approach to the

---

70  Kessler, *A Study of the Evangelical Alliance*, pp.66-9; Bromham, 'A More Charitable Christian Eschatology'.

71  T.R. Birks, *The Victory of Divine Goodness* (London: Rivingtons, 1867).

condition of the lost sit well with their traditional wording of that clause. Early on in *The Victory of Divine Goodness,* Birks asks the reader to 'suppose' that the fate of the unredeemed might 'combine, with the utmost personal humiliation, shame, and anguish, the passive contemplation of a ransomed universe, and of all the innumerable varieties of blessedness enjoyed by un-fallen spirits, and the ransomed people of God'. Such contem-plation, he adds, 'would be fitted, in its own nature, to raise the soul into a trance of holy adoration in the presence of infinite and unsearchable Goodness'.[72] Birks concedes that this sce-nario is 'nowhere in the Bible, in set terms, explicitly re-vealed'.[73] Even so, he goes on to infer from passages such as Philippians 2:11 that just as those who have been condemned at the last judgement must make 'unwilling acknowledgement of God's justice in their own sentence', so too they must expe-rience 'a compulsory but real perception of all other attributes of the Almighty', including his 'infinite wisdom and love'. De-spite their eternal conscious suffering, this means that they must also from time to time have an 'unutterably blessed' sense of God.[74] While Birks accepts that the co-existence of these two vastly contrasting states among the damned might be hard to grasp, he insists that 'if righteousness and grace co-exist for ever in the infinite perfections of the Most High, their exercise may co-exist for ever in his dealings even with those whose guilt requires that righteousness should assume the form of ir-reversible and lasting punishment'.[75]

At first, no one on the Alliance Executive Council seemed especially perturbed by the latest theological publication of their esteemed Honorary Secretary. Indeed, the matter was not raised until Monday, 10 May 1869. On that occasion, a letter was read out from the Treasurer, the city banker and philan-thropist Robert Bevan, who had sent his apologies for absence. The minutes record Bevan's letter as having asserted that Birks'

---

72  T.R. Birks, *The Victory of Divine Goodness* (London: Rivingtons, 1867), p.45.
73  Ibid.
74  Ibid., p.48.
75  Ibid., p.187.

views on hell were 'not compatible with the 8<sup>th</sup> Article of the Basis', and that for this reason, Bevan 'could not conscientiously continue in the Alliance with Mr. Birks'.[76] After some deliberation, the Council resolved to respond to Bevan by clearly defending Birks:

> [T]he Council, entertaining sincere respect for the conscientiousness which has induced … Mr Bevan to address them on the subject of his communication now read cannot but at the same time express their regret that he should have deemed it necessary to do so. They respectfully submit to Mr Bevan that since Mr Birks continues to avow his adhesion to the 8<sup>th</sup> Article of the EA doctrinal basis, and in the book referred to maintains the eternity of future punishment, and disavows the construction of the contrary put upon certain passages in it by others, they cannot deem it a part of their duty to call in question the sincerity of Mr Birks in the avowal of his continued belief in the doctrine in question, or to enquire how far (if at all) his speculations may be logically inconsistent with it. They therefore earnestly express their hope that Mr Bevan will not press the further consideration of the subject ….[77]

The strength of the Council's support for Birks at this stage is evident in the fact that at the same meeting, they appointed a special deputation to convey their wishes to Bevan in person.[78] Bevan, however, was not ready to let the issue rest. At the Alliance's Annual Conference in Derby on 25 November 1869, another letter from him was read out, in which he confirmed that unless it moved to condemn Birks' stance as irreconcilable with the Basis, he would be 'obliged to retire' from membership.

Immediately after this, Birks read a letter of his own, which expanded on one which had been written on 19 July and laid before the Executive at its meeting on 1 October.[79] This letter stated that Birks did not wish his name to be offered for re-election as Honorary Secretary. He gave as his principal reason for this the fact that despite the support of his colleagues on the Council, his office had now become 'an occasion of strife';

76 Executive Council Minutes, 10 May 1869.
77 Ibid., pp.6–7.
78 Ibid., p.7.
79 Executive Council Minutes, 1 October 1869.

he then added that he did not want to jeopardise the 'internal harmony' of the Alliance. He reaffirmed his allegiance to the Alliance's 'Basis, Principles and Objects', stressing that over the nineteen years of his service as Honorary Secretary, this had 'undergone no change'. However, Birks then went on in some detail to answer Bevan's objections, and in doing so, undoubtedly fuelled an already volatile dispute. 'I think it only right', he said, 'to add some parting words of caution against serious dangers which seem to me at this moment to imperil not only [the Alliance's] usefulness, but its very existence.' This dramatic tone was maintained as Birks proceeded to list six such threats to the Alliance's future. His concerns are worth quoting in full, because they highlight challenges which the Alliance had faced periodically up to that point, and which it continues to face today:

First, that it should cease to be evangelical, reflecting the grace and forbearance of the gospel of Christ, and should become in spirit an illegal and tyrannical body, in which a few members by the influence of their wealth, can impose their own private constructions of the Basis as a new test of peaceful membership on all the other members of the Organization.

Secondly, that it should cease to be an Alliance and become practically a Court of Inquisition summoning its members to its bar to entertain charges against them either of intellectual lunacy or of dishonesty in their own professions of faith.

Thirdly, that it should explain away its second article, the right and duty of private judgment, into the right and duty of a majority or even a minority of its members to impose their own private judgement on the right of interpretation of any article of the Basis as a law to exclude the rest from membership in the Alliance.

Fourthly, that it should reverse its own declaration and turn its summary of doctrines into a creed or confession practically more stringent than the creeds of the universal Church of Christ.

Fifthly, that it should contradict its own fundamental law, that no compromise of the views of any member on the points wherein they differ (including plainly all inferences from the Basis not named in it) is either expected or desired.

Sixthly, that contrary to its own professions it should claim to exercise the
functions of a Christian church and become a Court of ecclesiastical enquiry
into the orthodoxy and moral honesty of any or all its members.[80]

Plainly, Birks was invoking a cardinal principle of the Alliance.
The 'Right and Duty of Private Judgment in the Interpretation of the Holy Scriptures' had been enshrined in the Basis
largely in recognition of the damage done to evangelical unity
in the past through the forced imposition of dogma by one
party on another – not least on Dissenters by the Church of
England, and on Free Church adherents by state Protestant
churches on the continent.[81] Yet, the Basis of Faith clearly
stood as a testimony against unfettered *licence* in the understanding of doctrine. Bevan was arguing that in this respect,
Birks' claim that his views on hell remained consistent with the
Basis was not, in itself, enough. As Bevan saw it, Birks' reputation might have persuaded the Council to take this claim at
face value, but as the Executive of a voluntary association
defined by a statement of faith, it also had the right to apply a
more objective, corporate test. The key question was whether
it could do this without aping the 'Court of Inquisition'
described by Birks.

After Birks had finished reading his letter to the Conference,
the mood of the meeting appears to have changed. Whatever
the merits of his case, it seems that the apocalyptic terms in
which he expressed it, and the bitterness of his tone, aroused a
degree of sympathy for the absent Bevan. Certainly, the Conference formally expressed its 'deep regret' that 'anything
should arise likely to disturb the intimate relation which for
many years has so happily been maintained between themselves and their Treasurer'. It then went on to mandate the
newly-appointed Council to convene 'at the earliest possible
time' a special meeting in London, 'to take into their consider-

80 Executive Council Minutes, 25 November 1869.
81 For more on the historical background of 'the right to private judgment', see
D. Little, 'Reformed Faith and Religious Liberty', *Church and Society* (May/June
1986), pp.6–28.

ation the whole question'. It was clear that the subject could no longer be dealt with quietly.

The Special Meeting duly took place on Wednesday, 12 January 1870. Significantly, Bevan returned for this occasion, but Birks was not present. After the leading evangelical solicitor Robert Baxter had read various letters on the hell issue from Council members, he proposed that the British Organisation should recognise as its members only those who hold 'what are *actually understood* to be evangelical views with regard to the eternal punishment of the wicked' [our italics]. As if this were not pointed enough in its repudiation of Birks, the resolution added that the Alliance could not recognise as consistent with these views 'the assertion that there will be mercy in some form or other extended to the souls under the solemn sentence of eternal judgment'. It continued by criticising Birks' contention that the traditional model of hell was 'absolutely merciless' and that the God implied by such a model would have perpetrated 'an act of cruelty' inasmuch as he had created the vast majority of humankind for damnation. The resolution concluded that the publication of such views meant that Birks could not 'any longer be deemed a member' of the Alliance. After various amendments were discussed, further consideration of this proposal was adjourned until 16 February.[82]

In the meantime, the Executive Council met on 26 January and decided formally to accept Birks' previous resignation from his post as Honorary Secretary. The reasons they gave were that his opinions on hell had caused 'great pain to members of the Evangelical Alliance and other Christians, as being in their judgment discordant with the Word of God', and that the number of 'assaults' being made upon the Bible from other quarters obliged the Alliance to be seen to 'maintain the Divine truth and authority of the doctrine of the Sacred Scriptures'. To these ends, they expressed their 'satisfaction' that he had decided to step down from his post.[83] Despite all this, a letter was read out at the

---

82 Executive Council Minutes, 12 January 1870.
83 Executive Council Minutes, 26 January 1870.

same meeting from J.S.Blackwood, a Yorkshire-based Anglican
Vicar, in which he rejected a unanimous offer of Birks' now
vacant post. Explaining his reasons, Blackwood wrote that
despite personally disapproving of Birks' views, and despite
being the one who urged him to resign in the first place 'as an
offering upon the altar of peace', only 'great and grievous
discomfort and disturbance' would now ensue from any attempt
'to render our Executive Council a tribunal before which the
theological and other writings of a member are to be formally
impeached'. Such a course, Blackwood added, would be 'ruin-
ous to our peace, if not perilous to our association'.[84] It is a
measure of the rift that was opening up within the British
Organisation at this point that an editorial in the 1 February
issue of *Evangelical Christendom* (unsigned, but attributed by
Kessler to former editor Edward Steane) duly concurred with
Blackwood against the Executive:

> Mr. Birks … [has] alienated the minds of many brethren and must bear his own
> burden. We cannot, however, but observe with sadness, and deprecate the
> course of action attempted in this instance. No great success has ever attended
> the condemnation of books by any corporation – whether Popes, Councils,
> Convocations, or Committees; and of all conceivable bodies the Executive
> Council of the Alliance is, perhaps, the worst qualified and the least authorised
> to act as a Church Court, or to imitate the Holy Inquisition.[85]

The adjourned Special Meeting of the Alliance in fact took
place a week later than scheduled, on 25 February 1870. Blackwood was prominent in the proceedings, and read a new letter
sent to him by Birks dated 22 February. The full text of this
letter was subsequently published in the 1 March edition of
*Evangelical Christendom*, and appears to have swayed members
back towards a more conciliatory view. In this letter, Birks
pointed out that despite having tendered his resignation a full
seven months earlier, 'with no previous request from any
member of the Alliance, but of my own accord, as a sacrifice to

84 Ibid.
85 'The Evangelical Alliance and Eternal Punishment', *Evangelical Christendom*,
February 1870, p.35.

peace', he had still received no formal response from the Alliance. Acknowledging the difficulty that the Alliance had been facing on his account, he added that had he foreseen the problems that had been caused by his book, he would have resigned before publishing it. Yet, he emphasised, these problems had genuinely taken him by surprise:

> I expected, in the church at large, the gentle disapproval of some and the stronger dislike of others; but the idea never crossed my mind that it could possibly be made the ground for internal controversy within the Alliance. How could I guess that any thoughtful Christian, a lover of peace, should ever charge me with contradicting the Basis, when, holding exactly my present views, I had actively concurred in the addition of that very article [on eternal punishment], which I am so strongly alleged to contradict and oppose?[86]

Once Birks' letter had been read, Baxter informed the meeting that the motion he had proposed on 12 January had been withdrawn. A similarly condemnatory resolution in the names of H.M Matheson and General Alexander was then defeated by eleven votes to nine, but this more moderate text, drafted by R.A. MacFie MP, was carried:

> That the Council need not re-affirm – although they are ready, if need arise, to do so – the doctrine of the 8th article of the Doctrinal Basis inasmuch as, in declining or omitting action in the painful business for which they have been convened, they know, and desire it to be understood, that this cause by no means implies or involves the smallest degree of acquiescence in, or any unconcern in regard to, the individual opinions that have caused so great anxiety and regret, and must be viewed in connexion with the rule of the Alliance by which members are declared free from complicity in such cases.[87]

In the spirit of this resolution, the editorial in *Evangelical Christendom* for 1 March acknowledged Birks' integrity and sincerity, while courteously arguing against the specific position which he had advanced on hell. It recognised his intended distinctions from annihilationism, but nonetheless warned 'the

---

86  T.R. Birks, 'The Rev T.R. Birks to Rev Dr Blackwood', *Evangelical Christendom*, March 1870, p.69.
87  Executive Council Minutes, 25 February 1870.

champions of evangelical doctrine' to 'look to it that no weak defences are erected and relied upon for the maintenance of the truth'.[88] In similar vein, a letter from the Scottish Free Church minister Robert Candlish published in the same edition concluded, 'I think [Mr Birks] has drifted much further than he imagines from the common faith of evangelical Christendom ... But I give him all credit for uprightness and Christian honour, and would be disposed to leave the matter with himself.'[89]

If it was hoped that responses like this might help end the discord, such aspirations were shattered at the next meeting of the Executive Council, held on 30 March 1870. A letter was read out from Bevan and fifteen others, in which they resigned *en masse* from the Council, in protest at its unwillingness to censure Birks in any direct or public way, or to strip him of his actual membership.[90] Curiously, in view of his recently expressed generosity towards Birks, Candlish was one of the signatories. Reiterating their conviction that Birks' views were 'inconsistent' with the Basis, and that 'however unconscious of it, [he] does not hold what, in the words of the said Basis, are usually understood to be evangelical views in regard to the eternal punishment of the wicked', the correspondents declared that it was the 'bounden duty' of the Council 'to renew the testimony of the Alliance to the scriptural truth contained in the article in question, and this no less for the sake of Mr. Birks himself than for the warning of the unwary'. Dissenting

---

88 'The Doctrine of Everlasting Punishment', *Evangelical Christendom*, March 1870, p.66.
89 'The Rev Dr Candlish to the Rev Dr Blackwood', *Evangelical Christendom*, March 1870, p.72.
90 The fifteen in question were: Robert Baxter, the Scottish Liberal MP Arthur Kinnaird, Hugh Matheson, Clarmont Skine of St Peter's Chapel, Pimlico, General R. Alexander, Marcus Rainsford, Bevan's son J.A. Bevan, the independent Scottish episcopalian David Drummond, the Edinburgh botanist J.H. Balfour, the leading Scottish Free Church minister Robert Candlish, the Church of Scotland clergyman Andrew Thomson, the Dorset Anglican vicars John Glyn and G. Curme, the Oxford churchman J.Jordan, and Henry Beverley.

from the vote of the Council on 25 February, they reasserted Matheson and Alexander's defeated resolution, which had declared that article 8 of the Basis had been framed explicitly to combat annihilationism and 'universal restoration', and that 'the confessedly novel opinions' of Birks were 'equally incompatible' with the same article.[91] They then concluded by complaining that in this matter the Executive Council had conceded 'the utmost liberty to members of the Alliance to promulgate any opinions however at variance with true and natural meaning of the articles [of the Basis], provided only a verbal adherence to [them] be given'. In doing so, they wrote, it had lost a 'great opportunity' for 'vindicating the Scriptural basis of the Alliance, apart from which the organisation is hollow and valueless'.[92]

The Council responded to this body blow by referring the critical letter to a committee of six, including Blackwood and Edward Bickersteth. Having examined its provenance, the committee reported back to the Council on 27 April 1870 that two of its signatories were not members of the Council when the letter was submitted, and that one of these non-members was Bevan's own son! Of the remaining fourteen, eight had been absent from all of the meetings at which the Birks case had been considered. The report went on to confirm that when adopted conscientiously, the Basis was sufficient as it stood. Birks himself was acknowledged to have been truthful and honourable in his rejection of annihilationism and universalism, and to have 'unequivocally affirmed his adhesion to the whole Basis'. In any case, the committee urged that the Council should not assume legal powers that had not been assigned to it in respect of rescinding his membership. As a result, the committee hoped that the seceders would, on further reflection, 'perceive the injustice of their imputation' that the Alliance was ready to allow unlimited freedom to its members to interpret the Basis

---

91  Executive Council Minutes, 30 March 1870.
92  Ibid.

however they wished. These recommendations were duly accepted and entered into the minutes. At a later meeting, on 25 May, a letter was despatched to the seceders, expressing the hope that their split from the Alliance would be short-lived.[93] Sadly, no such official reconciliation appears to have taken place. Birks remained technically in membership, but played no further active part in the Alliance. Moreover, the impact of the Birks affair was so severe that no annual conferences were held in 1870 or 1872, and for the years 1871–4 annual reports were either withheld or significantly truncated.[94]

Although Birks himself had explicitly disavowed annihilationism and conditional immortality, through the 1870s and 80s prominent figures like Dean Farrar, Edward White and Henry Constable gained a degree of acceptance for them within Anglican and larger Free Church constituencies. Furthermore, even if evangelicals remained overwhelmingly opposed to these doctrines in the Victorian period, as the twentieth century progressed they would gradually gain a degree of acceptance until, in the year 2000, the Alliance's own theological commission would recognise conditionalism as a 'significant minority evangelical view'. We shall return to this development in chapter 12.

## Conclusion

The Basis of Faith was central to the Alliance's identity, but the Alliance never pretended that it could be exhaustive. Indeed, as the nineteenth century presented a series of tumultuous theological challenges – from Darwinism, through the baptismal regeneration debate and higher criticism to re-examinations of hell – it realised that its own doctrinal foundations would require regular appraisal and careful application. In practice,

---

93 Executive Council Minutes, 27 April 1870; *Evangelical Christendom*, 1870, p.199; Bromham, 'A More Charitable Christian Eschatology', pp.92–3.
94 Kessler, *A Study of the Evangelical Alliance*, p.69.

the Executive Council functioned as the British Organisation's key interpreter in these new contexts, even as it continued to affirm the essential transparency of the Basis when viewed in the light of Scripture's self-attestation and the established canon of evangelical thought.

The Alliance was quick to condemn modern 'rationalist' and 'secular' thinking when it appeared to threaten the gospel, and organised various committees, campaigns and rallies to counter this threat. Typically, however, it maintained a generous stance on the 'right to private judgment' and eschewed the more separatist and reactionary doctrinal strictures of what would come to be known as fundamentalism. In particular through the 'Birks affair', it came to acknowledge that as a voluntary association rather than a church denomination, it could not hope to run a 'court of enquiry' on the various specific doctrinal understandings of its individual members. Rather, it resolved to define its own position on contentious matters by principled dialogue and debate, both within its councils and conferences, and through the pages of *Evangelical Christendom*. As such, it showed itself willing to assimilate new ideas insofar as it deemed them to be consistent with the primacy of Scripture. Hence from its formation in 1846 to the end of the century, it would come to count theistic evolutionists, higher critics and those of more cosmic eschatological views among its membership – even if such groups would remain in the minority.

6

# In the Midst of the Universal Church

*The Alliance in Global Perspective*

Many of those who originally envisaged the formation of the
Evangelical Alliance saw it as a body that would be not only interdenominational but also international – a sign of the universality of the 'catholic' church. As we saw in chapter 3, the
possibilities for internationalism were severely curtailed by the
division between evangelicals in North America and Britain
over slaveholding. Yet the international instinct continued.
During a conference in New York, held from 5 – 11 May 1847,
an Evangelical Alliance for the USA was formed. As an indication of the desire for pan-national unity, the Basis of Faith from
the London Alliance conference was affirmed at the New York
meeting. Even so, this conference also made it plain that the
American Alliance was not subservient to Britain. Delegates
believed Christian union had existed – to a considerable extent
– in American churches long before the organisation of the Alliance in London.[1] This chapter will explore the internationalism
that Evangelical Alliance leaders attempted to sustain in the second half of the nineteenth century and the early years of the
twentieth century. It will also focus on the relationship between
evangelical unity and world mission. The role of the Evangelical

1 'The Evangelical Alliance for the United States of America', *The Christian Union and Religious Memorial*, Vol. 1, January 1848, pp.4–8. For the New York conference and sources see Jordan, *Evangelical Alliance for the United States of America*,
pp.63–5.

Alliance in world affairs changed because of the rise of the movement that was to produce the World Council of Churches. But the Alliance was an important pioneer of international expressions of Christian unity.

## Internationalist Forces

American evangelicals went to the Evangelical Alliance conference in London in 1846 hoping, as one of their number, Robert Baird, put it, to 'set forth a brief statement of doctrine ... a symbol of faith, in which all evangelical Protestants could unite'. Their aspiration had been to create a body that would promote Christian fellowship across 'all' nations. As we have seen, this idealistic dream had, however, been shattered because of strong views held by other nationalities – notably the British – about slavery. In 1851 Baird, who had spent sixteen years in Europe, asked a British Alliance audience whether Britain had no sin in relation to Ireland, India and China. Was Britain, he asked defiantly, 'immaculate'?[2] Although the Americans felt that British evangelicals refused to understand the difficulties of their position, they did engage in internal debate about slaveholding following the London conference. Some leaders proposed that an attempt should be made to distinguish between evangelicals who held slaves from 'benevolent' motives and those who did so 'for the sake of gain', with the latter group being excluded from Alliance membership. This approach had been mooted in London, but had failed to satisfy the British. American leaders such as Thomas Bond, editor of the powerful *Methodist Christian Advocate*, became convinced that the moral obligations arising from the London conference meant that the American Alliance must stand against slavery.[3]

The May 1847 Alliance meetings in New York followed this line, and affirmed that

2  Baird, *Address on the History*, pp.40–6.

3  Jordan, *Evangelical Alliance for the United States of America*, p.65.

we are ... persuaded that the great object of the Association, the promotion of
a larger Christian union, may be furthered by a frank expression of our sentiments on the subject of slavery: we therefore declare our deep, unalterable opposition to this stupendous evil, and we hold it to be the duty of all men, by all
wise and Christian means, to seek its entire extirpation and removal from the
land. Still the one object of the Alliance shall be steadily kept in view, which is
the promotion of Christian union and brotherly love.[4]

This stance meant that the American Alliance organisation lost
support in the southern States. In theory, northern evangelicals
should have been supportive of the Alliance, but because the
issue of slavery was largely shelved following the 1847 New
York conference, northern abolitionists were not satisfied.
Others in the northern states were unhappy about the way the
northern and southern churches were dividing; they saw the
Alliance as contributing to this division. As an organisation, the
American Evangelical Alliance made no progress; after its
inception it lasted for only three years. In the 1850s, however,
some American Alliance leaders sponsored public meetings,
and during the Civil War some Alliance spokesmen were in
communication with their British counterparts. After the
Civil War a number of Americans felt that the time was right to
begin planning for a World Evangelical Alliance conference.
This was held in New York in 1873.

Several international conferences of the Alliance were held
during the 1850s and 1860s, all of them in Europe. The European dimension will be examined in the next chapter. In 1851
there was a conference in London; it coincided with the Great
Exhibition in the city. Reference to international conferences
as 'Ecumenical Conferences' became commonplace.[5] Paris
was the venue in 1855, when 1,200 representatives from fifteen
nations gathered. A shared communion service was held. The
German Evangelical Alliance, formed in 1847, drew together a
number of leading evangelical theologians, such as E.W.
Hengstenberg, and in 1857 an Alliance conference was held in

4  'Evangelical Alliance for the United States of America', pp.6–7.
5  *Evangelical Christendom*, September 1858, pp.289–90.

Germany. This attracted special interest since Frederick William IV, King of Prussia, and a supporter of Protestant unity, welcomed the 900 delegates. At Berlin it was decided that an ideal place for Alliance meetings would be Geneva, with its Reformation heritage.[6] At the Geneva conference, held in 1861, delegates from Britain, Germany, France, Italy, Switzerland and America were welcomed. The British were referred to as those 'who extend [the Alliance's] operations far and near, who aid and support every branch of it'. James Davis was the energetic secretary of the British Alliance at that time. There was a message for America, 'at this moment tried even by bloodshed', expressing hope that 'the wound from which you have long been suffering may be gradually but finally cured', and pointedly looking to the time when 'your noble country shall include none but freemen'.[7]

Another international thrust in this period was provided by missionary conferences that were related to the Evangelical Alliance. At the annual meetings of the British Alliance in 1851 and 1852 there were suggestions for an international missionary conference. In 1853 a gathering of missionaries was held in conjunction with the meetings of the Alliance. The following year saw a conference of British missions and also a Union Missionary Convention held in New York. In 1860 an even more significant missionary conference was held in Liverpool,. The Liverpool event attracted 126 delegates, fifty-two of them directors and administrators from various missionary societies and others leaders from several denominations.[8] Lord Shaftesbury chaired the final session. Alliance leaders such as Sir Culling Eardley were prominent at these conferences. Eardley, who spoke French, had a strong sense of the universality of Christian witness. At the Geneva Alliance meetings of 1861 he described the privilege he felt at being 'in the midst of the universal church,

---

6 G. Carlyle (ed.), *Proceedings of the Geneva Conference of the Evangelical Alliance* (London: Hamilton, Adams & Co, 1862), pp.v–vi.

7 Ibid., pp.2–3.

8 *Conference on Missions Held in 1860 at Liverpool*, pp.4–9; W.R. Hogg, *Ecumenical Foundations* (New York, Harper & Brothers, 1952), pp.39–40.

in the midst of an assembly from which no one believing in a God of salvation is excluded'.[9] In the later 1860s further Alliance developments took place. An Evangelical Alliance was re-launched in the USA in 1866 and in the following year an international conference was held in Amsterdam.

A key figure in the new international impetus from the later 1860s onwards was a Swiss–American, Philip Schaff. The roots of Schaff's spirituality were in German pietism. He was a theologian and historian of the American German Reformed Church and became a professor at Union Theological Seminary, New York, in 1869. Schaff was initially critical of the Alliance, but from the time of the Berlin Alliance meetings in 1857 he became a strong supporter, and from 1865 until his death in 1893 he was a central personality in the international Alliance movement. Schaff's broad ecumenical vision derived from his Lutheran and Reformed connections and he envisaged the possibility of the ultimate coming together of the Roman Catholic, Protestant and Orthodox Churches in one body.[10] Together with another Presbyterian, Samuel Prime, editor of the widely read *New York Observer*, Schaff had a major share in the planning and executing of the international Alliance conference in New York in 1873. This conference, which will be looked at in more detail later, grew out of a desire, especially on the part of Americans, to give expression to the reality of an international evangelical movement.

## Obstacles to Internationalism

Within Europe, as well as transatlantically, pan-national relationships presented continuing challenges. As early as 1847, the Evangelical Alliance Council in Britain received a request

---

9  Carlyle (ed.), *Proceedings of the Geneva Conference*, p.7.
10  Jordan, *Evangelical Alliance for the United States of America*, p.75. See also Railton, *No North Sea*, pp.183-4. S.R. Graham, *Cosmos in the Chaos: Philip Schaff's Interpretation of Nineteenth-Century American Religion* (Grand Rapids: Eerdmans, 1995).

from the Swiss that the Alliance should receive into membership 'all the children of God who may be willing to join it'.[11] In
1851 the international Alliance conference in London
received a request from the Swiss Alliance to adopt a doctrinal
basis that said:

> The Alliance receives to membership every disciple of Jesus Christ, who, ac-
> cording to the Scriptures of the Old and New Testament, acknowledges that
> there is no salvation but in Christ, receiving Him as a complete Saviour and
> trusting entirely in him as the Eternal Son of the Father, 'God manifested in
> the flesh', who having procured eternal redemption for us, by His expiatory
> death, sends down the Holy Spirit upon those who believe, to accomplish the
> work of regeneration and sanctification.[12]

The background to this request was that many members of the
Brethren, who were strongly represented in the Lausanne area
of Switzerland, were unsympathetic to the existing Alliance
Basis, with its reference to ministry and sacraments. Discussions about this issue were cordial, but they highlighted the difference of view between a sectarian approach to ecclesiology
and the British Evangelical Alliance's commitment to the
spiritual unity of the church.[13]

Charles Barde, a minister of the Reformed Church in
Geneva, visited one Brethren leader in Lausanne and discovered
that the organisational approach of the Alliance was also inimical to Brethren. As Barde reported at the British Evangelical
Alliance Council meetings in Dublin in 1852, with their
commitment to 'open' meetings, Brethren felt able to join others in prayer only if no 'President' was formally appointed. The
Alliance representatives in Dublin considered the points made
by the Swiss about the Alliance statement of faith and decided
that they did not have any authority to change an international
basis.[14] Indeed, no change was made until 1912. In 1854 the

---

11  Executive Council Minutes, 29 September 1847.
12  *Evangelical Christendom*, August 1851, p.255.
13  *Evangelical Christendom*, December 1851, p.460.
14  *Proceedings of the Sixth Annual Conference*, 15, p.56.

Swiss Alliance made alterations to its own basis of faith. National
Alliances were free to do this, although such moves strained
wider pan-national links. Such problems were, however, the exception. A review of the work of the Alliance in 1864 spoke of
what it had done to 'demonstrate the catholicity of the Christian church'. The dream of a universal church had, said *Evangelical Christendom*, been a 'lofty abstraction', but hopes for deeper
communion and even 'ecclesiastical amalgamation' had been
raised as people met one another at Alliance meetings. [15] In 1864
the Pope condemned the Association for the Promotion of
the Unity of Christendom, which had attracted over 6,000
members from Protestant, Roman Catholic and Orthodox
churches. [16] The Alliance was certainly not open to union with
the Roman Catholic Church, but neither did it have sympathy
with those who opposed spiritual unity.

The 1860s saw new interest in international, especially
transatlantic, revivalism. *Evangelical Christendom* reported in
May 1858 that a revival movement had begun in the United
States that was attracting interest in British evangelical circles.
Before that, in 1857, James Caughey, the American Methodist
evangelist, was attracting large crowds to his preaching at Surrey Gardens, London. [17] It became clear later in 1858 and 1859
that this was an international revivalist movement, with areas in
Northern Ireland, Wales and Scotland – particularly close-knit
Scottish fishing communities such as those from Aberdeen to
Inverness – especially affected. Edwin Orr, an evangelist and
historian, sees this as a 'second evangelical awakening', although his account of revivals in Britain does not distinguish
between local spontaneous awakenings and carefully organised
evangelistic meetings. [18] In 1860 there were experiences of

15  *Evangelical Christendom*, January 1864, pp.1–2.

16  Rouse, 'Voluntary Movements', p.347.

17  Watts, *The Expansion of Evangelical Nonconformity*, p.657. On Caughey's work in
Britain in the 1840s see R. Carwardine, *Transatlantic Revivalism: Popular Evangelicalism in Britain and America, 1790-1865* (Westport: Greenwoood, 1978), pp.97–133.

18  Bebbington, *Evangelicalism in Modern Britain*, p.116; cf. Orr, *Second Evangelical
Awakening*.

revival in a few parts of England, notably in some fishing communities in Cornwall and Devon. There were also localised revival movements in Sweden and in some other European countries, but the greatest impact seems to have been in North America and Britain. The Evangelical Alliance, with its commitment to a broad vision of unity, played a crucial role, as Edwin Orr has argued, in this interdenominational and international movement through the period 1857-60.[19]

It was hoped that a revival of this kind would foster the coming together of evangelicals in different countries. The revival created, however, certain obstacles to unity. One problem was the frequent incidences of physical prostrations and other phenomena that were associated with some of the revival meetings. As we saw in the last chapter, James McCosh, an Alliance supporter and professor of philosophy at Queen's College, Belfast, was asked to write an analysis of the revival for *Evangelical Christendom*. In an attempt to overcome hesitations that were felt about the Ulster revival in other places, in 1860 the Alliance Council also requested the bishop of Down and Connor (as someone known to be sympathetic) to suggest those who could speak to English audiences about what had been taking place. Meetings were arranged in eleven venues and Charles Seaver, the bishop's nominee, had private conversations with the Archbishop of Canterbury and the bishop of London.[20] Barriers to mutual understanding were created by outbreaks of revival and the Alliance attempted to foster better communication in this area.

In addition to preparing the ground for the revival movement through its stress on unity, the Alliance also encouraged united prayer by its members. A widely publicised call to prayer was issued in 1858 at the annual Alliance conference

19 Orr, *Second Evangelical Awakening*, p.63. For a more critical assessment see J. Kent, *Holding the Fort: Studies in Victorian Revivalism* (London: Epworth Press, 1978). I.H. Murray in *Revival and Revivalism, the Making and Marring of American Evangelicalism, 1750-1858* (Edinburgh: Banner of Truth Trust, 1994), seeks to draw a distinction between revival and revivalism.

20 *Report to the Fourteenth Annual Conference*, p.7.

held that year in Liverpool. In 1860 American missionaries in Ludhiana, India, also invited English-speaking churches to unite in prayer during the second week in January. One of these Ludhiana missionaries suggested that in January1861 the Alliance should send out a more official call to churches around the world, not only to Alliance members, to pray.[21] The first Alliance 'universal week of prayer' was duly held, starting on 6 January 1861. The effects of the week were far-reaching, with tens of thousands of copies of a call to prayer being distributed in several languages for use during the first week in January each year. The intention of this was to transcend national divisions. International news was shared. Large prayer meetings in cities attracted most attention, but in many Swiss villages, to take one lesser-known example, people from the national Reformed church, members of free evangelical churches, and leaders of Brethren assemblies, prayed together – overcoming the doctrinal differences that had previously kept them apart.[22]

There was talk in the 1860s of denominational differences being forgotten, but Samuel Schmucker, who had been central to early pan-evangelical enterprises in America, was one of those who realised that united prayer without other actions was not sufficient. He pressed the Alliance to invite denominations to send delegates to a world conference on unity, suggesting, in an echo of proposals he had made in 1846, that such a conference should be convened every seven years. Schmucker's appeal was published posthumously in an Evangelical Alliance report of 1873, the year of the major Alliance conference in New York. The report covered the conference speeches, but added other items. The editor of the report noted that the plan by Schmucker was 'a proper subject for discussion at a conference and possibly for future action, though not by the Alliance as now constituted. The Alliance aims simply at a voluntary union of individual Christians of different churches

---

21  *Evangelical Christendom*, August 1860, p.447.
22  Rouse, 'Voluntary Movements', p.321.

without interfering with their denominational relations or assuming any power of ecclesiastical legislation.'[23] The vision, for many, remained one of spiritual unity. Denominational barriers appeared too strong to be pulled down.

## The 'One Catholic Church'

In later nineteenth-century America it seemed, however, that the lines of denominational demarcation were not as sharply drawn as they were in Europe. The secretary of the British Alliance, James Davis, visited the United States in 1870 and was received by President Grant. Commenting on the more open atmosphere he noted, Davis was not sure whether the absence of a state church or the impact of democratic institutions contributed to American Christianity's relative lack of strife over doctrinal positions. He was clearly delighted that American Christians wished 'closer fellowship with all in every land', and to draw towards 'every section of the one catholic church'.[24] Some American voices to be heard in the same period were self-assured about the American role in this process. Matthew Simpson, a Methodist bishop, spoke about the need for the world to be 'elevated' spiritually and considered that in such a process 'God cannot afford to do without America'. Although this was an extreme view, an American Presbyterian committee on 'the State of the Country' was confident that the future would see 'our Christian Commonwealth a praise among the nations, exemplifying and speeding the progress of the kingdom of our Lord and Saviour, Jesus Christ'. The respected Philip Schaff, who travelled in Europe and met leaders such as the Archbishop of Canterbury, considered that those from

---

23 *History, Essays, Orations and other documents of the Sixth General Conference of the Evangelical Alliance held in New York, October 2-12 1873*, p.742. For developments in this period and sources see Jordan, *The Evangelical Alliance for the United States of America, 1847-1900*, chapter 4.
24 *Deputation to the American Branch of the Evangelical Alliance*, pp.14–6; Minutes of the Executive Council of the Evangelical Alliance, 30 November 1870.

outside North America who conferred with American evangelicals would learn more in a few days about voluntary and self-supporting religion than they could in years in their own countries.[25]

Schaff's comments became sharply focused on the Europeans who arrived in America in 1873 to be part of the sixth general conference of the World Evangelical Alliance, the first such event to be held in the USA. More than 500 delegates gathered in New York from 2 – 12 October 1873 for this historic occasion. The eighty-strong British Alliance delegation was led by James Davis, who spoke of the Alliance as an 'ecumenical society', and by one of the Alliance's Vice Presidents, Lord Alfred Churchill.[26] There were one hundred speakers, with the main platform personalities and others who attended constituting a varied group of world evangelical leaders, including theologians from German universities such as Berlin, Bonn and Halle. America's President Grant hosted a reception. William Adams, who gave the opening conference address, was pastor of Madison Square Presbyterian Church, New York, and later President of Union Theological Seminary. Adams argued that despite differences over church organisation and despite national diversity, those present exhibited 'a real unity of faith and life' and a commitment to the 'holy catholic church and the communion of saints'.[27] A British Anglican delegate, R. Payne Smith, who had been recently appointed as dean of Canterbury, echoed this sense of the church universal. Payne Smith cast the Alliance as a counter to the dangers of Protestant individualism.[28] The Evangelical Alliance was thus

25 'The Report of Dr Schaff on the Alliance Mission in Europe', Evangelical Alliance, Document III, p.32, cited by Jordan, *The Evangelical Alliance for the United States of America, 1847-1900*, p.92; Minutes of the Executive Council of the Evangelical Alliance, 2 June 1869.

26 Minutes of the Executive Committee Council of the Evangelical Alliance, 21 November 1873.

27 W Adams, 'Address of Welcome', *Sixth General Conference of the Evangelical Alliance held in New York*, pp.65, 67.

28 R. Smith, 'Christian Union Consistent with Denominational Distinctives', *Sixth General Conference of the Evangelical Alliance held in New York*, pp.145-9.

conscious of its catholicity, both in denominational and geographical terms.

The broadly based spiritual unity that the Evangelical Alliance was seeking was expressed in a speech by Charles Hodge,
the well-known Princeton Seminary professor, whose writings were read by evangelicals on both sides of the Atlantic. A
conservative Presbyterian, Hodge saw the Alliance as held together by doctrine and experience. The tenets of the Alliance's
Basis of Faith were, for him, the scriptural beliefs held by all
evangelicals. Hodge was a strong proponent of Reformed theology. He also mentioned the importance of belief in the
Apostles' Creed and the doctrinal decisions of the first six Ecumenical Councils concerning the nature of Christ. Yet he was
adamant that Christians were united by their spiritual experience – by their worship, love and devotion to Christ. Indeed
his Alliance address was entitled 'The Unity of the Church
Based on Personal Union with Christ'. For Hodge there was a
divine command that Christians should be united, and this, he
believed, must be obeyed. His concern, however, was not for
structural union. Indeed, in 1870 he opposed attempts to re-
unify Presbyterians in the USA. Differences over matters of
doctrine constituted, in Hodge's view, legitimate reasons for
the existence of the historic denominations. What he wanted
was greater co-operation and, significantly, 'intercommunion'.
With reference to the Lord's Supper he asked: 'How can we re-
fuse to receive those whom Christ has received?'[29]

Which American denominations were to the fore in supporting Evangelical Alliance priorities in the 1870s? American
Presbyterians, as we have seen, were influential in promoting
the work of the Alliance. There was also support from Methodist and Congregational leaders. These denominations
tended to see American democracy and 'Free Church' life as
having provided an example for other parts of the world. Baptist leaders in the USA were, on the whole, less committed to

---

29 C. Hodge, 'The Unity of the Church Based on Personal Union with Christ',
*Sixth General Conference of the Evangelical Alliance held in New York*, pp.139-44.

the Alliance, since they had grave reservations about communion services that included those who had not been baptised
as believers. High-church episcopalians normally distanced
themselves from the Alliance. Schaff emphasised in 1872 that
the kind of union he had in view was 'as far removed from indifference to denominational distinctives as from sectarian bigotry and exclusiveness'.[30] Two years later Schaff indicated his
real priorities. He urged the cultivation of 'a truly evangelical,
catholic spirit' towards all Christians – 'all who love our Lord
Jesus Christ' – of whatever creed. It was not that Schaff wanted
to give up creeds. Indeed, he spoke of an 'ecumenical consensus' being expressed in the Apostles' and the Nicene Creeds.
Rather he wished for liberality of spirit. 'We must subordinate
denominationalism', he argued, 'to catholicity, and catholicity
to our general Christianity.'[31]

It was difficult for the sense of universality to be maintained.
Americans attended the world Alliance conferences in Europe,
but in 1884 they blocked moves towards forming an international Alliance committee that would act as a central executive.
This was a reversal of the position they had pressed for in 1846
and Philip Schaff, for one, resisted the new stance. His thinking
had become increasingly expansive: indeed, prior to coming to
Copenhagen he argued for Roman Catholic and Orthodox as
well as Protestant churches being valid expressions of the
church. He was, however, over-ruled by others. The isolation-
ist argument was that Americans should remain outside any
international committee that might give power to small
Alliances. By way of compromise, the international committee
became advisory, although even then the Americans were hes-
itant. It began to meet after Copenhagen.[32] In 1888 the New
York committee of the Alliance was asked to produce a draft
for the Alliance week of prayer. However, the Europeans did
not regard what was produced as substantial enough.[33] A

30  *Evangelical Christendom*, July 1872, p.216.
31  *Evangelical Christendom*, November 1874, pp.327-8.
32  *Evangelical Christendom*, December 1886, pp.395-6.
33  Executive Council Minutes, 14 June 1888.

further international Alliance conference took place in 1891
in Florence, and in 1893 Chicago was the venue. By this time
there was concern about the social mission of the church and it
was to this question that the 1893 conference gave most attention. At the same time, Schaff returned to his theme of a universal church that brought together Protestantism, Orthodoxy
and Catholicism.[34]

## Genuine Catholicity

From the 1880s to the period immediately before the outbreak of the First World War, there were great hopes among
many evangelicals for increased international co-operation.
Conferences at Northfield, Massachusetts, organised by the
American evangelist, D.L. Moody, inspired a new generation
of evangelicals such as John R. Mott. Moody was committed
to unity and to the increasing call, from the 1880s, for 'the
evangelisation of the world in this generation'. The same call
would shape and become the watchword of the international
Student Volunteer Movement.[35] The Alliance was growing
rapidly at this juncture, and its emphasis on catholicity mirrored this theme of the universality of mission. Alliance work
in France in 1878 was a testimony to 'true catholic unity'. At
an Alliance conference in 1881 the bishop of Liverpool spoke
of the Alliance's testimony to the essential unity of 'the whole
catholic church', and in 1884 there was a call from Philip
Schaff for 'genuine catholicity'.[36] But what did this mean?
When the Alliance celebrated its Golden Jubilee in 1896
with an international conference in London, there were
indications that moves towards organisational unity were

---

34 Executive Council Minutes, 14 September 1893; Jordan, *The Evangelical
Alliance for the United States of America, 1847-1900*, p.180.
35 C.H. Hopkins, *John R. Mott, 1865-1955: A Biography* (Grand Rapids:
Eerdmans, 1979), pp.70-1.
36 *Evangelical Christendom*, November 1878, p.346; 1 December 1881, p.367; 1
October 1884, p.316.

gathering momentum. Lord Polwarth, then President of the British Alliance, spoke about hopes for 'a vast reorganization of the outward visible churches of Christendom'. He offered, however, the Alliance vision of a union 'not of human organization, but of a spiritual nature'.[37] Conference speakers, who came from fifteen different countries – France, Germany, Switzerland, Italy, Hungary, Denmark, Holland, Norway, Russia, Armenia, Greece, Egypt, the USA, Canada and Australia – noted that the Alliance had contributed to improved relations between denominations. By this time Anglicans, Presbyterians and Methodists had followed the Alliance's lead in holding international conferences.[38]

Through interdenominational missionary conferences in London in 1878 and 1888, international evangelical co-operation was further strengthened. It seems very likely that the 1888 missionary conference built on the thinking of Schaff, who in 1884 had called for a new spirit of reconciliation, with each denomination contributing its own 'charism' and mission.[39] Almost all the main British and colonial missions – totalling fifty-five – were represented at the missionary conference, with 1,319 people from these societies participating. There were 219 delegates from North America, representing 66 societies, and 41 from continental Europe, representing eighteen societies.[40] Among the speakers were Schaff, Hudson Taylor of the China Inland Mission and Henry Drummond, an influential professor in Edinburgh. A paper by Gustav Warneck, a German professor of missions, argued that unity was 'a mere pious expression' if not recognisable in practice, and he suggested an organisation for that purpose.[41] The American missionary statesman Arthur T. Pierson, who is

---

37  *The Jubilee of the Evangelical Alliance*, p.22.
38  Ibid., pp.47, 49–50.
39  *Evangelical Christendom*, October 1884, p.315.
40  Hogg, *Ecumenical Foundations*, p.42.
41  J.Johnson (ed.), *Report of the Centenary Conference on the Protestant Missions of the World, held in Exeter Hall (June 9th-19th), London, 1888*, Vol. II (2 Vols; London: James Nisbet & Co., 1888), pp.431-7.

credited with articulating the Student Volunteers' credo, considered the 1888 conference 'the grandest ecumenical council ever assembled since the first council in Jerusalem'.[42] To dismiss the great ecumenical councils of the Christian church in this way was astonishing, but the conjunction of unity and world mission was undoubtedly significant.

In the 1890s mission was being increasingly interpreted not only in terms of spiritual endeavour but also social action. Josiah Strong, the General Secretary of the American Alliance in this period, was committed to the social mission of the church. The General Secretary of the British Alliance, A.J. Arnold, worked effectively with Josiah Strong, whose commitment to social action he shared. A close Anglo–American partnership was formed.[43] Both the American and British leaders considered that unity was important for mission. Strong aimed for federations of churches, or 'local alliances', working together to offer salvation for society as well as for individuals. He even envisaged 'men of all faiths and no faiths', serving in co-operation, a perspective not endorsed by the British Alliance.[44] Although it has been argued that the narrow basis of the American Alliance was a cause of its practical disappearance in the 1890s,[45] it is also arguable that it was a lack of a clear confession of faith that contributed to its demise. The British were strongly wedded to mission as explicitly Christian mission. J. Monro Gibson, a British Presbyterian, gave an address on divine love flowing into the world through the union of Christian people in unselfish devotion.[46] This was a call to translate unity into actions for the good of society.

---

42  *The Missionary Review of the World*, Vol. I, p.582.
43  C. Calver, 'Rise and Fall', p.159.
44  Executive Council Minutes, 14 November 1895; Jordan, *The Evangelical Alliance for the United States of America, 1847-1900*, p.182.
45  Rouse, 'Voluntary Movements', p.322.
46  *The Jubilee of the Evangelical Alliance*, p.181.

The turn of the century, however, was not marked by significant Evangelical Alliance advance. A.J. Arnold died in 1898 and Josiah Strong resigned from his role in the same year. Fresh energy for united evangelical action was coming at the turn of the century not from the Alliance but from the leaders of the missionary movement. From 21 April – 1 May 1900, an ecumenical missionary conference was held in New York; it attracted more than 4,000 people each day to the city's Carnegie Hall. For the first time the word 'ecumenical', referring in this case to the whole world, appeared in the actual title of a conference. William McKinley, the President of the USA, opened the conference with an address. Notable missionaries and mission organisers such as John G. Paton from the New Hebrides, Timothy Richard and Hudson Taylor from China (who represented, respectively, broader and more conservative thinking about mission in China), and John R. Mott and Robert E. Speer, both of whom were significant for the emerging ecumenical movement, were present. There were some women speakers, most notably Pandita Ramabai and Lilavati Singh from India. A total of 162 mission boards were represented, the largest representation being from the USA, with continental Europe second and Britain third. Over 170,000 people in total attended the meetings. The main emphasis was on audiences listening to addresses rather than on making plans for missionary action.[47]

## Edinburgh, 1910 and Visible Unity

Strategies that would profoundly affect world mission in the twentieth century, and which would also lead to the establishment of the World Council of Churches in 1948, were formulated a decade later. The World Missionary Conference in Edinburgh in June 1910 drew together 1,200 delegates. It would become a landmark in the history of the world church.

---

47  Hogg, *Ecumenical Foundations*, pp.45-7.

Much has been written about Edinburgh 1910 and the details of the conference do not need to be rehearsed here. The common verdict on the conference is that it was 'the birth place of the modern ecumenical movement'.[48] It built on the previous world missionary conferences and was also deeply influenced by the Student Volunteer Movement and the increasingly powerful Student Christian Movement. John Mott was the Edinburgh conference's Chairman. The conference's commission on co-operation and unity ventured to suggest the goal 'that we should be one in a visible fellowship'. The World Missionary Conference Continuation Committee, which continued to operate after Edinburgh, with J.H. Oldham from Scotland as its highly motivated and influential secretary, pursued the vision for mission and unity that was formulated in 1910.[49] This was a period when the Evangelical Alliance was driven to reconsider the nature of unity and also its implications for the work of mission. Henry Martyn Gooch, General Secretary from 1904, attempted to meet this challenge.

Two months before the Edinburgh conference, at a meeting of the British Evangelical Alliance held on 12 April 1910, J. Campbell Gibson, a moderator of the Presbyterian Church in England, referred to a conference that had been held in 1907 in Shanghai to celebrate the centenary of evangelical Protestant missionary activity in China. Gibson indicated that for him it was now time for the Evangelical Alliance 'to bring that Christian union, which is so much more real than it was, into some concrete form'. Those at Shanghai, he said, felt called 'to take practical steps to further the visible unity of the church of Christ'. This had radical implications. The practical steps envisaged, Gibson explained, included the coming together in union of all churches belonging to one type of ecclesiastical

---

48  K.S. Latourette, 'Ecumenical Bearings of the Missionary Movement and the International Missionary Council', in Rouse & Neill (eds), *A History of the Ecumenical Movement*, p.362.

49  K.W. Clements, *Faith on the Frontier: A Life of J. H. Oldham* (Edinburgh/Geneva: T. & T. Clark/WCC Publications, 1999).

order (for example Anglican, Presbyterian or Baptist) and the promotion of co-operation between all denominations. Gibson accepted that interim steps might not convey 'real catholicity', but he applauded the desire of Chinese leaders 'to regard each other as members of one church, bound together by the name of the one Lord'. His plea was that leaders in the churches at home should be enthusiastic when those in the 'younger churches' sought 'to flow together and form one great church' and did not feel bound by 'differences which we suffer from in the West'.[50] Gibson was issuing a farsighted call from the non-western world.

Six months later, in October 1910, Evangelical Alliance annual meetings were held in Dublin. The title of the conference was 'The Problem of Unity', and Prebendary H.W. Webb-Peploe, vicar of St Paul's, Onslow Square and a noted Anglican evangelical, and (from 1883) an Alliance honorary secretary, delivered one of the addresses. In the 1870s Webb-Peploe had been profoundly affected by teaching about the deeper spiritual life and had become a leader of the annual Keswick Convention, which attracted about 5,000 people each year and advocated consecration and personal holiness.[51] A prebendary of St Paul's Cathedral, Webb-Peploe was a dominant figure among evangelical Anglican clergyman in London. He spoke of himself as a strict churchman,[52] but he was also committed to the pan-denominationalism of Keswick's motto – 'All One in Christ Jesus'. Webb-Peploe brought the Keswick message about the power of the Holy Spirit to Alliance gatherings, and at the October 1910 Alliance meetings he argued in typical Keswick fashion for deeper spiritual unity.[53] The 1911 Annual Report of the Alliance showed that the Alliance Council was not uncritical of Edinburgh 1910, but on the other hand saw it as an

---

50 J. Campbell Gibson, 'China, and the Promotion of Unity', *Evangelical Christendom*, May-June 1910, p.62.

51 C. Price & I.M. Randall, *Transforming Keswick* (Carlisle: OM, 2000), chapters 3 and 4.

52 J.C. Pollock, *The Keswick Story*, p.111.

53 *Evangelical Christendom*, May 1891, p.167; *The Problem of Unity*, p.131.

'evident outcome of the early and later labours of the Alliance in the promotion of Christian Union and co-operation'.[54]

Doubts about the emphasis of Edinburgh 1910 were most prominently expressed by Bishop Evelyn Hassé of the Moravian Church in Great Britain. Hassé believed that the Alliance had been more effective in fostering unity than had Edinburgh. He commented in *Evangelical Christendom* in 1911 that delegates had come to Edinburgh 'in ignorance of the fact that there had been preliminary negotiations resulting in understandings and concessions and limitations which had never found public expression, but which, if they had been made known, would have called forth protests from many quarters'.[55] The reference here was to the fact that Edinburgh was inclusive, extending beyond evangelical Protestants, and that in order to secure the presence of Anglo-Catholics it had been necessary to exclude from discussions at Edinburgh any allusion to Protestant missions working in Catholic countries in Europe and Latin America. This troubled many evangelicals deeply. G. Campbell Morgan, minister of Westminster Chapel, London, said at the annual meeting of the British Alliance in May 1913 that he lamented the deliberate exclusion of mission in Latin America from consideration at Edinburgh. He saw this as 'a very significant and depressing sign of the time'.[56] From the evangelical point of view, it was also unsatisfactory that matters of doctrinal belief were not discussed at Edinburgh. This deficiency was later remedied through the Faith and Order Movement, which was formed in 1927 as a direct result of the Edinburgh conference.[57]

---

54 *Annual Report of the Evangelical Alliance*, p.9.
55 E.R. Hassé, 'The Problem of Unity', *Evangelical Christendom*, January-February 1911, p.2.
56 G. Campbell Morgan, 'The Present Need and Possibility of Christian Union', *Evangelical Christendom*, May-June 1913, p.102; cf. H.H. Rowdon, 'Edinburgh 1910, Evangelicals and the Ecumenical Movement', *Vox Evangelica* 5 (1967), pp.49-71.
57 T. Tatlow, 'The World Conference on Faith and Order', in Rouse & Neill (eds), *A History of the Ecumenical Movement*, chapter 9.

The Shanghai missions conference of 1907 continued to have an influence on British and American evangelical thinking. D.E. Hoste, director of the China Inland Mission, referred in 1911 to ideas on unification that had been discussed at Shangai. He commented: 'It is easy to say, "Let the Chinese arrange a church order of their own." Until such time, however, as the requisite experience and knowledge render them competent to do this, the missionaries are obliged to institute some ecclesiastical arrangements.' As a practical missionary thinker, Hoste recognised that foreign missionaries brought to China their own convictions about church order, and indeed he believed that there was value in the older traditions of the church being shared with new believers overseas. On the other hand, Hoste considered that inherited western views brought to China from outside should not be allowed to stand in the way of what might emerge as a new ecclesiastical identity in China. There was hope that the churches in China might be able to transcend divisions found among the missionaries. Given his position as leader of an interdenominational mission, it is not surprising that Hoste favoured 'recognition on the part of the several churches of each other's ministry' and also 'admission of alternative views in regard to the rite of baptism as a basis of church membership'.[58] The effect of the Edinburgh conference was to reinforce the belief that unity was important for mission. This drove the Alliance to engage more deeply with its own understanding of unity among evangelicals.

## A Parting of the Ways

During the course of the twentieth century, there were periods when tensions were evident between those who considered that unity should only be sought through associations of fellow-evangelicals and those whose outlook and approach

58  D.E. Hoste, 'Church Unity in China', *Evangelical Christendom*, May-June 1911, p.117.

were wider. The Evangelical Alliance has often been seen as one of the major bodies arguing for the first view. The second approach, which argues that all Christian denominations should be embraced within the quest for union, has been the defining characteristic of the ecumenical movement, a movement partly embodied in the World Council of Churches. Yet divergence of opinion between the Alliance and the post-Edinburgh ecumenical movement initially emerged during a debate in 1913 in which the Alliance seemed to be taking a position that was more inclusive. The issue was inter-denominational participation in Holy Communion. The Kikuyu Conference of June 1913, held in the Kenyan village of the same name, highlighted this issue. Kikuyu, however, was not a direct outcome of Edinburgh; an idea proposed there for a 'Federation of Missionary Societies' had, in fact, been talked about before 1910. But Kikuyu *was* part of a concern for unity found in some regions of Africa following Edinburgh,[59] and a Church of Scotland missionary in Kenya, J.W. Arthur, wrote in April 1913 to J.H. Oldham asking for advice on issues that might be brought up at Kikuyu.[60]

Those present at Kikuyu represented Anglicanism, Presbyterianism and other Protestant bodies. The proposals formulated, under the leadership of the bishops of Mombasa (W.G. Peel) and Uganda (J.J. Willis), included the idea of a Central Missionary Council for East Africa which would be pan-denominational. This proposal in itself generated virulent attacks from the Anglo-Catholic wing of the Anglican Church, the opposition from within Africa being led by Frank Weston, bishop of Zanzibar. There was particularly adverse re-action to a united service of Holy Communion at Kikuyu. *Evangelical Christendom* reported in the January–February 1914 issue that Kikuyu conference members (including non-Anglicans) 'received Holy Communion from the hands of a bishop. Immediately clamour was raised … The cry of heresy was

59  Hogg, *Ecumenical Foundations*, p.159.
60  Clements, *A Life of J.H. Oldham*, p.115.

raised against the bishops who attended the Conference.' For
*Evangelical Christendom* this kind of reaction represented 'Anglican exclusiveness'.[61] In July 1914 *Evangelical Christendom* returned to the subject, saying that the storm of protest about the
united communion service was deplorable and emphasising
that evangelicals had long been involved in intercommunion at
devotional conferences and at Evangelical Alliance events.[62]
During the golden Jubilee international Alliance conference
of 1896, two thousand people had participated in a communion service.[63]

In the period following the Edinburgh conference, with increased stress on unity, evangelicals were looking for more
openness to the practice of inter-communion. They therefore
regarded the step that had been taken at Kikuyu as altogether
right. An Alliance resolution was printed in *Evangelical Christendom*: it stated that the Alliance Council 'desires to record its
sense of gratitude for the excellent spirit of love and unity
which led fellow Christians of sister churches to join together
in a united Conference followed by the Lord's Supper at Kikuyu'. This was seen as 'carrying into practice some of the ideals
for which the Alliance has laboured during the past sixty-eight
years'. The hope was expressed that there might be similar
unity in other places.[64] The effect of Kikuyu, however, was to
engender greater caution among Anglicans, and even among
ecumenical statesmen like J.H. Oldham. Randall Davidson, the
Archbishop of Canterbury, was quoted by *Evangelical Christendom* in 1915 as having said 'we shall act rightly, in abstaining
from such services as the closing service held at Kikuyu'.[65]

It was inevitable, given such statements, that Alliance leaders
would see themselves as being at odds with the broader stream

61 'Kikuyu and Ideals of Reunion', *Evangelical Christendom*, January–February
1914, pp.17–9.
62 'The Kikuyu Conference – Its Bearing on False and True Unity', *Evangelical
Christendom*, July–August 1914, p.152.
63 *The Jubilee of the Evangelical Alliance*, pp.379–83.
64 *Evangelical Christendom*, July–August 1914, pp.148–9.
65 'The Kikuyu Statement', *Evangelical Christendom*, May–June 1915, p.109.

of ecumenical thinking that developed from Edinburgh 1910. For them Kikuyu was a sign of revival and spiritual openness, the like of which had not been evident at Edinburgh. Nonetheless, the Alliance leadership under Henry Martyn Gooch sought to have good relationships with the ecumenical movement. In 1921 the International Missionary Council (IMC), with John Mott as Chairman, was formed as a fruit of the Edinburgh conference. Gooch used Mott to prepare material for the Alliance Week of Prayer. In December 1938 Gooch wrote to Mott to express the hope of the Alliance that the World Missionary Conference beginning at Madras Christian College, India, would 'further through the work of Missions the unity of the Spirit'. Mott regarded this conference as a greater event than Edinburgh: it 'transcended our highest expectations', he wrote. Mott emphasised the need for a World Council of Churches that was built on a solid foundation. The letter from the Alliance was read at Madras and Mott replied to Gooch on 30 December 1938 to convey appreciation for 'the vital part' played by the Alliance members through their prayers.[66] The parting of the ways between the Alliance and the ecumenical movement was by no means total.

## Conclusion

To a large extent, the dedicated internationalism of the Evangelical Alliance in the later nineteenth century and early twentieth century mirrored the mood of the times. The increasingly significant role of the United States of America through this period was a sign of things to come, although Britain was still giving a major lead to international evangelicalism. Indeed, in 1912 the British Alliance introduced the name 'World's Evangelical Alliance' to describe the British Organisation, and this name was used until the 1950s. From the

---

66 Minutes of the Executive Council of the Evangelical Alliance, 22 December 1938; 26 January 1939; Hopkins, *John R Mott*, pp.684-9.

American side, Philip Schaff's determinedly catholic thinking was seminal. He opposed exclusiveness, lamenting that some polemical figures had 'exhausted the vocabulary of reproach and vituperation', and he argued in 1884 that evangelicals should 'look hopefully for a reunion of Christendom'.[67] Such thinking undoubtedly lay behind the marked broadening of the Alliance's theological scope during the late nineteenth and early twentieth centuries. However, it was world missionary leaders, most notably through the Edinburgh conference of 1910, who formed an international organisation that was the basis for the ecumenical movement and in particular for the World Council of Churches. Worldwide movements towards unity in the early twentieth century drew from earlier Alliance thinking, but the emphasis that came out of Edinburgh in 1910 on drawing denominations rather than individuals together meant that the Alliance's own emphasis on promoting unity through mutual love and evangelical affirmations was some-what overshadowed. Eventually, in fact, there was a parting of the ways. Nonetheless, the original Alliance desire for 'the promotion of a larger Christian union' continued to be a powerful factor within evangelical life in a number of nations, and played its part, therefore, in encouraging the realisation of a vision for greater unity within the global Christian community.

---

67 *Evangelical Christendom*, October 1884, p.315.

# 7

# To Anglicize, Gallicize or Americanize?

*The Alliance's Relationship to Europe*

There was a distinct European dimension present from the beginning of the Evangelical Alliance. At the London inaugural conference in 1846 representatives from continental Europe made a presentation in French at the final session. The European leaders included Adolphe Monod, Professor of the Theology faculty at Montauban University in France, August Tholuck, professor at Halle University, Germany, and Johann Oncken, the leader of the German Baptists.[1] The French representatives, who were active in discussions, committed themselves to forming a branch of the Alliance in France, Belgium, French-speaking Switzerland and other places where the French language was used. Other Protestant countries followed. Branches of the Alliance were formed in North and South Germany. Outside of the Protestant areas of Europe there were also initiatives. An Evangelical Alliance was formed in Constantinople in 1855. In Spain many of the leading evangelicals within the Protestant community united in forming an Alliance. The Spanish government saw the Alliance as the voice of Spanish evangelicals. This chapter will survey the international conferences of the Evangelical Alliance that were held on the continent of Europe;[2] and it will then look at the

---

1 Railton, *No North Sea*, pp.xvi–xviii.
2 See Ewing, *Goodly Fellowship*, pp.26–34.

place of mainland Europe in the life of the Alliance, and more
particularly at the European dimension of the Alliance's
British Organisation through the first half of the twentieth
century.


## Conferences in Europe

The Evangelical Alliance conference in Paris in 1855 was the
first International Conference of the Alliance held outside
the British Isles. George Fisch, originally from the Vaud region of Switzerland, who had followed Monod as pastor of
the independent church in Lyons, was a central figure. He had
left the French Reformed Church, and as President of the
French Alliance, Fisch encouraged French evangelicals to set
up free evangelical churches in France.[3] Twelve hundred people from fifteen nations came to Paris and discussed various
issues including religious liberty. At the close of the conference there was a united service of Holy Communion, led in
seven languages – French, English, German, Dutch, Italian,
Swedish and Danish.[4] Alliance members who gathered in
Berlin in 1857 were addressed by Frederick William IV, King
of Prussia, who hoped that 'there may descend upon all the
members of the conference an effusion of the Spirit of God,
like that which fell on the first disciples at Pentecost'.[5] Alliance work in Germany was animated by Eduard Kuntze, a
Lutheran pastor (formerly a curate at the German Savoy
Church in London) and G.W. Lehmann, a Baptist, both of
whom worked in Berlin. Baron Carl Bunsen, the envoy of the
Prussian court in London, fostered Anglo-German evangelical links. Many Lutherans were wary of such co-operation,
but F.W. Krummacher, court preacher in Berlin, assured
Germans at the 1857 conference that the Alliance was not

3 Kessler, *A Study of the Evangelical Alliance*, pp.17, 53.
4 *Evangelical Christendom*, October 1855, p.317.
5 E. Steane (ed.), *The Religious Condition of Christendom: The Conference Held in Berlin, 1857* (London, 1857), p.xiv.

seeking 'to Anglicize, Gallicize or Americanize the German people'.[6] European enthusiasm had limits.

The Reformed rather than the Lutheran heritage of evangelicals in Europe was recognised at the Alliance conference held in Geneva in 1861, and in conferences convened in Paris, London, Geneva and Edinburgh during 1864. At the 1861 Geneva conference speakers included the Reformed historian/theologian and Alliance supporter Merle d'Aubigné, who talked about John Calvin, the Genevan Reformer, as one who 'belongs to us all'. Twelve ministers from different denominations distributed the bread and wine at the communion service.[7] The conferences in 1864 celebrated the tercentenary of Calvin's death. In May 1864 a Calvin commemoration was held in the Freemason's Hall, London, when addresses were delivered by Anglican, Baptist, Methodist and Presbyterian figures who were well known within Evangelical Alliance circles – T.R. Birks, Baptist Noel, William Arthur and Thomas M'Crie. William Arthur, a noted Methodist, said that he was 'no admirer of that part of Calvin's views in which Calvin differed from the great majority of evangelical Christians', but, he continued, he heartily concurred in the 'great body of truth which Calvin taught'. Citing C.H. Spurgeon, he added that he would rather unite with someone who denounced Methodist Arminianism than with someone who praised Methodism's Arminian tradition but doubted redemption by Christ. There were cheers.[8] A distinctively European pan-evangelical heritage was coming to the fore.

A similar sense of connection with European history was to be found at Alliance conferences in 1867 and 1879. The Amsterdam conference in 1867 was intended to attract ministers, theological professors and other leaders. About 4,000 people attended the opening service, at which the preacher was Professor Van Oosterzee, Professor of Theology at the University

---

6 *Evangelical Christendom*, October 1857, pp.361, 366.

7 Carlyle (ed.), *Proceedings of the Geneva Conference*, p.205. For Merle d'Aubigné and the Alliance see Railton, *No North Sea*, pp.32–42.

8 *Evangelical Christendom*, July 1864, pp.348–9.

of Utrecht, an orthodox theologian who stood in contrast to many theologians in Germany and Holland. He spoke about the communion of saints. Hymns were sung in four languages – Dutch, German, French and English.[9] In 1879 the city of Basle, a recognised evangelical centre, was the venue for an Evangelical Alliance conference. The 2,000 members present (which included 250 from Britain and 50 from the USA) were reminded by John Stoughton, for ten years editor of the *Evangelical Magazine*, about the way the city had given refuge to English Protestant exiles in the sixteenth century. *The Times* covered each day of the Basle conference in detail and paid tribute to the Alliance's leaders. One editorial asserted: 'What they say is listened to, and what they purpose will be eagerly watched and aided, by a vast band of sympathisers in every country, and not least in our own.' The Alliance welcomed this 'friendly leading article'.[10] European evangelical developments were followed by opinion-formers in Britain.

European Evangelical Alliance conferences in 1884 and 1891 were groundbreaking. In Copenhagen, during 1884, Scandinavian nations were drawn in a new way into the sphere of Alliance activities. Some Swedish Lutherans, as will be seen below, were unsympathetic, but the conference was a success. The King and Queen of Denmark attended. Major General Field, one of the British Alliance secretaries, spoke of such 'ecumenical' assemblies as a manifestation of the unity of the Church of Christ.[11] At one of the sessions E.B. Underhill, secretary of the Baptist Missionary Society, referred to the protection given by a former king of Denmark to William Carey's Baptist mission in the Danish settlement of Serampore, India. Underhill made it clear that the British East India Company

9 *Evangelical Christendom*, September 1867, p.459; *Proceedings of the Amsterdam Conference of the Evangelical Alliance* (London, 1868), pp.xvi–xvii; cf., *Evangelical Christendom*, February 1871, pp.37–8, when doubt was cast on Van Oosterzee's belief in the eternity of the future punishment of the wicked.

10 *The Times*, 4 September 1879, p.4; 5 September 1879, p.5; 8 September 1879, p.11; Executive Council Minutes, 9 October 1879.

11 Executive Council Minutes, 23 October 1884.

had no sympathy for mission to Indian people. An Alliance resolution was passed expressing appreciation for support from Denmark.[12] At the Alliance conference of 1891 in Florence, which 1,200 people attended, Professor Mariona of the University of Florence spoke of how he had left the Roman Catholic Church as a result of his study of Hegel's philosophy, and described his belief in the gospel of Christ, leading to 'a mystical transformation of the heart'. He had not, however, joined any of the Italian evangelical churches, which he considered often looked like 'places of business'.[13] To have Mariona speaking was an adventurous attempt to increase European understanding. Another participant, Count di Campello, was working towards a Reformed Italian Catholic Church. The Alliance agreed to produce these unusual proceedings in English and Italian.[14]

## European Fractures

There were, however, fractures within European evangelicalism. In 1883 five German pastors who were not within the Lutheran Church wrote to the British Evangelical Alliance alleging that non-Lutherans were being excluded from the German Alliance. Alliance representatives from Bonn denied this, but feelings ran so high that there was talk of forming a new body that would be 'a real German Evangelical Alliance'.[15] In some countries the initial enthusiasm for an Alliance waned. The Alliance joint secretaries, Field and A.J. Arnold, found it necessary in 1882 to seek to revive Alliance work in Sweden and in Holland. The intention at that stage was that there should be an Evangelical Alliance conference in

---

12 *Evangelical Christendom*, October 1884, p.309; cf., J.H.Y Briggs, *The English Baptists of the Nineteenth Century*, p.234.

13 *Evangelical Christendom*, May 1891, pp.146-7; *Christendom from the Standpoint of Italy*, pp.56, 125-30.

14 Executive Council Minutes, 14 May 1891.

15 Executive Council Minutes, 13 December 1883.

Sweden, but discussions that took place throughout the whole of 1883 failed to resolve problems over Lutheran involvement. The Archbishop of Uppsala said that the Alliance committee in Sweden had insufficient standing and that 'scarcely any' key Lutherans would participate. In early 1884 the Stockholm committee finally agreed to stand aside in favour of a committee 'appointed by the Lutheran dignitaries', but even this was not acceptable to Lutheran leaders. The Archbishop of Uppsala finally wrote to Lord Polwarth, the President of the British Alliance, to say that it was advisable to postpone the conference for a few years.[16]

As an alternative to the Stockholm conference it was decided to hold the 1884 event in Copenhagen, and this move received support from the German, French, Swiss and British branches.[17] Philip Schaff made an important statement at Copenhagen which distinguished between genuine catholicity and 'negative liberalism which ignores or obliterates the distinction between truth and error'. In the face of growing liberal theological influence across the continent, Schaff argued for a 'deep conviction of the infinite grandeur of truth', despite the inability of any single Christian group to grasp its fullness.[18] It was not clear, however, what would happen to evangelical theology in Germany, in particular, given the rising tension between orthodox and liberal theological views. In the 1890s British Alliance representatives such as A.J. Arnold and F.B. Meyer attended German evangelical conferences at Bad Blankenburg,[19] and in 1899 Meyer spoke of the remarkable *Gemeinschaft* or 'fellowship meeting' movement in Lutheranism, although he was not sure if this would revive or split the church.[20]

---

16 Executive Council Minutes, 13 April 1882; 7 December 1882; 17 January 1884; 13 March 1884.

17 Executive Council Minutes, 25 April 1884.

18 *Evangelical Christendom*, October 1884, p.316.

19 Executive Council Minutes, 11 July 1895.

20 *Evangelical Alliance Quarterly*, 2 October 1899, p.20.

National issues exacerbated the problems faced by evangelicals in Europe. Because Britain and Germany took opposing stances on the Boer War, there was a degree of estrangement between British and German evangelicals. This was a blow to inclusive German Alliance leaders such as Count Bernstorff. The international conference of the Evangelical Alliance, which was to be held in Hamburg in 1902, had to be cancelled. The view in Britain was that the German Alliance had refused to have fellowship with the British.[21] In the annual report of the British Alliance for 1905 there was much concern that another year had gone by in which the postponed international conference had still not been held.[22] The conference was eventually convened in London in 1907, but the opportunity to engage with mainland European developments in a more significant way was lost. A number of church leaders were active in seeking to promote understanding between England and Germany and in 1910 'The Associated Councils in the British and German Empires for Fostering Friendly Relations between the Two Peoples' was launched. F.B. Meyer was a vice-President of the British Council's committee.[23] In this period Henry Martyn Gooch continued his travels in Europe, not only in Germany but also further east.[24]

The First World War, however, fractured attempts at Anglo-German friendship. John Clifford, a leading Baptist minister, peace supporter and internationalist, who in 1911 addressed an Evangelical Alliance audience of 3,000 people as President of the Baptist World Alliance,[25] told his London congregation in January 1914: 'A new era is coming nearer and nearer every year ... Militarism belongs to the dark ages; it is

21 *Evangelical Alliance Quarterly*, 1 July 1902, p.278.

22 *Report of the Council for the Year ending March 31st 1905* (London, 1905), p.16.

23 I.M. Randall, 'The Role of Conscientious Objectors: British Evangelicals and the First World War', *Anabaptism Today* 11 (1996), p.10.

24 H.M. Gooch, 'A European Travel-Talk', *Evangelical Christendom*, November-December 1911, pp.207-9.

25 Ibid., p.230.

not fit for our time. It must go. It is going.'[26] A mere seven
months later, following the outbreak of the First World War,
Clifford had dramatically changed his mind. 'The progress
of humanity', he informed his west London congregation,
'hinges upon this war ... We are forced into it.' There were
appreciative murmurs of 'Hear, Hear.'[27] A similar *volte-face* was
evident at London's Congregational Westminster Chapel. The
2,500 people who were at the Chapel on Sunday 2 August
1914 responded with applause to a statement from the minister, G. Campbell Morgan, a vice-President of the Alliance, that
anyone in Europe wanting war was 'accursed'. Yet a week later
the same congregation cheered a sermon by Morgan with the
message that war, though caused by man's wickedness, could
produce 'renewal of moral consciousness and the re-birth of
the soul'.[28]

This affirmation of the war was characteristic of many delivered by British evangelicals at this time. In September 1914
Gooch spoke of war as 'repugnant to the followers of the
Prince of Peace', but went on to affirm that many officers and
men, some of them members of the Evangelical Alliance, were
'fighting in the strength of alliance to Christ and his Word'.
H. W. Webb-Peploe, with his strongly internationalist Keswick
outlook, wrote in *Evangelical Christendom* at the same time of
the unity that he felt with Christians in Germany, while at the
same time asking for Alliance members to pray that German
militarism, infidelity and 'swell-headedness', as personified in
the Emperor, would be defeated.[29] Two months later, Gooch
commented on the fact that Alliance leaders in Germany were
writing and speaking in favour of the German cause. He made
it clear that he respected their devotion to Christ and their
honest convictions in what they said, and his conclusion was
that they did not know the full story of the events that led up to

26  *The Christian World*, 8 January 1914, p.7.
27  *The British Weekly*, 20 August 1914, p.525.
28  A. Wilkinson, *Dissent or Conform?: War, Peace and the English Churches,
1900-1945* (London: SCM Press, 1986), pp.24-5.
29  *Evangelical Christendom*, September-October 1914, pp.177, 188-9.

the war. Indeed, Gooch warned against believing evil of German brothers in Christ.[30]

Patriotic sentiments, however, meant that such sober statements were often ignored. The partisan spirit found among British Christians was reinforced by conceptions of spiritual warfare that appealed especially, though not exclusively, to evangelicals. Some, like John Clifford, portrayed the war in apocalyptic terms. A collection of essays, which included contributions from Clifford and A.F. Winnington-Ingram, Bishop of London, was produced in 1914 and entitled *Kaiser or Christ?*. Winnington-Ingram – who did not belong to the evangelical camp – preached a sermon in which he claimed that everyone who died in the war was a martyr, and he presented the struggle of the Allies in graphic terms as 'the Nailed Hand against the Mailed Fist'.[31] W.Y. Fullerton, the home secretary of the Baptist Missionary Society, conveyed this theme to the Alliance, contrasting the 'nailed hand of Christ', which he claimed would yet rule the world, with the 'mailed hand of man', and in particular the philosophy of force then prevalent in Germany.[32] Equally dramatic, and expressed in imagery not normally associated with conservative evangelicals, was the assertion by Campbell Morgan of Westminster Chapel that 'the sign of the cross is on every man that marches to his death'.[33] Evangelicals, with their cross-centred theology, tended to see the sacrifices made during the horrors of war as the way to victory. During the war the theme of victory, in which spiritual and national triumphs could become confused with each other, became more prominent among evangelicals than the emphasis on pan-national fellowship. Fractures were evident.

---

30  *Evangelical Christendom*, November–December 1914, p.242.
31  S. Mews, 'Spiritual Mobilization in the First World War', *Theology* (June 1971), p.259.
32  *Evangelical Christendom*, November–December 1914, pp.213–16.
33  Wilkinson, *Dissent or Conform?*, pp.5–7.

## Calls to Prayer

The priority for the British Evangelical Alliance during the First World War, however, was not rousing militaristic fervour; it was calling the British nation to united prayer. Monthly meetings for prayer that attracted over 2,500 people took place in the Queen's Hall, London. On occasions there was an overflow into All Souls Church, Langham Place, which was next door. It was the Alliance's strategy to use prominent denominational leaders to speak at these meetings in the hope that they would further the cause of spiritual renewal in Britain. In this, the Alliance's Executive Council was prepared to endorse co-operation with high church Anglicans.[34] In November 1914 the speakers included Winnington-Ingram, William Temple, who was to be appointed bishop of Manchester after the war, Luke Wiseman, a well-known Methodist leader, and F.B. Meyer. Different emphases were patently obvious. Temple, who was to use his enormous talents in part in the service of the ecumenical movement, argued that the war was underscoring the need for witness to the world through visible Christian unity, through a church that was 'one, catholic, and holy'. Meyer, who was to launch the premillennial Advent Testimony and Preparation Movement in 1917, proclaimed 'Marantha!' and pronounced: 'The war is the pre-travail out of which the New Age is about to be born. The Lord is at the doors.'[35]

Speakers at Alliance meetings for prayer in 1915 included the Archbishop of Canterbury, Randall Davidson, Lord Kinnaird and bishop Taylor Smith (the Chaplain-General, who addressed Alliance meetings in the Queen's Hall that were designed to promote family prayers in the nation). Gooch was delighted that the 2,700 people present included those

---

34  Executive Council Minutes, 25 March 1915.
35  *Evangelical Christendom*, November–December 1914, pp.230, 235; I.M. Randall, 'Cultural Change and Future Hope: Premillennialism in Britain following the First World War', *Christianity and History Newsletter*, No 13, June 1994.

from the high and low sections of the Church of England and from the Free Churches.[36] This initiated a movement for the National Revival of Family Prayers. Gooch considered that there was power in unity. He expressed his pride at the way in which the Alliance was uniting churches and Christians during the stresses of war. At the same time, the use of speakers from very different sections of the church could create difficulties. It might have seemed that F.B. Meyer, as the best-known international Keswick speaker, would have been unlikely to cause embarrassment to the Alliance. However, Meyer had travelled widely and had a broad view of spiritual experience. In May 1915 *Evangelical Christendom* strongly opposed the opinion expressed by Meyer that the war was bringing the churches together and that there was hope, within this process, for the Roman Catholic and Eastern churches to be 'purified'.[37]

Although the Alliance could see few signs of hope for such a wider Christian renewal, the way in which it adopted the strategy of prayer for the nation led to criticisms from those who felt it was compromising its evangelical beliefs. A.C. Dixon, an American who was minister of the huge Metropolitan Tabernacle, which had been founded by Spurgeon, accused the Alliance in 1917 of fraternising with 'sacerdotalists' and 'liberals'. Dixon was a member of the Alliance, but he was not a widely influential figure in Britain, and the Alliance did not seem to feel threatened by his attack.[38] It was in this period that the Alliance sought to increase pressure on the government for a 'Day of Prayer' to be held by national proclamation, but Lloyd George and Bonar Law were nervous that this would be a political problem. There were memories of the phrase used in the Victorian period, a 'Day of Humiliation', and the politicians feared that both allies and enemies would misunderstand such a concept.[39] It was only

36 *Evangelical Christendom*, July–August 1915, pp.129-30.
37 *Evangelical Christendom*, May–June 1915, pp.105-6.
38 *Evangelical Christendom*, May–June 1917, p.81.
39 A. Wilkinson, *The Church of England and the First World War* (London: SCM Press, 1996), p.67.

in 1918 that there was, finally, a Royal proclamation of a 'Day of Prayer'. The Alliance felt vindicated.

It was Campbell Morgan who, in 1917, gave what was perhaps the most thoughtful address at an Alliance prayer meeting on the evangelical view of the church and the nation. Morgan began by outlining what he saw as a dual allegiance. 'By birth I am British', he stated, 'and I thank God I am. But by grace I am a member of the holy catholic apostolic Church of Jesus Christ.' Morgan promoted love of one's nation, but also stressed that God was God of all nations. He warned against the 'incipient blasphemy ... which often lurks in our thinking – that God is *British*'. All attempts to prove the superiority of the British nation were, he considered, anti-Christian. Yet the churches had a responsibility for the nation. Morgan argued that British churches had a duty to 'ask the War Council to consider the *why* of what they do, as well as the *how* of the thing to be done', and that Christians should have words of rebuke and instruction. The church, he concluded, was called to a campaign: of *prophecy*, proclaiming the word of God; of *priesthood*, bearing upon her heart human sin; of *kingly authority*, leading the nation towards God's kingdom. The Alliance, in the crisis of war, believed that in a unique way it had drawn together Anglican bishops, Free Church leaders, military representatives, MPs and business people.[40] It had called the nation to pray.


## A Connecting Link

Following the end of the war, this leadership role in Europe was seen by the Alliance as continuing. During the 1920s the Alliance was active in supporting mission in Europe. In Russia, in the later nineteenth century, the Alliance had been involved in evangelistic outreach through evangelists such as F.W.

---

40  G. Campbell Morgan, 'The Church and the Nation', *Evangelical Christendom*, January–February 1917, pp.18–9; May–June 1919, p.54.

Baedeker, a German by birth, who became English by adoption and was well known for his travel guides. Developments in Russia from the Revolution onwards heightened Alliance concern. In 1923 Gooch asked whether the time had come for a 'step towards closer Christian Unity which would save England and the world from the tragedy of Russia under a Bolshevist Government'.[41] It was not obvious how this connection would be made, but there was a clear desire to unite against a common foe, as had been the case during the war. Yet the Alliance also made it clear in the 1920s that it did not see socialism as intrinsically anti-Christian. Rather, it was the measures of the Soviet government that were condemned. The Alliance was involved in campaigning for the freedom of Orthodox as well as evangelical believers in Russia. Adam Podin, who was the Alliance's main link with Russia in the 1920s, met regularly with Orthodox Church leaders.[42]

The British Alliance paid Podin's salary. He was a Baptist based in Estonia and his travels since before the First World War meant that he was widely known. His work, said the Alliance in 1913, was 'of an apostolic character'.[43] Podin had a great deal of freedom to preach and also to visit prisons, speak to prisoners – he had access to 4,000 prisoners – and distribute Bibles. In Estonia he began a Baptist seminary and set up an institution for lepers. In 1927 Henry Martyn Gooch visited the seminary in Estonia, speaking appreciatively of Podin's work, and addressed a united evangelical meeting in Sion Church, Riga, Latvia. Podin died during the Second World War.[44] The British Alliance also supported mission work in Poland, but there the complexities of the relationships between Baptists and other Protestants meant that the Alliance regarded it as

41 H.M. Gooch, 'Bolshevism and the Bible', *Evangelical Christendom*, March–April 1923, p.34.
42 *Evangelical Christendom*, January–February 1920, p.2; May–June 1922, pp.61–2; March–April 1923, p.39.
43 *Evangelical Christendom*, November–December 1913, p.206; Executive Council Minutes, 23 September 1920.
44 Ewing, *Goodly Fellowship*, pp.42–3.

impossible to be associated, as they were in Estonia and Russia, with Baptists. In 1937 the Alliance contributed substantially to the setting up of a Polish evangelical Bible school and a year later Gooch visited the school to establish a co-operative relationship.[45] The Alliance saw such moves as being expressions of its traditional concern for situations where evangelicals were in a small minority.

Concern for good relationships with evangelicals in Germany was a feature of the 1920s. The British Alliance asked in 1923 that there should be no more circulation of literature vindicating positions taken in the war, and emphasised the desire on the part of German Alliance leaders for a 'resumption of our post-war brotherhood'. German evangelicals also shared with their British counterparts the misery being felt by their people.[46] In 1926 a meeting was held with German Alliance leaders and there was a strong desire to lay aside past bitterness. The German-British axis was seen as crucial to the vision that Gooch in particular advocated – the vision of a strong link between evangelicals across Europe. For Gooch the Alliance was able to function as 'a connecting link' for continental Protestants, and he urged British evangelicals to take more interest in their 'Continental Brethren'. One of the leaders with whom the Alliance co-operated in this task of generating a European consciousness was J.H. Rushbrooke, a British Baptist who spoke German and who was to become secretary of the Baptist World Alliance.[47]

These activities by the Alliance were associated with the desire to establish Protestantism more firmly in Europe. Gooch spoke at celebrations at Augsburg in Bavaria in 1930 to mark the 400th anniversary of the Augsburg Confession of Faith. It is significant that Gooch was present there as an official represen-

---

45  Executive Council Minutes, 31 December 1935; 22 December 1938.

46  *Evangelical Christendom*, May-June 1923, p.87; November-December 1923, p.161.

47  *Evangelical Christendom*, July-August, 1929, p.123; November-December 1930, p.209.

tative of Protestant churches in Europe and America.[48] An international 'League' was formed on the continent of Europe for the 'Defence and Furtherance of Protestantism', and the President and secretary of this Protestant league were welcomed to the annual meetings of the British Evangelical Alliance in 1931. But the Alliance had connections with many evangelicals who were not part of the dominant Protestant churches in Europe – Lutheran and Reformed – and in October 1932 the Alliance's Executive Council noted the difficulties that the League had in recognising the Alliance. In the following month the relationship was terminated.[49]

One part of Europe in which the British Evangelical Alliance took a particular interest was Czechoslovakia, where in the 1920s evangelicals were welcoming into their congregations those who were leaving the Roman Catholic Church. At the invitation of the Evangelical Church of the Czech Brethren, Gooch visited Czechoslovakia in 1922, travelling by the Orient Express from Paris. He had been to Prague, the 'ancient and beautiful capital', 25 years before, and was delighted to see the evangelical progress that had taken place since then. *Evangelical Christendom* suggested that the way in which a new Czechoslovak national church had been formed, together with the way in which other Czechs had joined the Evangelical Church, meant that a new Reformation was in the making.[50] Czech leaders were invited to Britain. On one of his visits to Czechoslovakia, Gooch also visited Hungary and spoke at 'Alliance-Keswick' meetings, as they were termed, along with other English speakers. This period saw great interest in the possibility that countries in central Europe where there had been a long evangelical tradition but where Roman Catholicism had held sway, would see spiritual renewal.

Southern Europe also attracted much attention in the 1920s. Don Fernando Cabrera, the leader of the Evangelical

48  Ewing, *Goodly Fellowship*, p.56.
49  Executive Council Minutes, 27 October 1932; 24 November 1932.
50  H.M. Gooch, 'Articles on Czechoslovakia', *Evangelical Christendom*, July-August 1922, pp.91-3; September-October 1923, p.129.

Alliance in Spain, welcomed a British Alliance delegation in 1925. A capacity crowd filled the Church of the Redeemer, Madrid, for a special service. In Portugal, the Alliance worked with the International Missionary Council and it was a cause of satisfaction to the wider Alliance movement, with its desire to see Protestantism in the ascendancy, that the headquarters of the Portuguese Alliance were in a former Catholic convent in Lisbon. There were also Evangelical Alliance links with the Italian Waldensian Church, the traditional Protestant denomination in Italy, which dates back to the twelfth century. At Alliance meetings in London in 1927, Signor Janni of the Waldensian community expressed his gratitude to the evangelical Alliance for its support.[51] In 1931 Gooch visited Albania and spoke to groups made up of people from Islamic, Orthodox, Catholic and Protestant backgrounds. The Alliance was supporting witness within the variety of cultures and beliefs to be found in Europe.

## The March of Fascism

The Alliance in Britain looked forward to the 1930s with some optimism, speaking in 1929 of the continent of Europe coming to a new period of peace. The 'dark clouds' were seen as passing. Two years later the Executive Council of the Alliance agreed to thank Mussolini for his support of religious liberty in Italy. There had been 1,000 admissions to the Waldensian Church in Italy in the previous year and the outlook seemed highly promising.[52] A year later, however, the implications of the rise of fascism in Europe were becoming bleakly evident. The Alliance Council, on 27 April 1932, deplored the persecution of the Jewish people in Germany, who were suffering 'at the hands of those who profess and represent the Christian faith'. Some evangelicals in Germany, who

51 Ewing, *Goodly Fellowship*, pp.45-6, 111.
52 *Evangelical Christendom*, September-October 1929, p.162; Executive Council Minutes, 28 May 1931; *Evangelical Christendom*, September-October 1931, p.198.

protested to the British Alliance, received this resolution unfa-
vourably, but at a meeting in the Queen's Hall in London on 27
June 1933 the Alliance formulated a stronger resolution on the
subject. This stated that 'the discrimination now being exercised against the Jews is contrary to the basic principles of tolerance and equality which are accepted in the modern world
in relation to the treatment of religious and racial minorities'.
The Chairman of the Queen's Hall meeting, Lord Buckmaster,
described the treatment of the Jews in Germany as 'an act of
cruelty', the wrong of which it was 'impossible to describe'.[53]
The Alliance was again in the forefront of battles for human
rights.

The idea that Hitler was supportive of 'German Christians'
worried Evangelical Alliance observers in Britain, and plans to
create a united Protestant church, with a membership restricted to those of German blood, rang alarm bells. Gooch was
visiting Germany in July 1933 when all the churches were ordered to fly the Nazi swastika. Karl Barth's statement that the
liberties to be defended were those of the Word of God, was
quoted by the Alliance. In 1933, while Hitler was still courting
the Protestant church, the Executive Council warned that his
anti-semitism could develop into anti-Christianity.[54] From
then on the British Alliance concentrated on following events
connected with the rise of the so-called 'Confessing' Christians in Germany referred to at the time as 'the Confessional
Church'. Fifteen hundred 'Confessional' pastors read a declaration of defiance against the ecclesiastical arrangements put in
place by the Nazis, and Gooch went to Germany in the summer of 1934 to meet some of these leaders. After his return, the
British Alliance agreed a resolution, which was sent to Hitler as

53 Executive Council Minutes, 27 April 1932; *Evangelical Christendo*m, July-
August 1933, p.150.
54 *Evangelical Christendom*, May–June 1933, p.115; July–August 1933, p.132;
November–December 1933, pp.228, 234; J. R. C. Wright, 'The German Protestant
Church and the Nazi Party in the Period of the Seizure of Power, 1932-3', in D.
Baker (ed.), *Renaissance and Renewal in Christian History* (Studies in Church His-
tory, Vol. 14; Oxford: Blackwell, 1977), pp.393–418.

well as to church leaders, stating that what was happening in Germany was 'a conflict to maintain the fundamental principles of the Christian religion'. This echoed the thinking of Barth. Although the issues within the churches of Germany were complex, the Alliance made clear that the Confessional Church had its wholehearted support.[55]

In this period the British Alliance was continuing to seek to unite evangelicals in Europe. Reports in 1931 and 1932 stated that the Week of Prayer had never been so widely observed, especially in Europe, and attention was drawn to eighty places in Berlin where people had met for united prayer. *Evangelical Christendom* carried a regular 'European Intelligence' news section. Prayer items were being translated into most European languages in the 1930s. In the mid-1930s Gooch kept up his European travels, for example visiting southern Europe and attending a large evangelical gathering in Spain. When it was not possible to travel he found other ways of being involved. Gooch was instrumental in attempts to encourage the League of Nations to act over religious persecution in Russia.[56] The situation in Germany, however, was one that increasingly dominated the Alliance's European agenda.

By 1936 the British Alliance was seeking to help Jews leaving Germany and was taking a special interest in the German Confessional pastor, Martin Niemoller. In 1936 and 1937 Alliance representatives paid further visits to Germany and to Poland. Gooch, bishop Taylor Smith, who was a Keswick speaker and a vice-President of the Alliance, and J. Chalmers Lyon, a leading English Presbyterian who served as an honorary secretary of the Alliance, visited a number of people in 1936. In particular, they experienced the welcome and support of the Lutheran bishop Bursche, who was to be tortured and

---

55  *Evangelical Christendom*, July–August 1934, p.117; Executive Council Minutes, 25 October 1934; *Evangelical Christendom*, November–December 1934, pp.194–5. For further background see Hastings, *English Christianity*, chapter 22.

56  *Evangelical Christendom*, January–February 1931, p. 37; January–February 1932, p.34; Executive Council Minutes, 22 February 1934; 24 May 1934; 31 December 1935.

killed in the Second World War. When Barth was in London in 1937 the Alliance sponsored a meeting at the Russell Hotel to pay tribute to him. The speakers praised Barth's theology, his courage in opposing the Nazi powers – opposition that led to his dismissal from his post of professor of evangelical theology at the University of Bonn – and his significance for Europe. Barth, in his reply, said that declarations of sympathy from other churches were of little use. What was needed was a declaration from British churches that the beliefs of the Confessional Church were the beliefs of the universal church.[57]

During 1938 and 1939, as the situation in Europe deteriorated, the Alliance became more and more outspoken. An Alliance meeting in November 1938 adopted a further resolution. The Alliance statement spoke of 'the barbarous violence and cruel legislation inflicted upon the Jews in Germany'. It assured J.H. Hertz, the Chief Rabbi, of the desire of the Alliance to relieve the plight of Jewish refugees, and called on the British government 'to offer the widest possible asylum'.[58] Both at that point and during the war the Chief Rabbi expressed appreciation to the Alliance.[59] In its attempt to stand with Czechoslovakia, however, the Alliance found itself involved in the complexities of the developing conflict. At the end of 1938 it published a long, painful description by the Evangelical Church of the Czech Brethren of the dismemberment of their country. Within the report was a section that drew attention to the plight of two congregations under Polish occupation. One pastor had been evicted and the congregation dispersed. In March 1939, as a result of protests from bishop Bursche in Poland, *Evangelical Christendom* issued a disclaimer stating that the Czech situation was apparently not exactly as had previously been alleged. By the middle of 1939 the Czechs were under the rule of the Germans and were, an Alliance correspondent said, learning again from the country's late President – the

57  *Evangelical Christendom*, January–February 1936, p.24; March–April 1937, p.44.
58  Executive Council Minutes, 24 November 1938.
59  *Evangelical Christendom*, April–June 1943, pp.32–3.

Christian philosopher and politician, T.G. Masaryk – the message, 'Jesus, not Caesar'.[60] The march of fascism meant the Alliance could not hold European evangelicals together.

## War and Reconstruction

When the Second World War began, the reaction of church leaders was more restrained than during the First War. As Adrian Hastings puts it: 'For the church, as for the nation as a whole, war was seen by September 1939 as inevitable and just, but it was entered into soberly and rather sadly.'[61] As it did during the First World War, the Alliance organised large prayer meetings. Denominational leaders, together with representatives from Parliament, the City of London and the war services, as well as many church members, took part each month. Posters prepared by the Alliance were placed in the London underground system. In the Second War the Queen's Hall was destroyed by German bombardment, but Alliance prayer meetings for Londoners were held in the Methodist Central Hall, Westminster, and later in Caxton Hall. The Alliance Council again encouraged the Prime Minister and the Archbishop of Canterbury to designate specific Days of National Prayer. To the delight of the Alliance, a National Day of Prayer in May 1940 was very well supported, a sign of what has been termed the 'transient religious vitality' of the period.[62]

Some evangelicals, although believing that the power of prayer was a way to aid military victory, wanted to place stress on prayer for and continuing solidarity with German evangelicals. This was the stance of committed Europeans such as Gooch and J.H. Rushbrooke, although the latter also stated in 1941 that the German Baptists had never regarded Baptist believers in other parts of Europe as equal to themselves. As

---

60  *Evangelical Christendom*, November–December 1938, pp.186-7; March–April 1939, pp.48-9; July–August 1939, p.152.
61  Hastings, *English Christianity*, p.373.
62  Wolffe, *God and Greater Britain*, p.251.

evidence of a 'perverted racial feeling', said Rushbrooke, they had always taken preachers from other European countries to Hamburg to be trained.[63] George Bell, bishop of Chichester, who had talked to two representatives of German dissidents (one of them the German pastor, Dietrich Bonhoeffer), took on himself the task of suggesting a new direction in British policy, courageously expressing solidarity in 1942. He was, however, rebuffed by the British government. In the following year Bell took up the issue of Allied bombing, stating bluntly: 'To bomb cities as cities, deliberately to attack civilians ... is a wrong deed, whether done by the Nazis or by ourselves.' Such outspoken assertions by Bell aroused considerable hostility. *Evangelical Christendom* spoke of Bell's 'ill-timed criticism'.[64]

The war strained the broad vision of the Alliance in other ways. An unexpected ecumenical enterprise that emerged during the Second World War was 'The Sword of the Spirit', which was launched in 1940, with Cardinal Hinsley, the Roman Catholic Archbishop of Westminster, as its President. Meetings organised in London in 1941 were hugely successful, resulting in a remarkable demonstration of unity by leaders of the Catholic, Anglican and Free Churches. Hinsley himself was keen to have common prayer as well as united action between Catholics and Protestants – something that was authorised by the Roman Catholic Church in Holland – but he was ahead of his time. The Alliance discussed the ways in which it should respond to this initiative and felt that it was inappropriate to be involved with Roman Catholics who, as the Alliance saw it, did not support religious freedom.[65] It is likely that the participation of George Bell in 'The Sword of the Spirit' created barriers between himself and the Alliance, and in 1943 the Alliance

---

63 *Evangelical Christendom*, July–August 1941, p.98.
64 Hastings, *English Christianity*, pp.375–6; R.C.D. Jasper, *George Bell: Bishop of Chichester* (London: Oxford University Press, 1967), p.276.
65 S. Mews, 'The Sword of the Spirit: A Catholic Cultural Crusade of 1940', in W.J. Sheils (ed.), *The Church and War* (Studies in Church History, Vol 20; Oxford: Basil Blackwell, 1983), p.425. For Alliance discussions see Executive Council Minutes, 27 January 1941; 22 May 1941; 25 September 1941.

leadership responded cautiously to a request from Bell that representatives of the German Confessional Church should take part in the 1944 Alliance Week of Prayer. This was a particularly significant event, with 150,000 copies of the English language prayer programme alone being produced. It was agreed to invite Confessional Church representatives to be present, but despite the support given to the Confessional Church by the Alliance, not one of its members was invited to lead in prayer.[66]

The caution of the Alliance reflected its perception of itself as a responsible body that was not seeking to undermine the war effort. Although deeply concerned for liberty of conscience, it is striking that the Alliance seems to have given no attention to the position of British conscientious objectors (COs) in either of the two wars. At the same time, the Alliance was actively involved in helping refugees – Poles, Czechs, Armenians and Greeks. One enquiry by the Board of Trade into the convictions of British COs during the Second World War listed 1,716 Christadelphians, 145 members of the Plymouth Brethren, 140 Quakers, 112 Methodists, 73 Baptists, 66 Jehovah's Witnesses, 65 Congregationalists and 51 Anglicans.[67] The total number of COs was 16,500, making it probable that there were several hundred evangelicals who took this position of protest. Within the Alliance itself, however, there was to a large extent an alignment with the government's war policy. Following the end of the war services of thanksgiving were held, and the Alliance produced an appropriate form of worship for these services. At the same time, it joined in the calls for 'Christian Reconstruction in Europe'. It was in this pan-European role that it could exercise what it saw as its true ministry.

---

66  Executive Council Minutes, 28 October 1943.
67  J. Rae, *Conscience and Politics* (London: Oxford University Press, 1970), pp.250–51.

# EVANGELICAL ALLIANCE.

## BRITISH ORGANIZATION.

### ABSTRACT

OF THE

## PROCEEDINGS

OF THE

## FIRST ANNUAL CONFERENCE,

HELD IN

## EDINBURGH,

JUNE 10, 11, AND 12, 1847.

LONDON:
PARTRIDGE & OAKEY, PATERNOSTER-ROW,
AND 14, BUCHANAN-STREET,-GLASGOW (JOHN McCOMBE, AGENT).
EDINBURGH: J. JOHNSTONE. DUBLIN: CURRY.
AND ALL BOOKSELLERS;
AND AT THE OFFICE OF THE ALLIANCE, 2, EXETER-HALL, LONDON.
PRICE TWOPENCE.

Programme for the first annual conference of the British Organisation of the Alliance, Edinburgh, June 10th – 12th 1847

The Anglican clergyman Edward Bickersteth, one of the architects of the
Alliance

Silk handkerchief designed to mark the inaugural conference of the
Evangelical Alliance in London, 1846

Four early leaders of the Alliance.
Clockwise from top left: Baptist Noel, James Hamilton, Edward Steane,
W.S. Dodge (USA)

Entrance Hall of 19 Russell Gardens, the Alliance's Headquarters from 1912 until the Second World War

Henry Martin Gooch, General Secretary of the Alliance from 1904 – 1949. This picture was taken in 1925

British and European Alliance leaders at a special 80<sup>th</sup> anniversary garden party held in Russell Square Gardens, London, 1926. The British Alliance General Secretary, H. Martyn Gooch, is second from the right on the back row; his father, William Fuller Gooch, is also on the back row, second from left.

Gilbert Kirby, General Secretary of the Alliance from 1956-1966

Alliance leaders and civic representatives at an event held to mark the Universal Week of Prayer, Westminster Chapel, London, January 1948. Left to right: Martyn Lloyd Jones, J.A. Jagoe, Sir Stafford Cripps, the Dean of St. Paul's, H. Martyn Gooch, R.V.F. Scott.

Alliance General Secretary Roy Cattell being presented to the Duke of Edinburgh during a reception at the Alliance Club in Bedford Place, March 3rd 1953. The Club had been opened by the Alliance the previous October 'to serve the needs of men from overseas studying at the University of London.'

Martyn Lloyd-Jones (left) and John Stott in conversation following their disagreement at the Alliance Assembly, Westminster Central Hall, October 18, 1966

Alliance staff leadership in the late 1980's: Left to right, Back Row – Mike Morris, John Earwicker, Peter Meadows, Joel Edwards, Jonathan Markham. Front Row – Ian Coffey, Clive Calver, Ian Barclay.

Sir Fred Catherwood, President of the Alliance, 1992–2001

Joel Edwards outlining the Alliance's vision to become a 'movement for change', 2000

## Conclusion

For the Evangelical Alliance, the European dimension was a crucial one. There was a strong sense of a European evangelical community in the nineteenth century and of genuine catholicity, although at the same time national Alliances and denominational bodies were keen to preserve their own sense of identity. British evangelicals were active in supporting ventures in various parts of Europe. The reaction of the Alliance to the First World War mirrored the reaction commonly found in British society. There was a tendency for evangelicals to equate the cause of the nation with the cause of righteousness. This was not so marked in the Second World War, and the position of the Confessing Church in Germany meant that the sympathies of the Alliance crossed nationalist boundaries. Karl Barth was the European figure most often referred to by the Alliance. The most common view in the Alliance during both wars was that there should be an emphasis on prayer. In the inter-war years and in the period following the Second World War there were attempts by the Alliance, to rebuild the pan-European evangelicalism (including the Anglo-German sense of community) that had been shattered by the war.

A key feature of this process would be the resurgence of conservative evangelicalism in Britain and America in the later 1940s and 1950s. In 1948 the Alliance's Executive Council members asked Douglas Johnston, the secretary of the Inter-Varsity Fellowship and someone who was closely in touch not only with what was happening among students but also more widely, to speak to them. Johnston advised the Alliance to work with the churches in Europe that identified with Reformation beliefs. He encouraged the Alliance to keep in touch with pan-denominational organisations in America, the recently formed National Association of Evangelicals and also the American Council of Christian Churches.[68] This dual focus was in line with Alliance thinking, but in the event it would

---

68 Executive Council Minutes, 26 February 1948.

become difficult to implement. As we shall see in the next chapter, tensions over evangelical theology meant that from the 1950s the British Alliance would align itself more closely with America, and with the rest of the world, than it did with its European partner bodies. As they moved towards the formation of their own continental network in 1951, those partner bodies would evince the same ambition as Krummacher when he had disavowed attempts 'to Anglicize, Gallicize or Americanize' the Alliance. As far as the British Organisation was concerned, however, it would take rather longer for this vision of closer pan-European co-operation and unity to take root.

# 8

# Comprehensiveness Within the Truth

*The Alliance in the Early Twentieth Century*

At the annual meeting of the British Evangelical Alliance in 1912 a fresh declaration of faith was proposed and adopted. This set out a trinitarian statement – belief in 'One God', the Father, the Son, 'the Lord Jesus Christ our God and Saviour who died for our sins and rose again', and the Holy Spirit, by whom members of the Alliance 'desire to have fellowship with all who form the One Body of Christ'. It also affirmed 'the divine inspiration, authority and sufficiency of the Holy Scriptures'. The Evangelical Alliance's Executive Council saw this move as establishing 'comprehensiveness without compromise', the intention being to unite members of the Alliance under a Protestant banner.[1] The previous Basis of Faith was not replaced by the new one; instead the two were used in parallel. The period from 1912 to the Second World War was one in which the Alliance was faced with a number of theological challenges. The short version of the Basis of Faith was referred to on a number of occasions, for example in 1932, when Henry Martyn Gooch pointed out that two leading evangelical theologians, Handley Moule and James Orr, had assisted in the drawing up of the 1912 basis. Gooch also spoke at that point of the Alliance's commitment to the Bible, to the cross, to the presentation of the gospel and to service. The founders of

---

1 Kessler, *A Study of the Evangelical Alliance*, pp.73-4.

the Alliance, he insisted, had wanted it to be 'as wide as was
consistent with the widest possible interpretation of the word
evangelical' and had spoken of its aim as 'comprehensiveness
within the truth'. However, Gooch rejected compromise at the
expense of truth.[2] The Alliance's engagement with theological
issues in the first half of the twentieth century will be examined in this chapter.


## The New Theology

In 1907 R.J. Campbell, the minister of the City Temple,
London, who had succeeded the eminent Joseph Parker, published a book entitled *The New Theology*. He argued that
humanity and divinity were parts of one great consciousness,
and in so doing drastically revised the traditional concept of
Christ.[3] Controversy raged. The Alliance immediately
launched into the debate, producing a series of pamphlets in
1907, the first of which was by a lawyer, Sir Robert Anderson,
and was entitled *The New Apostasy*. The sixth pamphlet, under
the heading of what the Alliance began to term its own
'Tractarian Movement', was *The Virgin Birth*, by James Orr.
United meetings were also held under the auspices of the Alliance. Those convened in London were billed as being 'for the
reaffirmation of foundation Truths'. The Alliance Council was
surprised by the demand for the pamphlets. Enquiries during
the first part of 1907 came from different parts of the world and
there were calls to translate of some of the pamphlets into
foreign languages for circulation abroad. The Council

2 *Evangelical Christendom*, January–February 1932, p.41; May–June 1932,
pp.89-91. For James Orr see A.P.F. Sell, *Defending and Declaring the Faith: Some Scottish Examples, 1860-1920* (Exeter: Paternoster Press, 1987), pp.137-71; G.C.
Scorgie, *A Call for Continuity: The Theological Contribution of James Orr* (Macon:
Mercer University Press, 1988).

3 R.J. Campbell, *The New Theology* (London: Chapman & Hall, 1907); K.W.
Clements, *Lovers of Discord: Twentieth-Century Theological Controversies in England*
(London: SPCK, 1988), p.39.

appealed for £500 to mount a continuing campaign against 'the forces organizing for an attack on our common Christianity'. The Alliance Tractarian Movement was described as missionary in character, with pamphlets not only being sold but also given away to other agencies for special distribution.[4]

Campbell linked his new theology with a new view of the church's role in society. He identified himself with the Independent Labour Party and in his *Christianity and the Social Order*, also published in 1907, he argued that the kingdom of God was to be equated with the socialist order. P.T. Forsyth, the formidable Congregational theologian, insisted that Campbell had abandoned the theology of the cross.[5] Alliance leaders saw the Alliance's campaign as being in tune with the thinking of the evangelical world as a whole. As an example of popular feeling, it reported that at the 1907 Free Church Council Congress an elderly delegate, John King, had protested against a talk by Campbell and had asked – to a background of a mixture of cheers and cries of 'out of order' – for 'When I survey the wondrous Cross' to be sung. This was done.[6] *Evangelical Christendom* contrasted movements such as the Alliance, the Mildmay Conferences and the Keswick Convention in England, and the Northfield Conferences in the USA, all of which were committed to the 'fundamental truths of the gospel', with other movements in which such truths were 'belittled or re-stated'. The 'New Theology' was described as prominent among movements that were designed to 'meet the shallow views of modern thought, and to encourage the widening of so-called Christian Brotherhood at the expense of Christ and His Word'.[7]

---

4 *Evangelical Christendom*, March–April 1907, p.49; November–December 1907, p.132.

5 R.J. Campbell, *Christianity and the Social Order* (London: Chapman & Hall, 1907); Bebbington, *Evangelicalism in Modern Britain*, pp.198-9; K. Robbins, 'The Spiritual Pilgrimage of the Rev R.J. Campbell', *Journal of Ecclesiastical History* 30.2 (1979), 261-76.

6 *Evangelical Christendom*, March–April 1907, p.58.

7 Ibid., p.49.

The Alliance informed its constituency in 1908 that it had carried out an effective campaign against the New Theology through meetings and publications. At that stage the Alliance leadership seemed to be happy that the existing Basis of Faith was adequate and that the Alliance was standing for a clear standard of evangelical truth.[8] Two years later, however, a different approach was suggested. An article in *Evangelical Christendom*, 'The Problem of Unity in Relation to the Rising Generation', suggested that there was a need to retain 'all that is best in the conservatism of the past', while at the same time being 'ready to take into account the particular needs of the present day and the activities of the modern mind'. For the first time there was a suggestion that there should be a review of the position of the Alliance in relation to its basis of faith. Over the next two years thought was given to the formulation of a short and simple declaration of faith which had as its focus 'loyalty to the Person and claims of Christ as revealed in the Holy Scriptures'.[9] It was this process of re-evaluation that led to the new statement of 1912. There is no evidence that in making such a move the Alliance was seeking to align itself with newer theological trends. However, it is significant that this was the period which saw the publication and distribution of *The Fundamentals*, twelve volumes issued between 1910 and 1915 to defend 'fundamental' doctrines. The Alliance was, reluctantly, to be drawn into the 'fundamentalist' debate that ensued.

## Fundamentalist Battles

There have been a number of studies of the roots of fundamentalism. It has been seen as developing out of the apocalyptic premillennialism that gained prominence in the American churches in the 1880s.[10] Other contributory factors can be

---

8  *Evangelical Christendom*, March–April 1908, p.49.

9  H.N. Rodgers, 'The Problem of Unity and Relation to the rising Generations', *Evangelical Christendom*, November–December 1910, p.139.

10  See E.R. Sandeen, *The Roots of Fundamentalism: British and American Millenarianism, 1800-1930* (Chicago: University Press of Chicago, 1970).

identified, such as the response to social upheaval. Yet fundamentalism is properly viewed as a movement shaped by religious forces.[11] In Britain a controversy in Methodism, which had to do with an appointment to a teaching post, was the first significant fundamentalist controversy in a British denomination.[12] George Jackson, who expressed some higher critical views of the Bible, was chosen by the 1912 Wesleyan Conference to take the chair of Homiletics and Pastoral Theology at Didsbury College, Manchester. Those opposed to Jackson formed the fundamentalist Wesley Bible Union, and the harsh tone adopted by this group alienated many Methodists. Samuel Chadwick, the Principal of Cliff College, who was a leading figure in Methodism and a fervent evangelist, did not associate himself with the stridency of fundamentalism, and, as we shall see, fundamentalism was far removed from the thinking of liberal evangelicals, who were represented in Methodism by the Fellowship of the Kingdom.[13]

In 1915 as the Alliance prepared to celebrate seventy years of its existence, Henry Martyn Gooch expressed his understanding of the theological position of the Alliance. The vision, as he saw it, was of a 'reunited Christianity', with an Alliance that was 'free from stodginess, and yet based upon the ancient bonds of unity in the Church of God – the one Lord Jesus Christ, the Head of the Church, the one Faith and one Baptism'.[14] This seemed far removed from the spirit of the Wesley Bible Union, which in 1915 saw its main purpose as being to oppose 'destructive heresies'.[15] However, as in the 1870s and

11 The best introductions are G.M. Marsden, *Fundamentalism and American Culture: The Shaping of Twentieth-Century Evangelicalism, 1870-1925* (New York: Oxford University Press, 1980); and D.W. Bebbington, 'Martyrs for the Truth: Fundamentalists in Britain', in D. Wood (ed.), *Studies in Church History*.

12 D.W. Bebbington, 'The Persecution of George Jackson', in W.J. Sheils (ed.), *Persecution and Toleration* (Studies in Church History, Vol. 21; Oxford: Basil Blackwell, 1984).

13 I.M Randall, *Quest, Crusade and Fellowship: The Spiritual Formation of the Fellowship of the Kingdom* (Horsham: Fellowship of the Kingdom, 1995).

14 *Evangelical Christendom*, November–December 1915, p.249.

15 *Journal of the Wesley Bible Union*, January 1915, p.4.

80s, the Alliance found it necessary to engage with what it called 'The Fundamentals'. The World's Christian Fundamentals Association was formed in the USA in 1919, and it was at the American Northern Baptist Convention of 1920 that the term 'fundamentalist' was coined. W.B. Riley, a militant leader, said that Baptists had entered the controversy 'knowing that it was not a battle, but a war ... and that they will never surrender'.[16] On 1 November 1920 a conference took place at Alliance House in London that was reported under the heading 'The Fundamentals'. A representative group of invited evangelical leaders discussed attacks being made 'upon fundamental Truths of Evangelical Christianity, and the faithfulness of the record of God's revelation to man contained in the Holy Scriptures of the Old and New Testaments'.[17]

If R.J. Campbell had stirred up evangelicals in 1907, it was E.W. Barnes, through a sermon delivered at the British Association meetings, who became a focus for debate in the early 1920s. Barnes, who was to achieve fame later in the 1920s as a fiercely Protestant but also unorthodox bishop of Birmingham, argued in 1920 that the account of the Fall in Genesis had to be revised in the light of scientific thinking about evolution.[18] As a mathematician and a Fellow of the Royal Society, Barnes was an enthusiastic advocate of scientific advances, but there were those who were wholly unconvinced by the association in Barnes' mind between evolution and human progress. The evangelical weekly, *The Christian*, commented in September 1920 that Barnes' theology was 'a million miles removed from the apostolic gospel'.[19] It was a comment with which the Evangelical Alliance had sympathy. Barnes, in the view of the Alliance, had denied the historical truth of the early chapters of Genesis and

---

16 M. Marty, *Modern American Religion: The Noise of Conflict, 1919-1941* (Chicago: University of Chicago Press, 1991), p.170.

17 *Evangelical Christendom*, November–December, 1920, p.141.

18 *The Church Family Newspaper*, 10 September 1920, pp.8, 10. For Barnes see J. Barnes, *Ahead of his Age: Bishop Barnes of Birmingham* (London: Collins, 1979).

19 *The Christian*, 23 September 1920, p.2.

opposed the teaching of Paul founded on those chapters. To the question, 'Can a young man, a young women, trust their Bible?' the answer given by Barnes, said *Evangelical Christendom*, was 'No'. In the light of this, the Alliance arranged public meetings in 1921 to consider the themes of 'Science and the Bible', 'The Response of Revelation' and 'The Basis of Belief'.[20]

The question of evolution and creation did not, however, become a major issue within British evangelicalism. In America, by contrast, the so-called 'Monkey Trial' of 1925 was a major watershed. At the trial, the prominent lawyer and politician William Jennings Bryan led the attempt to prosecute the Tennessee teacher John Scopes for promoting biological evolution in his classroom. The judge who heard the case charged the jury to find Scopes guilty, but the fundamentalists were cast as objects of public derision, although they were technically the winners. Yet far from disappearing, fundamentalists in America focused their attention on local church life: in Mississippi and Tennessee, church growth in the period 1925-30 was twice as rapid as population growth.[21] Much to the disgust of fundamentalists in Britain, such as the editor of *The Journal of the Wesley Bible Union*, Harold Morton, many British evangelicals made a point of dissociating themselves from the fundamentalist battles of this period – whether over evolution or any other matter. Indeed, on the whole, evangelicals associated with the Alliance at this time deplored the kind of intolerance and vitriol that was a hallmark of fundamentalist rhetoric. Interdenominational fundamentalist organisations such as the Bible League (formed in 1892) existed in England, but the attitudes adopted by British

20 *Evangelical Christendom*, November–December 1920, p.141; January–February 1921, p.5.
21 J. Rogers, 'John Scopes and the Debate over Evolution', in R.C. White, et al., *American Christianity: A Case Approach* (Grand Rapids: Eerdmans, 1986), pp.143-8; Marty, *Modern American Religion*, p.32.
22 For British-American comparisons see especially G.M. Marsden, 'Fundamentalism as an American Phenomenon: A Comparison with English Evangelicalism, *Church History* 46.2 (1977), pp.215-32; Bebbington, 'Martyrs for the Truth', pp.418-20.

evangelicals towards those with whom they differed were generally fairly restrained.[22]

A somewhat neglected reason for this restraint was the contribution of the Evangelical Alliance. From its beginnings the Alliance had its 'Practical Resolutions' which said that when members had to 'defend any views or principles wherein they differ from Christian brethren who agree with them in vital truths', they would seek to 'avoid all rash and groundless insinuations, personal imputations, or irritating allusions, and to maintain the meekness and gentleness of Christ by speaking the truth only in love'. In 1924, when a British organisation called the Fraternal Union for Bible Testimony was being set up, the Alliance was anxious to draw attention to the Practical Resolutions and to emphasise that the Alliance was both 'supremely interested in fundamental truths' and yet was also 'in virtue of its basis, a protest against the fundamentalist who demands uniformity and denies the right of private judgment'. The concern of the Alliance was that in Britain and America a growing number of Protestant movements were emerging that were 'as harmful to true Christian Unity as the intolerance of the Roman Church'. The Fraternal Union drew in more moderate evangelicals alongside fundamentalists, but the Alliance was afraid that the tendency of such movements was separatist. The worst form of schism, as the Alliance saw it, was 'separation from any brother or sister in whom we acknowledge the Spirit of Christ to be dwelling'. This was precisely what some seemed intent on doing. They appear, said *Evangelical Christendom* in May 1924, 'to be concerned to create divisions in the evangelical ranks'. With an obvious reference to fundamentalism, the Alliance was defined as a 'central organisation' that sought to 'maintain evangelical faith, but not with a shut mind'.[23]

---

23  *Evangelical Christendom*, March–April 1924, pp.37–8; May–June 1924, pp.77–8.

## Anglo-Catholic Challenges

Whereas many fundamentalists turned their fire on other Protestants, whom they saw as compromising with liberal theology, the biggest challenge to Protestantism in the 1920s was the power of Anglo-Catholicism. After the First World War, huge Anglo-Catholic congresses were organised. These congresses began with one in 1920 that attracted 13,000 people and they peaked at a remarkable 70,000 people in 1937.[24] The period after the First World War saw forces coming together that assisted the Anglo-Catholic cause. Massive loss of life during the war brought such pressure to bear on the Church of England that in 1917 it authorised public intercessions for the departed.[25] Anglo-Catholics were delighted with this change. A new generation was finding itself drawn to Anglo-Catholic ceremony, with its emphasis on beauty and dignity. In 1917, as an evidence of the attractiveness of Anglo-Catholic ritual, Guy Rogers, who was a speaker at Evangelical Alliance events, stated that in his view the eastward communion position was quite acceptable. High-church clergy, when officiating at Holy Communion, faced east, with their backs to the congregation, in what was intended to symbolise priestly ministry, with a sacrifice offered to God. Evangelicals had traditionally opposed this on the grounds that the sacrifice of Christ had been offered in a final sense. They officiated at the north side of the communion table. So Rogers' change of view was a momentous departure from what was known as 'north end' evangelical practice.[26]

The most contentious issue to arise as a result of the advance of Catholic ritual in the Church of England was the perpetual reservation of the consecrated elements used in Holy Communion. Proposals to revise the Church of England's Prayer Book, presented to the National Church Assembly in 1923,

---

24 W.S.F Pickering, *Anglo-Catholicism* (London: Routledge, 1989), p.56; K. Hylson-Smith, *High Churchmanship in the Church of England* (Edinburgh: T. & T. Clark, 1993), pp.256-7.

25 Wilkinson, *The Church of England*, pp.176ff.

26 *The Record*, 12 July 1917, p.489.

allowed for the continuous reservation of the sacrament for the purpose of offering the elements to the sick and dying, but did not allow any services of worship before the reserved sacrament. The proposals did not satisfy advanced Catholics in the Church of England, but it was Protestant opposition that was most noticeable. At a meeting convened by the Alliance in the Royal Albert Hall in 1925, Sir William Joynson-Hicks, the Home Secretary (known as 'Jix'), a vice-President of the Alliance, gave a stirring speech, punctuated by applause, in which he claimed – with dubious historical warrant – that Nonconformists, as well as members of the Church of England, claimed a heritage in the Book of Common Prayer. Joynson-Hicks referred to 'Ecclesiastical Bolshevism' by Anglo-Catholics. His speech was later printed as *The Reformation: A Clarion Call to Britain*.[27] At a similar Alliance meeting in 1926, also held in the Royal Albert Hall, even Bishop E.W. Barnes of Birmingham was applauded for his battle against advanced Anglo-Catholicism in the parishes in his diocese. The Alliance was described as standing, in this conflict, for 'Fundamental Truth'.[28] Given that Barnes could be seen as an ally, the conflict illustrated the difficulty of defining the limits of comprehensiveness.

The most visible campaign against the Revised (or Alternative, or Deposited) Book was that led by the retired bishop of Manchester, E.A. Knox. Alliance House was used as a venue for meetings between Knox and Free Church leaders. Over 300,000 signatures were obtained protesting against the changes to the Prayer Book. Hensley Henson, the bishop of Durham, famously ridiculed the campaigners as 'an army of illiterates generalled by octogenarians',[29] but for the Alliance the warfare against Catholic tendencies was serious business and its

27 *Evangelical Christendom*, January-February 1925, p.45; G.I.T. Machin, 'Reservation Under Pressure: Ritual in the Prayer Book Crisis', in R.N. Swanson (ed.), *Continuity and Change in Christian Worship* (Studies in Church History, Vol. 35; Woodbridge, Suffolk: Boydell & Brewer, 1999), pp.447-52.
28 'True Fundamentalism and Dead Orthodoxy', *Evangelical Christendom*, March–April 1926, pp.33-4.
29 Hastings, *English Christianity*, p.206.

strategy was far from uninformed. The Alliance, and those with whom it worked to oppose the Revised Prayer Book, recognised that they did not command much support in the higher echelons of the Church of England. Randall Davidson, the Archbishop of Canterbury, wanted to see a workable solution to the problem of liturgical indiscipline. The House of Bishops voted 34-4 in favour of the Revised Book. The voting proportions in the House of Clergy were similar. Efforts were directed, therefore, to the House of Commons. A preparatory meeting of MPs opposed to the Revised Book was held on 30 November 1927, with Joynson-Hicks presiding, and in the debate itself, on 15 December, Joynson-Hicks gave a speech that apparently did much to sway the House. He argued that the provisions of the Revised Book would inevitably lead to worship of the reserved sacrament; the revision measure lost by 238 votes to 205.[30]

A further attempt was made to pass the measure in Parliament in 1928, but this also failed. The Alliance was concerned during this period not to lose supporters within the Church of England. But it considered that it had played a unique role in 'acting as a liaison office' so that leaders from different schools of thought and denominations could keep in touch with one another. 'One of the greatest weaknesses in the campaign against the Deposited Book', said *Evangelical Christendom* in January 1928, 'was the scattered character of the opposing forces.' The Alliance considered that the appeal it had made to Free Church Councils to consider the situation had awakened Free Church interest, and that this had been crucial in determining the outcome. This was certainly an important factor: the votes of Free Church members of Parliament were of decisive importance. *Evangelical Christendom* summed it up this way: 'Evangelicals in the National and Free Churches were linked together and under God's guidance the House of Commons spoke frankly and soberly the mind of the Nation.'[31] For

---

30  Machin, 'Reservation under Pressure', pp.456-60.
31  *Evangelical Christendom*, January-February 1928, p.18.

a period in the middle and later 1920s the evangelical Protestants who associated with the Alliance were able to mobilise a national campaign. The victory was rather a hollow one, however, since in 1929 Cosmo Lang, who had recently become Archbishop of Canterbury, made it clear that any liturgical practices that had been embodied in the rejected book were acceptable.

After 1928 some of the paranoia about a Catholic take-over of the Church of England subsided. There was continued Alliance watchfulness, however, not least because of conversations that went on at Malines, France, during the 1920s between some high church Anglicans, most notably Viscount Halifax, Walter Frere and Charles Gore, and a few progressive Roman Catholics such as Dom Lambert Beaudouin.[32] In 1928, when the conversations had come to an end, Halifax published his Notes, which provoked the Alliance to amazed comment. *Evangelical Christendom* stated that few had believed 'the revered Viscount' when he reported that in the conversations the Anglican members took the view that it was possible to reconcile the Thirty-Nine Articles of the Church of England with the Decrees of the Roman Catholic Council of Trent of the sixteenth century. Now it seemed that this was indeed the position of the Anglican participants. It was impossible, in the view of the Alliance, to square the outlook of the Anglican conversationalists with the Reformation tradition.[33] In 1930 the official Roman Catholic attitude to the Malines conversations was that they were conducted without ecclesiastical mandate. By this time, Henry Martyn Gooch was taking the view that Anglo-Catholicism had been very influential among the bishops and the clergy in general, but that lay people were not impressed.[34] The Alliance staked out a central evangelicalism that it believed lay people in the churches understood and appreciated.

---

32  Hylson-Smith, *High Churchmanship*, pp.273-5.

33  *Evangelical Christendom*, January-February 1928, p.19.

34  *Evangelical Christendom*, November-December 1930, p.210.

# A Broader Evangelicalism

The Alliance found it all the more necessary to define the evangelical centre ground because of the growth of what was often termed liberal evangelicalism. In 1906 conversations between some younger evangelicals in the Church of England led them to the conclusion that existing leaders of the evangelical party were too rigid in their attitudes to scholarship and social questions. A 'Group Brotherhood', as it was called, soon grew from six like-minded clergy in the Liverpool area. This 'Liverpool Six' provided the nucleus for an Anglican network that pioneered a broader or liberal evangelicalism.[35] In 1922 the Church Missionary Society (CMS) suffered a schism when a number of CMS supporters who objected to the way the CMS was willing to co-operate with high-church enterprises formed the Bible Churchmen's Missionary Society.[36] In the wake of this event the Group Brotherhood decided to establish itself publicly as the Anglican Evangelical Group Movement (AEGM). Cyril Bardsley, the General Secretary of the CMS, was active in liberal evangelical ranks. The AEGM was committed, as its manifesto stated, to showing that its members, 'while clinging to the fundamental spiritual truths of evangelicalism, recognised that old doctrines had to be set forth in modern language'.[37] At that point membership was 300 and growth over the next decade meant that by 1935 the AEGM's clerical membership was 1,454, with the claim being made in its *Bulletin* that about 10% of active Anglican clergy were members.[38]

Although the Alliance made reference to liberal evangelicals as early as 1916, substantial comment on the movement first appeared in the early 1920s. In 1922 Gooch, while not

---

35 A.E. Smith, *Another Anglican Angle: The History of the AEGM* (Oxford: Amate, 1991).

36 D.W. Bebbington, 'Missionary Controversy and the Polarising Tendency in Twentieth-Century British Protestantism', *Anvil* 13.2 (1996).

37 *The Church Family Newspaper*, 20 July 1923, p.4.

38 *Bulletin*, October 1933, p.4; April 1935, p.13.

referring explicitly to the troubles in the CMS over broader theology, probably had this in mind when he wrote that the present time was 'unfortunate to raise issues on the question of theories of inspiration'. He argued that the Bible itself did not establish any particular theory of inspiration and that it was difficult to reach agreement on this matter.[39] This was in 1923, the same year in which an AEGM volume called *Liberal Evangelicalism: An Interpretation* appeared. In reviewing this volume in *Evangelical Christendom* in March 1923 Gooch reiterated Alliance comprehensiveness and noted that some of the contributors to the volume were personal friends of his (Guy Rogers had been a speaker at the Alliance week of prayer that year). Yet his tone was not affirmative. Two months later Gooch, although welcoming the way the AEGM was supporting church reunion, suggested that in some of its pamphlets the AEGM had not thought out the implications of its theological position.[40] Canon Vernon Storr, a canon of Westminster Abbey and a considerable theologian, soon emerged as the leading figure in the AEGM. Storr argued in two early AEGM booklets dealing with biblical authority that the Bible was God's progressive self-revelation, a story of religious experience and not a book entirely free from mistakes. He considered that scholarship enhanced its spiritual value.[41]

By the end of 1923 the Alliance, despite its regard for some of the liberal evangelical leaders as 'men of high spiritual attainment', and 'servants of Christ, at whose feet we would willingly sit and learn', was increasingly critical of the new movement. There was deep suspicion in Alliance circles about the participation of E. W. Barnes. Vernon Storr was seen as having no place in his theology for the personal return of Christ. By this stage, members of the AEGM such as R.T. Howard, Principal of St Aidan's College, Birkenhead, were aligning

---

39 *Evangelical Christendom*, January–February 1922, p.1.

40 *Evangelical Christendom*, March–April 1923, pp.40, 59; May–June 1923, pp.61–4.

41 V.F. Storr, *The Bible* (London, [1923]), pp.7, 16; V.F Storr, *Inspiration* (London, [1923]), pp.5, 16.

themselves with the cause of Prayer Book revision. This did
not help the AEGM in the eyes of the Alliance. Gooch quoted
Guy Rogers' statement that Liberal Evangelicalism is 'adventurous through its *loyalty to the primitive Gospel*. It seeks to bind
adventurous souls in a living fellowship that they may march
together in obedience to the Spirit'. For Gooch, this statement
about loyalty to the gospel was not consistent with AEGM
literature. Gooch's article concluded:

> To the plain man if adventurous souls accept the plain teaching of Scripture
> and follow it with the Spirit's guidance, we are with them; but if they treat
> Scripture as something to be made to fit in with the prevalent spirit of the age,
> then we are bound to protest, and prefer to venture our all upon the Truth that
> is revealed in God's Word written.[42]

The Alliance was clearly not inclined to align itself with the
liberal evangelical cause.

Yet the Alliance did not wish to be regarded as an obscuran-
tist body. In 1924 *Evangelical Christendom* carried an article that
had as its over-riding aim the positioning of the Alliance
within the mainstream of Christian orthodoxy. The Anglican
Lambeth Conferences, it was noted approvingly, had laid down
as doctrinal standards 'Holy Scripture, the Apostles' and Nicene Creeds and the two sacraments of the gospel with the
Christian ministry holding a commission from Christ'. The
article argued that it was 'impossible to deny the doctrine of
the Nicene Creed without undermining fundamental doctrine'. It also took the view that the sacraments could not be
overlooked without breaking with historic Christianity. In
common with Alliance tradition, it was stated that the Alliance
had 'no wish to narrow the faith or to make too rigid the
boundaries of the Church of Christ', but that it could not accept that those holding to the historical standards of the church
'are to be considered obscurantists'.[43] The growing tension

---

42 'Liberal Evangelicalism', *Evangelical Christendom*, November–December 1923,
pp.153-4.
43 'The Fundamentals: What is at Stake', *Evangelical Christendom*, July–August
1924, pp.105-6.

with the liberal evangelicals eased somewhat in 1925 when a second major AEGM volume, *The Inner Life*, was published. It contained essays on spirituality, and *Evangelical Christendom* welcomed what it saw as a different ethos within the volume.[44] Rapprochement was, however, short-lived. In January 1926 Gooch reported in *The Life of Faith*, the Keswick Convention's mouthpiece, on an AEGM meeting he had attended. His account, while it accepted that there were in the AEGM men of 'undoubted spirituality', was highly critical.[45] George Buchanan, who had been a speaker two years previously at the Alliance's week of prayer, replied on behalf of the AEGM. He stated trenchantly that if Gooch wished to follow 'die-hard' conservatism he could do so, but 800 AEGM clergy were prepared to follow the Holy Spirit.[46] In spite of its commitment to catholicity the Alliance had failed to bridge the divide between evangelical groups in the Church of England.

Much less attention was paid by the Alliance in this period to liberal-conservative tensions felt by evangelicals in other denominations. This is probably because of the Alliance's focus on Anglo-Catholic strength, which primarily affected Anglicans. A divided Anglican evangelicalism was not well placed to counter Anglo-Catholicism. Methodism had a liberal evangelical movement that enjoyed considerable inter-war influence – the Fellowship of the Kingdom (FK). This had leaders such as Leslie Weatherhead, minister of the City Temple, but the Alliance had no links with FK. Within Methodism, the Alliance felt the closest sympathy with eirenic evangelicals such as Samuel Chadwick. The evangelical perspective of Chadwick meant that he appreciated a range of churchmanship. He said that if he had not been a Methodist he would have been a Roman Catholic and that he could see himself as an Abbot of a monastery.[47] In 1922, as a member of the Alliance Council,

---

44  *Evangelical Christendom*, January-February 1925, p.24.
45  *The Life of Faith*, 20 January 1926, p.61.
46  *The Life of Faith*, 27 January 1926, p.87.
47  N.G. Dunning, *Samuel Chadwick* (London: Hodder & Stoughton, 1933), p.20.

Chadwick spoke about the testimony the Alliance had borne 'to the catholicity of the Christian religion and the evangelical quality of the Christian faith'. He declared that the evangelical position, with its 'comprehensiveness and disregard of denominational distinctives, and its over-riding of all kinds of sectarian barriers, suits my catholic spirit down to its very roots'.[48] For the Alliance, this statement summed up the kind of Methodism it wished to affirm.

Baptists did not have an identifiable liberal evangelical group such as the AEGM or FK. There were Baptists of broader views, such as T.R. Glover, a classical scholar who was a Fellow of St John's College, Cambridge. Fundamentalists fulminated against Glover's election to the presidency of the Baptist Union in 1924. But few Baptist leaders were inclined to disrupt the denomination.[49] Those within the Baptist denomination to whom the Alliance looked for support were neither on the fundamentalist nor on the liberally inclined wings. The Alliance leadership regarded three prominent Baptist speakers at Keswick in the 1920s as embodying moderate evangelicalism. They were F.B. Meyer, then in his seventies but still an inveterate promoter of Keswick spirituality, Graham Scroggie, minister of Charlotte Chapel, Edinburgh, and W.Y. Fullerton, home secretary of the Baptist Missionary Society. In 1924 Scroggie, by then the leading teacher at Keswick, was enthusiastically quoted in *Evangelical Christendom*. Scroggie said that 'any one who fairly interprets and wholeheartedly accepts the Apostles' Creed is loyal to the evangelical faith'. On the vexed question of the nature of the inspiration of Scripture, Scroggie stated that it was 'enough that evangelicals agree on the fact of the unique and inclusive inspiration of Scriptures, leaving theories to the enlightened judgment of the individual'. The Alliance's stance was that anyone laying on others burdens greater than that imposed by loyalty to Christ and his teaching was 'an

---

48  *Evangelical Christendom*, May-June 1922, p.69.
49  D.W. Bebbington, 'Baptists and Fundamentalism in Inter-War Britain', in K. Robbins (ed.), *Studies in Church History,* pp.316-20.

enemy of the truth'.[50] Although the Alliance was not prepared
to embrace a liberal evangelical agenda, it remained broad.

In this approach the Alliance was in tune with the spirit of
the Keswick Convention. The Convention, with its emphasis
on the spiritual life, had a moderating influence on British
evangelicalism. There were deep suspicions by fundamentalists
in the 1920s that theological modernists were engaged in a
'Capture Keswick' campaign, and that Stuart Holden, the
Keswick Chairman, was sympathetic to modernism. Yet *Evangelical Christendom* was convinced in 1928 that there was no
foundation for the charge of 'incipient modernism' at
Keswick.[51] Keswick's venerated leaders, such as Meyer, combined evangelicalism with openness. At the Alliance's week of
prayer in 1925 Meyer said that the High churchman and the
Low churchman met at the point of mystical experience, 'the
life which is hidden with Christ in God'. Here, he argued,
Thomas à Kempis and Luther were united. This spiritual experience Meyer saw as 'the birthright of all holy souls'.[52] In 1927
Meyer made it clear in a report on American fundamentalist
battles that his sympathies lay with those outside the conflicts
who 'longed for the deeper aspects of spiritual truth'.[53] For the
Alliance there was evangelical centre ground that was neither
too broad nor too narrow. Even so, liberal evangelicals were
judged by the Alliance to have compromised the evangelical
faith. In 1934 the Alliance maintained that the weakness of the
liberal evangelical approach had to be met by the 'definite presentation of the gospel of Christ as it is revealed in the Holy
Scriptures'.[54]

50 *Evangelical Christendom*, November–December 1924, p.188.
51 *Evangelical Christendom*, May–June 1928, p.90; *The Life of Faith*, 30 May 1928,
p.601; I.M. Randall, 'Capturing Keswick', *The Baptist Quarterly* 36.7 (1996),
pp.331–48.
52 F.B. Meyer, 'The True Centre of Christian Unity', *Evangelical Christendom*, January–February 1925, p.14.
53 *The Baptist Times*, 3 November 1927, p.773.
54 *Evangelical Christendom*, January–February 1934, p.30.

## Theological Trends in the 1930s

By 1934 the Alliance had been following for some time the activities of another 'Group Movement', the Oxford Group. Although this Group began to take shape in the early 1920s when
Frank Buchman, an American Lutheran minister, started to
meet informally with students in Cambridge and then in Oxford, it attracted wider attention in 1928. It was in that year that
the name 'Oxford Group' began to be used, and the *Daily Express* made allegations about the Group's practice of public confession of sin. In 1928 *Evangelical Christendom* welcomed the
Group's use of the methods of the Methodist class meeting, 'the
waiting upon God of the Quakers' (seeking personal guidance
each day), and 'an out-and-out devotion to the Person of our
Lord and Saviour'. In 1931 Group members sought 'wholeheartedly to recapture that quality of life which vibrates through
the Apostolic Age'.[55] In the early 1930s, the Group created a
huge impact through house parties attracting thousands of
mainly young people, and through its effective mobilising of
teams of 'life-changers'. Questions were being raised, however,
about the movement's lack of any clear theological position.
The Group's philosophy was that Christianity should be
presented in a way that maximised its relevance, especially
through personal testimonies. Undoubtedly the Group's stress
on communicating the essence of faith, together with its
interdenominationalism and its European-wide vision,[56]
appealed to the Alliance. But the Alliance expressed no further
support for the Group after it held a meeting in 1936 at the
Albert Hall when there were apparently many testimonies, but
at which prayer and Scripture were entirely absent.[57]

---

55 *Evangelical Christendom*, March–April 1928, p.55; November–December 1931,
p.241. See D.W. Bebbington, 'The Oxford Group Movement Between the Wars',
in W.J. Sheils & D. Wood (eds), *Studies in Church History* Vol. 23 (Oxford: Basil
Blackwell, 1986), pp.495–507.
56 I.M. Randall, '"We All Need Constant Change": The Oxford Group and Mission in Europe in the 1930s', *European Journal of Theology* 9.2 (2000), pp.171–85.
57 *Evangelical Christendom*, January–February 1932, pp.40–41; July–August 1932,
pp.145–6; July–August 1936, p.157.

A more significant movement for the Alliance in the 1930s was what was termed 'Biblical Theology' or 'Neo-Orthodoxy'. Nathaniel Micklem, who from 1932 was Principal of the Congregational Mansfield College, Oxford, and whose comments were noted by the Alliance, referred in 1927 to a 'very important quasi-Fundamentalist movement' associated with Karl Barth and Emil Brunner, on the continent.[58] At that time few in Britain would have been aware of Barth or Brunner. Two years later *Evangelical Christendom* reflected on the importance of Barth for European theology. Barth's approach was contrasted with a German theological tradition that had made little of the historic foundations of faith and had indulged in 'wild criticism of the Gospel records'. 'Now Karl Barth', said the article, 'comes forward with emphasis on the objective facts of Revelation and on the Truth of the Bible account of Christ.' Barth's stress on reading scripture from the standpoint of 'revelation' was applauded, and the Alliance considered that this revived study of the Bible was having an impact on Germany.[59] Later, as we have seen, the Alliance would utilise the reports of Barth on the state of the church in Germany in relation to the rise of Nazi power, but its primary interest in Barth was spurred by his work in the area of biblical theology.

By 1930 the British Alliance was unhesitatingly supportive of Barth. *Evangelical Christendom* spoke in January 1930 of Barth as teaching a 'revived Calvinism' and saw him as 'one of the greatest religious forces in Germany'. His Calvinism was seen not so much as concerned with the doctrine of election as with the transcendence of God, and with biblical revelation. By this stage, Barth's theology was being referred to in theological circles as a 'theology of crisis', but from the Alliance's perspective its main (and welcome) characteristic was that it pointed theology away from the 'subjective teaching which had become so common in Germany and which had resolved

---

58  *The Congregational Quarterly* 5.3 (1927), pp.327–8.
59  *Evangelical Christendom*, September–October 1929, p.162.

itself largely into every man following his own feelings'.[60]
*Evangelical Christendom* carried a further report on Barth at the
end of 1930. 'There is no doubt', it stated enthusiastically, 'that
as a personality Karl Barth has magnetic qualities. He im-
presses, he wins confidence, and he leads. Students flock
around him ... Undoubtedly he is leaving a deep mark on the
religious thought of Germany.'[61] In 1930 few of Barth's writings were available in English and the Alliance would have
been relying for its information partly on reports from Alliance
leaders in Germany and partly from the views of those of its
British members who were reading German theological material. Books in English on Barth by a Presbyterian minister, John
MacConnachie, appeared in 1931 and 1933. Barth approved of
these.[62]

The British Alliance's reliance on its German counterparts
was evident in the early 1930s. An analysis of the spiritual vitality of the German churches, which drew from German
sources, was made in 1932. The analysis concentrated on the
strength of the various schools of theological thought. On the
one hand the schools that had been prominent were considered to be declining. These included approaches that concentrated on psychology or on the study of religions. On the
other hand, and to the delight of the Alliance, there was a
'Luther renaissance', with younger scholars seeking a deeper
understanding of the Reformation. Most encouraging of
these developments was the approach of Karl Barth. 'In opposition to almost all theological movements of the last century', said *Evangelical Christendom*, 'it aims at regaining a
central position for the great objective facts of Salvation, the
redemption of the world wrought by the Incarnation of the
Godhead, as applied to theological and ecclesiastical work,
thus giving a mighty new impulse especially to the preaching

60  *Evangelical Christendom*, January–February 1930, p.35.
61  *Evangelical Christendom*, November–December 1930, p.226.
62  J. MacConnachie, *The Significance of Karl Barth* (London: Hodder & Stoughton,
1931); J. MacConnachie, *The Barthian Theology* (London: Hodder & Stoughton,
1933), p.9 (for Barth's comments).

of the Gospel'.[63] By contrast with later conservative evangelical wariness of Barth,[64] this endorsement by the Evangelical
Alliance is significant. When Barth was appointed to the post
of Professor of Evangelical Theology at Bonn University, the
January 1935 issue of *Evangelical Christendom* went so far as to
suggest that 'a new Acts of the Apostles is being written in
Germany'.[65]

Nor did the Alliance deal only with Barth at a distance. On
22 March 1937, as Barth was returning to Switzerland from
Aberdeen, where he had delivered the Gifford lectures, the Alliance held a reception for him at the Russell Hotel, London.
The Archdeacon of London, E.N. Sharpe, who was associated
with the Anglican Evangelical Group Movement, was asked by
the Alliance to extend a welcome to Barth. In his speech,
Sharpe spoke of Barth's 'brave stand for the truth of God'.
W.R. Matthews, the Dean of St Paul's Cathedral, also spoke. He
said that he did not profess either completely to understand
Barth's theology, or to agree with what he did understand, but
he saw in Barth's writings a profoundly serious mind. 'Barth',
said Matthews, 'had sounded a trumpet for Europe'. The next
speaker, J.A. Hutton, editor of the popular *British Weekly*, concentrated on the contribution of Barth in bringing people
'face to face with God'. Carnegie Simpson, Professor of
Church History at Westminster College, Cambridge, who in
his writing had urged the view that evangelical and catholic
traditions had substantial areas in common, gave a passionate
speech. He said that there was 'no man in Europe whom he
would more gladly come to meet than Barth, who had stood
for the supremacy of God and for the rights of man and the liberty of conscience'. W. Talbot Rice and Henry Martyn Gooch
spoke on behalf of the Alliance's council, expressing their support for Barth's work. In response, Barth argued that the

63  *Evangelical Christendom*, July–August 1932, p.139.
64  For an account and appraisal of this later wariness about Barth, see B. Ramm,
*The Evangelical Heritage: A Study in Historical Theology* (Grand Rapids: Baker Book
House, 1981 [1973]), pp.108–22.
65  *Evangelical Christendom*, January–February 1935, p.29.

church in Germany was fighting against a new religion – the new German state under Hitler – and that all churches should identify with this struggle.[66]

Others in Britain besides the Alliance were prepared to do precisely that. Nathaniel Micklem, who in the 1930s was the most influential Congregationalist espousing a fresh Reformed theology, kept in close touch with developments in Europe and was regarded by the Alliance as having a keen knowledge of the situation. On 4 March 1938 Mansfield College, Oxford, at Micklem's initiative, staged a reception for Barth on the occasion of his receiving an Oxford honorary degree. A few weeks after Barth's visit to Oxford, Micklem, accompanied by Alec Whitehouse (a Mansfield student who would become a leading Barthian scholar), visited Germany and met Confessing Church representatives.[67] The Alliance's deep interest in Barth continued up to the Second World War. In 1939 *Evangelical Christendom* quoted extensively from an article Barth had written in *The Christian Century* (Chicago) in which he stated that what was at stake in Germany was the call to practice 'the truth that God stands above all other gods' and in which he explained that it was because of this that he could not begin his lectures in Bonn with the salutation to Hitler. The theological conflict, he argued, 'contained within itself the political conflict'.[68] Barth was presenting a vision of a theological task that affected the whole of life.

By contrast with the Alliance's admiration for Barth, there were those within the evangelical constituency who were dismissive. Martyn Lloyd-Jones, minister of Westminster Chapel from 1938, considered the reading of Barth and Brunner a waste of time.[69] Yet there were similarities between Barth and

---

66 *Evangelical Christendom*, March–April 1937, p.44.
67 E. Kaye, *Mansfield College, Oxford: Its Origin, History and Significance* (Oxford: Oxford University Press, 1996), p.208; W.A. Whitehouse, *The Authority of Grace* (Edinburgh: T. & T. Clark, 1981), vii; *Evangelical Christendom*, January–February 1937, p.44.
68 *Evangelical Christendom*, November–December 1939, p.206.
69 I.H. Murray, *D. Martyn Lloyd-Jones: The Fight of Faith, 1939-1981* (Edinburgh: Banner of Truth Trust, 1990), p.137.

Lloyd-Jones. Both were deeply committed to the revival of Reformed theology. Both saw God at work in the world in ways that were not comfortable and which showed the folly of easy optimism. Both represented a reaction against subjective religion. Speaking at the Alliance's week of prayer in 1939, Lloyd-Jones stressed the difference between subjective knowledge and objective revelation, and argued for the foundation for faith being found in the word of God. In the same address he condemned 'spiritual smugness'. When the war came a few months later, Lloyd-Jones saw it as entirely possible that the war was God inflicting judgement on the British nation. 'What if war has come', he asked in one sermon, 'because we did not deserve peace; because we by our disobedience and godlessness and sinfulness had so utterly abused the blessings of peace?'[70] This renewed sense of the sovereignty of God would have a powerful influence on evangelical theology over the course of the next two decades. As we shall see, Lloyd-Jones would play a crucial part in the unfolding history of the Alliance and would in some respects challenge the validity of the Alliance's commitment to comprehensiveness.


## Conclusion

In 1921 Henry Martyn Gooch argued for the 'Catholicity of the Gospel' a catholicity that he saw embodied in the Alliance, with its pan-denominational witness.[71] At this point the Alliance had made clear its stance over theological liberalism through its campaign against the New Theology. It had also reasserted its longer-running opposition to the Anglo-Catholic movement. On several fronts the 1920s brought fresh challenges. The Alliance may have resisted the narrow spirit of fundamentalism but Anglo-Catholics were opposed at national level and Liberal Evangelicalism was seen

---

70 Ibid., p.26.
71 *Evangelical Christendom*, May-June 1921, p.71.

as a threat to the Alliance's attempts to create an evangelical platform that was comprehensive within the truth. Some liberal evangelicals staked out ground that the Alliance considered was beyond acceptable evangelical limits. It seems that up to the Second World War it was Karl Barth whom the Alliance found to be the most promising theologian in Europe. It may be, however, that this was the stance of Gooch and was not one that was widely shared. Yet it was the consistent policy of the Alliance to argue for a proper openness in evangelical thought and to resist a narrower line. John Stott would adopt a similarly moderate stance in the debate about the rise of fundamentalism during the Billy Graham crusades of 1956.[72] Stott entered the discussion determined to repudiate the fundamentalist label and distance himself from mechanical ideas of biblical inspiration. In a book published by the Alliance in 1956, *Fundamentalism and Evangelism*, Stott stated that the personalities of the Bible's authors were 'fashioned, enriched and fully employed'.[73] In 1942 J.C. Mann, assistant bishop of Rochester, who was presiding at the annual meeting of the Alliance, referred to the ability of Gooch to 'rope in one and another': he had, said Mann, created a truly 'catholic' platform. Indeed, he suggested that there were few platforms that were quite so catholic as that of the Alliance. It was catholic, Mann believed, because it was first of all evangelical – it had been founded upon evangelical truth. In the light of the vision of comprehensiveness within the truth, it is significant that Mann regarded as evangelical all those who followed Christ Jesus as Saviour and Lord.[74]

---

72 I.M. Randall, *Educating Evangelicalism: The Origins, Development and Impact of London Bible College* (Carlisle: Paternoster Press, 2000), pp.98–100

73 J. Stott, *Fundamentalism and Evangelism* (London: Evangelical Alliance, 1956), p.6.

74 *Evangelical Christendom*, July–September 1942, p.68.

# 9

# A Body of Responsible Enthusiasts

*The Alliance and Modern Evangelism*

The story of evangelism in Britain in the nineteenth and twentieth centuries has not yet been fully analysed, although considerable attention has been given to the growth of evangelical life in the nineteenth century. There were spontaneous revivals, but increasingly there were also organised methods of evangelism such as house-to-house visitation. The late nineteenth and early twentieth-century period was marked by confidence about evangelism, by 'an ebullient spirituality ... that generated mission'.[1] Attempts at outreach were often initiated by local churches or sponsored by denominations, but some were interdenominational. Of the latter, the most notable was the London City Mission (LCM), which was established in 1835.[2] By the 1880s, there were 460 people on the staff of the LCM. Two years before the formation of the Evangelical Alliance, the influential and distinctly evangelical Young Men's Christian Association (YMCA) was formed.[3] In the 1840s, when the Evangelical Alliance emerged, there was an excitement about the fulfilment of prophecy and about international revival.[4] A further wave of interdenominational and transnational evan-

---

1 D.W. Bebbington, 'Evangelism and Spirituality in Twentieth-Century Protestant Nonconformity', p.1.

2 See Lewis, *Lighten their Darkness*.

3 For the YMCA see Binfield, *George Williams and the YMCA*.

4 Wolffe, 'The Evangelical Alliance in the 1840s', p.341.

gelistic activity followed in 1858-9 and was expressed in a more organised way in campaigns led by D.L. Moody and Ira D. Sankey in Britain in 1873-5. This chapter will begin with the nineteenth-century background and will then analyse more fully the relationships that existed between the Alliance and the fresh evangelistic impetus that occurred in the mid-twentieth century.

## Nineteenth-Century Evangelistic Activity

According to J.W. Ewing, the Alliance from the outset was like 'a lighthouse flashing out the glory of the gospel'. In 1845 Edward Bickersteth delineated the message of the gospel and thus the message of the Alliance as 'the incarnation of the Son of God: His work of atonement for us sinners – a finished work: His mediatorial intercession for which He ever lives: His supreme sovereignty and reign … The justification of the sinner by faith alone'.[5] The mid-1850s saw several initiatives taken by the Alliance. One hundred ministers were involved in evangelisation in Ireland, although it was reported that this project was hampered by 'violence and persecution'.[6] There were weekly Sunday evening services in Exeter Hall over a period of three months. The interest in these was such that hundreds of people whom the Exeter Hall could not accommodate were turned away. It was suggested that two-thirds of those who attended did not regularly worship in any church. As a result of these successes, Edward Steane, as an honorary secretary of the Alliance, called in 1856 for intensified activity to reach non-churchgoing people in Britain. This helped to prepare the way for the further evangelistic impetus of the years 1857 to 1859. In Tyneside, for example, the revival of this period, with its interdenominational character, was described as an 'Evangelical Alliance revival'.[7]

5  Ewing, *Goodly Fellowship*, p.41.
6  Minutes of the Evangelical Alliance Conference in London, 1853.
7  Kessler, *A Study of the Evangelical Alliance*, pp.58-61.

In his analysis of the '1859 revival', Edwin Orr argued that it confirmed the doctrinal basis laid down by the Alliance in 1846. 'The Evangelical Alliance view of Christian unity (namely that as soon as a sinner accepts Christ as Saviour he becomes one with all the members of the Body of Christ throughout the earth)', Orr wrote, 'was so widely adopted that it led to a practice of fraternal fellowship having the force of a major doctrine.'[8] It does seem that in this period many evangelicals inclined towards the idea of spiritual unity advocated by the Alliance. 'There is something very remarkable', said *Evangelical Christendom* in 1858, 'about this revival of religion. There is no exclusiveness in its operation. From the most demonstrative Methodist to the dignified and orderly Episcopalian, all participate in the baptism of the Spirit with equal rejoicing.'[9] This was probably an overstatement. J.B.A. Kessler similarly overstates the degree of commitment to spiritual unity when he suggests that after 1859 'everybody' accepted the idea in principle.[10] Yet for Kessler the 1859 revival contributed to a period of decline for the Alliance, since its primary objective – spiritual unity – was widely seen as having been achieved. Giving attention to evangelistic outreach, however, cannot be equated with decline. Certainly Alliance activities evolved. In the 1860s, for example, Alliance-sponsored speakers were involved in debates with secularists.[11]

Interdenominational evangelism of the kind that the Alliance affirmed was given a further boost from June 1873 to August 1875 through the British evangelistic campaigns of D.L. Moody and his singer and co-evangelist, Ira D. Sankey. F.B. Meyer was one of the future Alliance figures who felt the impact of Moody's approach. George Bennett, the founder-secretary of the York YMCA, had written to Moody about the possibility of his coming to Britain, but Bennett was taken by surprise when, in June 1873, Moody and Sankey unexpectedly

8  Orr, *Second Evangelical Awakening*, p.126.
9  *Evangelical Christendom*, August 1858, p.288.
10  Kessler, A Study of *The Evangelical Alliance*, pp.63-4.
11  Executive Council Minutes, February 1869.

arrived in England. The Americans headed for York and there established Priory Street Baptist Church as their base. In his role as Priory Street's pastor, Meyer was fascinated to discover a new, expansive approach to evangelism – an approach that freed him from what he saw as conventional forms of worship. Later, Meyer was to describe how, through Moody, he saw 'a wider, larger life, in which mere denominationalism could have no place'. Meyer was deeply involved in Baptist life, becoming (among other things) President of the Baptist Union, but in his pioneering ministry at Melbourne Hall in the 1880s he was determined that there should be no 'marked denominationalism'.[12] In this Meyer was signalling a trend towards a wider view of the mission of the Church.

The Alliance in Britain gave the evangelistic efforts of Moody and Sankey wholehearted support in the 1870s, with the Alliance's Executive Council speaking in November 1875 of the united evangelistic activity, prayer meetings and interchurch co-operation that had been taking place as 'a harbinger of awakening and revival'.[13] C.H. Spurgeon, who, as we have seen, had a complex relationship with the Alliance, was sufficiently supportive of the evangelistic thrust to host Moody and Sankey in his huge Metropolitan Tabernacle at the Elephant and Castle, London. It is significant that in 1876 when this spirit of evangelistic co-operation was strong, Hugh Price Hughes, who would become a leading Wesleyan Methodist minister and promoter of the progressive Forward Movement in Methodism, joined the Alliance.[14] In 1878, at an international exhibition in Paris, the Alliances of Europe sponsored a 'Salle Evangélique' that attracted 100,000 visitors. Well-known British figures such as Lord Shaftesbury gave talks. The outreach was seen as a 'testimony to true catholic

---

12 I.M. Randall, 'Incarnating the Gospel: Melbourne Hall, Leicester, in the 1880s as a model for holistic ministry', *The Baptist Quarterly* 35.8 (1994), pp.394-5; I.M. Randall, 'Mere Denominationalism: F.B. Meyer and Baptist Life', *The Baptist Quarterly* 35.1 (1993), p.20.

13 Executive Council Minutes, 12 November 1875.

14 Executive Council Minutes, 14 June 1876.

unity'.[15] The Billy Graham meetings and crusades of the 1940s and 1950s were to promote a similar concept of broadly based unity, in part by reactivating the Moody and Sankey ethos.

## Twentieth-Century Revivalist Movements

The twentieth century began with a united campaign which was entitled the 'Simultaneous Mission', and which was organised by the Free Church councils of England and Wales. During ten days in January and February 1901 London audiences were addressed, and missioners then moved elsewhere throughout the country.[16] A National Free Church Council (NFCC) had begun in 1892, with a special congress in Manchester. This was connected to a loose network of local councils, and a Welsh body was formed around the same time. Later, in 1919, a Federal Council of Evangelical Free Churches was co-ordinated and by 1940 this had joined with the NFCC in the Free Church Federal Council. During the first half of the twentieth century, these Free Church councils would emerge as key agents for joint evangelism and social action, and in the process would divert a significant degree of strength and support from the Alliance.[17] This is not, however, to suggest that the two movements were mutually exclusive: the Methodist Hugh Price Hughes and the Baptist John Clifford were prominent in the development of the Free Church councils, but as we have seen, were also both active within the Alliance. Besides, revival and mission were hardly demarcated concerns. The Welsh Revival of 1904-5, for example, was another influential interdenominational movement within British evangelicalism which engaged the attention of both the Free Church councils and the Alliance. Evan Roberts was the principal and most controversial figure in the Welsh Revival.

---

15 *Evangelical Christendom*, November 1878, p.346; *Report Presented to the Twenty-First Annual Conference of the Evangelical Alliance*, p.10.

16 E.K.H. Jordan, *Free Church Unity: History of the Free Church Council Movement, 1896-1941* (London: Lutterworth Press, 1956), pp.66-72.

17 On the Free Church councils see Jordan, *Free Church Unity*.

Several evangelical leaders from other parts of Britain travelled to Wales in 1905 to hear and meet Roberts. Although the strain of the ministry he had undertaken meant that Roberts withdrew from public preaching after a comparatively short time, the challenge of the revival spirit continued in a number of quarters.[18] At the Alliance conference of 1907 there was reflection on the state of the nation, and it was pointed out that 'the masses' – the reference was particularly to urban areas – were alienated from the churches. In south London it was reckoned that only one in twelve men and one in ten women attended church.[19] Evangelists to working class people were, however, emerging in this period. George Jeffreys, the founder of Pentecostalism's Elim Church, together with his brother Stephen, both of whose roots were in the Welsh Revival, led Pentecostal evangelistic and healing campaigns that attracted large audiences in the 1920s.[20]

It seems that towards the end of the First World War there was a growing expectation within evangelicalism that spiritual renewal might be imminent. At the Islington conference for evangelical Anglican clergy held in London in January 1918, Webb-Peploe, by then a venerable a Keswick Convention leader, spoke about Christ as the foundation for renewal 'of society, of ecclesiastical matters, and of individual spiritual life'. Webb-Peploe's focus was on Anglicanism, but other denominations were thinking in similar terms. John Kent describes the period 1921-8, and especially 1922-6, as the years of the last 'flicker' of expansion in modern Methodism, and attributes it in part to the efforts invested in traditional evangelism, supremely by the 'ageing Victorian revivalist', Gipsy Smith.[21] Methodism's Cliff College, in the Derbyshire Peak District,

18  B.P. Jones, *An Instrument of Revival: The Complete Life of Evan Roberts* (South Plainfield: Bridge Publishing, 1995); B.P. Jones, *The King's Champions* (Cwmbran, Gwent: Christian Literature Press, 1986).

19  *Maintaining the Unity: Report of the Eleventh International Conference of the Evangelical Alliance* (London, 1907), p.151.

20  See D.W. Cartwright, *The Great Evangelists* (Basingstoke: Marshall Pickering, 1986).

21  J. Kent, *The Age of Disunity* (London: Epworth Press, 1966), p.6.

was also crucial. Gipsy Smith regularly visited its Whitsun
Conventions. During the period of Samuel Chadwick's powerful leadership as Principal, in the years before, during and after the First World War, there was a strong emphasis on revival.
A new mood of hope prevailed in the Cliff College constituency after the war, thanks in part to what Chadwick called a
'Pentecost' at the College in October 1920. At a Cliff College
mission in Chesterfield in May 1922, in which 60 missioners
took part, it was reported that there were 3,000 conversions.
Local Free churches were drawn together in united mission.[22]

Discussions about the possibility of a wider interdenominational revival in Britain in the early 1920s were brought into
sharp focus by events in East Anglia. In the autumn of 1920
Hugh Ferguson, minister of London Road Baptist Church,
Lowestoft, visited Douglas Brown, minister of Ramsden Road
Baptist Church, Balham, to ask if he would conduct a mission
in Lowestoft. From March 1921 when the mission began, there
was a sense of unusual spiritual revival. In July 1921 Ferguson
and John Hayes, vicar of Christ Church, Lowestoft, reported at
Keswick that a revival had come to East Anglia. The subject of
revival was also taken up at a meeting of the Evangelical Alliance in January 1922, when J.E. Watts-Ditchfield, Bishop of
Chelmsford, presided. The speakers on that occasion included
Charles Raven, later Regius Professor of Divinity at Cambridge.[23] In the wake of this event, the Alliance, keen to affirm
that it had always been 'intensely evangelistic in its aims and
operations', arranged a 'Week of Witness' in the period of Pentecost.[24] Each night preachers spoke in churches other than
those of their own denomination, as a sign of evangelical unity.
There was a particular emphasis within the Alliance on
personal evangelism. Larger scale Alliance events took place
in 1924 in connection with the British Empire Exhibition in
Wembley. The Alliance co-operated with other bodies to hold

---

22 *Joyful News*, reports of 1922; *Joyful News*, 15 July 1925, p.3; Dunning, *Samuel Chadwick*, p.190.
23 *The Record*, 10 January 1922, p.39.
24 *Evangelical Christendom*, July–August 1923, p.100.

meetings, addressed by evangelists such as Gipsy Smith, in the large conference hall of the Exhibition.[25]

The 'Week of Witness' was observed by Alliances in a number of countries. A report from Mussoorie, India, noted that the Anglican Lambeth Conference of 1920 had enunciated principles of intercommunion and that steps in this direction were to be encouraged in India. The Alliance's call to united witness was seen as 'calculated to further the cause of unity'. In response, Anglican clergymen and Free Church ministers in Mussoorie had united. The example of what had happened at Kikuyu was cited. There was prayer for revival at well-attended services in the various churches in the Mussoorie district. At a united missionary service, representatives of the Church Missionary Society, the Methodist Episcopal Church and the Presbyterian Church gave addresses.[26] Although this report from India seemed to be heavily biased towards western Christian influences, in the same period the Alliance paid tribute to the remarkable work of Pandita Ramabai, an Indian who attempted to conduct mission in an Indian way. As well as being an outstanding Christian teacher and scholar, she founded a school where, as the Alliance put it, 'hundreds of girls were educated. Widows, deserted wives and famine victims won her sympathy and help. Her school grew into a regular colony with some two thousand members ... Her Mukti Colony is unique in India.'[27]

One aspect of spiritual revival that the Alliance attempted to foster in Britain – what Ewing called 'the world-wide revival of the keeping of the Holy Day' – was not destined to flourish. The Alliance, in its early period, had highlighted Sunday observance through a book entitled *The Pearl of Days*, written by a Scottish labourer's daughter. The Alliance not only promoted the book, which sold widely, but also had it translated into several languages. At various points, the Alliance enlisted the support of

---

25  Ewing, *Goodly Fellowship*, p.47.
26  *Evangelical Christendom*, July–August 1923, p.100.
27  Ewing, *Goodly Fellowship*, p.103.

the Archbishop of Canterbury for its campaigns over Sunday observance, and in 1922 was in tune with churches as a whole in opposing the decision of the London County Council (LCC) to open public parks in London on Sunday for games.[28] At a meeting called by the Alliance in early 1923 to address the issue the Queen's Hall was filled, with an overflow in All Souls, Langham Place, and at these meetings resolutions were passed condemning the LCC. Some evangelicals, however, were coming to doubt the strict Sunday observance position. In the 1930s Edward Woods of Croydon, an evangelical bishop with broader views, supported Sunday opening of cinemas and chaired a committee that selected films to be shown on Sunday evenings. The Evangelical Alliance joined with the Lord's Day Observance Society in opposing Sunday opening of cinemas, but there was limited support for the campaign.[29]

## New Evangelistic Forces

Although British evangelicalism reached its nadir around 1940,[30] evangelistic activity was by no means absent in Britain in the later 1930s. The National Young Life Campaign (NYLC), which was founded in 1911 by the brothers Frederick and Arthur Wood, was a significant interdenominational movement in inter-war evangelicalism, attracting enterprising evangelists to its ranks. It claimed 13,000 young people in membership in 1947.[31] In 1938 10,000 boys were attending interdenominational boys' Crusader classes and 6,000 were in girls' Crusader classes each week.[32] Towards the end of the

---

28  Ibid., 83; *The British Weekly*, 13 July 1922, p.309.

29  Bebbington, *Evangelicalism in Modern Britain*, p.211; J. Wigley, *The Rise and Fall of the Victorian Sunday* (Manchester: Manchester University Press, 1980), p.193.

30  Bebbington, *Evangelicalism in Modern Britain*, p.252.

31  *The Christian*, 24 April 1947, p.1. For the Wood brothers, see F.P Wood & M.S. Wood, *Youth Advancing* (London: National Young Life Campaign, 1961).

32  See J. Watford, *Yesterday and Today: A History of Crusaders* (St. Albans: Crusaders' Union, 1995), and H. Roseveare, *On Track: The Story of the Girl Crusaders' Union* (St. Albans: Girl Crusaders' Union, 1990).

Second World War, the Alliance, partly influenced by outreach such as that undertaken by Methodists in their Commando Campaigns, committed itself to a campaign of evangelism.[33] A younger British evangelist who had been influenced by the Wood brothers was Tom Rees. At the end of the war, Rees, who had worked for the Children's Special Service Mission (CSSM) and an active evangelical Anglican church in Sevenoaks, Kent, initiated large-scale meetings in London, particularly orientated towards young people.

Rees' first major campaign in the capital was called 'Faith for the Times', and ran for a fortnight at the Albert Hall. Accompanying him were others who would go on to exercise powerful evangelistic ministries in their own right: Alan Redpath, F.T. Ellis and Stephen Olford. Later in 1945 Rees organised a month of meetings at Westminster Central Hall. He planned to return there the following year, but when the United Nations requisitioned the building for the period he had planned, they offered him an alternative venue of his choice and he opted for the Albert Hall! Rees would go on to hold more than fifty weekly rallies there, as well as speaking at other large London venues like the City Temple. Guest speakers at these meetings included C.S. Lewis, Martyn Lloyd-Jones, who had taken over from Campbell Morgan as minister of Westminster Chapel, and the highly regarded Methodist preacher, W.E. Sangster, of Westminster Central Hall, who was a supporter of the Evangelical Alliance. These meetings drew many young people, although backing from London ministers was less obvious.[34] Rees was an important promoter of the unity for which the Evangelical Alliance stood, and there is no doubt that he paved the way for the visit to Britain of an even more significant advocate of united evangelical outreach.

In the spring of 1946 an American evangelist, Billy Graham, then aged twenty-seven and at that time virtually unknown outside the USA, was part of a small team of Youth for Christ

33  Executive Council Minutes, 22 June 1944.
34  J. Rees, *Stranger than Fiction* (Frinton-on-Sea, 1957), pp.24–5.

(YFC) emissaries who came from the USA to Britain charged with the task, as they saw it, of saving Britain out of a spiritual 'abyss'.[35] Roy Cattell assisted Tom Rees as his executive officer. Cattell, who would later become the Alliance's General Secretary when he was in his early forties, was a businessman who was active in interdenominational affairs as a leader of the Hendon Crusaders Bible Class. From 1944 he was involved in organising wider evangelism in London. Rees and Cattell gathered about sixty clergy and lay people to meet the Americans at the Bonnington Hotel in London. Evangelistic events across Britain began to be scheduled. Not all British evangelicals welcomed the invasion of American-style revivalism that they saw as taking place. Stanley Baker, for example, the evangelistically minded minister of Bordesley Green Baptist Church in Birmingham, was unconvinced that the way to reach the 95% of people in Birmingham who allegedly did not attend church was through 'surplus saints', as he labelled them, from America. Billy Graham convinced him otherwise, and Baker was so motivated that he engaged in frantic telephoning of his acquaintances, urging support for Graham's Birmingham youth meetings. Numbers attending quickly rose to 2,500.[36]

The initial YFC British tour, which lasted forty-six days, was followed by six months of mission that Graham conducted throughout Britain from October 1946. Accompanied by Cliff and Billie Barrows as his musical team, Graham spoke in twenty-seven centres and on 360 occasions – an average of about two meetings a day. He had made four further transatlantic trips by 1949 and T.W. Wilson, one of his close friends and colleagues, also spent several months in Britain. Support for Wilson was forthcoming from prominent businessmen as well as ministers.[37] The idea of a crusade in Britain was already

---

35  Report by Wes Hartzell on the British trip by Billy Graham and his colleagues, in Collection (CN) 224, Box 1, Folder 17, Billy Graham Archives, Billy Graham Center, Wheaton, Illinois, USA. Also W Martin, *The Billy Graham Story: A Prophet with Honour* (London: Hutchinson, 1992), pp.94–5, 106.

36  Report by Billy Graham, (CN) 318, Box 54, Folder 13, Billy Graham Archives.

37  *The Christian*, 8 April 1948, p.9.

germinating, and it was this that would draw Graham into the orbit of the Evangelical Alliance. Graham's comment to George Beverly Shea, his associate and someone emerging as a leading gospel singer in America, was: 'There is a feeling among some of us that we should go back again some day and hold a campaign not directed primarily to youth'.[38] In 1947 British Youth for Christ was inaugurated and Billy Graham was in Britain for the second YFC annual conference in 1948. Tom Rees noted in 1948 that there had been a marked increase in co-operation between many churches and Christian leaders in Britain.[39] Inspired by experiences in the United States, Rees purchased Hildenborough Hall, a large country house in Kent, and turned it into an influential Christian conference centre. Roy Cattell was manager of Hildenborough Hall and was therefore at the centre of the continuing evangelistic developments of the period. Lindsay Glegg, an evangelical business-man, saw in Rees an embodiment of Moody's ministry.[40] American influences were becoming stronger.

The years 1946 to 1949 were notable for the fresh evange-listic impetus coming from Billy Graham and his associates, and for new appointments within the Evangelical Alliance. Hugh Gough, then rural dean of Islington and later bishop of Barking and Archbishop of Sydney, became an honorary sec-retary in 1946, and a year later Gilbert Kirby, who would be-come Alliance General Secretary, joined the Executive Council. These were key figures in a time of transition. Gough warned in 1947 that continual tramping over the same soil could turn a path into a rut.[41] There was to be a new stress on relevant forms of evangelism. A statement

---

38 G.B. Shea, *Then Sings My Soul* (Old Tappan/London: Hodder & Stoughton, 1968), p.95.

39 *The Christian*, 29 April 1948, p.6.

40 *The Christian*, 24 January 1946, p.9; 27 April 1951, p.3. I am indebted to Maurice Rowlandson for his help with information about this period, especially about Roy Cattell.

41 H.R. Gough, 'One Great Evangelical Fellowship', *Evangelical Christendom*, Jan-uary–March 1947, pp.1–2.

issued by the Alliance in 1947 covered a number of issues, but
only one of these was printed in capital letters. The Alliance
called for 'a return to true EVANGELICALISM, that evangelicalism which has at its heart the EVANGEL, the gospel of
salvation, free for each and every one to accept'.[42] Hugh
Gough made it clear in 1948 that in his view it was time for a
complete change in the policy and leadership of the Alliance.[43] When Gooch retired in 1949, and received an OBE, it
was stated that the Alliance would continue to promote unity,
assist persecuted Christians, be involved in evangelistic work
and emphasise prayer.[44] This suggested continuity, but
changes were afoot. The enterprising Roy Cattell was
appointed to a secretarial role to 'put the Alliance on the
map', and would soon make his presence felt.

## The Alliance and British Evangelism

At the meeting of the Executive Council of the Alliance on
27 July 1950, the fourteen members present – who included a
number of new faces such as Geoffrey King, minister of the
East London Tabernacle – expressed their optimism about
the future. The experience of the past year had been encouraging, and there was particular stress on the role of Cattell,
who was taking on the task of building up the work of the
Alliance.[45] The momentum increased. Lt.-Gen. Sir Arthur
Smith, the Executive Council Chairman, reported at a meeting in February 1951 that plans were moving ahead for a
major evangelical 'Exhibition' and associated public meetings
during the national Festival of Britain to be held later in
1951. Cattell had met with a group of evangelists. It was
suggested that the slogan for the campaign, which would ultimately draw in 160 evangelical organisations, should be 'For

42  *Evangelical Christendom*, April–June 1947, p.31.
43  Executive Council Minutes, 28 October 1948.
44  *Evangelical Christendom*, October–December 1949, p.85.
45  Executive Council Minutes, 27 July 1950.

Such a Time as This'.[46] At a further meeting, in May, names
of missioners were mentioned. These included John Stott,
who became rector of All Souls Church, Langham Place,
London, in 1950 at the age of twenty-nine, and in the same
year started a training school in All Souls to equip church
members for active evangelism. Cattell, with typical enthusiasm, wrote in *Evangelical Christendom* that the Alliance's contribution would 'undoubtedly form one of the most
impressive of the various acts of witness being arranged in
connection with the Festival of Britain', and that the display
of evangelical unity and strength would be 'of a character and
on a scale never before seen'.[47] Evangelical confidence was
certainly evident.

Other evangelistic preachers who were utilised during the
Exhibition campaign were Tom Rees and his brother Dick,
Alan Redpath and Stephen Olford, both of whom would become known as effective Baptist pastors and evangelists, and
W.E. Sangster, who was by then a vice-President of the Alliance. On two nights 7,500 people filled the Methodist Central Hall, Westminster Abbey and Westminster Chapel. On 27
September 1951, as the Alliance's Executive Council considered the results of the campaign, it was agreed that 'many societies had come into close contact with others doing similar
work' and that the seeds of closer co-operation between
evangelical agencies had been sown. It seemed to the Alliance
leadership that the Alliance now had 'a great opportunity to
be of still greater service to the evangelical world', although it
was also recognised that the Alliance had the problem, which
was to be a continuing one, of how to encourage united activities without 'appearing to dictate' (as it was put) to other
societies. Further suggestions were made. The Alliance's week
of prayer could, it was thought, be a launch pad for larger
events. Meetings for prayer were held in Baptist Church
House, Southampton Row, and were therefore small in scale,

---

46 Executive Council Minutes, 22 February 1951.
47 Executive Council Minutes, 24 May 1951; T. Dudley-Smith, *John Stott: The
Making of a Leader*, p.296; *Evangelical Christendom*, May 1951, pp.33-5.

but there was interest in using Westminster Central Hall again. Sangster, the Central Hall minister, was preparing a letter to be sent to all those who had responded during the Exhibition. Lindsay Glegg, who was present at the Alliance executive, floated the idea of the Alliance organising nation-wide evangelistic campaigns. Tom Rees, also present, considered that this could be done using local missioners. United witness in 1953 or 1954 was discussed.[48] The creative ideas emanating from Rees to use British evangelists, however, would be overshadowed by more widely publicised initiatives in mass evangelism in America.

As Rees' Executive Officer, Roy Cattell was in close touch with evangelistic developments that were taking place in America as well as in Britain. It was at Graham's Los Angeles Crusade of 1949, when such celebrities as Stuart Hamblen, a popular cowboy singer, Louis Zamperini, an Olympic track star, and Jim Vaus, a wiretapper with underworld connections in the USA, were converted. All of this guaranteed Graham's position as America's foremost evangelist. At an Alliance meeting held on 22 November 1951 – attended by Hugh Gough, J. Chalmers Lyon (a Presbyterian minister in London), Ernest Kevan (the Principal of London Bible College), Gilbert Kirby (Kevan's colleague at London Bible College), Frank Colquhoun (the Alliance's Editorial Secretary) and Roy Cattell – it was reported through an intermediary called Ralph Mitchell that Graham had signalled his willingness to address church leaders on evangelism.[49] Negotiations, which took place during the period March–July 1952, were far from straightforward. Alliance leaders also met with Geoffrey Fisher, Archbishop of Canterbury, who indicated that the Church of England would not officially support a campaign conduced by Graham alone, although it would not oppose such a venture. A meeting was subsequently held with Francis House and Bryan

---

48  Executive Council Minutes, 27 September 1951.
49  Executive Council Minutes, 22 November 1951; F. Colquhoun, *Harringay Story*, pp.17–8.

Green of the British Council of Churches (BCC), the ecumenical body that had been set up in 1942.[50]

Further to these discussions, Roy Cattell went to the USA with the Alliance's Treasurer, J.H. Cordle, and spoke with the Graham team. The ideas being put forward as a result of the BCC discussions included the idea of a pilot crusade, but Graham was not prepared to co-operate in such a scheme. In view of this, the Alliance decided that there should be no further official co-operation with the BCC in arranging what became the Greater London Crusade at Harringay Arena from March–May 1954. The intriguing statement was made that a campaign of the kind proposed was best sponsored by 'a body of responsible enthusiasts outside ecclesiastical organisation'.[51] The fact that such responsible enthusiasts could be drawn together in Britain was due in no small measure to bodies such as the Keswick Convention, the Inter-Varsity Fellowship and Hildenborough Hall, to new Alliance leaders such as Gough, Kirby and Cattell, and to Graham's influence in Britain during the later 1940s. An outstanding example of someone with many connecting links was Gilbert Kirby. In addition to his lecturing role at London Bible College, Kirby was at this time pastor of Ashford Congregational Church, and was involved in the Alliance, in Hildenborough Hall, and in Martyn Lloyd-Jones' fellowship for ministers.[52]

The committee which planned Harringay in the period leading up to 1954 included Lindsay Glegg, minister of Down Lodge Hall, Wandsworth, and a Keswick young people's speaker who had interests in evangelical groups such as Christian Endeavour and Crusaders. He was immoderately described in an American YFC report in 1946 as one who 'probably has more influence on British Christian life than any other man'.[53] Also on the committee were Tom Livermore,

---

50  Executive Council Minutes, 22 May 1952; 24 July 1952.

51  Colquhoun, *Harringay*, p.27.

52  For the role of London Bible College in this period see Randall, *Educating Evangelicalism*, chapter 4.

53  CN 224, Box 1, Folder 17, Billy Graham Archives.

who had used Graham as the main speaker in a much ac-
claimed mission to his own parish, St John's, Deptford, in 1947
and was involved in Youth for Christ,[54] and Joe Blinco, who
had invited Graham to his Methodist Church in Southampton
and who would later join the Graham team. As a result of Graham's visits to Birmingham between 1946 and 1949 he forged
a lasting friendship with Alfred Owen, the Chairman of the
large engineering firm Rubery, Owen & Co. Owen became a
powerful evangelical force through his work for Birmingham
YFC, and then as treasurer of the Harringay Crusade.[55] Another businessman, Oliver Stott, was active in supporting Graham's visits to Britian, and in fact hosted him on his first night
in England. A key figure within the Harringay team was
Maurice Rowlandson, an Evangelical Alliance staff member
whose personal history as Billy Graham's representative in
Britain was to be so closely intertwined with the evangelist's
work that his autobiography was entitled *Life with Billy*. This
association started when Rowlandson met Graham at a London YFC presentation in 1948.[56]

There was some confusion as to the role of YFC in the period when preparations were being made for the Harringay
Crusade. Roy Cattell had a meeting with Tom Livermore and
Eric Hutchings, the director of British Youth for Christ, at
which they discovered that YFC in America was thinking of
sending teams to Britain to participate in an evangelistic effort.
Nothing more came of this and it seems likely that Graham
discouraged YFC from becoming involved in a large-scale enterprise at the time of the Harringay Crusade. The next step
was to bring Graham to London for preparatory meetings. In
March 1952 he spoke to about 700 British church leaders at a

---

54  *The Christian*, 20 March 1947, p.11.

55  D.J. Jeremy, 'Businessmen in Interdenominational Activity: Birmingham
Youth for Christ, 1940s-1950s, *The Baptist Quarterly* 33.7 (1990), pp.336-43; D.J.
Jeremy, *Capitalists and Christians: Business Leaders and the Churches in Britain,
1900-1960* (Oxford: Clarendon, 1990), pp.397-410.

56  M. Rowlandson, *Life with Billy: An Autobiography* (London: Hodder &
Stoughton, 1992), p.11.

reception in Church House, Westminster. His speech was carefully calculated to play down any idea that America had the answers to the problems of Britain. Graham stated, in an address that was widely circulated, that as he looked around 'and particularly as I think of America', he was desperately afraid. He went on to argue that both America and Britain faced perils from within, the threat of communism from outside and the imminent possibility of God's judgement. He saw the period 1920-40 as one of spiritual drought in America, characterised by a church that was 'prayerless and powerless', and by 'super-sensational, hyper-emotional' evangelism. Mass evangelism, he stated, was only one form of outreach and was largely ineffective unless conducted in full conjunction with churches in any given district.[57] The reference to unacceptable styles of evangelism was designed to assure British church leaders that this was not what he would promote.

## Harringay and its Aftermath

The scale of the Greater London Crusade at Harringay Arena was unprecedented. It attracted an aggregate attendance of over two million at all associated meetings, including 120,000 at Wembley Stadium on the closing day of the campaign, 15,000 of whom had to be accommodated on the pitch itself. In addition, demand for final day tickets was so great that the Alliance had to arrange an overflow rally for a further 55,000 people at White City. Although Billy Graham was open to the idea of employing what he called a 'different technique' in Britain, his method of making an appeal at the end of his address and then linking up those who came forward and 'made a decision' with a counsellor, was the method used at Harringay.[58] It would become standard practice in much mass evangelism in Britain. Graham received the approval of

---

57  B. Graham, *The Work of an Evangelist* (World's Evangelical Alliance: London, 1953), pp.7-12; *Evangelical Christendom*, May 1952, p.40.

58  Executive Council Minutes, 24 September 1953.

Geoffrey Fisher, Archbishop of Canterbury,[59] and Leslie Weatherhead, minister of the City Temple, London. Weatherhead was widely quoted when he said: 'what does fundamentalist theology matter compared with gathering in the people we have all missed and getting them to the point of decision?'[60] In this period Graham, as he received support from church leaders who were not evangelicals, made it clear that he did not wish to draw people out of their existing churches.[61] Such evangelical reservations about Graham as there were in Britain tended to come from some in the Calvinistic camp. Martyn Lloyd-Jones declined to take part in ministers' meetings held in conjunction with Harringay. He included in his prayer at Westminster Chapel on 1 March 1954 the 'brethren' who were 'ministering in another part of the city', but spoke of reports from the campaign as 'most confusing'.[62] Yet looking back on Harringay, the author John Pollock emphasised the unity in evangelism and prayer that had come out of Graham's crusade.[63] This was exactly what the Evangelical Alliance hoped would happen.

The members of the Executive Council of the Alliance were convinced, by the end of the Harringay Crusade, that – as Sir Arthur Smith, the Chairman, put it – 'all other aspects of the work of the Alliance was [sic] secondary to the follow up of the Greater London Crusade'. There were suggestions of another major campaign, although it was recognised that this would need 'a vast sum of money and enormous headquarters'. The Executive Council did not commit itself to this plan, but the thirteen members present did agree that 'the Evangelical Alliance should regard evangelism as its primary task'. The Alliance was seen as having a 'tremendous responsibility, which if it did not undertake nobody else would'. Military figures such as Lt.-Gen. Sir William Dobbie and Major Batt were

---

59 In the *Canterbury Diocesan Notes*, June 1954.
60 Martin, *Billy Graham Story*, p.181.
61 *Christian Century* 77.7 (1960), p.188.
62 Murray, *D. Martyn Lloyd-Jones*, p.338.
63 J.C. Pollock, *Christianity Today*, Vol. 2, No. 15 (1958), p.11.

attracted by the idea of an ongoing spiritual crusade. With pastoral leaders such as John Stott, Ernest Kevan and Gilbert Kirby on the Executive Council, however, it was unlikely that the Alliance's agenda would be solely evangelistic in nature. It was also agreed that 'the Alliance had a vital responsibility of ministry to the clergy and the churches to foster and strengthen the spiritual life of the churches'.[64]

It was never likely that the Alliance would concentrate exclusively on mass evangelism. During the 1950s, through Kenneth Hylson-Smith and others, it was heavily involved in the running of a students' hostel, the Alliance Club, in London. It also sponsored film evangelism in prisons – a project initiated by Billy Graham's close friend Oliver Stott. The Alliance Club was mainly for overseas students. The Duke of Edinburgh visited the Club in 1953. By the end of the decade hundreds of students from many different countries had been given accommodation in the hostel. The film ministry, which was the responsibility of Maurice Rowlandson, was one of the major activities of the Alliance's Extensions Department. Over a period of five years every penal establishment in England, Wales and Scotland was visited.[65] Lindsay Glegg proposed to the Alliance in November 1954 a follow-up convention for the Graham Crusade to be held at Butlins Camp, and this became an annual event – the Filey holiday week convention. It was widely recognised that the Graham Crusades of 1954 in London, together with a further highly influential Scottish crusade in the Kelvin Hall, Glasgow, in the following year, had made a major contribution to a change in evangelical outlook. The sponsorship of Harringay by the Evangelical Alliance could have substantially narrowed Graham's support, but in the event evangelical Christianity was given a significant boost. In what was to be the last issue of *Evangelical Christendom* in September 1954, it was suggested that Harringay had indeed marked a turning point in the history of the Alliance.[66]

---

64  Executive Council Minutes, 25 March 1954.

65  *Evangelical Alliance Broadsheet*, Autumn 1961, p.5.

66  *Evangelical Christendom*, September 1954, p.65.

For Cattell, who liked to operate on a grand scale, Harringay had been a dream come true. Alliance staff numbers rose sharply as a direct result. After publication of *Evangelical Christendom* came to an end, a more popular style of magazine called *Crusade* was launched. Although its title confirmed an initial relation to the Harringay campaign, it was not a direct publication of the Alliance. For its part, the Council of the Alliance began at the same time to issue the *Evangelical Broadsheet* – a regular digest of about eight pages. Although there was a remarkable flurry of activity, it was evident that the level of Alliance staffing could not be maintained. Peter Hemery, a businessman who was brought in to look at the Alliance's affairs, dismissed most of the existing staff and set out in a letter to Maurice Rowlandson of 5 October 1954 his view that unless new projects were undertaken the Evangelical Alliance had 'a very frail future'. He believed that the only true Alliance matters were in the field of hostels and in the organising of the week of prayer. A smaller movement called the 'Movement for World Evangelisation' (MWE) was running the Filey Convention. The first Convention attracted 1,700 people, of whom 1,200 were under thirty-five years old. Hemery wondered whether the holiday camp group Butlins might link up with evangelical ventures directed at youth, but he did not see the Alliance as capable of running such a project.[67]

There had been plans to unite the Evangelical Alliance with the MWE, and Cattell had been earmarked as the probable secretary of the merged organisation. There had, however, been concern about Alliance overspending during the later period of Cattell's secretaryship. When it became clear that plans regarding the future were not coming to fruition as he had hoped, Cattell resigned from the Alliance and embarked on training for Anglican ministry. He was a curate at Christ Church, Beckenham, and then became Vicar of Moulton, Northamptonshire. At the point of Cattell's resig-

---

67 P. Hemery to M. Rowlandson, 5 October 1955. I am grateful to Maurice Rowlandson for this letter.

nation, some of the Alliance's council members were disturbed to learn that there was talk of Ben Peake from the Movement for World Evangelisation being appointed as Secretary of the Alliance. It emerged that there was opposition to this move and indeed a growing opposition to the merger as a whole.[68] By March 1956 it was clear that it was going to be impossible to merge the two bodies. Steps were taken to find a new General Secretary for the Alliance and Gilbert Kirby was persuaded by Hugh Gough to allow himself to be considered. Kirby was appointed as General Secretary from 1 November and together with his team, which included a gifted editorial secretary in Timothy Dudley-Smith (later bishop of Thetford and also well known for his hymns), and the entrepreneurial Rowlandson, he set to work mapping out the future of the Alliance.

Under Kirby's leadership evangelism continued to be seen as a fundamental commitment of the Alliance. Developments in the 1960s will be explored in chapter 10. It was accepted by some commentators in the late 1950s that Harringay had not been the beginning of a revival and that new ways forward in evangelism would need to be explored.[69] Kirby, who was intimately acquainted with the strengths and weaknesses of the Alliance, consistently took the view that its strength was the role that it could play in encouraging evangelicals to put evangelism and spiritual revival at the top of their agenda. Its weakness was that it was often able to bring only limited influence to bear when evangelicals disagreed. In the light of this, he attempted to bring evangelical leaders together in conferences. In 1959 Kirby wrote about the way in which evangelicals co-operated in mission through such organisations as the interdenominational overseas missionary societies, Keswick, the Children's Special Service Mission, the Inter-Varsity Fellowship and 'a host of kindred societies'. In the same issue of the Alliance's *Evangelical Broadsheet*, however, he referred to 'our

---

68 Honorary Secretaries of the Alliance to Sir Arthur Smith, 3 January 1956.
69 *Crusade*, March 1959, p.5.

sadly divided evangelical ranks'.[70] This aspect of the British
evangelical scene caused Kirby much concern and it was a situation he consistently sought to improve.

Kirby also worked hard to draw evangelicals together to engage in more effective mission overseas. He became secretary
of the Evangelical Missionary Alliance (EMA), which was
formed in November 1958, and which drew together forty
missionary societies and eight evangelical training colleges.
Within two years there were seventy societies and colleges in
EMA membership. John Savage, who was a member of the Executive Council of the Evangelical Alliance, was vice-Chair-
man of the EMA. As had been the case earlier in the century,
the challenge of Christian mission to a world that suffered
from divisions caused by ethnicity and by the unequal distribution of wealth raised the question of the divided state of Christianity. Reference was made in *Crusade* in 1960 to the role of
the missiologist Stephen Neill, who was working for the
World Council of Churches in Geneva. The editorial comment in *Crusade* reflected the continued view of the Alliance
about the unity of the church, a view that was at odds with that
of the WCC. 'The Church of Christ *is* one', was the argument,
'and our experience of that unity does not wait for a formal reunion of our churches'.[71] A body of enthusiasts united by the
Spirit, with a minimal structure such as that of the EMA, was
seen as the right kind of missionary expression.

## Conclusion

The evangelistic successes of the nineteenth century created
within British evangelicalism a belief that a certain style
needed to be adopted in order to be effective. The Moody and
Sankey method, which was adopted and adapted by Billy
Graham, was to be influential for at least one hundred years.

---

70  *The Evangelical Alliance Broadsheet*, Winter 1959, pp.1-3.
71  *Crusade*, March 1960, p.5.

There were new initiatives in the early decades of the twentieth century, most notably among youth, but it was the Billy
Graham crusades that were to bring fresh hope to many evangelicals. The beginnings of Graham's influence in Britain can
be located in the year immediately after the Second World
War. This was also a period that saw the re-vitalisation of the
Evangelical Alliance. New leaders such as Hugh Gough were
pleading for united action. In 1946 Gough stated: 'It is essential
that we should develop a deeper sense of our unity as members
of Christ's Holy Catholic Church. Evangelical individualism
has obscured the corporate spirit and our church life has been
sorely impoverished thereby.' Gough saw the post-war Alliance as a rallying point for all evangelicals who wished to combine their evangelistic efforts.[72] The earlier Alliance vision of
catholicity was still to be found. But the high hopes of the
mid-1950s, that responsible enthusiasts could come together
in broadly based evangelistic endeavour, would not be sustained. Indeed, as we shall see in the next chapter, just twelve
years after Harringay evangelical unity would be strained to
the limit.

---

72 *Evangelical Christendom*, January–March 1947, pp. 1f.

# 10

# Benevolent Neutrality

*The Alliance and the Ecumenical Movement*

Hugh Gough represented the thinking of a new wave of younger post-war leaders within the Alliance. In early 1947 he wrote: 'It is essential that we should develop a deeper sense of our unity as members of Christ's holy catholic church. Evangelical individualism has obscured the corporate spirit and our church life has been sorely impoverished thereby.'[1] Gough's comments were prompted by the formation of the World Council of Churches (WCC), which was then in process. Inevitably, the issue highlighted the question of evangelical relationships with the wider church. In 1946 the Alliance had stated that it had nothing but goodwill for the British Council of Churches and the WCC, calling them 'great and representative bodies'. At the same time, however, it had stressed that it was itself distinctively evangelical.[2] A request from the WCC in 1947 to merge WCC and Alliance weeks of prayer was duly rejected. Even so, Gough chose to reiterate the traditional Alliance theme of catholicity, and was keen to stress that although it was an association of individuals, it did not encourage individualism. The Council of the Alliance followed Gough's article later in the same year with an 'Evangelical Charter'. Some saw this as a statement of opposition to the World Council of

---

1 *Evangelical Christendom*, January–March 1947, pp.1–2.
2 *Evangelical Christendom*, April–June 1946, p.50.

Churches, but Gough denied the charge. Instead, he insisted, 'The World Council of Churches is out to achieve something which does not yet exist and that is the union of churches. We in the Alliance are out to demonstrate and foster something which already exists and that is the unity of the Spirit amongst all Christian people.'[3] As Kessler notes, the Alliance in 1846 was actually trying to achieve something that did not yet exist just as much as the World Council of Churches in 1948. Both were trying to *manifest* unity rather than merely *recognising* it. Having said this, their means to this end were undeniably different.[4] In fact, closer examination shows that these distinct approaches to unity led to enormous tensions.

## The Alliance and the World Council of Churches

The Alliance's Evangelical Charter of 1947 stated:

> As the World's Evangelical Alliance is an alliance not of churches, nor of church societies, but of individual Christians, its relationship with the World Council of Churches is clear. The World Council of Churches may (as some believe) have come into existence partly as a result of the prayers and witness of the World's Evangelical Alliance, but its objective is entirely different. The Alliance advocates the close unity of Protestantism and works for a more real fellowship between all evangelicals. It believes that here in real spiritual unity (a unity which already exists) and not in an outward uniformity (a uniformity which would have to be imposed against insuperable difficulties) lies the hope of revival and Christian victory.[5]

The first point of distinctiveness, that the Alliance was not an alliance of churches or church societies, was one that would not continue. By the 1960s, churches would be invited to join. Second, it is difficult to see the clear difference between the Alliance's advocacy of 'the close unity of Protestantism' and the early goals of the WCC. Although the ultimate objective of the

3 *Evangelical Christendom,* July–September 1947, p.79.
4 Kessler, *A Study of the Evangelical Alliance,* pp.91–2.
5 *Evangelical Christendom,* July–September 1947, p.79.

WCC was broader Christian unity, it was essentially a
Protestant initiative and brought together Protestants. Finally,
there is a supposed contrast between spiritual unity and outward uniformity. In fact, the WCC never stated that it was in
favour of uniformity, and the early leadership of the WCC was
certainly committed to spiritual as well as organisational oneness.

Although the issue of ecumenism would become highly
contentious among evangelicals, this was not so obvious in
1948. Kessler records that at least two (unnamed) members of
the British Alliance were present at the 1948 conference in
Amsterdam at which the World Council of Churches was
formed.[6] Moreover, in January of the following year this comment appeared in an *Evangelical Christendom* editorial:

> True evangelicals assure us that these dangers – 1) false union outside of the
> truth, 2) reunion with Rome, 3) formation of a super-church – have so far
> been successfully avoided. The Council (of the Alliance), therefore feel that
> the right policy for evangelicals is to avoid opposition to the World Council,
> but courageously to point out wrong tendencies and carefully and prayerfully
> to foster that unity of the Spirit, which already exists between all true believers
> and is something infinitely deeper than the outward form of union which the
> World Council has brought into being. If evangelicals oppose the World
> Council of Churches or abstain from co-operating with it, the Council may
> well be captured by the Modernists or the Ritualists, but if we play our part we
> may be an instrument in the hand of God for reviving the churches.[7]

Kessler regards this pronouncement as ambiguous. It could
mean, he suggests, that evangelicals were urged to co-operate
with other Christians in order that the World Council's
attempts at forming an organisational unity might by God's
grace be so deepened and extended as to result in a true unity
of the Spirit. However, it could also mean that evangelicals
were expected to inject into the World Council's basically
man-made and inessential unity the real unity that existed only
between true believers.[8] Frankly, it is harder to draw the second

---

6  Kessler, *A Study of the Evangelical* Alliance, p. 92.

7  *Evangelical Christendom,* January–March 1949, p. 1.

8  Kessler, *A Study of the Evangelical Alliance,* 92.

inference than the first, although it was hardly surprising that an Alliance pronouncement would give priority to the unity of the Spirit. Certainly, Hugh Gough's conviction in 1948 was that the Alliance could provide spiritual inspiration for the WCC and should continue to adopt a middle, or bridge, position.[9]

In the autumn of 1949 the Alliance Council looked again at the question of its attitude towards the WCC, but did not feel able to give full support to the new movement. Nonetheless, it is clear that the Alliance's leadership did not wish to be seen as being in conflict with the WCC, and resolved that 'the Alliance, for the time being therefore, will adopt an attitude of benevolent neutrality'.[10] In the meantime, steps were being taken by evangelicals in the USA to seek to set up a world evangelical fellowship – a plan that had, of course, faltered in 1846.[11] The Evangelical Alliance of the post-war period in Britain still carried the cumbersome and confusing title 'The World's Evangelical Alliance (British Organisation)'. This suggested some ambiguity as to the balance of its national and international status. There was a feeling, as the Alliance Council acknowledged in late 1949, 'that the Alliance is too much centred on Britain'. Evangelicals in some countries, however, understandably misconstrued the words 'British Organisation' as meaning that the entire Alliance was British-run. 'This', the Alliance Council conceded, 'tends to hold them back from closer co-operation with the parent body and in some cases has led to a national organization being formed with the same aims and objects as the Evangelical Alliance, but adopting another name in order to keep its national identity.'[12] There was pressure on the British Organisation, therefore, to foster transnational co-operation. From the British perspective, the World Council of Churches was undoubtedly a stimulus to thinking about wider evangelical unity, even if moves towards a world

---

9 Executive Council Minutes, 17 November 1948.

10 'The New Alliance', *Evangelical Christendom*, October–December 1949, p.86.

11 See Howard, *The Dream that Would Not Die*.

12 'The New alliance', *Evangelical Christendom*, October–December 1949, p.86.

fellowship were not made simply in response to the creation of the WCC.

In North America, however, there was a significant new evangelical movement dedicated to promoting evangelical unity. The American branch of the Evangelical Alliance had officially ceased to function in 1944 and a fresh body, the National Association of Evangelicals (NAE), had been formed.[13] This was to affect British evangelicals significantly. In 1946 Martyn Lloyd-Jones called a meeting at Westminster Chapel at which Harold J. Ockenga, the President of the NAE, was the speaker. This provoked Alliance fears that the NAE might be about to create a new pan-evangelical organisation in Europe. Hugh Gough went to see Lloyd-Jones about this, but he was non-committal about the American plans.[14] Lloyd-Jones did, however, persuade the NAE to consult Alliance leaders. It was understood that the NAE would wish to proceed on narrower and more exclusive lines than the Alliance.[15] In 1948 a meeting about possible world links was held in Clarens, Switzerland, and in preparation for that meeting Gough and Henry Martyn Gooch met in London with Lloyd-Jones and E.J. Poole-Connor, who in 1922 had founded the Fellowship of Independent Evangelical Churches (FIEC). Differences over policies of evangelical co-operation and the ecumenical dimension became increasingly apparent in the summer of 1948.[16] By the end of the year the FIEC had made it plain that it could not condone the way in which the Alliance invited to its platform those whose views were, from the FIEC standpoint, divergent from the Alliance's doctrinal basis.[17] This was a foretaste of divisions to come.

---

13  Howard, *The Dream that Would Not Die*, pp.26-7.
14  Executive Council Minutes, 25 April 1946; 25 July 1946.
15  Executive Council Minutes, 1 July 1948.
16  Executive Council Minutes, 22 July 1948; 23 September 1948.
17  Executive Council Minutes, 25 November 1948.

## The World Evangelical Fellowship

Given the differences of opinion in Britain, American interest
in the creation of a pan-evangelical body became crucial. It
was the outlook of the Americans, who were generally critical of the wider Christian scene in America outside evangelicalism, which would have a major influence on discussions in
the period 1948 to 1951. At the preliminary discussions in
Clarens, the view was expressed that the weakness of the
World Council of Churches was that it did not in any way
bind the members of the participating churches to the Basis
of Faith agreed upon by the delegates. From 7 to 10 March
1950 an International Delegate Conference was held at
Hildenborough Hall in Kent, the centre that had been set up
by the British evangelist, Tom Rees. Those who attended included representatives from twelve countries in Europe, including the British Evangelical Alliance organisation. There
were also delegates from the NAE in America. Lt.-Gen. Sir
Arthur Smith, Chairman of the British Alliance, was elected
Chairman of a new international committee and (partly in
view of the problems of 1846) it was agreed that a 'basis of
belief would be the foundation stone', while each affiliated
group would have freedom in 'the application of this basis to
their national situation'. [18]

More concrete steps towards a world fellowship were taken
at a conference at Gordon Divinity School in Boston, USA,
4–8 September 1950, at which it was recommended to set up
an International Association of Evangelicals. The agreed purpose of this body was: (i) to witness to evangelical and historic
Christianity; (ii) to encourage and promote fellowship among
evangelicals; (iii) to stimulate evangelism and promote united
evangelical action in all spheres. The proposed statement of
faith was as follows:

---

18  *World Evangelical Fellowship Bulletin*, No. 2 (1964), pp.1-2.

1   The inspiration and entire trustworthiness of the Holy Scriptures as originally given and their supreme authority in all matters of faith and conduct.
2   One God eternally existent in three Persons, Father, Son and Holy Ghost.
3   The deity of our Lord Jesus Christ, his virgin birth, his sinless human life, his divine miracles, his vicarious and atoning death, his bodily resurrection, his ascension, his mediatorial intercession, and his personal return in power and glory.
4   The salvation of lost and sinful man through the shed blood of the Lord Jesus Christ and regeneration by the Holy Spirit by faith apart from works.
5   The indwelling of the believer by the Holy Spirit enabling him to live a godly life and to witness to the Lord.
6   The resurrection both of the saved and the lost; they that are saved into the resurrection of life and they that are lost unto the resurrection of damnation.
7   The spiritual unity of all believers in our Lord Jesus Christ, composing his church, the Body of Christ.

This form of words drew to some extent from the 1846 Alliance statement of faith. There were some significant changes, however – most notably the omission of the statement about the right to private judgement, and the lack of an article on the ministry and the sacraments. By the 1950s, private judgement was not the issue that it had been a century before, and the new statement also reflected a loss of the sense of churchmanship among evangelicals. Perhaps even more significant was the insistence of evangelicals from the USA that the word 'infallible' should be inserted into the first article so that it read: 'The Holy Scriptures as originally given by God, divinely inspired, infallible, entirely trustworthy and the supreme authority in all matters of faith and conduct.' During this period of doctrinal debate and organisational development the involvement of the NAE was a notable feature. The NAE formed a Commission on International Relations with Harold Ockenga as Chairman and J. Elwin Wright (who had led a body called the New England Fellowship) as executive secretary. The purpose of this group was to encourage worldwide evangelical co-operation. Together with NAE leader Clyde W. Taylor, J. Elwin Wright was requested to make a world tour to contact evangelicals in as many countries as possible. From 12 October 1950 to 28 January 1951 Taylor and Wright undertook a punishing schedule, visiting Tokyo, Manila, Hong Kong, Bangkok, Calcutta, Bombay, New Delhi, Beirut, Damascus, Amman, Jerusalem, Athens, Rome, Zurich, Geneva, Marseilles, Barcelona, Paris, Amsterdam and London.[19]

This flurry of activity generated further interest. The international committee formed at Hildenborough Hall met in January 1951 at Woudschoten, a student conference centre on the outskirts of Zeist, near Utrecht, in the Netherlands. It was recommended that the name of the new body should be the World Evangelical Fellowship. The committee invited evangelicals from around the world to an international convention at Woudschoten in August 1951. Among the speakers was John Stott, rector of All Souls' Church, Langham Place, London who expounded the theme of 'The Holy Spirit and the Church'. The name World Evangelical Fellowship was approved. Because some who were present were wary of joining a group opposed to ecumenical endeavour, it was stated that the Fellowship was 'not a council of churches, nor is it in opposition to any other international or interdenominational organization. It seeks to work and witness in a constructive manner, ever maintaining the truth in love'.[20] There were still fears, however – particularly among evangelicals in Europe with whom British Alliance leaders had traditionally enjoyed good relationships – that the body might 'become ultra-fundamentalist and adopt a belligerent attitude towards the ecumenical movement'.[21]

19  Gilbert Kirby to Everett Cattell, 6 May 1965, cited by Howard, *The Dream That Would Not Die*, p.29. See also, Kessler, *A Study of the Evangelical Alliance*, pp.95-8.

20  N. Goodall, *The Ecumenical Movement* (London: Oxford University Press, 1964), p.153.

21  *Evangelical Alliance Broadsheet*, Autumn 1962, p.5.

Although most delegates affirmed the need for a worldwide fellowship of evangelicals, when the proposal to establish WEF was voted on there was not unanimity. Eleven countries were in favour, but Germany abstained, and France, Denmark, Norway and Sweden opposed it since they wanted the Alliance to continue as before. Indeed, Spain was the only continental European country that joined WEF. One of the main concerns among the Europeans was that the word 'infallible' implied too mechanical an understanding of biblical inspiration. There were also concerns that co-operation with those who might not hold to the Basis of Faith in its entirety was being prohibited. These objections led to some hesitation among representatives of the British Alliance, but they decided to join nonetheless.[22] A constitution was drawn up consisting of the following five points:

1   Belief without mental reservations in the basic doctrines of our faith as expressed in the statement of faith.
2   Acceptance into active co-operation with us of all who hold these doctrines and give evidence of loyalty to them, though there may be differences in conviction on other points of doctrine or of ecclesiastical policy.
3   Obedience to the commands of Scripture by renunciation of all co-operation with unbelief in or apostasy from these doctrines.
4   Recognition of the complete autonomy of every constituent national or area-wide body within the Fellowship.
5   Dedication to a programme of mutual helpfulness in the propagation of the gospel, the defence of Christian liberties and the attainment of objectives which are of common concern.

As well as the creation of a world evangelical fellowship, evangelical division also resulted from the Woudschoten conference. In 1952 representatives from several European countries

---

22  Executive Council Minutes, 24 July 1952.

met in Germany and established their own separate European Evangelical Alliance. The breach with WEF would not be healed until 1968, up to which point WEF was able to make little headway in Europe. The stance of WEF towards the World Council of Churches also created divisions of opinion. In 1962 it held a conference in Hong Kong and at that conference the delegates from the United States suggested that article 3 of the constitution, which already spoke about the limits of co-operation, should read: 'Obedience to the commands of Scripture by avoidance of any association which would compromise its loyalty to the statement of faith.' Many of the delegates present, however, felt that to adopt wording like this would mean that WEF would find itself in open conflict with the World Council Churches. This may have been the thinking of some who proposed the amendment, but after considerable discussion the proposal to change article 3 was dropped.[23] The neutrality of the British Alliance towards ecumenism was being maintained, but the conflict being played out on the world stage would soon become public in Britain.

## Roots of Division in Britain

As we have seen, the seeds of division over ecumenism lay in the 1940s. The anti-ecumenical convictions held by some British evangelicals during this period found institutional expression in the establishment in 1952 of the British Evangelical Council (BEC), then known as the British Committee for Common Evangelical Action. This was formed in St Columba's Free Church in Edinburgh. Its founders were G.N.M. Collins and Murdoch Macrae of the Free Church of Scotland and T.H. Bendor Samuel and E.J. Poole-Connor of the Fellowship of Independent Evangelical Churches. W.J. Grier of the Irish Evangelical Church, which became the Evangelical Presbyterian Church of Ireland, also later joined

---

23 Kessler, *A Study of the Evangelical Alliance*, pp.99-100.

the BEC. Strong elements within the BEC had separation from larger denominations at the core of their identity. The Free Church of Scotland and the FIEC gave official backing to the BEC. Carl McIntyre, the leader of the International Council of Christian Churches – a fiercely anti-ecumenical organisation based in North America – hoped that a British branch of the ICCC could be formed. Indeed, it was a conference held by McIntyre in Edinburgh in 1952 that stimulated the Free Church of Scotland to approach the FIEC about forming a new joint fellowship of evangelical churches. However, the BEC did not wish to be an appendage of an American body, aspects of whose spirit and stance its own leaders did not find acceptable.[24]

At this stage, the Evangelical Alliance was far more involved in evangelistic endeavour than it was in thinking about ecumenical issues. It was prepared to have dialogue with the British ecumenical body, the British Council of Churches, but this dialogue was focused on issues concerned with evangelism and the role of Billy Graham. In the mid-1950s, there was no reason to suppose that the BEC was going to play a significant part in British evangelicalism. Martyn Lloyd-Jones, who would later become a major supporter of the BEC, was quite willing to be associated in the 1950s with the Evangelical Alliance. Lloyd-Jones was the main speaker, for instance, at an Alliance day conference held in 1957 at Westminster Chapel. E.J. Poole-Connor, writing to Lloyd-Jones to thank him for his contribution on that occasion, took exception to the fact that Hugh Gough, who had also spoken, had contemplated co-operation with the World Council of Churches. Gough's efforts to argue for a bridge between evangelicals and the ecumenical movement were dismissed by Poole-Connor as 'the vaguest platitudes'.[25] Although Lloyd-Jones attended a luncheon

24  H.R. Jones, 'The Doctor and the British Evangelical Council', in H.R. Jones (ed.), *D. Martyn Lloyd-Jones: Unity in Truth* (Darlington: Evangelical Press, 1991), p.8.
25  E.J. Poole-Connor to D.M. Lloyd-Jones, 20 June 1957, cited in Murray, *D. Martyn Lloyd-Jones*, p.306.

arranged by the BEC in the Cora Hotel, Bloomsbury, in 1954, he did not join the organisation. This may be because he was opposed to para-church organisations, but it is more likely that he was wary of the BEC's relationship with the ICCC. He may also have considered that evangelicals had not had time to reflect on the issues involved in ecumenism.[26]

Such reflection was, however, taking place. In 1959 Gilbert Kirby, as General Secretary of the Alliance, published an article entitled 'Oecumenical Problems'. In it, he wrote: 'It is clear that spiritual unity can and does exist quite apart from ecclesiastical union. The great interdenominational missionary societies, the Keswick Convention, the Children's Special Service Mission, the Inter-Varsity Fellowship, the Evangelical Alliance and a host of kindred societies all bear witness to this fact.' He also referred to 'our sadly divided evangelical Ranks'.[27] The BEC was, at this point, seeking permission from Lloyd-Jones to print one of his sermons on revival, but the BEC had not yet been able to enlist Lloyd-Jones to its cause. The alternative visions of the Alliance and the BEC were, however, to become more evident in the early 1960s. An important assembly of the WCC was held at New Delhi in 1961. Although some evangelicals were present, evangelicals as a whole were seen as being opposed to the ecumenical movement because for them 'Christian unity is invisible' and because the WCC was being viewed by many evangelicals as theologically modernist and as seeking relations with Roman Catholics.[28] In his report on New Delhi, Kenneth Slack, General Secretary of the BCC, saw that assembly as formulating a conception of unity that 'departs wholly from any idea that Christian unity is a wholly "spiritual" idea'.[29]

---

26 Jones, 'The Doctor and the British Evangelical Council', pp.10-12.

27 *Evangelical Alliance Broadsheet*, Winter 1959, pp.1, 3.

28 J. Lawrence, *The Hard Facts of Unity: A Layman Looks at the Ecumenical Movement* (Naperville: SCM Book Club, 1961), p.65.

29 K. Slack, *Despatch from New Delhi: The Story of the World Council of Churches, Third Assembly, New Delhi, 18 Nov.–5 Dec. 1961* (London: SCM Press, 1962), p.79.

Despite all this, the Alliance itself desired a measure of organisational unity. Its stance continued to be an inclusive one, with a call being made in 1963 that in view of 'the growing influence of the ecumenical movement, evangelicals should overcome some of their petty differences and unite around the great fundamental verities of the Word of God and give evidence to the world of the spiritual unity that they already have in Christ'.[30] The way in which evangelicals united was more than by affirmation of their spiritual bonds, although at times Kirby appeared not to be sure how visible unity should be expressed. One method was by united celebration of the Lord's Supper. The 3,000 who gathered in the Royal Albert Hall in January 1963 for the united communion service arranged by the Alliance were, from the perspective of the Alliance, a visible demonstration of unity.[31] Both in 1962 and in 1963, Kirby reflected in *The Evangelical Broadsheet* on the prospects for unity. He recognised that evangelicals were divided in their assessment of the ecumenical movement, but considered that the Spirit was pointing Christian people towards spiritual unity. Evangelical Christians had been rediscovering the effectiveness of such unity when expressed in positive action. In some areas local Evangelical Fellowships had come into being and, through their agency, Bible Rallies and Conventions had been held. There had been a drawing together of evangelical societies, particularly in overseas mission. Over seventy societies and Bible colleges were by then linked together in the Evangelical Missionary Alliance. Kirby's appeal in 1963 was that in the light of 'the growing influence of the Ecumenical movement, evangelicals should overcome some of their petty differences and unite around the great fundamental verities of the Word of God and give evidence to the world of the spiritual unity that they already have in Christ'.[32] One united initiative in this

---

30  *Evangelical Alliance Broadsheet*, Summer 1963, supplement.

31  *The Christian*, 18 January 1963, p.1.

32  *Evangelical Broadsheet,* Summer 1963, Supplement to the National Association of Evangelicals Convention.

period was of enormous encouragement to Kirby. A 'Union and Communion' statement was prepared by an Alliance theological study group and signed in 1962 by forty evangelical leaders.[33] This was followed by a united communion service in the Royal Albert Hall. Ernest Kevan and John Stott preached. Some had told Kirby that to organise such a service was 'irresponsible', and others had expressed misgivings, but after the event the Alliance office had been deluged with letters expressing deep appreciation of the service.[34]

For all the success of the Albert Hall event, other evangelicals, however, were thinking seriously by this time in terms of more thoroughgoing, structural unity. In the period 1963 to 1965 J.I. Packer, who had been deeply involved in the revival of Reformed theology in Britain, served as a member of the Anglican-Methodist Unity Commission discussing the report *Conversations Between the Church of England and the Methodist Church*. Packer began to contemplate a comprehensive state church that excluded liberals but included Anglo-Catholics. Lloyd-Jones found this a disappointing development and stated his belief in the need for more independent evangelical churches.[35] In a parallel development at a Nottingham Faith and Order conference in 1964, 550 delegates from fifteen denominations passed a resolution inviting BCC member churches to work for unity by 1980. For the first time, evangelicals were represented in some strength at such a conference.[36]

Tensions were growing. Kirby, who was more acutely aware of the problems within evangelicalism than almost anyone else, began, in 1962, to plan for a National Evangelical Conference. This was eventually held in 1965. By this stage, Kirby had enabled churches as well as individuals to affiliate to the Alliance and 6,000 evangelical churches were invited to send delegates: 1,155 registrations were received. Anglicans formed

---

33  *Crusade,* December 1962, pp.18, 27.

34  *Evangelical Broadsheet,* Winter 1963, p.2.

35  Murray, *D. Martyn Lloyd-Jones,* pp.498–506.

36  *The Christian,* 25 September 1964, p.1.

the biggest group, with Baptists not far behind, followed by members of FIEC churches. The National Assembly of Evangelicals, as it was called, was held in Church House, Westminster. A number of Baptists, Methodists and Congregationalists who attended had begun to question whether their position in their denominations was tenable. For his part, Kirby stated: 'The evangelical is the loyalist in his denomination – our denominations owe their origins to the very things that we hold dear ... There is good historic evidence for staying in until we are thrown out.'[37] The Assembly decided to set up a representative Commission of nine people to study evangelical attitudes to ecumenism, denominationalism and a possible future united evangelical church.[38] A report was to be prepared by the Commission for the planned 1966 Assembly. Kirby wanted a balanced picture of evangelical views. Due deference must not, he suggested in July 1966, be given to the right wing or the left wing of evangelicalism.[39]

## Evangelicals in Disarray

In planning for the 1966 National Assembly of Evangelicals, Gilbert Kirby took a calculated risk by asking Martyn Lloyd-Jones and John Stott to play a prominent part in the opening session. What Lloyd-Jones said on that occasion did not surprise Alliance leaders. Indeed, he was asked by the Alliance to state publicly what he had said in private. Lloyd-Jones had put his views to the members of the commission and the members of the commission believed that he should have the opportunity to state his position. According to several commentators at the time and subsequently, Martyn Lloyd-Jones was advocating at the opening public session of the 1966 assembly that evangelicals should leave their denominations if

---

37	*The Christian*, 8 October 1965, p.1.
38	*Crusade*, December 1965, pp.18–9.
39	Executive Council Minutes, 27 July 1966.

those denominations were 'mixed' – that is, theologically compromised by liberalism.[40] Others, including Lloyd-Jones' biographer Iain Murray, have denied this.[41] If secession was implied at all, however, Lloyd-Jones did not specifically use the term 'separate' or 'secede'. As far as he was concerned, the key issue was the broader one of the doctrine of the Church. 'I would dare to suggest tonight', he said to his Alliance audience, 'that we find ourselves in a new situation. And the new situation has very largely been caused by the rising and revival amongst us of what is known as the ecumenical movement, which began in 1910, but has become a pressing problem to us as evangelicals, especially since 1948.'[42] It should be remembered, as Kessler notes, that just a month beforehand the British Council of Churches had covenanted for organic church union in Great Britain by Easter 1980, and that this may have served to make Lloyd Jones' statements all the more cutting.[43] Lloyd-Jones did refer to denominations being 'prepared to put everything into the melting pot in order that a new world church might come out of it' and spoke of Methodists and Anglicans, Congregationalists and Presbyterians as 'well on with their negotiations'.[44] As Robert Amess comments, the fact that a 'world church' has never shown any sign of emerging has not lessened the impact that Lloyd-Jones made.[45]

But Lloyd-Jones was not simply being negative. Indeed, he castigated evangelicals for being negative and being 'defensive in their denominational relationships'. On the one hand

---

40  For a recent expression of this viewpoint, and an account of its provenance, see D. W. Wright, 'A Review Article [of] *Evangelicalism Divided*…[by] Iain H. Murray', *Reformation and Revival,* 10:2 (Spring 2001), pp.121-36.

41  Murray, *D. Martyn Lloyd-Jones*, pp.513-33.

42  Evangelical Alliance, *Unity in Diversity: The Papers Given at the National Assembly of Evangelicals at Westminster, London, in October, 1966* (London: Evangelical Alliance, 1967), p.9.

43  Kessler, *A Study of the Evangelical Alliance*, p.107.

44  Evangelical Alliance, *Unity in Diversity,* p.9.

45  R. Amess, 'Evangelicals and the Ecumenical Movement' (unpublished M.Phil Thesis, Open University, 1998), p.154. I am indebted to the thesis by Robert Amess in this section.

Lloyd-Jones regarded the position of evangelicals as 'pathetic', 'tragic', and 'serious', especially in view of the ignorance that prevailed among evangelicals about the changing attitudes of Protestants to the Roman Catholic Church. On the other hand, Lloyd-Jones believed that 'evangelical people have got an opportunity today such as they have never had'. The opportunity, as Lloyd-Jones saw it, was to stop being only an evangelical wing in what he believed would become a 'comprehensive, total, national, territorial church', and instead to 'start afresh' and 'go back to the New Testament'. This kind of call was not new. It had been the vision of the Brethren movement in the nineteenth century. What made this occasion significant was the passionate call issued by Lloyd-Jones for a fellowship or association of evangelical churches, which would be free from what he saw as the compromises entailed in ecumenical or wider denominational involvement, and which instead would express 'evangelical ecumenicity'. It was inconsistent, in Lloyd-Jones' view, for evangelicals to unite with those with whom they agreed only on secondary matters. 'Why is it', he asked, 'that we are so anxious to hold on to our inherited positions?'[46]

As Robert Amess points out, to blame Lloyd-Jones for personally wrecking the serene waters through which evangelicalism seemed to be sailing at the time of the 1966 Assembly would not be just. It cannot be fairly argued, he suggests, that Lloyd-Jones abused the platform he was offered. He had been requested to express his view and he made it clear that he was not saying anything he had not previously said to the Alliance commission on church unity.[47] Neither was he directly responsible for what followed. John Stott, who was chairing the meeting, brought the evening to a sensational end by adding his own comments. Both history and Scripture, asserted Stott, were against what Lloyd-Jones had said. 'Scripture', Stott continued, 'is against him; the remnant was within the church not

---

46  Evangelical Alliance, *Unity in Diversity*, pp.11-3; Murray, *D. Martyn Lloyd-Jones*, pp.523-5.
47  Amess, '*Evangelicals and the Ecumenical Movement*', pp.155-6.

outside it. I hope no one will act precipitately.'[48] The outcome
of these events is not in dispute. 'One immediate consequence
was a deep division both between Anglican evangelicals and
many of their non-conformist brethren, but also among
non-conformist pastors and churches.'[49] But that meeting did
not cause the division. One Baptist writer commented about
that evening: 'I went to the Central Hall, that night, disillusioned with the Baptist Union, desiring closer unity with
evangelicals.'[50] This kind of comment indicates something of
the atmosphere of the times. There were evangelicals who
were disillusioned with denominations, even when, as with the
Baptist Union, the majority of those who were within a denomination were evangelical. This disillusionment would lead
not only to secessions from denominations but to the emergence of new churches – something that would in turn result
in the forming of new denominations.

The 1966 Assembly continued with other business. The report prepared for the assembly referred to the option of 'a
united evangelical church on denominational lines'. The commission stated that it had found no widespread support for
such a move. Rather, it encouraged 'evangelical churches of
varying traditions' to form effective fellowships both locally
and nationally.[51] In the debate that followed, points were made
on both sides of the argument, with some supportive of secession. Still, a large majority adopted the report of the commission. Positions had, however, publicly polarised and attitudes
were palpably hardening. *The Church of England Newspaper*,
which represented an inclusive position, dismissed what
Lloyd-Jones had said as 'nothing short of hare-brained'.[52] The
reporter for *Crusade*, influenced no doubt by Gilbert Kirby's

48  Murray, *D. Martyn Lloyd-Jones*, pp.523–5; E. Davies, '18 October 1966: Its context, message and significance', in *Foundations*, No. 37 (1996), p.11.
49  Davies, '18 October 1966', p.11.
50  B. Howlett, '18 October 1966: I was there …', *Foundations*, No.37 (1996), p.16.
51  *Report of the Commission on Church Unity to the National Assembly of Evangelicals* (London, 1966).
52  *The Church of England Newspaper*, 28 October 1966, p.5.

restraint, was content to call the opening session of the assembly 'adult stuff'.[53] Looking back over a decade later, Kirby felt that encouraging Lloyd-Jones to put his case had been 'probably one of my biggest mistakes'.[54] Evangelicals committed to separation from theologically 'mixed' denominations would associate increasingly with the BEC. Morgan Derham, who followed Kirby as the General Secretary of the Alliance, commented gloomily that evangelicals were being pushed to make a choice between denominations and individualistic anarchy.[55]

## The Aftermath of the Assembly

Hopes of conciliation within the evangelical constituency were largely dashed at a packed meeting of the Westminster Fellowship of ministers in November 1966 when Lloyd-Jones made the issues clear. There was, he said, an unmistakeable cleavage between those who believed in staying in their denominations and those who saw no purpose in so doing. From now on, he added, he would offer his help only to ministers already out of their denominations or thinking of leaving.[56] The stance taken by Lloyd-Jones gave a huge boost to the FIEC and the BEC. In 1967 Westminster Chapel, which had previously been in the Congregational Union, joined the FIEC, and the numbers at the BEC's 1967 conference mushroomed to 2,700 when Lloyd-Jones spoke. The same year saw the launch of *Evangelical Times,* a monthly 'separatist' newspaper edited by Peter Masters, previously a member of Westminster Chapel. Two main reasons were advanced in favour of its appearance. First, it would meet the need for a means of communication between thousands of churches, missions and assemblies in Britain that were wholly evangelical, self-governing, unaffiliated to denominational bodies and usually

53  *Crusade,* December 1966, p.33.
54  *Crusade,* October 1979, p.56.
55  *Crusade,* October 1966, p.13.
56  Murray, *D. Martyn Lloyd-Jones,* pp.528-31.

strongly opposed to ecumenicity. Secondly, it would serve as a contrast to existing popular Christian journals that adopted a benevolent or at best strictly neutral attitude towards the ecumenical movement.

Meanwhile, Anglican evangelicals were travelling in a different direction. The historic National Evangelical Anglican Congress held at Keele University in April 1967 declared the following:

> The initial task for divided Christians is dialogue at all levels and across all barriers. We desire to enter this ecumenical dialogue fully. We are no longer content to stand apart from those with whom we disagree. We recognize that all who 'confess the Lord Jesus Christ as God and Saviour according to the Scriptures and therefore seek to fulfil together their common calling to the glory of the one God, Father Son and Holy Spirit (World Council of Churches Basis) have a right to be treated as Christians, and it is on this basis that we wish to talk with them.[57]

The older evangelical view, that ecclesiology was a 'secondary' matter, was being questioned – not least because of the neo–Puritan movement's emphasis on the church.[58] It was perceived at the time that Keele, with its new stress on the visible church and on wider ecclesiastical involvement, would loom large in the annals of Anglican evangelicalism.[59] The Alliance's position, as a force for evangelical unity, was under threat. Morgan Derham considered that it was essential for the Alliance to find ways of restoring belief in pan-evangelical co-operation. The Alliance attempted to do this by encouraging the formation of regional and local evangelical fellowships, conferences and meetings of ministers. Anglican evangelicals were involved in such events. For instance, one of their leaders, Michael Cole, was prominent at a Northern Alliance Conference in 1967.[60]

---

57 National Evangelical Anglican Congress, *Keele '67, The National Evangelical Anglican Congress Statement*, p.37.
58 C. O. Buchanan, *Is the Church of England Biblical?* (London: Darton, Longman & Todd, 1998), pp.6–7.
59 *The Christian*, 14 April 1967, p.2.
60 Executive Council Minutes, 27 July 1967.

These attempts did not, however, placate the separatist wing. At a meeting of the Alliance's Executive Council in October 1967 it was reported that resignations had been received from John Caiger and T.H. Bendor-Samuel, both of whom 'were finding themselves in a difficult position, due to their positions in the Westminster Fellowship and the British Evangelical Council respectively'. At the same meeting considerable discussion took place regarding 'the increasing activity of the separatist movement associated with the BEC'. There had been meetings between Alliance and BEC leaders with the aim of establishing a working relationship,[61] and it was decided by the Alliance Executive Council that it would be good to meet again and to come to an agreement on 'professional etiquette'. It was noted that very few individuals or churches had withdrawn from the Alliance.[62] In the same period Roland Lamb, who had been a Methodist minister, was appointed as part-time secretary to the BEC in order to promote what was at the time a growing movement.

The major figure within the separatist constituency was, however, Lloyd-Jones. Sir Fred Catherwood, Lloyd-Jones' son-in law and a deacon of Westminster Chapel at the time, speaks of Lloyd-Jones' 'passionate plea for evangelical unity'. He comments on the result of Lloyd-Jones' concerns:

> Evangelicals divided instead of uniting. In retrospect it is easy to say that he should have left it there. But the vocal minority, who wanted to translate his plea into a united evangelical church, also wanted him as their leader, and he was identified with them and lost to the evangelical majority.[63]

One result of the October 1966 debacle and the events that followed was that the separatists were perceived as a single-issue party.[64] It was not obvious to the bulk of evangelicals that the ecumenical movement was as central to the

---

61  Executive Council Minutes, 25 May 1967.

62  Executive Council Minutes, 14 December 1967.

63  F. Catherwood, *At the Cutting Edge* (London: Hodder & Stoughton, 1995), p.65.

64  Amess, 'Evangelicals and the Ecumenical Movement', p.158.

ecclesiastical scene as the separatists seemed to believe. Alan Gibson, who became the General Secretary of the BEC, wrote in 1988: 'Perhaps that was one weakness of evangelical beliefs in 1966 – they gave more credence to the power of the ecumenical movement than it merited.'[65]

## The Doctrine of the Church

Despite the rupture that had taken place in evangelicalism, there were continuing relationships between those who differed on the ecumenical movement. An attempt was made in 1970 to engage in constructive dialogue on the subject through a day conference in London on the 'Doctrine of the Church'. This brought together thirty-four evangelical leaders. The event was held at the Alliance offices, but was not officially sponsored by the Alliance. At a time when evangelical Anglicans were widely thought to have taken on the Keele agenda to the detriment of pan-evangelical concerns, it is significant twelve Anglican clergy were present, and that they formed the largest denominational group at the conference. Included among them were Raymond Turvey from St George's Church, Leeds, who was a co-chair of the conference, J.I. Packer from Tyndale Hall, Bristol, and Colin Buchanan from St John's College, Nottingham. These three had been invited to speak, but others in attendance included Alan Stibbs from Oak Hill College, London, Michael Saward from the Church Information Office, and R.T. Beckwith and J.W. Wenham from Latimer House, Oxford. It had been hoped to have a residential conference, but the publication in 1970 of the book *Growing into Union*, part-authored by Packer and Buchanan, and espousing evangelical–Anglo-Catholic co-operation, had caused fresh tension within British evangelicalism.[66]

---

65 A. Gibson, *Holding Hands in the Dark* (St Albans, 1988), frontispiece.
66 C.O. Buchanan, E.L. Mascall, J.I. Packer, & The Bishop of Willesden, *Growing into Union: Proposals for Forming a United Church in England* (London: SPCK, 1970), p.255.

Free Church leaders at the conference were divided between those who were separatist by inclination and those who were open to wider denominational involvement. The Baptists included David Pawson from Guildford, one of the sponsors of the conference, Robert Horn from Horley Baptist Church, who was a speaker, Paul Helm from the University of Liverpool, Graham Harrison from Newport, and Ron Luland from Bedford. Some of these Baptists were within the Reformed constituency. John Doggett represented the Strict Baptists. There were no members of the Methodist, Congregational or Presbyterian denominations present, apart from Iain Murray, an independent Presbyterian, and D.O. Swann, an independent Congregationalist. FIEC/independent representatives included Leith Samuel from Above Bar Church, Southampton, who was a co-chair, David Middleton from Surrey Chapel, Norwich, who was a speaker, Michael Buss from Tollington Park Baptist Church, and Alan Gibson, then a pastor in Winchester. Harold Rowdon and H.L. Ellison, both of whom were well known for their Bible College teaching, represented the Brethren, and John Lancaster and Eldon Corsie the Elim Pentecostal denomination. John Laird, the former General Secretary of Scripture Union, was the Chairman. Morgan Derham and Gordon Landreth, past and present General Secretaries of the Alliance, were also in attendance. Landreth acted as secretary to the conference, and it is symbolic of the Alliance's 'benevolently neutral' policy on ecumenical matters at this time that his role was essentially one of quiet note taking.

The main speakers presented their papers. From the Anglican side, Colin Buchanan argued that *Growing into Union* had not changed the situation among Anglican evangelicals. As had been set out at Keele, they wished to be involved both in Anglican affairs and in relationships with other evangelicals. Packer acknowledged the mistrust and pain that had been caused by the book's publication. He had spent much of his life with Free Church evangelicals and hoped that the conference would result in greater understanding. Regarding the nature of the church, Packer questioned whether apostolic practices were norms for all time. Earlier generations had been divided over this matter. On the ecumenical issue, Packer argued that it was legitimate to talk to people in the ecumenical movement and in the Church of Rome. These were highly complex bodies and it was extremely difficult, in his view, to simplify what was going on within them. Packer saw any approach that put everything in unduly black and white categories as 'sectarian'.[67]

In response, David Middleton said that Free Church evangelicals had hitherto thought that evangelical unity was more important than denominational unity, but the attitude of evangelical Anglicans was throwing doubt on this assumption. He wondered whether the uniqueness of Scripture as the authority for the church had been betrayed in *Growing into Union*. Robert Horn took up the question of episcopacy. It had been thought that evangelical Anglicans regarded episcopacy as of the *bene esse* of the church, but it seemed that the new approach was to regard it as of the *esse* of the church – that is, as intrinsic and indispensable rather than merely preferable. In *Growing into Union* fellowship seemed to be on the basis of the episcopacy rather than the gospel. 'Regarding future relationships among evangelicals', said Horn, 'church issues could not be isolated and all interdenominational activity was affected by the present tensions, including the work of Societies like Scripture Union, I.V.F., etc'. He asked how evangelical Anglicans related their position to these societies and whether they had faced the implications of the new lack of consensus among British evangelicals.[68]

Both Buchanan and Packer responded to these statements. Buchanan accepted that there were different views of the doctrine of the church among evangelicals – hence the conference. He asked Free Church evangelicals to accept the integrity of their Anglican brethren. He added later that the

---

67 Evangelical Alliance, Record of a Private Day Conference on the Doctrine of the Church, 8 September 1970, pp.1–3.

68 Ibid., pp.3–4.

two Anglo-Catholics they had worked with, Graham Leonard and Eric Mascall, were serious about sharing real theological concerns. Packer asserted that it was wrong to say that *Growing into Union* placed Scripture and tradition on an equal footing. Scripture must test tradition. On the subject of church order, episcopacy had been defended in *Growing into Union* as a 'meaningful sign' of the identity of the church. Confession of the faith and the sacraments were also signs. Finally, he acknowledged that there were omissions in *Growing into Union*. The way of conversion had not been spelled out. Justification by faith had also received a barely adequate treatment.[69]

The ecumenical issue became a focus in subsequent discussion. Some who considered ecumenical involvement to be a mistake believed that through ecumenical discussions in which evangelicals took part evangelical orthodoxy was being diluted. Leith Samuel said he had hoped that Anglican evangelicals would 'stand together with all evangelicals when the question of the church was in the melting pot', but that now they 'were looking the other way'. H.L. Ellison took the view that there were not two standpoints, Anglican and Free Church, but three. The third he believed was that of the radical reformation. This might have seemed to complicate matters further. There was, however, sufficient common ground for the conference members to suggest that a small working group should go on discussing the issues. It was proposed that Gordon Landreth should discuss this with Roland Lamb so that future initiatives should, if possible, have the co-operation of the BEC.[70] This conference illustrated that at the beginning of the 1970s deep feelings of suspicion and of distrust, as well as genuine doctrinal differences, had emerged among British evangelicals. At the same time, however, there at least remained a willingness to talk together. The inclusive vision of the Alliance had suffered a severe blow, but it was not dead.

---

69  Ibid., pp.4-5.
70  Ibid., pp.8-10.

# Conclusion

After the Second World War, issues connected with the ecumenical movement were raised by the creation and increasing
role of the World Council of Churches. For the Evangelical
Alliance the ecumenical vision was not new, although its priority had traditionally been spiritual. What divided evangelicals increasingly in the 1950s and early 1960s was the
question of whether the vision for unity should also be
churchly. The World Evangelical Fellowship took a narrower
position. In Britain, Martyn Lloyd-Jones espoused a strongly
anti-ecumenical stance, and this helped to polarise evangelicals in the mid-1960s. For a time it seemed that separatism
would pose a major challenge to the Alliance's traditional role
as a body that included all shades of evangelicals. Despite all
this, as the 1970s progressed, mainstream evangelicals, and a
growing charismatic evangelical constituency, would see the
separatists somewhat marginalised. After the death of
Lloyd-Jones in 1981, these separatists would lack a leader or
leaders of the stature they needed. Separatists themselves tend
to agree with this analysis: 'One obvious difference between
1966 and 1996', writes Geoffrey Thomas, 'is the figure of Dr
Lloyd-Jones ... Our greatest weakness is a lack of an awakening ministry in the nation.'[71] In the meantime, evangelicals
within most of the historic denominations would see
their own influence increase. Indeed, as we shall see in the
remaining four chapters, a more avowedly inclusivist Alliance
would emerge from the crisis of 1966, and would gradually
recover to become a powerful force within British Christianity.

---

71  G. Thomas, 'Then and Now: 1966–1996', *Foundations* No. 37 (1996), p.32.

11

# The Other Side

*The Alliance and Renewal from the 1960s to the early 1980s*

As the 1960s brought dramatic challenges to established norms, so evangelicalism in Britain was profoundly affected by the rise of the charismatic movement. The two developments were not unconnected; as Nigel Scotland observes, they both indicated a new hunger for spiritual reality:

> The 1960s ... saw the emergence of the hippie culture which was a reaction to the materialism of the 'never had it so good' post-war years under Harold Macmillan. Prompted by Timothy Leary, people began to take drugs in the hope of getting in touch with some deeper level of reality. Others followed the example of the Beatles and began to look East for meaning. The Maharishi and the practice of meditation became the focus of many hopes in a country which was losing its way spiritually. The charismatic experience which began to emerge in England in the 1960s was to some extent part of this environment. On the one hand, it was a reaction away from enlightenment thinking. On the other, it reflected the widespread quest of the time for the exotic and the culturally new. Western evangelicalism was very much a one dimensional affair in which the middle classes, reinforced by Intervarsity paperbacks, looked for 'sound' teaching. But for most, there was little in it beyond a certain satisfaction of having been able to bend one's mind around a 'good word'. At the same time existentialist thinking which emphasised the importance of the present moment prompted people to seek new experiences and the growing popularity of television increased their desire for deeper emotional and spiritual satisfaction.[1]

---

1 N. Scotland, *Charismatics and the New Millennium* (2nd edn; Guildford: Eagle, 2000), pp.36-7.

Of course, these cultural interactions were not immediately apparent, and early participants in the charismatic movement were far more concerned with its potential for transforming their understanding and experience of God the Holy Spirit.[2] In 1963, speaking as General Secretary of what was now popularly referred to by the initials 'EA', Gilbert Kirby drew attention to an encouraging trend. A good many Christians, he noted, were 'applying themselves to the detailed study of the biblical doctrine of the Holy Spirit, and we can but hope that this will clarify evangelical thinking on this vital matter'. Kirby recognised that there were long-standing disagreements over the 'baptism of the Spirit', the filling of the Spirit and spiritual gifts – not least between classical Reformed evangelicals and Pentecostals. Since its rise in the United States in the first years of the twentieth century, Pentecostalism had generally adopted evangelical doctrine, but its emphasis on Spirit baptism as a 'second blessing' after conversion, and on speaking in tongues as 'initial evidence' of that baptism, had caused friction.[3] The Alliance was, in fact, no stranger to such friction. As early as 1908 the apologist Sir Robert Anderson argued in *Evangelical Christendom* that Pentecostalism 'subordinates the great facts and truths of the Christian revelation to the subjective experience of the Christian life'.[4] Campbell Morgan of Westminster Chapel suggested a year later that the 'tongues movement' was evil.[5] At the start of the 1960s, the charismatic movement was beginning to bring Pentecostal emphases into mainline denominations – hence its technical identification as 'neo-Pentecostalism'. Now, however, Kirby trusted that the

2  For a detailed account of the rise of the charismatic movement during this period see P. Hocken, *Streams of Renewal: The Origins and Early Development of the Charismatic Movement in Great Britain* (rev'd edn; Carlisle: Paternoster Press, 1997 [1986]).

3  For more detail see W.K. Kay, *Pentecostals in Britain* (Carlisle: Paternoster Press, 2000).

4  *Evangelical Christendom*, March–April, 1908, p.48.

5  *Evangelical Christendom*, March–April 1909, p.37.

Alliance would respond more eirenically: the days were gone, he hoped, when evangelicals would write booklets dismissing Pentecostalism, or its newer expressions, as 'a delusion of the Devil'. He also looked for 'increasing charity' from Pentecostals, so that those who had not travelled by the same pathway might be seen as equally committed to 'the deepening of spiritual life'.[6] Kirby's desire was for a greater openness to the Spirit that would lead to renewal.

This chapter will look at the theme of renewal in relation to the Alliance. The charismatic movement may have been a fresh form of spirituality, but it was not the only expression of renewal in the 1960s and 1970s. There were also attempts to find ways forward in evangelism. In 1966 the Alliance's National Assembly of Evangelicals set up a commission to look at mission. The report of the commission was published in 1968 and was entitled *On the Other Side*. The introduction referred to the danger of passing by 'on the other side' (Lk. 10), to Jesus and his disciples coming 'to the other side' (Mk. 5), venturing into unknown territory in mission, to the disciples casting their nets 'on the other side' (Jn. 21) in a change of strategy, and to crowds finding Jesus 'on the other side' (Jn. 6). Taken together, the thrust of these passages from the gospels, and the thrust of the report, was the need to cross over boundaries. For the authors, the call was to Christians to be willing to 'alter traditional methods' in their evangelism.[7] This chapter will look at the report and its consequences, and also examine the way in which, in the 1970s, evangelism was increasingly linked with social action. Finally, we shall see how the Alliance itself was seeking, in the later 1970s and early 1980s, to find a renewed vision.

---

6  G.W. Kirby, 'In All Things – Charity', *The Evangelical Alliance Broadsheet*, Winter 1963, p.2.

7  Evangelical Alliance, *On the Other Side: The Report of the Evangelical Alliance's Commission on Evangelism*, (London: Evangelical Alliance, 1968), pp.13-4.

## Spiritual Unity in Action

As the 1960s began the Alliance seemed to be operating with a strong and united team. Gilbert Kirby was advocating 'Spiritual Unity in Action' as a core value for the Alliance. In the Annual Report for 1959-60 he explained that the work of the Alliance at that point fell into two categories. There were special projects, such as the hostels in London, the evangelistic film work led by Maurice Rowlandson, the extensions secretary, the production of a monthly magazine edited by David Winter, *Crusade*, and the organisation of the week of prayer. Alongside this Kirby described what he termed the strategic work of the Alliance, speaking for evangelical Christians and acting in their interests. The Alliance provided a 'platform' on which evangelicals united, he said. In this respect its twenty-strong Executive Council was important. In 1960 it drew together Anglican evangelical clergymen such as John Stott, Kenneth Prior, Maurice Wood, L.F.E. Wilkinson and Frank Colquhoun, Baptist ministers such as Geoffrey King, Ernest Kevan and John Caiger, a Presbyterian in Tom Allan from Glasgow, Methodists such as Howard Belben, the secretary of the FIEC and T.H. Bendor-Samuel, missionary leaders like John Savage, and prominent military laymen such as Lt.-Gen. Sir Arthur Smith (the Chairman), Lt.-Gen. Sir William Dobbie and Major W.F. Batt. By their united contribution, the Alliance's leaders played, as Kirby saw it, a unique role in co-ordinating evangelical witness.[8]

This witness was varied. The emphasis in many evangelistic presentations of this period in Britain was on seeking to present an apologia for the Christian faith, and the Alliance was prominent in this. In 1961 it organised a National Bible Rally at the Royal Albert Hall to mark the 350th anniversary of the Authorised Version of the Bible – at this time the most widely used version among evangelicals. Sir Kenneth Grubb, President of the Church Missionary Society and a well-known

---

8 *Evangelical Alliance Annual Report, 1959-60*, pp.1-2.

figure within the World Council of Churches, was the chairman. Speakers brought a range of perspectives. Robert (later Sir Robert) Boyd, then lecturer in physics at University College, London, spoke on 'A Scientist and his Bible'. Another speaker was D.J. Wiseman, Professor of Assyriology at London University, whose subject was 'An Archaeologist and his Bible'. Martyn Lloyd-Jones gave a typically rousing biblical address.[9] The Alliance also involved itself in overseas mission. Overseas tours were undertaken, especially by A.J. Dain (the overseas secretary), and after he left to take up a position with the Church Missionary Society of Australia these contacts were to some extent taken up through the growing Evangelical Missionary Alliance (EMA). Initially the Evangelical Alliance and the EMA shared a number of key personnel, with John Caiger as Chairman of the EMA, Kirby as secretary and Col. C.D.O. Pugh as secretary of both bodies.

In 1962 Gilbert Kirby gave an illuminating survey in the Alliance's publication, *The Evangelical Broadsheet,* of spiritual trends in Britain at that point. Pre-war theological liberalism he saw, rather optimistically, as being 'as dead as the dodo'. There were certainly signs in theological circles of growing evangelical influence. Kirby highlighted the fact that Bible and theological colleges in which the main emphasis was upon the authority of the word of God were filled. With this new emphasis on the Bible had come a renewed interest in the Reformed faith. The writings of Calvin and of the Puritans were being re-published by the Banner of Truth Trust and were being read again. Another feature to which Kirby drew attention was the renewed interest in and discussion of the nature and character of evangelism. He highlighted a tendency amongst evangelical Christians to reassess the place of mass evangelism in the churches' programme. Partly as a result of the revival of Reformed thinking and thus of the awareness of doctrines associated with divine sovereignty, the methods employed in mass evangelism had, Kirby noted, been under fire in some quarters. The relationship

---

9  We are grateful to Maurice Rowlandson for the programme of this evening.

of evangelism to the sovereignty of God was being frequently
debated in evangelical circles in the early 1960s. Kirby argued
that whatever particular views evangelicals might hold in relation to these issues, the fact remained that the Spirit had awakened the church to the need for evangelism.[10]

Kirby was also concerned for unity within local churches.
The 1960s saw the accentuation of the generation gap, and for
Kirby this could have serious consequences for unity. He
pointed out that in the post-war years the accent had been on
youth. Through government agencies huge sums of money
were being spent on local youth committees and facilities for
recreation. The church, too, had become increasingly absorbed
in catering for youth. By the early 1960s there were many more
Christian youth movements than there had been before the war.
Many facilities were provided for young people in local
churches. Kirby did not wish to question the importance of
young people in the churches, but saw dangers in any tendency
among youth to dominate the scene and for youth activities, and
even youth movements, to become an end in themselves. A
New Testament church, he argued, was a family, and different
generations had to live together. The tendency, he observed, had
been one of segregation. In some churches separate Bible studies
were being provided for different age groups. Kirby questioned
whether 'this is in fact following the pattern of New Testament
Christianity'.[11] The charismatic movement was to appeal to a
younger generation, intent on rediscovering the dynamic of the
New Testament churches. Despite Kirby's hopes for unity, this
movement would contribute to increased tensions.

## The Third Person of the Trinity

'When we come to deal with the doctrine of the third Person
of the blessed Trinity', said Kirby in 1964, 'our tendency to be

10 G.W. Kirby, 'The Post-War Years', *Evangelical Alliance Broadsheet*, Summer
1962, pp.1-3.
11 Ibid., pp.1-3.

unbalanced once more shows itself.' He argued that evangelicals found it difficult to show equal enthusiasm for the gifts of
the Spirit and the fruit of the Spirit, and suggested that in some
quarters there was a greater emphasis on the importance of
'ecstatic utterances' than seemed to be the case in the New Testament.[12] This was certainly a period when there was great
interest in spiritual gifts. It was in 1962 that many evangelicals
in Britain became aware of this 'new Pentecostal' movement in
mainline Protestant churches. An American Episcopal clergyman, Dennis Bennett, had announced in 1960 to his parish in
Van Nuys, California, that he had received the baptism of the
Spirit and had spoken in tongues. The experiences at Van
Nuys were publicised through a magazine entitled *Trinity*,
backed by a Pentecostally minded Episcopalian and edited by
Jean Stone, a member of Bennett's congregation. Copies of
*Trinity* were distributed to a number of British evangelicals in
March 1962. Interest was further stimulated later that year.
Philip Hughes, a respected Anglican evangelical scholar and
editor of the journal *Churchman*, visited California and wrote
about 'indications of a new movement of the Holy Spirit'.[13]

The Alliance was quick to respond to this new development. It was reported that in 1963 at a quarterly seminar that
brought evangelical scholars together under the auspices of the
Alliance, 'scholarly papers have been read by evangelical theologians, dealing with different aspects of the work of the Holy
Spirit'. Although this seminar was limited in size, it included a
cross-section of denominational life – Anglicans, Methodists,
Baptists, Congregationalists, members of the Christian
Brethren, and Pentecostalists.[14] One issue raised in these discussions was whether any new emphasis on the gifts of the
Spirit would of necessity lead to the forming of new denominations – as had happened with many who were caught up in
the Pentecostal movement at the beginning of the century – or

---

12  *The Evangelical Alliance Broadsheet*, Summer 1964, pp.2-3.

13  'Editorial', *Churchman*, September 1962, p.131.

14  *The Evangelical Alliance Broadsheet*, Winter 1963, p.2.

whether, as with the Anglican priest Alexander Boddy in his ministry in Sunderland, renewal could come within the denominations.[15] For Kirby, it was a healthy sign that the rediscovery of the doctrine of the Spirit had associations with a renewed interest in the doctrine of the church. Evangelical Christians, in his experience, had not been renowned for their sense of churchmanship. Instead, they had often been marked by excessive individualism. It was as a counter to this individualistic and fissiparous tendency that Kirby, in line with the historic catholicity of the Alliance, tried to bring people together. He spoke of 'countless private consultations between evangelical leaders', most of which could not be written about, that were taking place in the boardroom of the Alliance in 1963.[16]

The relationship between the Alliance and this new expression of spiritual renewal was not, however, only at the level of discussion. The Alliance shared the charismatic movement's concern for revival and applauded the 'Nights of Prayer for Revival' being held in the early 1960s. These had their beginnings in the early 1950s when George and May Ingram, who had been missionaries with the Church Missionary Society in India (George received an MBE for his work among 'untouchables'), became involved in the prayer committee for the forthcoming Billy Graham Crusade. The Ingrams developed a friendship with Colin Kerr, a well-known Keswick speaker and the vicar of St Paul's, Portman Square, where some of the prayer meetings were held. From 1957 they led monthly 'Nights of Prayer for Worldwide Revival' and began to produce news-sheets which by the time of George Ingram's death in 1969 had a print-run of 6,000 copies. In 1959, the centenary of the 1859 revival, Ingram attended Westminster Chapel regularly to hear a series of sermons on revival preached by Martyn Lloyd-Jones. In the same year, Ingram launched the Anglican Prayer Fellowship for Revival (APFR), and he and

---

15 E. Blumhofer, 'Alexander Boddy and the Rise of Pentecostalism in Great Britain', *Pneuma* 8.1 (1986), pp.31–40.

16 *The Evangelical Alliance Broadsheet*, Summer 1962, pp.1–3; Winter 1963, p.2.

others began to concentrate on prayer that the clergy of the parish of All Souls, Langham Place, which was Ingram's parish, would experience the baptism of the Spirit. Ingram understood this as an experience of entire sanctification, although others who were close to him saw Spirit-baptism as linked with the gift of tongues. The new Pentecostal outlook developed partly out of a concern for revival.[17]

Martyn Lloyd-Jones met with Michael Harper, a curate at All Souls, Langham Place, and with other Anglicans who were affected by the new charismatic movement. He spoke about the subject in an address to the annual meeting of the Evangelical Library in December 1963. Although he had serious questions about aspects of what was happening at that time, he affirmed the longing for deeper spirituality.[18] Neither Lloyd-Jones nor Gilbert Kirby held the view that the charismatic gifts were confined to the apostolic age. It was on other grounds that Kirby raised questions about the exercise of spiritual gifts. He was concerned, rather, about what he saw as a danger of distortion in the assessment of gifts. In February 1964 Kirby wrote in *Crusade* and later in the year in *The Evangelical Broadsheet* about what he took to be the major dangers posed by the new developments within evangelicalism. One was the claim that speaking in tongues was essential 'initial evidence' of the experience of the baptism of the Spirit. The other was the danger of dismissing tongues, since, Kirby believed, 'whenever and wherever God pours out his Spirit in abundance there are unusual manifestations'.[19] From the beginning therefore, the Alliance showed its sympathy towards renewal within historic denominations. This gathered strength through the leadership of Michael Harper, who left his curacy at All Souls and, in September 1964, became the first General Secretary of the Fountain Trust, an interdenominational body formed to encourage renewal.

---

17  These developments are dealt with in Hocken, *Streams of Renewal*, pp.70-74.

18  Murray, *D. Martyn Lloyd-Jones*, pp.480-82.

19  *Crusade*, February 1964, p.33.

Bridge-building was also taking place with the Pentecostal denominations, some of whose leaders were perplexed about charismatic phenomena breaking out in Anglican and Baptist contexts. From the later 1950s the Alliance had been making its own links with Pentecostalism. Through Gilbert Kirby's initiative, individuals from Pentecostal churches and then Pentecostal churches as bodies, became involved in the Alliance.[20] In the 1960s and 70s, some Pentecostals continued to have reservations about the Alliance's neutral stance on the ecumenical movement. Furthermore, when John Stott was proposed as President of the Alliance for the period 1972-4 some Pentecostals voiced their reservations on the grounds that he was too cautious about the gifts of the Spirit. But for a period in the mid-1960s evangelicals from differing backgrounds expressed an openness to renewal – an openness due, as Alliance Council member A. Morgan Derham put it, to the prevailing 'formality and dullness' of evangelical worship and spirituality.[21] In the 1970s, there were to be deep divisions within the ranks of those who in the 1960s seemed to be part of one movement. Following an international charismatic conference in Guildford in 1971, which brought together Protestants and Catholics, *Crusade* suggested that 'neo-Pentecostalism' had become 'the most important single development in British church life since the War; possibly this century'.[22] In 1975 however, *Restoration* magazine was launched, and in its pages proponents of new charismatic streams began to challenge the inclusive renewal that the Alliance had sought to foster.[23] As the magazine's title suggested, these streams taught the necessity of restoring the New Testament church as a prerequisite of Christ's return – hence their collective identification as the 'restorationist' movement.[24]

---

20 Executive Council Minutes, 23 May 1957.

21 *The Christian*, 10 December 1965, p.2.

22 *Crusade*, September 1971, p.1.

23 A. Walker, *Restoring the Kingdom: The Radical Christianity of the House Church Movement* (Guildford: Eagle, 1998), especially chapters 2-5.

24 For background see Walker, *Restoring the Kingdom*.

## Evangelical Assemblies

Evangelical Alliance leaders could not foresee that restorationism would spawn a number of new denominations in Britain in the 1970s. Far more challenging in the 1960s, as we saw in the previous chapter, were tensions over the ecumenical movement. Yet it is a mistake to think that this issue dominated the Alliance. When, in spring 1964, Gilbert Kirby announced the plans that were being made for 'the first Evangelical Assembly', due to be held in the Autumn of 1965, he envisaged that it would 'draw together for consultation and mutual edification evangelical Christians from the different churches and denominations'. Delegates from local churches or groups of churches would handle business. The sense of leading a genuinely national movement was strengthened in this period through successful residential ministers' conferences. Also, the united service of Holy Communion at the Albert Hall was being repeated in 1964. At the proposed conference there would be devotional sessions, Bible readings and preaching services. Kirby hoped that the number of churches linked to the Alliance would greatly increase and that those who attended could therefore be seen to be widely representative of the evangelical life of the nation. Far from ecumenical issues being high on the agenda, Kirby did not mention them. Rather, he considered that the main topics dealt with by speakers at the main meetings could be related to revival and evangelism.[25]

It is possible that Kirby was seeking to divert attention away from the growing tensions within evangelicalism by focusing on the areas that could unite evangelicals. However, at an Alliance Executive Council conference on 29 January 1965, he told the twenty people present, who represented the Alliance's 'inner circle', that he believed 'we have reached a most exciting stage in the history of the Evangelical Alliance'. He was pleased with the activities of the Alliance, mentioning in his report to

25  *Evangelical Alliance Broadsheet*, Spring 1964, pp.1–3.

the council the work of the Alliance clubs, the Alliance's theological study group under the Chairmanship of John Stott, and a successful youth conference at which almost all evangelical youth societies were represented. But Kirby's vision went beyond individual ministries, however important. The reason why, as he put it, he believed the Alliance had been 'called to the kingdom for such a time as this', was that evangelical Christians were seeking for ways to express their common concerns and that there was 'no other body geared to meet the aspirations ... apart from the Alliance'. Kirby did not think he would be overstating the case if he referred to 1965 as 'a year of destiny' as far as the Alliance was concerned.[26]

By the summer of 1965 Kirby was comparing the forthcoming conference in the capital to the 1846 London conference at which the Alliance had been inaugurated. Since then, he said, there had been many vicissitudes in the life and work of the Alliance, but he contended that the work had been revived and given fresh impetus. Kirby suggested that the conference was being held at an opportune moment considering 'the present spiritual and moral state of the nation as a whole'.[27] John Stott was conveying the same message, commenting on the 'paganising tendencies' at work in Britain and lamenting the fact that the lessons Billy Graham had taught in 1954 had been largely forgotten.[28] It was also timely to have a conference, Kirby believed, because evangelicals were 'under fire', being dismissed as 'fundamentalists' and 'obscurantists'. His earlier optimism about liberal theology being dead had been misplaced. With the publication of John Robinson's *Honest to God* in 1963, and the rise of the so-called 'Death of God' theology, Kirby admitted that evangelicals were out of step with much theological thinking. A further factor making the conference important was that some evangelicals had misunderstood one another and drifted apart. Kirby hoped

---

26 *Report of the Executive Council Conference held at the Alliance Club, Newington Green, 29 January 1965.*

27 *Evangelical Alliance Broadsheet*, Summer 1965, p.3.

28 *Decision*, June 1964, p.8.

for deeper unity so that 'the voice of evangelicalism in Britain can be heard'.[29]

The theme of unity did, in fact, come close to dominating the 1965 assembly – a development that would set the stage for the 1966 assembly.[30] About 1,000 delegates attended the 1965 assembly and in his report to an Alliance conference, held on 27 January 1966, Kirby said that he was convinced 'that we cannot exaggerate the significance of this event'. It was widely regarded as encouraging.[31] Four things in Kirby's report highlighted its significance. First, he wrote, evangelicals were looking for a forum to meet and discuss, and this had been provided. In the second place, the Alliance had found a way to act as a mouthpiece of evangelical opinion. A third significant feature was that those who had come had been delegates from churches and societies. Although there had been criticisms of this, Kirby believed it had given the conference authority. Finally, a Christian Unity Commission had been set up. From Kirby's perspective, the Alliance's 'Assembly at Westminster' ranked alongside the annual assemblies of the major denominations and of the British Council of Churches. He recognised that in a future assembly there would be a need to have more debate, and he accepted that the path ahead would not be easy. Kirby's hope, however, was that the Alliance could steer a middle course and 'give due deference to the views of our Right Wing and our Left Wing'.[32] Within a few months, however, this hope would be dashed.

## Renewal of Mission

The 1966 assembly took place just after the end of Gilbert Kirby's period as General Secretary of the Alliance. Morgan Derham, who took over from him, had the task of finding a

29 *Evangelical Alliance Broadsheet*, Summer 1965, p.3.
30 *Evangelical Alliance Broadsheet*, Spring 1966, p.1.
31 Brady, 'Gilbert Kirby', p.10.
32 *Report to the Evangelical Alliance Council Conference, 27 January 1966.*

way forward for the Alliance. Derham had been a Baptist minister in West Ham and in Barking, and had then worked for Scripture Union. He realised how essential it was that after the break of 1966 the Alliance should find ways of restoring belief among evangelicals that the Alliance could be the place where all those who shared a common concern for the gospel could come together. In this task he looked to the work of a Commission on Evangelism set up by the 1966 Assembly, whose members were seeking a renewal of mission under the direction of the Holy Spirit. The Assembly resolution said that in view of the 'urgent spiritual need of the nation' the Assembly 'dedicates itself anew to the task of evangelism, recognizing its need for a scriptural experience of the Holy Spirit'.[33] The background of renewal was evident. The Commission was to recommend the best means of reaching unchurched people, bearing in mind the need to co-operate with existing evangelistic endeavours where possible 'and specifically to promote a new emphasis on personal evangelism'. The membership was designed to reflect the Alliance's constituency. Two members were Anglican clergy, two were Baptists ministers, one was a Pentecostal minister and three, including two women, were Bible College staff or staff of evangelical societies.[34] Morgan Derham ensured that the group that was set up was orientated towards younger evangelical leaders. All the members were under forty.[35]

The resulting report, entitled *On the Other Side,* was published in 1968. Its first part surveyed the situation within British society. Particular attention was paid to three areas: young people and education, urbanisation, and the mass media. In view of the ways in which young people were taught in the British educational system, with an increasing stress on encouraging young people to question and search for satisfactory answers in all areas of life, the report argued for informal

33 Evangelical Alliance, *On the Other Side*, p.11.
34 Ibid., pp.11-2.
35 Kirby, 'On the Other Side', unpublished notes (1975).

discussions with young people about the Christian faith. These should be characterised by understanding, honesty and openness. The report argued that evangelicals must be willing to distinguish between the true historical Christian faith and traditional trimmings and prejudices.[36] The section on urbanisation and industrialisation analysed features of city life: anonymity, a secular outlook, concern for 'the here-and-now', and indifference to spiritual values. On the mass media, the report found a serious shortage of those willing and able to dedicate themselves in an imaginative and radical way to the task of presenting and applying the gospel in this arena. The conclusion of this sociological part of the report was that Christians were often out of touch with the world that they sought to win and too many evangelical Christians were 'depressed, introspective and downhearted'. In place of this mood, the report called for a renewed confidence that the gospel was relevant and suggested that the insecurity and fluidity of society could provide the context for large numbers of people to turn to Christ.[37]

The remainder of the report dealt with the theology and practice of evangelism. Questions had been raised in the 1960s about the effectiveness of mass evangelism. Billy Graham had returned to Britain in 1961 for a Crusade in Manchester, stating that Britain was 'either on the brink of a catastrophic moral declension or on the verge of a spiritual revival'.[38] Clearly seven years on from Harringay, it seemed that there was limited evidence of a change in national life. In June 1961 the Crusade was being heralded in Graham's own *Decision* magazine as a 'mass evangelistic effort on a scale unknown in the history of the Christian church', but by November 1961, when a British edition of *Decision* was launched, its pages spoke of British alienation from the churches (less than 10% attending) and of rampant immorality.[39] When Maurice Rowlandson, on behalf

---

36  Evangelical Alliance, *On the Other Side*, pp.24–33.

37  Ibid., pp.33–59.

38  *Decision*, August 1961, p.10.

39  *Decision*, June 1961, p.16; November 1961, p.2.

of the Billy Graham Evangelistic Association, approached the leaders of the Evangelical Alliance in 1963 about a further invitation to Billy Graham to come to Britain, they surprised him with 'a unanimous and categorical rejection'.[40] In retrospect, it appears that this negative response was at least partly prompted by the unease about Graham's methods that would come to be more fully expressed in *On the Other Side*. The refusal meant that an independent lay-council was convened. This managed to achieve 100 signatures to a parchment to invite Billy Graham to come to Britain, and he duly accepted. When Gilbert Kirby heard about this, he contacted Rowlandson to ask why the Alliance had not been asked to issue the petition. Rowlandson had taken the initial refusal still to apply, but the lay-council agreed to put things back in the Alliance's hands. As a result, the Alliance became the official sponsor of what would be the Greater London Crusade of 1966 – the crusade at which, famously, the pop singer Cliff Richard was converted. The Executive Committee of the Crusade met at the Alliance headquarters.[41]

There were indications that fresh theological thinking was taking place. Section 2 of *On the Other Side* argued that belief in God as Lord of creation and the desire to follow Christ 'both impel the Christian to be identified with the world. This means a genuine, a full, and a Christian participation in the life of the world'. The report called for a commitment to the social implications of the gospel.[42] Drawing on new research, its assessment of the effectiveness or otherwise of local churches' engagement in evangelism was that much preaching was out of touch with actual human needs. On the other hand, the report recognised that there was a growing interest in evangelism in theological college programmes. There were evangelistic agencies taking up the challenge of work outside the churches, especially in schools, colleges and universities, but other sectors

40  Martin, *Billy Graham Story*, p.318.
41  Report to the Evangelical Alliance Council Conference, 27 January 1966.
42  Evangelical Alliance, *On the Other Side*, pp.60–88.

of the population were not being reached. Evangelicals had not fared well in inner-city areas. Existing churches, the report continued, had been 'signally unsuccessful in reaching non-white members of the community with the result that separate places of worship are springing up'.[43] The growth of the black churches, which was to have such a significant impact on the evangelical scene in Britain, was beginning to be noticed.

Perhaps the most controversial aspect of the report was its critical comments about crusade evangelism. Maurice Rowlandson found the critique of mass evangelism very hard to understand and accept, and considered that *On the Other Side* 'put the clock back on evangelism for at least the next ten years'.[44] Certainly the survey that the members of the Alliance Commission undertook was significant. It showed that with regard to mass evangelism 'the recurring theme was that the crusade did not make a lasting effect on the complete outsider'. The report spoke of a declining confidence among churches and ministers in the crusade method. It suggested that in the future crusade meetings should concentrate more on instruction than inspiration and that it might be better not to have an open appeal in the meetings.[45] Not surprisingly, this section of the report caught the attention of the press. An Alliance Assembly was held in 1968 to consider the report and this Assembly received more prominent coverage on radio and in the national press than the previous assemblies. Reporters were keen to find evidence of direct criticism of the Billy Graham Crusades, but Morgan Derham was anxious to stress that good relationships between the Alliance and the Billy Graham Evangelistic Association were not at risk.[46] Nonetheless, new directions in mission were being proposed.

------

43  Ibid., 89–161.
44  Rowlandson, *Life with Billy*, pp.95, 115.
45  Evangelical Alliance, *On the Other Side*, pp.143, 16–9.
46  *Evangelical Alliance*, January–April 1969, pp.5–8.

# A Service Agency

Morgan Derham left the Alliance to work for the United Bible Societies at the end of December 1968. His successor was Gordon Landreth, an Anglican lay reader, who had been in Malawi with the Overseas Civil Service and had then worked for the Inter-Varsity Fellowship as secretary of the Graduates' Fellowship.[47] This was a time of reappraisal of the work of the Alliance. In July 1968 Derham had written a paper that suggested that the Alliance should be 'a compact information and service agency' and should move out of the world of evangelical politics, stop holding national assemblies and acknowledge the self-sufficiency of most evangelical groups and movements. There should be continued support for relief work and for groups that were part of the Alliance family, such as the Arts Centre Group. It was a time, in Derham's view, when the wider evangelical world was 'breaking up into self-sufficient groupings', with evangelicals in the Church of England likely to become less distinctive and to find their needs met within Anglicanism, with independents regarding the Alliance as a hindrance, and with the Baptists likely to be left as the only major denominational group in the Alliance family. Thus Derham could not see the Alliance being able to continue in its traditional role of promoting evangelical unity.[48]

In some respects the picture was not as bleak as Derham had privately painted it. From 1966 to 1968, 117 congregations of various types joined the Alliance, representing an increase of 28% in church affiliation.[49] In 1967 the circulation of *Crusade* was over 21,000 – an increase of 20% from 1964. Another significant development in this period was the establishment and growth of an Alliance department, led by Mary-Jean Duffield, which became known as TEAR Fund (originally EAR – the Evangelical Alliance Relief Fund; the new, serendipitous

---

47 *Evangelical Alliance*, Summer 1969, p.3.
48 A. Morgan Derham, 'The Role of the Alliance', a confidential statement, 10 July 1968.
49 Annual Report given by the Rev. Morgan Derham, 1968.

acronym was suggested by Peter Meadows). In the first instance, the department grew out of a need to distribute an increasing number of donations for relief work. Initially, these
were sent to Hong Kong, but money was subsequently directed towards projects in the Congo, India and Vietnam. The
Alliance was seeking to show that the dichotomy between 'the
social and the spiritual Gospel' was a false one.[50] TEAR Fund
was to grow at a remarkable rate and during the 1970s, under
George Hoffman, it became the best known evangelical
agency in Britain engaged in global social action.[51] The Alliance set up Commissions on World Mission and on witness in
new towns. Two important reports – *One World, One Task* and
*Evangelical Strategy in the New Towns* – were published. Both
had an impact in the 1970s. While, therefore, it was true to say,
as *Crusade* did in 1970, that there had been a serious rift between evangelicals in the mainline denominations and some of
those outside,[52] there were still many ways in which evangelicals continued to work together.

The specific initiatives taken during the period of Gordon
Landreth's secretaryship focused mainly on evangelism in Britain and elsewhere. In 1972 John Bird, who was then the pastor of
Duke Street Baptist Church, Richmond, was appointed to the
full-time staff of the Alliance as Director of Evangelism. The Alliance was keen that Bird should visit local churches and area
evangelical fellowships to discuss ways in which evangelism
could be promoted locally.[53] Bird took on a wider brief a year
later – to lead an Alliance national evangelistic project entitled
POWER. This was a call to intercession centred on the Alliance's week of prayer. It was also a call to evangelism. A
programme of church-based outreach lasted from Easter 1974

---

50  *The Evangelical Alliance Broadsheet*, Spring 1967, p.5; *Evangelical Alliance*, Summer 1969, pp.18-21.
51  See T. Chester, *Awakening to a World of Need* (Leicester: Inter-Varsity Press,
1993), p.23.
52  Editorial, *Crusade*, August 1970, p.1.
53  *idea*, Autumn 1972, p.1. *idea* was published by the Information Department,
Evangelical Alliance.

to Easter 1975. POWERpacks were produced by the Alliance for local churches and Bird addressed ministers' meetings around the country.[54] Along with this, Landreth helped to revive the Evangelists' Conference, which had originally been hosted by Tom Rees at Hildenborough Hall and which became an increasingly important forum for those involved in local mission.[55] In this period, there was also a deliberate emphasis within the Alliance on the relationship between evangelism and socio-political action. Patrick Sookhdeo was employed by the Alliance to promote evangelism in multi-ethnic areas, and the Alliance also supported the work of the Evangelical Race Relations Group.[56] Internationally, Landreth served as Secretary of the European Evangelical Alliance. He was also a member of the Lausanne Committee for World Evangelisation. This had arisen out of the momentous Lausanne Congress of 1974 – an international meeting of leading evangelicals which had done much to re-establish socio-political action as an indispensable partner to personal conversion in the presentation and reception of the gospel.[57]

In 1976 a small group of denominational leaders met with Alliance leaders and in due course it was agreed that there should be a 'Nationwide Initiative in Evangelism' (NIE). The chief mover of NIE was the Archbishop of Canterbury, Donald Coggan, but he was prominently supported by the Methodist evangelical leader, Donald English, and by Baptist spokesmen such as David Russell and David Pawson.[58] Partly in response to these discussions, the Alliance began to talk about presenting the 1980s as a decade of evangelism. At a residential conference of the Alliance on 30 and 31 January 1978

---

54  *idea*, Summer 1974, p.5.

55  P. Lewis, 'Renewal, Recovery and Growth: 1966 Onwards', in Brady & Rowdon, (eds), *For Such a Time as This*, p.182.

56  *idea*, Summer 1974, p.2.

57  J. Stott (ed.), *Making Christ Known: Historic Mission Documents from the Lausanne Movement, 1974-1989* (Carlisle: Paternoster Press, 1996).

58  D. McBain, *Fire Over the Waters: Renewal Among the Baptists and Others from the 1960s to the 1990s* (London: Darton, Longman & Todd, 1997), pp.80-81.

involvement in NIE was discussed in more detail. Gordon
Landreth reported that evangelicals had been asked to play a
major role in choosing the Initiative Committee. At this conference, the Anglican theologian, James Packer, gave a paper in
which he argued for the contextualising of the gospel. He
commended what was going on in the charismatic movement,
especially the sense of local church community, which he saw
as vital.[59] At a meeting of the Executive Council on 12 September 1978 it was agreed that Clifford Hill, the Alliance's Secretary for Evangelism and Church Growth, would work as
closely as possible with the NIE Secretary. The leading Methodist NIE supporter, Donald English, who would launch the
initiative in 1979 as President of the Methodist Conference,
was a guest at this meeting. He considered that NIE and Alliance ideas were virtually identical and hoped that there would
be agreed spheres of co-operation.[60] Although the extent of
Alliance involvement in an ecumenical enterprise provoked
debate, the Alliance was clearly seeking to serve the wider
church in its mission.

## Renewed Vision

There was a feeling of renewed energy in Alliance circles in the
early 1980s. At a day conference of the Alliance Council on 22
July 1980 Gilbert Kirby spoke of evidence of God at work in
the independent churches, including Pentecostal churches and
house fellowships.[61] At a time when many groups were 'doing
their own thing', said Kirby, the Alliance had a unique opportunity to co-ordinate efforts.[62] Partly by way of response, in
January 1981 reports were given at the Alliance Executive

---

59  Minutes of the Residential Session of the Executive Council of the Evangelical Alliance held on 30 and 31 January 1978.
60  Minutes of a Special Meeting of the Executive Council of the Evangelical Alliance, 12 September 1978.
61  Minutes of a Day Conference of the EA Council, 22 January 1980.
62  G. W. Kirby 'The Role of the Evangelical Alliance', unpublished paper, 1980.

Council by David Abernethie, Gilbert Kirby, Michael Barling and Clive Calver on – respectively – the independent evangelicals, the denominational evangelicals, charismatic renewal, and the youth scene and the 'House Churches'. David Abernethie said that he had taken soundings among independent evangelicals and had found an optimistic note. There were 435 FIEC churches with 25,000 members and numbers were increasing at the rate of about ten churches per year. The charismatic influence was being felt. There was a new concern for evangelism. Within the independent network there was support for London Bible College and Scripture Union, and also for the Evangelical Alliance – although there were worries among some that it had become too broad, and that *Crusade* was 'brash, crude and cruel'. Despite this, independents were largely committed supporters of TEAR Fund.[63]

Gilbert Kirby gave a report on evangelicals in the denominational churches. He saw disarray among evangelicals, with Anglicans in particular being 'self-contained and self-sufficient'. Within the renewal movement there was debate regarding various gifts, attitudes to Roman Catholics and a general failure of the leaders to relate to one another. Kirby saw the charismatic movement as having caused a general 'loosening up' in church life, particularly in worship, the sharing of ministries and the adoption of modern language. On the whole, the Anglicans were more responsive to change than the Free Churches, and there was also a tendency for restorationist groups (often also dubbed 'House Churches' in this period) to break away from the mainstream. Michael Barling, an Anglican involved in the renewal movement, said that new features within this group included less emphasis on tongues and healing, increased stress on prophecy, teaching and evangelism, and a decline in big central meetings. Looking to the future, Barling anticipated prophecy and its role being debated, evangelism being seen as a demonstration of God's power as well as

63 'A Review of the Evangelical Scene in Britain': Note of a discussion at the Executive Council of the Evangelical Alliance, 20 January 1981.

proclamation, new hunger for teaching in the renewal movement, and new emphases on community and lifestyle. Barling's
plea was that there should be a coming together of what he
called 'credal Christians', whether Protestant, Catholic, evangelical or charismatic. This was at a time when the Alliance was
asking for a clearer confession of faith than that contained in an
interim NIE statement.[64]

Clive Calver, the director of British Youth for Christ
(BYFC), surveyed the youth scene. In order to achieve a
broader unity among younger evangelicals from varied church
backgrounds, he reported, the Spring Harvest festival had been
launched in 1979. Morgan Derham recalled that in the 1960s
he had not believed bridges could be made between independent and inclusivist evangelicals. But Roger Forster,
founder of the Ichthus Fellowship in London and typical of the
new generation of evangelical leaders, felt that diversity need
not cause polarisation. David Pawson, a Baptist charismatic
who had chaired the commission that produced *On the Other
Side*, similarly wanted to move beyond the past debates.[65] In
view of this new mood, an Alliance Task Force was set up to
consider the future. Chaired by Morgan Derham, it reached
the startlingly radical conclusion that the way forward was
through a new representative body to replace the Alliance. It
was proposed that a conference of evangelical leaders be called
to take the process further.[66] As we saw in the last chapter, in
1970 there had not been sufficient common ground to bring
evangelicals together for a residential conference. Some of
those on both sides of the divide that had been evident in 1970
were now prepared to make a fresh effort. Thus from 9–11 September 1981 fifty-two evangelical leaders met at High Leigh
to discuss the Alliance's willingness to put its future on the line
if this would help unity. There was no one present from the
United Reformed Church or from Assemblies of God, but

64　*idea*, Spring 1981, p.3.
65　'A Review of the Evangelical Scene in Britain': Note of a discussion at the Executive Council of the Evangelical Alliance, 20 January 1981.
66　Executive Council Minutes, 14 May 1981.

apart from that the major denominations and evangelical groupings in England – though not in the rest of Britain – were represented. Gerald Coates of the Pioneer network acted as spokesman for the House Churches and Peter Lewis from Nottingham emerged as the main speaker from the independent wing. A new mood of co-operation was emerging.[67]

The discussions at High Leigh covered such topics as the Bible, the nature of the church, mission and the charismatic movement. The suspicion that there were evangelicals selling out on the gospel did not seem to have been substantiated. A year later, at a further conference arranged by the Alliance, it was reported that there was now even more open fellowship between evangelical leaders. David Watson of York, the most prominent Anglican charismatic leader, and Robert Horn, later General Secretary of the Universities and Colleges Christian Fellowship (UCCF), spoke on approaches to co-operation. It was plain in the early 1980s that the Alliance was providing a unique forum in which evangelical leaders – Anglican, charismatic, conservative and Reformed – were interacting constructively in a way which had not been the case for almost two decades. In the light of this development, it appeared that there was no overwhelming case for the demise of the Alliance. So when Gordon Landreth announced that he was moving to a new job at Trinity College, Bristol, the search began for a new General Secretary. This time there was no ambiguity about the kind of person who was wanted. Kirby, who was then President of the Alliance, set out the criteria. He (or possibly she – there were now a few women on the Council) would need to 'gain the ear of Christian people up and down the country', would be 'a reasonably young person, although not without some experience', would be theologically aware, would 'hold the respect of the vast majority of evangelicals', and would be 'acceptable to charismatics and non-charismatics'.[68]

---

67 Notes of an Alliance conference, 9–11 September 1981.
68 *idea*, Winter 1982/83, p.1.

## Conclusion

The period of the 1960s and 1970s was one that threw up considerable challenges for the Alliance. New movements brought fresh energy but also fresh tensions. Both in the area of spirituality and of evangelism there was a move away from traditional paths, a development that reflected the changing mood in society. As we have seen, the Alliance was open to renewal on several fronts: there was a willingness to go over to 'the other side'. Yet at the same time, it was struggling to deal with the divisions within British evangelicalism. Gilbert Kirby managed to keep many evangelicals together through his emphasis on evangelism, but unity became harder after the divisions of the 1966 Assembly. It would be wrong, however, to think that the Alliance was moribund in the 1970s. The idea of the service agency, which Morgan Derham proposed, suggested a still important role. However, Derham's ideal for the Alliance was that there should be someone at the helm who was a 'promoter'.[69] With the new confidence about the future of the Alliance that emerged in the early 1980s it became possible to envisage such a person. The steady bridge building that Gordon Landreth had undertaken was about to bear fruit in a powerful coming together of those who had been on different sides of the charismatic renewal debate. It might have seemed impossible to find the kind of 'catholic' mix that was being sought by the Alliance at the end of 1982 as it began to contemplate a new General Secretary. Yet Clive Calver's experience with BYFC was taken to have equipped him well for the role, and he was duly appointed in 1983.

---

69  Derham, 'The Role of the Alliance'.

# 12

# A Deepening of Evangelical Unity

*The Resurgence of the Alliance in the 1980s and 1990s*

The Alliance announced in the Spring 1983 edition of its bulletin, *idea*, that 34-year-old Clive Calver had been appointed General Secretary, and that he was one of the youngest men to hold the position in the Alliance's 137 year history. *idea* emphasised Calver's ability to motivate others and to encourage people and organisations to develop their full potential.[1] There was some surprise in the evangelical world that the Alliance should turn to someone of Calver's age, but it was to become clear that Calver could fulfil the kind of influential role the Alliance's senior advisors had in mind.[2] The period of Calver's secretaryship, from 1983 to 1997, was to be one in which the Alliance grew rapidly. In the early 1980s, the number of individual Evangelical Alliance members was between 900 and 1,000. In the mid-1990s individual membership of the Alliance reached 56,000. The number of churches in membership grew from under 1,000 to almost 3,000 in the same period.[3] In 1990 the members of the Executive Committee of the Evangelical Alliance, as they reflected on the progress that had been made in the previous seven years, affirmed that it

---

1 *idea*, Spring 1983, p.1.

2 J. Capon, *The Baptist Times*, 11 January 1996, p.7.

3 Historical Membership Statistics for the Evangelical Alliance produced in 2000.

remained committed to what they saw as five activities that
have been at the heart of the Alliance since 1846. These were
the promotion of true Christianity, the encouragement of
evangelism, the stimulation of prayer, the maintenance of biblical truth and the engendering of Christian action in society.[4]
This summary did not convey the Alliance's 'grand object' in
1846, which was 'manifesting and promoting the unity of
Christ's disciples' (see chapter 3), but the stress on active
involvement in society was true to the Alliance's history.

## In Continuity with the Past

A brief look at Calver's career up to 1983 might have led to
the conclusion that he would be interested in producing a
forward-looking and active Alliance and would have relatively little interest in continuity with the past. From a
Brethren background, he was converted at the age of nineteen, under the ministry of future Ichthus Fellowship leader
and Alliance Vice-President, Roger Forster. At that time he
was involved in political activities (with the young Liberals)
and in community work in East London. He then studied at
London Bible College, where he met his wife, Ruth, a
daughter of Gilbert Kirby, and he subsequently led evangelistic teams for several years. In 1975 Calver became director of
British Youth for Christ and was a member of the planning
group for the annual conference of British evangelists. Calver
and Peter Meadows were instrumental in launching the phe-
nomenally successful Spring Harvest festival in 1979. At the
time of his appointment as General Secretary of the Evangelical Alliance, Calver was already a member of the Executive
Council and was the programme director for Billy Graham's
Mission England crusade in Britain. He was known internationally, having made several visits overseas, including a

4 Minutes of the Executive Committee of the Council of Management, 14
November 1990.

preaching tour in America and Canada. In his local area at the time, Milton Keynes, he was an elder of a recently formed Free Church.[5] Clive Calver seemed to be a classic evangelical activist.

At the same time, Calver was well aware, especially through Gilbert Kirby, of the story of the Alliance in the 1960s and 1970s. At a meeting in 1983 of the Executive Committee of the Council of Management, a body that had been set up in response to a desire to make the structure of the Alliance more effective, Calver reviewed the recent history of the organisa-tion. He stressed that the Alliance was an umbrella for corpo-rate evangelical action and not another society. He made particular reference to the critical events of 1966, when the late Martyn Lloyd-Jones was associated with the advocacy of the separation of evangelicals from mixed denominations and, on the other hand, evangelicals such as John Stott advocated re-maining in denominations. For Calver, there was a need for the Alliance as a non-denominational uniting body. He reminded the Alliance committee members of the review that was un-dertaken in 1981 of its role and future, a review that had con-cluded that there should be a metamorphosis of the Alliance, out of which would emerge a body that would be more repre-sentative of evangelical groupings. Calver considered that the new moves taking place within the Alliance were in continuity with this decision. The council of management would be operating as a widely representative body dealing with policy and issues of theological and denominational importance, and the Executive Committee of the council would deal with strategy, finance, staffing and new projects.[6]

Soon Calver was also exploring the more distant past. He spoke later of discovering for himself 'exactly what the heart-beat of the Evangelical Alliance was', and his conclusion was to have considerable significance for its future direction. As a result

---

5  *idea*, Spring 1983, p.1.

6  Minutes of the Executive Committee of the Council of Management, 14 October 1983.

of his historical study, Calver began to champion two causes. The first to which he dedicated himself was the dream of united evangelical action espoused by the Alliance's founding fathers. The second was the recovery of the concern of Victorian evangelicals such as Lord Shaftesbury and William Booth to have an effective social impact.[7] In his public statements in 1984 Calver was clearly committed to setting the tone. The Alliance received high profile exposure at Spring Harvest in that year – membership increased by almost 50% as a result of the 1984 Spring Harvest meetings.[8] Calver was clearly also aware of the need to make evangelical views known through the media. He took the view that many in the media were struggling to find a cohesive, representative voice, because evangelicalism has been so divided. In 1983 and 1984 Calver visited conferences, such as the charismatic leaders' conference and the annual conference of the largest Pentecostal denomination, the Assemblies of God, in order to achieve the kind of radical realignment of evangelicals and the co-operation that he envisaged.[9] This concern for a broad-based unity was a contemporary expression of the Alliance's founding vision – 'One Body in Christ'.

Enthusiasm for evangelical unity was clearly growing in this period, although tensions were also evident. One of Calver's first major achievements was a conference entitled 'Leadership 84', which took place at the Pontins Holiday Camp at Brean in Somerset. This brought together about a thousand evangelical leaders. It was, as Peter Lewis commented, 'a significant event in the deepening of evangelical unity'.[10] Calver reported to the Evangelical Alliance Executive Committee after 'Leadership 84' that the overwhelming majority of those returning questionnaires had commented very positively, but there had also been negative responses, especially from some Anglicans,

---

7 *idea*, June/July/August 1997, p.22.

8 Minutes of the Executive Committee of the Council of Management, 17 April 1984.

9 Minutes of the Executive Committee of the Council of Management, 15 December 1983; 24 October 1984.

10 Lewis, 'Renewal, Recovery and Growth', pp.187-8.

Methodists and United Reformed Church participants. In particular, it had been suggested that the Alliance had a disproportionately low percentage of members from the Anglican constituency and it was noted that there had been a lack of senior Anglican leaders attending the conference. There had also been complaints that the style of worship did not take account of Anglican tradition. It had also been suggested that Methodists and URC members were not adequately represented within the Alliance and that this constituency felt disquiet about the growing charismatic emphasis. In response to Anglican concerns, Calver had discussions with John Stott, who indicated his willingness to represent the Alliance to the evangelical Anglican constituency. Calver was also in discussion with Howard Mellor from the Methodist Cliff College. The URC's Group for Evangelism and Renewal (GEAR) was unconvinced about joining the Alliance.[11] It had been formed to promote broad-based charismatic renewal rather than evangelicalism per se, and was concerned that such a move might alienate more liberal charismatics within its constituency. Meanwhile, in the attempt to reach out to new groups, the Alliance was struggling to retain some of its own more traditional constituency.

It was seeking to draw from its past not only in the sphere of evangelical unity but in the way it was emphasising social action. In 1985 the Executive Committee was informed that the Shaftsbury Society was concerned to encourage the church in Britain to greater involvement in social and community affairs. The Alliance was in touch with Fran Beckett, who later became the Chief Executive of the Shaftesbury Society. It was suggested that the Alliance should draw together member societies with a particular interest in this field to discuss raising finance. George Hoffman of TEAR Fund was also raising the profile of social issues.[12] In addition, the Alliance was building

11 Minutes of the Executive Committee of the Council of Management, 17 April 1984.
12 Minutes of the Executive Committee of the Council of Management, 7 November 1985.

on its concern to campaign for religious liberty and was, as *Christianity Today* noted later, achieving visibility and credibility with the media and political leaders in Britain. Journalists began to contact the Alliance for its views on a broad range of issues. The challenge for the Alliance in this period was to ensure that the information and the comments it gave to the media were a product of thorough research and could take their place in the arena of debate about issues of public policy.[13]

## The Multi-Ethnic Dimension

One issue with which the leadership of the Evangelical Alliance was increasingly determined to engage was the multi-ethnic nature of British evangelicalism in the 1980s. Calver was challenged by a black church leader, Philip Mohibir, who later recalled how he had summoned up all his courage to ask Calver why there was only one black-led church in membership of the Alliance. Mohibir had come to Britain from the Caribbean in the 1950s. His work became international, but in the early 1980s he returned to Britain. Having issued his challenge to Calver he waited for the rebuttal and the polite telling off he had come to expect from British evangelical leaders, but instead Calver asked Mohibir to 'help me to change things'. Some painfully honest exchanges followed.[14] The result was constructive. In April 1984 the West Indian Evangelical Alliance (WIEA), which was later renamed the African and Caribbean Evangelical Alliance (ACEA), was launched. A congregation of 450 people attended the launch at Rye Lane Chapel, Peckham. The report in *idea* noted that there were approximately one million West Indians in Britain and that the WIEA was seeking to represent evangelicals from 150 different West Indian church groupings and some 1,500 churches.[15]

---

13  *Christianity Today,* 9 December 1996, p.29.
14  *idea* June/July/August 1997, p.22.
15  *idea,* Summer 1985, p.3.

At the launch, Brian Mills, who was leading the prayer and evangelism department of the Alliance's work, made a public apology on behalf of the white evangelical community 'for not treating our West Indian brethren as we should have done'. He made it clear that in his view there was a need to 'repent of deep-seated prejudices and coldness of heart which have created distance between us and to work out how our unity in Christ can find practical expression in the days ahead'. Philip Mohibir, who was then the newly elected Chairman of the WIEA, endorsed this approach. Mohibir spoke of 'a divided world torn apart by class differences and racial and sexual discrimination' and urged evangelicals to 'unite in order to become an authentic Christian witness in our torn and divided society'.[16] A year later the Alliance leadership discussed proposals from Mohibir for the development of the WIEA and agreed that office facilities, part-time secretarial help and other financial assistance would be provided to the WIEA by the Alliance, that two Alliance staff would be representatives on the WIEA committee, and that the WIEA would function autonomously within the Alliance.[17] A new structure was being put in place to seek to meet the needs of a new societal situation.

Joel Edwards, pastor at the New Testament Church of God, Mile End, who was for ten years a probation officer with the Inner London Probation Service, succeeded Philip Mohibir in 1988. Edwards had met Mohibir at Spring Harvest the year before, an indication of how larger evangelical events were acting as bridge-building occasions. Although Edwards had studied at London Bible College in the early 1970s, and had made many friendships that would later prove strategic,[18] to an extent he had lost touch with the wider British evangelical world after college, and his reconnection came through 'Leadership 84'.

16 Ibid.
17 Minutes of the Executive Committee of the Council of Management, 13 March 1986.
18 Joel Edwards, *Lord, Make us One – But Not All the Same!* (London, Hodder & Stoughton, 1999), chapter 3.

At the time of his appointment as General Secretary of the WIEA, Edwards spoke of 2,000 'black-led churches' – the number was growing and also more were being discovered – that had little contact with white Christians. Edwards believed the situation must change.[19] One project that was indebted to WIEA involvement was the Evangelical Enterprise Unemployment Consultancy, which secured a voice for the black churches on bodies like the Inner London Education Authority. When Edwards became the Alliance's UK Director in 1992, he reflected on the 'significant strides forward' that the African Caribbean Evangelical Alliance (ACEA, as it was by then called) had made. It had given the black church community a 'focal point and coherence where needed', and had 'let down the drawbridge between the black church and the wider Christian community'.[20]

ACEA continued its work under Ron Nathan, who joined the Alliance in 1991 as Community Initiatives Consultant.[21] Like Edwards, he stayed in the post four years, moving in 1996 to undertake Master's study at Westminster College, Oxford. He saw his most important achievement as having been 'to help the black church to see its potential as a community development agency for social change'.[22] By the later 1990s, those attending black-led or black majority Pentecostal churches (belonging to a variety of denominations), which were especially strong in inner-city areas, formed over 7% of church attendees in England as a whole, with many black Christians, in addition, to be found in other churches.[23] Mark Sturge, who became the new leader of ACEA in 1996 at the age of thirty-one, was the pastor of the Caribbean Fellowship at Kensington Temple, London, and had studied at London Bible College. He was determined to continue the policy by

19  *idea*, Summer 1988, p.7.
20  *idea*, September–October 1992, p.11.
21  *idea*, August–September 1991, p.6.
22  *idea*, June–August 1996, p.9.
23  Brierley (ed.), *UK Christian Handbook*, 9.16, 12.3.
24  *idea*, November–December 1996, p.2.

which black-led churches would 'engage with what other churches are doing for the sake of the gospel'.[24] The identity of the black-majority churches was further enhanced by the production of a directory of churches.

## Alliances for the Nations

In the later 1980s, the Alliance was also seeking to recognise diversity within the different parts of the United Kingdom. The development of this UK-wide vision merits a detailed study of its own; here we offer a summary, conscious of significant ongoing growth and change at this level even as we write. In 1987 it opened a Belfast office to encourage co-operation on specific projects such as ministries to those with addiction problems, and community care schemes. Howard Lewis, a Presbyterian minister who had worked in Belfast all his life, took responsibility for Evangelical Alliance Northern Ireland, and by 1992 it represented some 22,000 evangelicals in the province.[25] At that stage, one Ulsterman, Sir Fred Catherwood, was taking a prominent role in the Alliance. He was born in 1925 in County Londonderry and followed a career path that included posts in industry as managing director of the British Aluminium Company and John Laing and Sons Ltd. He was also Chairman of the National Economic Development Council and of the British Overseas Trade Board. As a Member of the European Parliament, Catherwood was strongly pro-Europe (*Pro-Europe?* was the title of one of his books) and was vice-President of the European Parliament in 1989. As the President of the Evangelical Alliance from 1992, he made it clear that he did not like to conform, a tendency that he attributed to his resistance as an Ulsterman to 'being put in a mould'.[26] Catherwood embodied the spirit of the Alliance, which was seeking to affirm national and transnational identity.

25  *idea*, November–December 1992, p.6.
26  *Alpha*, October 1992, 25; *idea*, April–May 1992, p.11.

Developments in Wales also illustrated what was being attempted. Arfon Jones, who was appointed co-ordinator in
1989 for the newly formed Alliance in Wales, spoke about the
promotion of unity among evangelicals and churches in Wales
as one of the major challenges ahead. He commented on the
way in which the number of evangelicals in Wales was growing
and also becoming more diverse, suggesting that there was an
urgent need for a movement that would encourage evangelicals to work together. Jones, a former national youth officer
with the Union of Welsh Independents, was deeply committed to Welsh life. The Alliance in Wales was set up intentionally
as a bilingual movement, reflecting the trends that were evident
in the wider church and society of the period.[27] It would,
according to Jones, seek to respond to the unique needs of both
small chapels and large city congregations and would 'act as a
catalyst for evangelistic and social action'. In Jones' view,
the difficulties and challenges faced by Welsh churches were
markedly different from those in England. Hence the focus on
shaping an Alliance that would, in his words, 'grow from the
soil of the Welsh churches'.[28]

Three years later, a Scottish Evangelical Alliance was
launched, following three years of consultation among evangelical leaders in Scotland. Colin Sinclair, director of Scripture Union in Scotland, and Chairman of the steering group of church
leaders behind the formation of the new Alliance, explained in
*idea* in 1992 that the Scottish Alliance would provide 'a framework for evangelicals throughout the country to unite in prayer,
mission and active concern about our country'. Responsibility
for oversight of the Alliance would be with a forty-member
council of management drawn from across the denominations
in Scotland. The Scottish Alliance, which was to become even
more strategic with the setting up of a Scottish Parliament, had
as its vision the provision of a forum where evangelicals from

---

27 See D. Densil Morgan, *The Span of the Cross: Christian Religion and Society in
Wales, 1914-2000* (Cardiff: University of Wales Press, 1999).
28 *idea*, November–December 1989, p.16.

different denominations and different parts of the country could work together. Ian Coffey, then field director of the UK Evangelical Alliance, highlighted the fact that the Alliance had begun in 1846 as a result of initiatives from Scottish church leaders and emphasised the rightness of Alliance members in Scotland having their own council, executive and staff. He looked forward to the rich contribution they would make.[29] The danger was that the UK Alliance would not hold together so strongly as the national Alliances developed, and when Joel Edwards was appointed UK director in 1992 an Alliance press release made clear that he would work with Alliances in Northern Ireland, Scotland and Wales to promote evangelical co-operation across cultural and national boundaries.[30]

## Ecumenical Issues

As a body committed to unity, the question of co-operation with ecumenical ecclesiastical bodies remained a challenging one for the Alliance. By this period the acrimonious debates about withdrawal from all those involved in theologically mixed denominations, which had characterised the 1960s, were rare. Nonetheless, there was sensitivity about the extent to which the Alliance could officially associate with the ecumenical movement. In June 1988, at a meeting of the Executive Committee, two Baptists who were present, Robert Amess – who would later become the Alliance Chairman – and Ian Coffey reported that the British Council of Churches (BCC), the British ecumenical body, planned to cease operation in its present form by 1990, and then to set up new ecumenical structures at local, regional, national and UK levels. The Executive Committee noted that a consultative process to examine different proposals for a new structure had been in process. A major evaluation had taken place at a conference at Swanwick in 1987, and it was now envisaged that specific proposals would be

---

29  *idea*, April–May 1992, p.2.
30  Evangelical Alliance News Release 21 August 1992.

available in the Autumn of 1989. The BCC had also requested the Alliance's involvement in providing written questions, comments and criticisms in connection with their proposals.[31]

This ecumenical development, which took the title 'Not Strangers but Pilgrims', offered hope of a broader expression of Christian unity than had been the case with the BCC – a unity that included black-led churches and Roman Catholics. Against a background of failed unity schemes, such as the Covenant proposals of the 1970s and early 80s which had sought to bring five major denominations closer together, this 'Inter-Church Process' (ICP) seemed to some to be more hopeful.[32] Alliance members welcomed the fact that the new body would operate under a basis of faith that would be trinitarian, but noted that it would not be as complete as the Basis of Faith of the Alliance. The purpose of the new body would be to encourage Christians to work together in local areas on social issues and evangelism. It would have three levels of membership: full membership for denominations only, associate membership for groups like the Alliance which could assent to the basis of faith, and observer membership for groups which could not assent to the Basis of Faith. After discussion about the BCC's invitation, it was agreed that Kenneth Prior, Robert Amess and Ian Coffey should prepare a list of questions for the BCC and that these should be referred to the Executive Committee before sending them to the BCC. Clive Calver advised Alan Gibson of the British Evangelical Council (BEC) of this decision.[33]

The concern to keep the BEC informed showed the desire of the Alliance to guard the evangelical constituency from another damaging period of polarisation over ecumenism. A meeting between representatives of the Inter-Church Process and Alliance representatives on 25 May 1989, by which time definite proposals about new 'ecumenical instruments' (*The*

---

31  Minutes of the Executive Committee, 22 June 1988.

32  C.J. Ellis, *Together on the Way: A Theology of Ecumenism* (London: British Council of Churches, 1990), pp.4–5.

33  Minutes of the Executive Committee, 22 June 1988.

*Next Steps for Churches Together in Pilgrimage*) had been published,[34] explored the possibilities in more detail. Those who attended the meeting recommended on 25 July 1989 that the Evangelical Alliance should seek a consultant relationship with the ICP, and the Executive agreed to adopt this approach. It was considered that the ICP would appear attractive to many Alliance supporters and that it could be damaging to the Alliance not to have some sort of relationship with the Process. However, it was regarded as important to communicate to Alliance members that any relationship it might have with the ICP would be entered into realistically in the light of past experience of evangelicals with ecumenical bodies. The conviction among Alliance leaders at that stage was that a relationship with ICP would enable the Alliance to take part in discussions where otherwise evangelical standpoints could be ignored. It was noted that the WIEA had opted for observer status in the new ecumenical process, and in view of the regret expressed by the WIEA that there had not been a joint response to the ICP from the Evangelical Alliance and themselves, it was agreed to formulate a joint approach.[35]

Although the Alliance was able to develop constructive relationships with leaders within the ICP, and indeed in the 1990s Alliance council members such as David Coffey, the General Secretary of the Baptist Union, would be involved in Churches Together in England, it was decided in 1990 that the Alliance could not accept an invitation to become a member of the Council of Churches for Britain and Ireland. This decision followed months of intensive discussion. This had not, however, led to divisions within the Evangelical Alliance. It was the unanimous view of the Evangelical Alliance council

---

34 D. Palmer, *Strangers No Longer* (London: Hodder & Stoughton, 1990), pp.69–80.
35 Minutes of the Executive Committee, 25 July 1988.

that it would be impossible for the Alliance, based as it was on a credal confession, to enter into membership with a body whose basis of faith was significantly different. Also, it was recognised that the Alliance incorporated evangelicals holding differing views about ecumenism and that in the light of this Alliance membership of the new ecumenical council would be inconsistent. The obvious retort was that the Alliance had been seeking for 150 years to draw together individual Christians, local churches, denominations and agencies. Why should it, therefore, distance itself from a new initiative in the sphere of unity? The reality was, as Executive members saw, that for most evangelical Christians in the UK the Evangelical Alliance had a distinctive role. Besides, Alliance leaders made it clear that they wished ongoing dialogue with officers of the new ecumenical councils on matters of mutual interest and concern.[36]

## Evangelical Unity

It was in the field of evangelical unity that the Alliance felt more confident. There was awareness in the 1980s of the need to reach out across some of the divides created by certain strands within the charismatic movement. In particular, the rise of churches that claimed to have restored New Testament church life in a way that the denominations had failed to do. Terry Virgo, one of the leaders of this 'restorationist' or 'House Church' strand, was typical in suggesting that denominational leaders overseeing churches would simply defend the status quo. He spoke about safe denominational churches enjoying a little renewal.[37] In order to foster dialogue, the Alliance arranged a meeting in 1987 at the Friends Meeting House, London, addressed by John Stott and Gerald Coates, a House Church leader, like Virgo. A decade previously, Stott had publicly apologised to Michael Harper, the Anglican charismatic renewal leader, for the way he had allowed their friendship to

---

36 Minutes of the Executive Committee, 14 November 1990.
37 *Restoration*, November–December 1981, pp.9–12.

become 'tarnished' due to disagreements over charismatic issues.[38] In 1987 Stott was seeking to demonstrate, through appearing on a platform with a House Church leader, that 'we belong together in the body of Christ'. It was a statement that echoed the classic Alliance concern for the reality of the 'one body in Christ' to be expressed. Coates stated that the coming together indicated that after years of often-hostile separation, Anglicans and House Churches (later known as 'New Churches') were learning to express their love to one another without abandoning their own distinctives.[39]

This 'coming together' was reflected in the composition of the Alliance's Council. The forty-five members at the end of the 1980s represented some fourteen denominational streams, including Assemblies of God, Baptist, Church of England, Elim Pentecostal, Methodist, New Testament Assembly, New Testament Church of God, Presbyterian, United Reformed Church, Salvation Army and House Church and independent streams. A further leadership conference, 'Leadership 89', was organised in conjunction with MARC Europe, to consolidate the new sense of unity. At that stage the Alliance's leadership team was Mike Morris (Secretary for Social and Foreign Affairs), John Earwicker (Prayer Secretary), Peter Meadows (Communications Secretary), Joel Edwards (General Secretary of the WIEA), Jonathan Markham (Administrative Secretary), Ian Coffey (Field Director), Ian Barclay (Minister at Large), and Clive Calver (General Director).[40] Denominationally, the bias of this group was towards Free Church life, with Ian Barclay being the only ordained Anglican clergyman.

The priority for the Alliance, however, was to reinforce a sense of pan-denominational evangelical identity. It was a viewpoint that fitted well with the increasing ambivalence on the part of many younger evangelicals towards denominational 'labels'. A report in *idea* in mid-1991, entitled 'Under the Spot-

38 *idea*, Winter 1975, p.6.
39 *idea*, Spring 1987, p.12.
40 *idea*, May-June 1989, p.16.

light', captured the feeling of the time. It noted that the new
Archbishop of Canterbury, George Carey, was an evangelical.
The most recent church census had revealed what was described
as 'dramatic evangelical church growth', with evangelicals apparently comprising 45% of Protestants in church in Britain on
Sundays. Evangelical social action was also bringing evangelicals
'into the glare of the media spotlight'. From the *Daily Mirror* and
the *Sunday Times*, continued the report, to BBC and ITN, the
media were trying to understand evangelicalism. Journalists
were 'tying themselves in knots attempting to unravel evangelists from evangelicals and New Churches from charismatic
Anglicanism'. Alliance representatives were in front of micro-
phones and cameras answering questions about worship styles,
healing, evangelism and growing churches. Spring Harvest was
by that stage a focus of media interest. It had become the largest
event of its kind in Europe, having grown from 2,700 people in
1979 to 80,000 in 1991. For most of that time, there had been
little interest from religious correspondents, but now journalists
were keen to visit, write about and film it.[41]

Internally, the period 1991-2 saw changes that were designed to keep the Alliance in touch with its own constituency
and aid united action. Alan Martin, formerly general director of
Scripture Union, retired as Chairman of the Alliance's Council
after six years of service. He had given strong support to Calver
in a period of massive change. The new Chairman of the
Council of Management was Derek Copley, Principal of
Moorlands Bible College near Bournemouth. The Chairman
of the Executive Committee was Mark Birchall; he had taken
early retirement from a City of London stockbroking firm to
concentrate on evangelical Christian work, and was the Chair
of the Church of England General Synod's evangelical group.[42]
A Church Life team was formed in this period under the leadership of the former Prayer Secretary, John Earwicker. Also in
the team were David Abernethie, who had been minister of

---

41  *idea*, June-July 1991, p.1.
42  *idea*, August-September 1991, p.6.

Cheam Baptist Church and who was Pastoral Development Secretary, and Brian Mills, who had been the Alliance Prayer Secretary in the 1980s, and had returned to that role from local church ministry. Colin Saunders, the Management and Finance Director, explained in August 1992 that this 'major realignment of the Evangelical Alliance' would further improve communication and service to members, and would facilitate greater co-operation and united action among evangelicals.[43]

In March 1994 a fresh development took place within evangelicalism with the publication of a historic 8,000-word declaration entitled 'Evangelicals and Catholics Together: The Christian Mission in the Third Millennium'. A core group of seven Roman Catholics and eight evangelicals in North America had produced the document, which set out areas of common affirmation, hope, searching, action and witness. The document recognised that evangelicals and Catholics 'constitute the growing edge of the missionary expansion at present and, most likely in the century ahead', it affirmed the Apostles' Creed as a uniting credal statement, and it included the soteriological proposition that we are 'justified by grace through faith because of Christ'.[44] Among the well-known representatives of the Catholic and evangelical communities involved in drafting the document was Charles Colson, a prominent voice in American evangelicalism. Prior to its release the statement was endorsed by a number of other eminent figures, including James Packer, a theologian held in high regard by evangelicals in Britain and America. Joel Edwards said that at first he was doubtful about the statement, but his considered view was that while evangelicals had to take seriously theological issues dividing Catholics and Protestants they did not need to be 'locked in a time warp' as far as attitudes to others were concerned. The Alliance could associate with Roman Catholic agencies on social issues while insisting on the importance of doctrine.[45]

---

43 Evangelical Alliance News Release, 21 August 1992.

44 J.I. Packer, 'Why I Signed It', *Christianity Today*, 12 December 1994, pp. 34-7.

45 *Alpha*, February 1995, p. 33.

Attitudes were changing in Britain as well as in America. In response to the papal encyclical on commitment to ecumenism, *Ut Unum Sint*, the 'Faith and Unity' Committee of the Baptist Union of Great Britain wrote: 'Amongst most (if not yet all) of our people, there is a sense of a growing unity with Roman Catholics, a unity based on the one Lord Jesus Christ, the bond of love and the mutual study of Scripture.'[46] The response rightly stated that not all Baptists, whether in the Baptist Union or outside it, shared such sentiments. Indeed, the Baptist Union convened a forum on the question and published a book by several authors, including Robert Amess, conveying the differing viewpoints. Issues that caused the Protestant Reformation continued to be raised.[47] Nor was the Baptist Union 'faith and unity' perspective uncritical. It was accepted that serious theological issues remained. Yet it is highly significant that at the Baptist Union assembly in 1995, when denominational policy on ecumenical involvement was debated, the vote was 91.21% in favour of continuing the Baptist Union's membership of Churches Together in England. This represented a commitment by evangelical Baptists in England (the church census of 1989 found that 84% of Baptist churches identified themselves as evangelical) to working within an ecumenical body with Catholics as full members.[48]

It was against this background that in 1996 Calver spoke of the evangelical constituency as 'in many respects a broad church'. His own definition of an evangelical was succinct. An evangelical, in his view, was someone who believed that the Bible was the word of God and that Jesus was the Son of God, who held to the traditional credal statements of the church and who owned a commitment to Jesus Christ as their Saviour,

---

46  Baptist Union of Great Britain, 'A Response to the Papal Encyclical *Ut Unum Sint* from the Faith and Unity Executive Committee of the Baptist Union of Great Britain', April 1997. *Ut Unum Sint* is published by the Catholic Truth Society, 1995.

47  M.I. Bochenski, (ed.), *Evangelicals and Ecumenism: When Baptists Disagree* (Didcot: Baptist Union, 1993).

48  See Christian Research Association, *Prospects for the Nineties*, p.28.

Lord and King. Within this broad church, Anglicans and Baptists accounted for 60-65% of Alliance membership. Calver considered that evangelical Anglicans were again involving themselves in the life of the Alliance, while on the other hand the Alliance had strong support from New Church leaders. In 1987, leading New Church supporters of the Alliance – Roger Forster of Ichthus, Gerald Coates of Pioneer and Lynn Green of Youth with a Mission – joined the popular songwriter Graham Kendrick to launch 'March for Jesus'. The specific origin of this new street-based mix of procession, performance and evangelism did not deter many in the historic denominations from participating, and by 1990 estimates suggested that some 250,000 marchers had taken part in towns and cities across the British Isles. In 1994 'March for Jesus' went global, with 177 nations and between 10 and 12 million Christians taking part.[49] For all this success, however, questions were being raised about whether the Alliance, during Calver's time, had become 'a mainly charismatic body' with non-charismatics feeling left outside – questions which Joel Edwards acknowledged in December 1996. Even so, for Edwards' own part, there was no tension. He considered that he held to all the fundamental things that made him Pentecostal, but also to all the fundamental things that made him evangelical.[50] This was an affirmation of the evangelical 'broad church' and illustrated the nature of the deepening evangelical unity of the period.

## Social Involvement

Although its traditional concern for unity was still evident, the Alliance was able in the later 1980s and 90s to give more attention to Christian action in society.

An example was Evangelical Enterprise, an unemployment consultancy launched by the Alliance and the WIEA to com-

49 *The Baptist Times*, 11 January 1996, p.8; Scotland, *Charismatics and the New Millennium*, pp.319-20.
50 *Christianity*, December 1996, p.24.

bat unemployment. It was announced in Autumn 1987 that the Alliance had created a new department to oversee the unemployment consultancy, which was seen as especially crucial because of government interest in the project. The project co-ordinators were Michael Hastings, who was concentrating on inner cities, and Michael Weatherley, who was focused on the wider community. Together, they were seeking to help churches and Christian groups discover how to start or expand training and unemployment projects in their localities. The Department of Employment pledged £150,000 to support the project's first two years. The aim was to provide direct links between concerned Christians and the support available from the Department of Employment, local authorities and charitable trusts and foundations. There would then be expert monitoring and back-up once church training and employment schemes were operational.[51]

Further steps followed. In 1989 Calver insisted in *idea* that through its increasing support of Christian action in society the Alliance was 'keeping faith with its past'. He spoke about leading national figures who had played a role in the Alliance's affairs. Many of these figures gave their weight to Alliance campaigns – not least those waged on behalf of religious freedom in Russia, Austria and Turkey. Calver remarked that a recent visit by Mike Morris to Turkey was a belated follow-up, since Alliance members had negotiated the original provision of religious liberty from the Sultan of Turkey in the 1850s.[52] In 1990 the Alliance's investment in social affairs was further increased when the social and foreign affairs department was divided and Mike Morris was given responsibility for foreign affairs.[53] It was recognised that the socio-political issues in Britain were complex and required expertise. The Movement for Christian Democracy was formed in 1990 and David Alton MP, someone identified with issues such as abortion law

---

51  *idea*, Autumn 1987, p.2.
52  *idea*, January–February 1989, pp.8–9.
53  Minutes of the Executive Committee, 27 March 1990.

reform, commented on how it had introduced Catholics and evangelicals to each other.[54]

Martyn Eden, who had been a university lecturer in politics and social administration and then Director of Christian Impact (formerly the London Institute for Contemporary Christianity), was appointed in 1990 to the Alliance's Home Affairs department, previously run by Morris. It was Eden's task to encourage Christians to become more involved with local as well as national issues. From his perspective, evangelicals were increasingly aware of issues like Sunday trading, abortion and embryo experimentation. He believed that the work in recent years of evangelical events and agencies such as Spring Harvest, the Jubilee Centre and CARE Trust had helped evangelicals to become more socially aware and active. His commitment was to widen that concern to issues such as homelessness, housing and education.[55] The vision that had led to the setting up of the London Institute for Contemporary Christianity, which was that Christians should be helped to integrate their faith into every dimension of their lives and to penetrate the secular world for Christ, was being carried over to the Alliance.

Even more attention was given to social action from 1992, when Fred Catherwood became President of the Alliance. 'British Churches', he insisted in October 1992, 'are not doing enough to combat racism and nationalism.' He urged that Christian teaching which presented the church as 'a universal church of all races and all classes' should be coming across very powerfully. Still, however, he did not believe that it was being communicated with sufficient impact.[56] In the summer of 1993 *idea* was delighted to report that Catherwood was leaving politics to spearhead an Alliance campaign to address Britain's moral, social and spiritual problems. He would be working

54  D. Alton, preface to C. Colson & R. J. Neuhaus, (eds), *Evangelicals and Catholics Together: Working Towards a Common Mission* (London: Hodder & Stoughton, 1996).

55  *idea*, September–October 1990, p.5.

56  *Alpha*, October 1992, p.25.

full-time as President of the Alliance and would devote his energy to 'encouraging evangelicals to be more effective in their social care and faith evangelism, particularly in the inner cities'. Although he had enjoyed being a politician, Catherwood believed that evangelical churches and organisations were closer to 'the human wreckage of today's society'. They were dealing, he said, with 'the traumas of wrecked marriages, reaching out to teenagers who roam the estates, and caring for elderly people who have been abandoned by their families'. His commitment was to encourage this work.[57]

A nationwide tour was planned for 1994 and other visits were made by Catherwood to meet local church leaders around the UK and to address church congregations. Under the auspices of the Alliance, he aimed to stimulate co-operation among evangelical churches and societies and the launching of new ventures in areas such as community care, evangelism and employment training. The name given to these new ventures was Christian Action Networks (CANS). In *CAN News* in 1996 Catherwood reported that he had visited twenty-five cities over the past three years, and in each case had seen a project that set a standard in its field. Evangelicals ran these projects. Whether, said Catherwood, 'it was debt counselling or jobs for the jobless, someone had cracked the problem with which others were still struggling'. The way in which the CANS were developing gave Catherwood hope that this would be a significant advance in evangelical social action. His idea of networks was not simply that the churches in a city should know where to find help when they had to care for a needy person. Rather, he wished to build and use a national network so that all churches could have access to the expertise available in Britain that was relevant to their particular kind of activity.[58] It was a vision that was in continuity with that of a Victorian evangelical reformer such as Shaftesbury.

---

57  *idea*, June–August 1993, pp.1–2.
58  *CAN News*, No. 1, 1996, p.1.

## From 1966 to 1996

In spite of the obvious success that the Alliance was enjoying in the mid-1990s, it was with some trepidation and with considerable care that plans were made for a major Assembly to mark the Alliance's 150th anniversary in the Autumn of 1996. The magazine *Christianity*, reporting on plans for the Assembly, asked a pertinent question. Given the memory of previous assemblies (in fact, only rather unclear versions of the assembly of 1966 lived in the memories), and given the evangelical tendency to be fissiparous, why should the Evangelical Alliance risk another such gathering? The answer given by Joel Edwards was that the final years of the millennium were a *kairos* moment for evangelicals. Given the window of opportunity that existed – the degree of working together in society and the interest that was being generated – evangelicalism, he argued, must define itself clearly and agree a wide ranging agenda.[59] To an extent this had already been happening over the previous years, but the assembly was to be a high profile occasion.

The Assembly was also the culmination of a year of celebration. In January 1996 the *Church Times* reported that the Evangelical Alliance was celebrating its 150th anniversary at Wembley with more members and more national influence than at any time in its history. The Archbishop of Canterbury, it observed, was the most prominent participant among the 2,400 people at the first in a series of celebration nights. The *Church Times* also noted that as final preparations were being made for the Evangelical Alliance event it emerged that Clive Calver had been to Downing Street for private talks with John Major, the Prime Minister. It was the social agenda that was apparently in view. The Alliance was attracting the attention of politicians because of its involvement in coalitions, forums and agencies addressing issues like drugs, disability and education.[60]

---

59 *Christianity*, December 1996, p.24.
60 *Church Times* 12 January, 1996, p.5.

Other newspapers saw the meeting with the Prime Minister in strictly political terms. John Major had become aware of the changing face of the Church of England, with claims being made that one in four Anglicans were evangelical, and he now wished to ascertain the political views of evangelicals. Two prominent evangelicals accompanied Major at the meeting – Lord McColl, his Parliamentary Private Secretary, and Michael Alison, a Church Estates Commissioner.[61]

The Assembly was held at the Bournemouth International Centre and attracted 3,000 delegates. Clive Calver's keynote speech took up the theme of unity. He appealed to delegates to 'override their differences and focus on what they have in common'. The unity that Calver urged seemed to be evident in the results of a wide-ranging survey of some of the 4,000 congregations and groups in membership of the Alliance. More than eight out of ten of the churches that responded considered that the growing gap between the rich and poor in Britain was unjust, and that a worthwhile goal for the millennium would be a significant reduction in homelessness. The survey also revealed that 96% of evangelical congregations believed homosexual practice to be wrong. An almost identical proportion, 95%, said that sexual intercourse outside marriage was wrong. Calver described the results as 'a clear re-statement of traditional Christian morality and values' and added that the new millennium would require a new kind of evangelicalism, which would in fact be a return to the old evangelicalism of William Booth, Charles Spurgeon, Dr Barnardo and Lord Shaftesbury, all of whom had helped to change the face of their society.[62]

The stress on social issues at the Assembly was striking. The Bishop of Hull, James Jones (subsequently Bishop of Liverpool), launched a campaign for the doubling of child benefit to parents who attended parenting courses. He called for politicians to match the rhetoric about the family with policies that

---

61  *Daily Telegraph*, 6 July 1996, p.4.

62  *idea*, January–March 1997, p.8.

strengthened the family. National and local media took up the Bishop's speech and he became involved in several hours of radio and television interviews. Fred Catherwood similarly addressed social issues in his speech to the Assembly. He blamed the rise of an underclass in Britain on the greed of many of those in employment whose interests, he said, were purely in tax cuts, at the expense of the unemployed. He called for the restoration of full employment, arguing that work was necessary for the dignity of the individual. Steve Chalke, a Baptist minister whose involvement in social action included the launch of Oasis Trust, and who was regularly on television, closed the Assembly. He described how many of his television colleagues perceived evangelicals as 'bigoted and uninformed', preaching the Bible in a vacuum, and not against the background of life. This, however, had not been the kind of approach seen at Bournemouth. Rather, evangelicals who looked outwards, not inwards, had marked the Assembly. Such a shift of perspective, declared Chalke to great applause, represented the kind of evangelicalism to which he wanted to belong.[63]

## Conclusion

Clive Calver was determined to effect change when he became General Secretary of the Alliance in 1983. This change was not, however, a departure from Alliance tradition. Over the next ten years he encouraged the diversity of the Alliance, a theme that had been present from the beginning of its life. He also worked hard to achieve the deepening of evangelical unity. An article in the American periodical *Christianity Today* in December 1996 summarised the objectives of the Alliance, 150 years after its commencement, as the promotion of unity in the church, the encouragement of united prayer and evangelism, and the enabling of Christians to act as salt and light in

---

63  Ibid., p.9.

society. It was the last point that was most important to Calver. 'As evangelicals have begun to depart from an inherited policy of self-imposed isolation', he said, 'they have emerged from their comfortable ghettos to grapple with the needs of contemporary society.'[64] The fact that the highly respected Catherwood committed himself to Christian Action Networks helped to persuade evangelicals to give this social thrust a strong measure of support. Evangelical renewal and growth had given to evangelicals a much greater confidence. Alliance leaders and others managed internal tensions within evangelicalism so that they did not cause serious division. Calver, who left Britain in 1997 to take up a new post as President of World Relief in the USA, had helped to change the face of British evangelicalism. The growth of the Alliance's membership and profile during his period in office had been unprecedented. There had been several richly gifted General Secretaries before him, but none had made a greater impact.

---

64  *Christianity Today*, 9 December 1996, p.30.

13

# A Knife–Edge Exercise

*Theology and Ethics in the Recent History of the Alliance*

## The Formation of ACUTE

In late 1992 Clive Calver paid a visit to Jerusalem. As we have seen, Calver had led the Alliance into remarkable growth throughout the preceding decade. Even so, while in Israel he realised that something was missing. Moreover, he was sufficiently well versed in the formation of the evangelical worldview to appreciate that this deficit was not new. On arriving back in Britain, he articulated it thus, in a report entitled 'The Jerusalem Paper':

> The last decade has witnessed transformation and growth within the Alliance. [But] the emphasis [of this paper] is on an [outstanding] strategic area of weakness, *viz.,* EA's lack of proper theological undergirding for what it is attempting to do. In 1846, our forefathers began by establishing a clear theological foundation. They then proceeded to establish a vehicle for evangelical unity and inquired as to what its prime functions and practical outworkings should be. The great Scottish secessionist Thomas Chalmers raised the objection that the Alliance could become a 'do nothing' society. He would not retain that fear today. However, the opposite objection is sometimes raised – 'EA does a great deal, but what is its undergirding raison d'être? Has it thought through the correct theological basis for its attitudes and activities?'

Calver went on to suggest reasons why such issues were arising. 'Much of the ground for this concern', he wrote, 'emanates from the fact that the majority of EA's present leadership are

activists at heart. Their desire is to build on the basis of evangelical unity those achievements which can be viewed as measur-
able gains.' This pragmatic approach, he stressed, had much to
commend it: 'It can be argued that the current membership
growth indicates popular estimation of the value of what is
being achieved by EA's coalitions, staff and specific initiatives.'
Even so, he concluded, 'it is also observable that little emphasis
is placed on relating ... doctrinal perspectives to our current
cultural and theological situation.'[1]

Calver's recognition of the detrimental effects of evangelical
activism on serious theological reflection echoed a prominent
theme of David Bebbington's, *Evangelicalism in Modern Britain*.
In the wake of the Wesley-Whitefield revival, with its characteristically 'utilitarian' approach to mission and ministry,
Bebbington notes that for many evangelicals, 'Learning [came
to be] regarded as a dispensable luxury.' Hence,

> At the beginning of the nineteenth century Independent ministers were
> trained not in theology or Greek, but simply in preaching. It would have been
> 'highly improper', according to a contributor to their magazine, 'to spend, in
> literary acquisitions, the time and talents which were so imperiously de-
> manded in the harvest field'.[2]

Such pragmatism, notes Bebbington, fuelled the flexible, ad
hoc ecclesiology of early Methodism and the contingency of
most Free Church evangelical approaches to liturgy and worship during this period.[3] As Os Guinness has observed, it also
reflected the wider economic and social changes that were
afoot in Britain during the same era:

> Through hard work, commonsense and ingenuity, evangelicals prospered and
> dotted the countryside and towns not only with mills, but also with church
> buildings. The Protestant work ethic took hold. A by-product, however, was
> an indifference to ideas in general and theology in particular. If God had

---

1  C. Calver, 'The Jerusalem Paper', Evangelical Alliance archive, London, dated
28 November 1992, pp.1-2.

2  Bebbington, *Evangelicalism in Modern Britain*, p.12.

3  Ibid., pp.65-6.

blessed the industrial enterprise with success, what need was there of theological sophistication? Pragmatism became a pronounced characteristic of evangelicalism, and has remained so ever since.[4]

The same entrepreneurial perspective has also been identified as a key feature of evangelicalism by David Wells. Wells argues that the ambitious drive of many early evangelicals achieved much in terms of evangelism, church building and statistical growth, but also 'produced some savage anti-clericalism, for example, not just because of undercurrents of anti-intellectualism but also because the insurgent leaders were "intent on destroying the monopoly of classically educated and university trained clergymen"'.[5] This vigorously populist legacy is now evident, suggests Wells, in the proliferation of the evangelical 'religious marketplace', with increasing numbers of parachurch ministries and agencies competing for support and money – most of them too preoccupied with their own 'bottom line' to engage in serious collaborative theological reflection. He also sees the same legacy manifested in the ever-expanding 'church growth' sector, where results are given greater weight than theology, and competition tends to come before co-operation.[6] This fragmented picture more generally bears out what Kenneth Hylson-Smith has called evangelicalism's 'built-in tendency to be centrifugal rather than centripetal'. By its very nature, Hylson-Smith remarks, evangelicalism 'encourages individuality, stresses personal faith and promotes distinctive individual or group expressions of faith and practice'. No doubt, such characteristics ensure a large measure of personal and corporate creativity; but, warns Hylson-Smith, they also 'almost guarantee divisiveness'.[7]

4 O. Guinness, *Fit Bodies: Fat Minds: Why Evangelicals Don't Think and What to Do About It* (London: Hodder & Stoughton, 1995), p.58.

5 D.F. Wells, *God in the Wasteland: The Reality of Truth in a World of Fading Dreams* (Leicester: IVP, 1994), p.65.

6 Ibid., pp.65-87.

7 K. Hylson-Smith, 'Roots of Pan-Evangelicalism, 1735-1835', in Brady & Rowdon (eds), *For Such a Time as This*, p.137.

As a keen student of evangelical history, Clive Calver no doubt had all these forces in mind when he wrote of pragmatism as a decidedly mixed blessing, and of the theological dangers that could befall an Alliance whose activist leadership had achieved such impressive numerical gains in so short a time. In this sense, his 'Jerusalem Paper' resonated with concerns expressed by the lawyer John Langlois and the theologian Bruce Nicholls when they had helped to form the World Evangelical Fellowship's Theological Commission eighteen years before – namely, that too many practical evangelical initiatives turn out to be 'shallow, resulting in a ripple lasting only a generation'. [8] Calver's solution to all this was to propose a new theological advisory group for the Alliance – a group that would become known as 'ACUTE'.

The 'Jerusalem Paper' recommended the appointment by the Alliance of a part-time theological consultant who would be chiefly responsible for servicing an 'Evangelical Unity Commission' comprised of Alliance staff, Council members and specialist academics. At various times in the past, there had been sub-committees, groups and individuals appointed to deal with theological concerns. As we have seen, the 'Infidelity Committee' of the 1870s and 80s had a brief to combat 'rationalism', while in the 1960s John Stott had chaired a 'Theological Committee' whose main achievement had been the revision of the Basis of Faith. As the media profile of the Alliance rose in the 1980s, Calver had been increasingly invited to discuss doctrinal questions on radio and in the newspapers: he emerged, for example, as a leading voice against both the pronouncements of David Jenkins, the liberal Bishop of Durham, on the virgin birth and the resurrection, and the 'Sea of Faith' movement initiated by the radical Anglican philosopher, Don Cupitt. Calver's new vision, however, was for something rather more ambitious and proactive. Although the key issues outlined for consideration by the Commission were largely 'intra-ecclesial' – ranging from reassessment of the Alliance

---

8 Langlois quoted in Fuller, *People of the Mandate*, ch. 10.

Basis of Faith, through ecumenism and charismata to separat-ism – Calver also noted that 'theology is not merely internal, but external in its application'. Concentration, he urged, 'must also be given to EA's role in representing evangelical theology to secular society'.[9] This tension between internal 'peacemak-ing' and wider prophetic witness would become more appar-ent as the Commission developed.

On 2 December 1993, almost a year to the day after the 'Jerusalem Paper' had been presented to senior staff and members of the Alliance, the inaugural meeting of the 'Com-mission on Unity and Truth among Evangelicals' (CUTE) took place at the Alliance's headquarters in London. The Commission was to be co-ordinated on a part-time basis by Dave Cave – a Baptist minister well known for his work on urban theology and mission. By the end of the meeting, it had been agreed to replace the rather unfortunate acronym CUTE with ACUTE – the 'Active Commission on Unity and Truth among Evangelicals'. 'Active' was soon replaced by 'Alliance'.

Before tracking the subsequent agenda of ACUTE, it is worth noting that even the very act of its formation set the Alliance apart from most other non-ecclesiastical Christian or-ganisations in the UK and, one presumes, the world. In a report presented to the Bible Society in January 1997, Mark Bonnington analysed the structures and processes of theologi-cal reflection in a number of Christian agencies, most of which were evangelical in outlook. While the majority of groups sur-veyed expressed a strong commitment to biblical and theologi-cal reflection on their work, Bonnington found that only 14% actually had a leading committee charged with offering such reflection, and only 17% a nominated individual who had been allocated this task.[10] ACUTE's was thus a rare birth, even while it apparently embodied the aspirations of many within the

9  Calver, 'The Jerusalem Paper', pp.9-12.
10  M. Bonnington, 'The Bible and Christian Organisations', A Report Presented to the Bible Society Comprising the Results of the Salt and Light Research Pro-ject, January 1997, Summarised by Roy McCloughry, October 1999.

Christian community. The 'Jerusalem Paper' had clearly envisaged it as providing much-needed scriptural and doctrinal reflection at the nexus of the academic world, the church and the mission field, and in doing so saw it as speaking for many who are otherwise too busy, or too under-resourced, to generate such reflection for themselves. Indeed, as Bonnington put it in his report, '[Christian] organisations are large, complex and action-orientated ... Usually there is no consistent hermeneutical strategy and when occasions for interpretation do occur, their relationship to the "organisation" is not clear.'[11]

ACUTE was to be tied firmly to the Alliance's Basis of Faith, but Calver recognised that the *application* of that Basis in particular cases could not always be straightforward, and would require very much the sort of holistic hermeneutical endeavour defined by Bonnington. As we saw in chapter 5, this interpretative challenge had been recognised by the Alliance from its earliest decades, as it had sought to grapple with debates on such matters as revival, higher criticism and hell. At the turn of the 21$^{st}$ century, the range of issues which impinged on the delicate balance of evangelical unity and truth would, if anything, appear even greater than it had in the days of the Ulster outpouring, Darwin, the Tübingen School and T.R. Birks. In his introductory remarks to the first ACUTE meeting, Calver stressed that the new Commission had been mandated to 'work through' issues 'which divide evangelicals', and to report directly to the Executive. In order to do this effectively, it had been composed, he said, to reflect the denominational and doctrinal diversity of the Alliance's membership. Calver then added the startling comment that the Commission would constitute 'the single greatest influence on Alliance policy'.[12]

In the years since its inception, it must be said that this bold vision of theological discourse driving Alliance strategy and forward planning looks to have been somewhat hyperbolic.

---

11  Bonnington, 'The Bible and Christian Organisations', pp.17-8.
12  Minutes of the Commission on Unity and Truth Among Evangelicals, 2 December 1993.

Even so, ACUTE, and the wider theological work it has spawned, has made a valuable contribution, not only to the output of the Alliance as a whole, but to its essential self-understanding as an organisation. This has been borne out by the fact that the original half-time appointment of Dave Cave, which ran from 1993-6, was expanded after he returned to pastoral ministry and was replaced by the co-author of this book, David Hilborn. An ordained minister of the United Reformed Church (URC), Hilborn came to the Alliance having done his doctorate under Anthony C. Thiselton, the leading evangelical hermeneutics scholar, and having pastored at the City Temple in Holborn – the place where the Baptist Union had sought to resolve the Downgrade controversy in April 1888, where R.J. Campbell had initiated the 'New Theology' debate, and where Tom Rees had led many of his evangelistic rallies after the Second World War. Hilborn's role now includes the running of an in-house 'Theology Department' within the Alliance, whose brief beyond ACUTE per se is to handle members' inquiries, liaise with the media, train staff in theological matters relevant to their work, oversee a dedicated page on the Alliance website and brief managers on doctrinal topics, as appropriate.

ACUTE has grown to comprise a Steering Group of twenty theologians. Having been chaired by the other co-author of this history, Ian Randall, this body now meets under the Chairmanship of Professor David Wright of Edinburgh University. It convenes at least three times a year for half a day and aims to reflect the breadth of the Alliance's constituency while maintaining a high level of theological expertise. Roughly half the Group are academic theologians working in theological colleges and university departments, or involved regularly in theological education. The remaining half consists of pastors, teachers and practitioners working more directly 'in the field', but committed to serious theological reflection.

From its inception, ACUTE has pursued its brief in a range of ways. From time to time, it has published reports on key issues of concern to evangelicals and/or the wider church. Latterly, these have been produced and marketed in collaboration with Paternoster Press. At other times, it has generated internal discussion documents and research papers to aid the Alliance Council in its decision-making. It has also been responsible for gathering evangelical leaders together in order to debate and reflect on specific theological tensions. Indeed, once it had been formed, ACUTE very soon found that it had to convene such gatherings as a matter of urgency.

## The 'Toronto Blessing' Debate

We saw in chapter 5 that the Alliance played an important role in the so-called 'Ulster Revival' of 1859, covering the issue extensively in *Evangelical Christendom* and engaging the renowned scholar James McCosh to write a paper on it. In the latter half of 1994 a growing constituency of mainly charismatic evangelicals began to invoke the Ulster Revival and other revivals as precedents for a new spiritual movement – a movement that became known as the 'Toronto Blessing'. However, whereas the 1859 revival had attracted overwhelming support from the Alliance, 'Toronto' soon threatened to divide it, and thereby to undermine much of the progress made under Clive Calver in the preceding eleven years. As such, it represented a major test of the Alliance's ability to strike a biblical balance of unity and truth, and a formative challenge to its newly established theological commission.

The phrase 'Toronto Blessing' first appeared in the public domain courtesy of the *Times* journalist Ruth Gledhill. In an article printed on Saturday 18 June 1994 Gledhill reported that it was becoming popular as a nickname for a 'religious craze' of 'mass fainting' that had 'crossed the Atlantic to cause concern in the Church of England'.[13] As it was, the 'craze' to which Gledhill alluded had several antecedents, involved rather more than 'mass fainting', and went on to prompt

13 R. Gledhill, 'Spread of Hysteria Fad Worries Church', *The Times*, 18 June 1994, p.12.

debate and discussion well beyond the Church of England. Gledhill's geographical reference was to the Toronto Airport Vineyard (TAV) – a church led by John and Carol Arnott, and overseen by the influential charismatic evangelist and teacher John Wimber. Wimber's Association of Vineyard Churches (AVC) had grown remarkably through the 1980s to become a force within North American evangelicalism. TAV had started as an independent congregation, but contact with Wimber in the late 1980s led the Arnotts to place it within the Vineyard network. During the same period a number of Vineyard churches were planted overseas, and Wimber made a significant impact on historic churches beyond the USA and Canada – not least within Anglican and Baptist member congregations of the Evangelical Alliance in the UK.[14]

Peter Wagner, Wimber's friend and former Fuller Seminary colleague, had defined the distinctive approach of Wimber and the Vineyard as 'Third Wave' renewal. This term was coined to suggest that it represented a development from the 'first wave' of classical Pentecostalism, and from the 'second wave' of the post-war charismatic movement. According to Wagner, the 'Third Wave' borrowed extensively from these two earlier developments but differed from one or both of them on certain key points. In contrast to classical Pentecostalism, it disavowed the notion that the baptism of the Holy Spirit is a second work of grace subsequent to conversion. Rather, it expected multiple fillings of the Holy Spirit consequent upon new birth, some of which were akin to what others would call 'baptism in the Spirit'. Also in distinction from classical Pentecostalism, it viewed the gift of speaking in tongues not as 'initial evidence' of Spirit baptism, but as one of many gifts given by God to the Church – a gift that may be granted to some and not to others. In comparison with both First and Second Wave renewal, the model of ministry developed by Wimber and the Vineyard

---

14 For a helpful account of Wimber's ministry and its impact on the UK, see Scotland, *Charismatics*, pp.199-250. Also D. McBain, *Charismatic Christianity* (Basingstoke: Macmillan, 1997).

placed particular emphasis on the power and demonstration of the Holy Spirit's work in 'signs and wonders' such as healing and deliverance. In addition, it claimed to be more overtly committed to 'body ministry' – that is, to a corporate expression of spiritual gifts and a team ethos in ministry, as distinct from either the 'anointed man'/'faith healer' focus of much classical Pentecostalism, or the clergy-driven ecclesiology of many historic denominations.[15]

As well as these defining features, Vineyard-style meetings through the 1980s had begun to exhibit other marked elements. From at least 1986 significant instances of 'holy laughter' were recorded, along with already-established phenomena like slumping or falling to the floor, trembling and weeping.[16] Despite the growth and profile of this Third Wave/Vineyard movement, with its high degree of charismatic openness, by the early 1990s, a number of its pastors and leaders appear to have been seeking fresh impetus and 'anointing'. In late 1993 Arnott and various colleagues visited key figures in the 'Argentinean Revival' – a significant wave of evangelical church growth centred on Buenos Aires.[17] While they were looking towards South America, another Vineyard leader, Randy Clark of the St Louis Vineyard in Missouri, was experiencing a radical personal transformation under the ministry of Rodney Howard-Browne.

Rodney Howard-Browne had come to the USA from his native South Africa in 1987. A child of devoutly Pentecostal parents, his American ministry gained considerable momentum in 1989 when laughter and 'slaying' or falling down in the

---

15  C. Wagner, 'Third Wave', in S. M. Burgess, G.B. McGee & H. Alexander (eds), *Dictionary of Pentecostal and Charismatic Movements* (Grand Rapids: Zondervan, 1988), pp.843-4.

16  M. Robertson, 'A Power Encounter Worth Laughing About', in K. Springer (ed.), *Power Encounters Among Christians in the Western World* (San Fransisco: Harper & Row, 1988), pp.149-57; W.J. Oropeza, *A Time to Laugh: The Holy Laughter Phenomenon Examined* (Peabody: Hendrickson, 1995), p.17.

17  G. Chevreau, *Catch the Fire* (London: Marshall Pickering, 1994), p.23; Oropeza, *A Time to Laugh*, p.22; D. Roberts, *The 'Toronto' Blessing* (Eastbourne: Kingsway, 1984), p.31.

Spirit became more prominent in his evangelistic meetings.[18] While such things were hardly unknown in Vineyard circles, Randy Clark found them occurring around Howard-Browne at a level of intensity that deeply impressed him. Clark had been virtually burned-out by a demanding pastorate, and this condition appears to have prompted him to overlook doubts about Howard-Browne's style and theological background. Very much a classic 'front man' Pentecostal, Howard-Browne had also trained and ministered in the 'Rhema' and 'Word of Faith' constituencies – key engines of the so-called 'prosperity gospel' movement. Indeed, it was in Tulsa, Oklahoma – a major Word of Faith centre – that Clark first encountered Howard-Browne in August 1993, and duly ended up on the floor laughing.[19] Subsequently, as Arnott and other Vineyard leaders returned from Argentina, Clark informed them of what had happened to him, and of the effect it had begun to have on his congregation, some 95% of whom had 'fallen under the power' on his return from Tulsa. At this same meeting, Arnott invited Clark to visit TAV in the New Year.[20] Clark accepted, and on Thursday 20 January 1994 he led a 'family night' at the airport church. As he called people forward for prayer, large numbers manifested a range of dramatic physical phenomena, from falling and then 'resting' in the Spirit, to laughing, shaking, prostration and healing. Within weeks, word of what was happening had spread, visitors to TAV were increasing, and some had begun to fly in from overseas to investigate.[21]

Back in St Louis, during April and May 1994, Rodney Howard-Browne led a series of equally spectacular meetings, some of which were attended by Terry Virgo, leader of the British-based charismatic network New Frontiers International – a member body of the UK Alliance. Along with other

18  Roberts, *The 'Toronto' Blessing,* p.85.
19  'Rumours of Revival', *Alpha,* July 1994, p.46; Oropeza, *A Time to Laugh,* p.22, citing R. Riss, 'History of the Revival, 1993-1995'.
20  Chevreau, *Catch the Fire,* pp.23-4.
21  Roberts, *The 'Toronto' Blessing,* pp.20-21.

Britons who had attended TAV during this period, Virgo reported what had been happening to his colleagues, and various outbreaks of 'Toronto-style' manifestations began to occur in the UK.[22] Two further Alliance member bodies – Queen's Road Baptist Church, Wimbledon, and the Ichthus Fellowship in South London – had already started to experience such manifestations when Eleanor Mumford, of the Vineyard's own Putney congregation, met with leaders of the high-profile Anglican charismatic church Holy Trinity, Brompton (HTB), on Tuesday 24 May.[23] After reporting on a recent visit to TAV, Mumford saw key members of 'HTB's' leadership team rendered virtually immobile as they, too, fell, shook, rested and laughed.[24] Significantly, Sandy Millar, the Vicar of HTB, had to be called to this meeting from another which he was attending at the same time at the Evangelical Alliance. The following Sunday, Eleanor Mumford preached at HTB with similar effect,[25] and news that hundreds of largely upper middle class Knightsbridge churchgoers were rolling around as if 'drunk' and 'helpless' at services soon caught the attention of the press – hence the interest of the *Times*, and Ruth Gledhill's coinage of the term 'Toronto Blessing'.

Within weeks, the Blessing had spread to hundreds of churches across the British Isles, and estimates were suggesting that between 2,000 and 4,000 congregations had embraced it by the end of 1994.[26] The Blessing became one of the biggest

22  T. Virgo, *A People Prepared* (Eastbourne: Kingsway, 1996), pp.13-4.

23  R. Warner, *Prepare for Revival* (London: Hodder & Stoughton, 1995), pp.2-3; P. Dixon, *Signs of Revival* (Eastbourne: Kingsway, 1994), pp.19-21.

24  Roberts, *The 'Toronto' Blessing*, p.25; 'A Day By Day Diary of What We Have Seen', *HTB in Focus*, 12 June 1994, p.3; M. Fearon, *A Breath of Fresh Air* (Guildford: Eagle, 1984), pp.115-6.

25  E. Mumford, 'Spreading Like Wildfire', in W. Boulton (ed.), *The Impact of Toronto* (Crowborough: Monarch, 1995), pp.17-9. For a fuller transcript, see 'A Mighty Wind from Toronto', *HTB in Focus*, 12 June 1994, pp.4-5.

26  M. Fearon, 'Principal of Laughter', *Church of England Newspaper*, 11 November 1994, p.8; C. Price, 'Surfing the Toronto Wave', *Alpha*, May 1995, pp.6-9; G. Coates, in *Rumours of Revival* (Video), Milton Keynes: Nelson Word, 1995. C. Gardner, 'Catching a Glimpse of God's Glory', *Joy*, March 1995, pp.17-8.

stories covered by the British Christian media in recent times, and remained so through 1995 and into early 1996. It also appeared frequently as a subject of debate and discussion in the secular press – not only in the religious pages, but in the news sections too. As such, the Toronto Blessing very quickly came to engage the time, attention and pastoral capacity of the Evangelical Alliance more than any unprogrammed issue since Martyn Lloyd-Jones and John Stott famously clashed over evangelical church allegiance in 1966.[27] The Blessing, too, soon proved highly contentious. It seemed to many – not only liberals, traditionalists and conservatives, but also some established charismatics – to represent a dangerously potent and fast-breeding strain of fanaticism which could seriously destabilise the church. Even those who rejected this view, and who instead championed the Blessing, sometimes did so with a zeal that only provoked further polarisation. Not surprisingly in view of its provenance, arguments about the Blessing were most numerous and most heated among evangelicals.

As the twentieth century unfolded, the majority of Pentecostals and charismatics came readily to identify with evangelicalism's typically high view of Christ and Scripture, its commitment to conversion, its activism and its objective view of atonement. Granted, not all evangelicals – and especially not those in more classically Reformed circles – were happy to confirm this identity, and a good deal of familiarly heated debate arose as a result. Even so, in all but the most separatist and fundamentalist quarters, it is clear that a degree of tolerance and mutual co-operation developed in the British context during the 1970s and '80s – a development which owed a great deal to the work of the Evangelical Alliance. With the rise of Toronto, however, old fault-lines were once again exposed, and concerns that had either been sublimated or suppressed for the greater cause of unity, were reiterated. Many of those who welcomed the emergence of 'Toronto' were confirmed in their view that those who opposed it had an insufficiently dynamic

---

27 See chapters 10 and 11.

understanding of the Holy Spirit. Similarly, opponents tended to present the Blessing as evidence of a long-held conviction that despite its protestations to the contrary; the charismatic movement in fact relied too much on experience, and not enough on Scripture. Prominent among the former group were established charismatic leaders like Virgo, Sandy Millar, Gerald Coates and Rob Warner. Among the latter were known anti-charismatic detractors such as Christian Research Ministries, Tricia Tillin,[28] and the Derbyshire Baptist minister Alan Morrison, whose Diakrisis organisation launched a range of fierce broadsides against the Blessing from July 1994 onwards.[29] Then again, while the Blessing predictably incurred the scorn of many separatist Reformed evangelicals, it was also challenged by the self-professed charismatics of the Centre for Christian Ministry, by the 17th World Pentecostal Conference, and a group of Sheffield-based charismatic scholars who would go on to produce a stinging critique of the Blessing's theology.[30]

This fractious atmosphere put the Evangelical Alliance under considerable pressure. Not surprisingly, given his own background and vision, Clive Calver sought to foster a balanced, constructive outlook. Invited to address a conference organised by Holy Trinity, Brompton in early August 1994, he took the opportunity to assess the new movement and its implications for British evangelicalism:

> Just after this move of God started I was in a set of churches and they said, 'Is this an awakening?' And I said, 'No. An awakening is what God does in the

28  Christian Research Ministries report, cit. S. Dube, 'Holy Spirit "Blessing" Dismissed as Demonic', *Western Mail,* 5 September 1994; T. Tillin, *Looking Beyond Toronto: The Source and Goal of Pentecost* (Banner Ministries, 1994), S. and C. Thompson quoted in J.A. Beverley, 'Toronto's Mixed Blessing', *Christianity Today,* 11 September 1995, pp.23-6.

29  A. Morrison, *We All Fall Down* (Crich: Diakrisis, 1994).

30  Centre for Contemporary Ministry, *Charismatic Crossroads*; L. Pietersen (ed.) *Mark of the Spirit? A Charismatic Critique of the Toronto Blessing* (Carlisle: Paternoster Press, 1998); J.L. Grady, 'Classical Pentecostals Wary of the "Toronto Blessing"', *Charisma,* November 1995, pp.41-2.

world when he turns society around as he did in the 18th century.' They said, 'Is this revival?' I said, 'I don't think so. Revival is what God does when he brings the world into the church.' They said, 'Is this renewal?' I said, 'Yes, definitely. It's as important as this: you have never had an awakening in history that hasn't started in renewal and revival.' Now I want to see an awakening. I want to see God touch our nation and to see God turn our society upside down and inside out. But he won't start in society. He'll start with the people of God.[31]

Realising its responsibility, the Alliance mandated ACUTE to organise three major forums on the Blessing in 1994-5.[32] While some on the separatist wing of evangelicalism dismissed them as fronts for an Alliance overrun by charismatics,[33] they in fact engaged a representative proportion of leaders from that 42% of the Alliance's membership which around this time did not define itself as charismatic.[34]

The first of these gatherings took place at the Ibis Hotel near London's Euston Station on 19-20 December 1994. Alongside Calver and Joel Edwards, the 23 leaders who attended included 'Toronto sceptics' like David Abernethie of Above Bar Church, Southampton, Robert Amess of Duke Street Baptist Church, Tony Baker of Bishop Hannington (Church of England), Hove, Alan Gibson of the British Evangelical Council, the Welsh theologian R. Tudur Jones and the leading Anglican conservative evangelicals Philip Hacking and Stephen Sizer. Those present who were more favourable to the new movement included Faith Forster of Ichthus, R.T. Kendall of Westminster Chapel, Bryn Jones of Harvest Time and Rob Warner – then at Herne Hill Baptist Church but soon to move on to Queen's Road, Wimbledon.

---

31  Quoted in *HTB in Focus*, 14 August 1994, p.10.

32  For summaries of these Consultations, see entries for 19-20 December 1994, 2 June 1995 and 21 December 1995 in Part II of D. Hilborn (ed.), *Toronto in Perspective: Papers on the New Charismatic Wave of the mid-1990s* (Carlisle: Paternoster Press, 2001).

33  A. Morrison, 'No Great Surprise', *Evangelical Times* (Letters), September 1995, p.18; 'Comment', *Evangelical Times*, September 1995, p.2.

34  This figure is derived from a 1998 survey of 848 Alliance member churches, the results of which were published in the Spring 1999 edition of the Alliance's churches' magazine, *Ear*, p.1.

The forum began with three short talks on revival. R.T. Kendall expounded Acts chapter 2 as the cardinal text for consideration of the Blessing. Tudur Jones then spoke of revival in church history, and Derek Tidball, Principal of London Bible College, continued with a reflection on the tensions that have often challenged the church at such times. There was then a period of open response and discussion before the meeting divided into four groups, each of which expressed a variety of opinions. Later on the first day, Stephen Sizer and Rob Warner were asked jointly to draft a statement that might reflect the theological consensus, mood, hopes and fears of those present. They worked on this into the early hours of the next day, and eventually presented a paragraph, 800-word text to the meeting. Under the guidance of Clive Calver, this was endorsed by all but one of those present.

The 'Euston Statement' itself began by stressing the need 'not only to evaluate' the Blessing, but also 'to make clear distinctions between primary and secondary convictions among us as evangelicals, even though we differ in our initial interpretations of these experiences'. It proceeded to define agreed primary convictions as the authority and divine inspiration of Scripture, the atoning work of Christ, the 'vital need' for personal conversion, and the prerogative of active witness and service in the world. It then rejoiced that God had poured out his Spirit in revivals, and that these had been 'intrinsic to the evangelical heritage' shared by those present. The text moved on to emphasise the need for a unity of Word and Spirit in evangelical life and action. With particular concern for the outworking of this unity in the evangelical context, it acknowledged that in the past, evangelicals had sometimes failed adequately to listen to one another, and 'to denigrate and caricature those with whom we disagree'. In the Euston consultation, the statement declared, 'we have sought to ask questions of ourselves and one another, without compromising the integrity of our consciously held differences'.

Dealing particularly with the manifestations related to revivals, the statement noted that they should be seen as 'secondary'. In and of themselves, it explained, 'they cannot … prove that a movement is or is not a work of God'. The final test must be 'the lasting, biblical fruit'. Acknowledging that the Toronto experience had not yet been 'integrated with theological reflection', clause 7 expressed thanks for those who had known 'genuine life-changing encounters' as a result of it, while regretting that 'some have neglected the discipline of biblical preaching in the face of current manifestations'. Warning against the dual dangers of imbibing 'the existentialist spirit of our age' along with the Toronto Blessing, and dismissing it out of sheer 'enlightenment rationalism', the text urged that the 'absolute truth of the gospel' should be guarded 'without compromise'.

The Euston Statement closed by deducing that the church in the UK was not yet experiencing revival, but accepted that many during the foregoing months had known significant 'enrichment'. This, the text went on, encouraged 'hope that we may be in a period of preparation for revival'. Concluding that any evaluation of the Toronto phenomena could only be 'provisional' at that point, the statement called for a group within the Evangelical Alliance 'to continue to provide evaluation and theological reflection on these developments within the church'. It then urged this group and others assessing Toronto to apply the eighteenth century revivalist theologian Jonathan Edwards' classic tests for a genuine work of God: exaltation of Christ in people's understanding; undermining of Satan's purposes; a fostering of greater regard for Scripture and truth; a cultivation of seriousness about the things of God, and of greater love for God, fellow Christians and the world as a whole.

The Ibis Hotel meeting and the Euston Statement received extensive press coverage. The Statement itself may have been less sharp-edged and detailed than many other declarations on the Toronto movement which were produced from more partisan quarters, but it remains one of the few documents published at that time which can claim a genuinely 'conciliar' and 'ecumenical' evangelical authority.[35]

The Blessing was at the height of its popularity when, six months on, the Alliance convened a second forum on the issue at its headquarters in Kennington. This time, some sixty leaders were present. Speakers for the day were David Coffey (Baptist Union General Secretary), David Noakes (Marlow Christian Fellowship lay leader), Roger Forster (Ichthus Fellowship founder), R.T. Kendall (Westminster Chapel) and Andrew Walker (King's College, London). Setting the scene for the consultation, Walker traced the provenance of the Blessing, after which he suggested that the Blessing was now moving, on analogy, from an 'Acts 2' phase to an 'Acts 15' phase – 'from the first stage of blessing to the church council phase of reflection'. The Alliance Consultation, he suggested, could represent an important development in this respect.

David Noakes then proceeded to present the Toronto movement as a severe challenge to the charismatic church. Although a charismatic, Noakes conceded, 'We have lost our way somewhat' and described many of the manifestations associated with the Blessing as being 'demonic'. By contrast, Roger Forster suggested that the new movement was not yet worthy of the term 'revival', but that it could legitimately be seen as a 'time of refreshing'. He suggested that most of the manifestations could be shown to have biblical precedent, and pointed out that Scripture could at times appear even more radical in this sphere than what had been occurring – e.g. in the levitation of Ezekiel. Through it all, however, Forster was insistent that the phenomena should be interpreted and explained, lest the movement fall foul of mystical obfuscation.

R.T. Kendall then surprised some by testifying that although he had been initially hostile to the Blessing, the personal transformations of his wife and son while sitting

---

35  We are using the term 'ecumenical' here in its general, biblical sense of Christian co-operation. Martyn Lloyd-Jones regularly spoke of 'evangelical ecumenicity', and this comes close to what we are implying.

under the ministry of Rodney Howard-Browne had forced him to revise his opinion. 'It just so happens', he said, 'that I believe Rodney is a man of God. God uses crude men who are not so literate ... and who stick their foot in it.' Recognising the use that was being made of Jonathan Edwards on both sides of the Toronto debate, Kendall pointed out that the New England theologian, in his sermon 'True Grace as Distinguished from the Doctrines of Devils', showed that the one thing the devil cannot do is to produce a true love for the glory of God. Kendall was ready, he said, to affirm that such love and glory were present in the new movement. Summing up, David Coffey appealed to Matthew chapter 18 as he called both for a deeper examination of the theological issues at stake in the Blessing, and a strengthened commitment to evangelical unity. The latter prerogative was vital, he said, at a time when political and social commentators were offering no clear solutions to society's loss of confidence.

The Whitefield House consultation ended with a request from those present that ACUTE undertake further work on Toronto, and in December 1995 it duly hosted a third consultation on the matter.[36] Held once again at Whitefield House, this meeting was addressed by Rob Warner, Brian Edwards (Chairman of the Fellowship of Independent Evangelical Churches' Theological Commission), Philip Hacking, and Dave Cave. By this point, the impact of the movement was waning – a fact reinforced by a recent split between the Toronto Airport Vineyard and the Vineyard Association.

Warner did not discuss this split, but was in any case at pains to stress that the Blessing could not be characterised as a homogeneous movement. Rather, he argued, it had often been successfully assimilated with existing denominational emphases, whether with classical Pentecostal approaches at leading 'Toronto church' Sunderland Christian Centre, or with the

---

36 Quotations from the consultation are taken from transcripts of the talks given. These transcripts have been published on the Evangelical Alliance website: www.eauk.org

distinctive liturgy of Anglicanism in parishes up and down the country. Warner added that while some non-charismatics had been 'judicious, measured and constructive' in their critique of the movement, others had been more 'intemperate'. To these he replied firmly: 'A movement of God cannot be properly evaluated by caricature. A work of God cannot be undone by such caricature. Smears, distortion and guilt by association are not devices of good evangelical theology. Are you opposed to emotionalism and manipulation? So am I. Are you equally opposed to what Paul described as "holding to the form of religion while denying its power"? So am I.'

Brian Edwards was considerably less sanguine about the Blessing, depicting it as symptomatic of the drift of many evangelicals away from commitment to the inerrancy and sufficiency of Scripture towards a more 'inductive' hermeneutic. 'From whatever perspective you begin', he opined, 'an honest biblical exegete will admit that any attempt to justify from the Bible such phenomena as "slaying in the Spirit", which has flippantly been referred to as "carpet time", uncontrolled hysterical laughter and various animal noises, reveals either an ignorance of or a disregard for sound principles of hermeneutics.' Against this model, Edwards called for a reaffirmation of traditional doctrines of Scripture and the historic evangelical approach to hermeneutics. Philip Hacking echoed Edwards' concerns about the place of the Bible. He warned that the Blessing was 'only the tip of an iceberg' concealing a deeper threat to evangelical integrity – namely, a relinquishing of the 'final authority of Scripture'. Some of the Blessing manifestations were, he said, 'so far removed from Scripture that I find it very difficult to accept the movement as being divinely inspired'.

In summing up, Dave Cave detailed the work done by himself, ACUTE and the Alliance on the Blessing since its rise. The Commission had sent representatives to a number of major consultations on the issue, he confirmed, and had gathered an extensive archive related to it. Even so, he concluded, 'The time and energy which have been expended on the "Toronto

Blessing" appear not only to have put evangelical against evangelical, but also to have diverted us from our two main tasks – to glorify God and to go out into all the world and preach the good news.'

Drawing on the benefit of hindsight, in early 2001 David Hilborn collected a series of essays from prominent evangelical thinkers on the impact of the Blessing, and added to them a detailed chronology of the movement based on the Alliance archive. He also incorporated statements on it from various Christian bodies around the world. Contributors included David Pawson, Margaret Paloma and Stephen Sizer. Extracts from the resultant book, *Toronto in Perspective*, were posted on the Alliance's web site prior to publication. Among these extracts was Hilborn's own introductory essay. Referring to Toronto as a paradigmatic 'crisis' of evangelical definition, discernment and unity, he went on to assess the part played by the Alliance in dealing with this crisis:

> Against [the] fraught backdrop [of the Toronto controversy], the role and work of the Evangelical Alliance became crucial. No doubt the Blessing spurred many conferences, consultations, studies and statements, but the truth is that these tended to reflect the views of one 'side' or another in the debate, and thus tended to reinforce, rather than ameliorate, existing differences. Of course, some of those who took it upon themselves to attack the movement saw themselves in a 'prophetic' role – warning the church against a perilous deception. As such, any attempt at dialogue or co-operation with proponents of Toronto was presented by them as a compromise to be avoided.[37] On the other hand, there were those in the forefront of the movement who, when it was at its height, saw little point in having to justify something so self-evidently 'of God' to those whose theological presuppositions ensured that they would always be set against it. As the largest pan-evangelical body in the UK, the Alliance was probably the only organisation which could seriously hope to work through and beyond these polarities, and thereby reiterate a unity which could be neither cheap nor monolithic, but which would be grounded in genuine biblical collegiality.[38]

---

37  See, for example, Morrison, 'No Great Surprise', p.18.
38  D. Hilborn, 'Evangelicalism, the Evangelical Alliance and the Toronto Blessing', in Hilborn (ed.), *Toronto in Perspective*. Viewable at www.eauk.org

## Evangelical Identity and Practice

As the Toronto Blessing faded from the headlines, ACUTE
undertook, in 1996, to revisit one of the most pervasive and
foundational questions in the history of the Alliance – the
question of evangelical identity. In preparation for the
Bournemouth National Assembly of the same year, it produced a document called 'What is an Evangelical?'[39] This was
presented as 'setting the scene for a serious debate', and offered
broad brush-strokes rather than detail. Even so, the working
group that produced the report stated that it was meant to
stand within a healthy, well-established tradition of evangelical
self-examination. Specifically, they added, it had been necessi-
tated by the challenges of the postmodern age. Echoing
Calver's concerns in the 'Jerusalem Paper' of 1993, the authors
asserted that 'evangelicalism generally has become light-
weight on the theological front', and that it was consequently
under-equipped to deal with the intellectual challenges being
presented by contemporary philosophy. One way in which it
had already been compromised, they contended, was in the
increasing ambivalence of some of its representatives towards
statements of faith. In certain parts of the evangelical constituency, they wrote, these had been reduced to little more than
'flags of convenience' – mere ciphers which often concealed
'all kinds of mental reservations' about their actual meaning.[40]

Another postmodern trend cautioned against by 'What is an
Evangelical?' was an 'increasing tendency to base fellowship on
friendship rather than on truth'. 'Evangelical love is the hallmark of evangelicalism at its best', wrote the working-group,
'but we must never put the cart before the horse. It is truth that
leads to fellowship, not fellowship or friendship that establish
or condition what is the truth'. Seeking to chart a biblical
course through the 'twin errors of rigidity and laxity', the
report underlined the need to recover the scriptural

---

39 ACUTE, *What is an Evangelical?* (London: Evangelical Alliance, 1996).
40 Ibid., pp.2-3.

understanding of the gospel, and to glean the wisdom of past generations of evangelicals on this subject: 'The story of the Evangelical Alliance and other evangelical bodies', it suggested, 'provides us with rich oral and written material to learn from. The issues we face today are not new. The way our predecessors faced them and the conclusions they drew must provide us with teaching material for facing them again, albeit in our different era.' Predicting that the outcome of this endeavour would be an evangelicalism which was unafraid to state negatives as well as positives, but which was 'as inclusive as possible', the report surmised that pursuing such a goal would always be 'a knife-edge exercise'.[41]

After reiterating and briefly expounding the tenets of the Alliance Basis of Faith, the authors of the report stressed that 'evangelicalism is not just about orthodoxy, but also about orthopraxis'. An evangelical 'ethos and behaviour pattern', it continued, 'ought to arise out of our evangelical beliefs if it is to mean more than mental assent'. In concrete terms, this implied an active love and study of Scripture, a regular life of prayer, a genuine pursuit of holiness, a passion for spiritual life, evangelism and revival, mutual honesty and openness, and a social demonstration of gospel love. With such commitments, the report concluded, evangelicals might hope to be 'in the forefront in the rising challenge of a post-modern age, in which human nature is the same as the day it fell in Adam'.[42]

The emphasis of 'What is an Evangelical?' on practical demonstration as well as doctrinal correctitude was taken up shortly afterwards, when the Alliance Council was encouraged to adopt a 'modern language' revision of the original 'Practical Resolutions' passed at the inaugural conference in 1846. These resolutions had often lacked prominence, but would be highlighted as the agenda of the Bournemouth National Assembly began to be worked out. Already, ACUTE had provided a briefing paper for the Alliance Council on the theological and

---

41  Ibid., pp.3-5.
42  Ibid., pp.6-8.

social issues arising from the launch of the National Lottery in November 1994, and had persuaded them to advise Alliance members on biblical grounds against playing the Lottery or taking grants from it for church and charitable projects.[43] Subsequently, it would advise the Council on the arguments for and against the Alliance tithing its own income on to other organisations and projects.[44] (Largely on the grounds that it was itself reliant on gifts and offerings intended for its own and not others' work, the Council declined to pursue this as a systematic procedure, although it did commend tithing a proportion of its income to less well-endowed Alliances abroad.) Later, too, it would also host a day conference for fifty key leaders to explore the so-called 'prosperity gospel', and would begin work on a major report on the matter.[45] In 1997-8, however, one issue would test ACUTE and the Alliance's commitment to the balance of orthodoxy and orthopraxis more sharply than any other – homosexuality.

## Homosexuality and Transsexuality

David Hilborn's first major task on arriving at the Alliance in July 1997 was to complete work begun by Dave Cave and an ACUTE study group on the vexed subject of homosexuality. Since the time of the Wolfenden Report in 1957, and more particularly since the passing of the Sexual Offences Act in 1967, British society at large had adopted an increasingly liberal attitude towards same sex relationships, and gay and lesbian sexual activity. By the late 1990s, this liberalisation moved on apace as the new Labour administration took steps to repeal Section 28 of the Local Government Act banning the promotion of homosexuality by Local Education Authorities, to reduce the gay male age of consent to 16, and to lift restrictions

---

43  Minutes of Executive Council, September 1994.
44  Minutes of Executive Council, September 1997, February 1998.
45  This conference took place at Whitefield House in June 1998. The book, edited by Andrew Perriman, is scheduled for publication in 2002.

on homosexual people serving in the armed forces. Gay couples were also beginning to win cases establishing their parity with married couples in respect of key employment and financial rights.[46]

This wider shift had also been reflected in the Christian community, with books like Derrick Sherwin Bailey's *Homosexuality and the Western Church* (1955) and Norman Pittenger's *Time for Consent* (1967) paving the way for the formation of the Lesbian and Gay Christian Movement (LGCM) and the serious consideration, by liberal-majority denominations like the United Reformed and Methodist Churches, of whether they should follow the United Church of Christ (USA) and the United Church of Canada in officially approving the ordination of sexually active lesbians and gay men. Even within the evangelical world, some had begun during the last years of the century to question whether the traditional, absolute rejection of sexually active same sex relationships should be maintained.[47] Most prominent among this group was Michael Vasey, a lecturer at the Anglican evangelical college St John's, Durham. Vasey's 1995 book *Strangers and Friends* invoked a wide range of historical, sociological and psychological research to argue that an authentic understanding of the relevant scriptural texts on homosexuality might allow that certain forms of homoerotic intimacy 'are not contrary to the Christian vision of human life but close to themes and instincts that are an integral part of biblical and Christian tradition'.[48] The frankness and thoroughness with which Vasey put his case did much to convince the Alliance that it needed to formalise its own position on the issue.

The resultant book was called *Faith, Hope and Homosexuality*, and represented ACUTE's first collaboration with Paternoster Press of Carlisle. Launched at a Westminster press conference

---

46 ACUTE, *Faith, Hope and Homosexuality* (Carlisle: Paternoster, 1998), pp.1–4.
47 Ibid., p.ix, n.4.
48 M. Vasey, *Strangers and Friends: A New Exploration of Homosexuality and the Bible* (London: Hodder & Stoughton, 1995), p.237.

in January 1998, it attracted more media interest than any Alliance initiative for decades. All the main national broadsheet newspapers carried stories on it; David Hilborn and Joel Edwards were both interviewed for the main BBC national radio news programmes, and were busy for a number of days afterwards providing comment to local journalists. Joel Edwards had written in the Preface of the book that 'Homosexuality may well be the single most divisive issue in the Western church today'; the phenomenal media coverage accorded to it seemed to bear this observation out.[49]

The book itself began by stating that it had been written with three main aims: (i) to respond to the arguments of the gay lobby in general; (ii) to enable Christians, and evangelicals in particular, to relate more pastorally to homosexual people; and (iii) to affirm groups, like the True Freedom Trust, that were ministering alongside lesbians and gay men who wished to refrain from lesbian and gay sexual activity. Having set out the contemporary social and ecclesiastical context, *Faith, Hope and Homosexuality* moved on to consider the witness of Scripture on same sex relationships. Although it conceded that homoerotic sexual practice was hardly the most frequently mentioned sin in the Bible, and although it accepted that the most common contexts of such practice in the ancient world were not wholly identical to its most common contexts today, it nonetheless emphasised that authentic interpretation must still concur with 'the classical view of the biblical witness – namely, that homoerotic sexual activity is wrong'. From Old to New Testament, it added, 'sexual activity outside marriage comes to be seen as sinful, and homosexual practice is presented as a stock example of sexual sin'.[50]

Statistically, ACUTE challenged the common assumption that anything up to 10% of people are gay. Rather, it quoted the most reputable secular surveys of western societies as showing that little more than 2% of the population had had any kind of

49  ACUTE, *Faith, Hope and Homosexuality,* p.vii.
50  Ibid., pp.19–20.

homosexual experience.[51] In the face of growing opposition, ACUTE then reaffirmed the established theological distinction between sexual orientation and sexual practice, arguing that while the former may predispose people to sins of the 'eye' and 'heart', the church could only practically order its ministry on the basis of the latter. Despite the historical revisionism of scholars like Vasey and James Boswell, it also defended this distinction as underlying the ethics and discipline of the church down the ages.[52]

While the report acknowledged that it was largely reiterating the classical evangelical stance for the current age, ACUTE did challenge its own constituency to act with greater pastoral sensitivity towards homosexual people than it had been known to do in the past. In their concluding section, the authors expressed their earnest prayer that God's 'love truth and grace would characterise evangelical responses to debates on homosexuality, both now and in future'. They also repudiated homophobia 'insofar as it denotes an irrational fear or hatred of homosexuals', and wrote of their 'deep regret' for 'the hurt caused to lesbians and gay men and the church's past and present hatred and rejection of them' – although they resisted the idea that 'to reject homoerotic sexual practice on biblical grounds is in itself homophobic'. The report went on to call upon evangelical congregations to 'welcome and accept' sexually active homosexual people, 'but to do so in the expectation that they will come in due course to see the need to change their lifestyle in accordance with biblical revelation and orthodox church teaching'. In keeping with this, it then defined persistent homoerotic sexual activity without repentance to be 'inconsistent with faithful church membership', and rejected services of blessing for gay partnerships as 'unbiblical'.[53]

Although never likely to win plaudits from more liberal quarters, *Faith, Hope and Homosexuality* was widely recognised

51  Ibid., pp.21-4.
52  Ibid., pp.25-7.
53  Ibid., pp.33-4.

to have stated the evangelical view with sensitivity, as well as with clarity and conviction. As a URC minister, Hilborn had been engaged for a number of years in the human sexuality debate within his own denomination, and was well acquainted with contrary arguments and testimonies. He had talked with Michael Vasey and various LGCM representatives in different settings, and it was significant that when interviewed about the book, Richard Kirker (LGCM Secretary) recognised its more compassionate tone, even while repudiating its basic doctrinal view.[54] Following the book's launch, dialogue continued on a number of related fronts. The Alliance kept up contact with gay ministry groups on both sides of the debate; it also lobbied the European Union with regard to its Equal Treatment Directive, whose incorporation into British Law threatened the right of Christian organisations to decline to employ practising homosexuals and others who did not accord with their ethical and theological convictions. Furthermore, in the year 2000, the orthodoxy-orthopraxis balance was starkly tested again when one of the Alliance's most prominent Council members, Roy Clements, resigned his membership having come out as a gay man, and when Courage, an evangelical trust engaged in the pastoral care of homosexuals, was reported to have abandoned its previously traditional view.[55]

*Faith, Hope and Homosexuality* provided a helpful framework for the first report published by a newly formed 'Policy Commission' of the Alliance in 2000. Appointed to deal principally with 'issues of an ethical nature with national or international implications' as distinct from the more directly theological remit of ACUTE, the Policy Commission was overseen by Martyn Eden (Public Affairs Director) and co-ordinated by Don Horrocks, a former bank manager engaged in doctoral research at London Bible College. The Commission's initial

---

54  Richard Kirker and Joel Edwards, Interview, *The World Tonight,* BBC Radio 4, 20 January 1998.
55  'Counselling Group Changes Heart on Gays', *Church of England Newspaper,* 30 March 2001, p.3.

study was entitled *Transsexuality* and was prompted by increasing claims for full legal recognition of those who had undergone gender reassignment surgery. Based on detailed research conducted by an expert working group of ethicists, scientists and lawyers, the report acknowledged that transsexual men and women had suffered undue hurt at the hands of the church, but that 'authentic change from a person's sex is not possible and an ongoing transsexual lifestyle is incompatible with God's will as revealed in Scripture and in creation'. While expressing opposition 'in principle' to discrimination against transsexual people in relation to human rights and employment, the report nonetheless argued against transsexuals being allowed to amend their birth certificates, except in rare 'intersex' cases involving a genuine medical mistake. Such amendment of so vital a document, wrote the working group, was 'fundamentally flawed, open to abuse, and tending to undermine accepted realities by condoning illusion and denial'.[56]

## The Nature of Hell

As we saw in chapter 5, the 'Birks Affair' of 1869-70 made the theology of hell a litmus test of the Alliance's identity. It forced the British Organisation to examine the hermeneutical limits of its doctrinal basis; it also raised fundamental questions about the right to private judgement, the criteria of membership, and the power of the Council to discipline those deemed to hold unorthodox views. As it happened, Birks' specific ideas would remain esoteric, but their more generally perceived affinity with the positions known as annihilationism and conditionalism ensured that the legacy of his case would continue to weigh upon the Alliance into the latter part of the twentieth century.

By the time the Alliance revised its Basis of Faith in 1970, the view that the unredeemed would eventually be destroyed,

56 Evangelical Alliance Policy Commission, *Transsexuality*, pp.84-7.

rather than eternally punished by God, had gained some
ground in evangelical circles. So, too, had the closely related
notion that the immortality of the soul was a Platonic rather
than a biblical concept, and that eternal existence was a gift
related to faith in Christ rather than an intrinsic feature of
humanity as a whole. In 1941 Harold Guillebaud, from
the Church Missionary Society, had argued the case for
conditionalism in a study called *The Righteous Judge,* while Basil
F.C. Atkinson, the widely respected Cambridge librarian and
Inter-Varsity Fellowship leader, had influenced a number of
evangelical students towards a similar view before committing
that view to paper in his 1964 book, *Life and Immortality.* Both
of these texts had been published privately, but John Stott, who
chaired the Alliance Theological Committee that refashioned
the Basis of Faith from 1967 onwards, knew them.

Among several other changes, the revised version of the
Basis dropped the references to 'the immortality of the Soul'
and 'the Eternal Punishment of the wicked' which had been
insisted upon by the American delegation to the inaugural
conference in 1846. Instead, it left Alliance members to infer its
position on hell from two new clauses on human sin. The first
of these affirmed 'the universal sinfulness and guilt of fallen
man' as a just cause of God's 'wrath and condemnation'. The
other declared Christ's substitutionary sacrifice on the cross to
be the only basis of redemption 'from the *eternal consequences* of
sin' (our emphasis). The mention of sin's effects being 'eternal'
here certainly echoed traditionalist language. Even so, it did
not necessarily exclude conditionalists, who typically argue
that although the *instrument* of punishment may itself be everlasting (as in 'eternal fire'), the *outcome for any specific individual* is
terminal (i.e. consummation by the fire).[57]

If the new Basis thus suggested a certain ambiguity with respect to hell, this appeared to be reflected in 1988 when Stott
published a 'Liberal–Evangelical dialogue' with his fellow

---

57 For a representative account of this argument, with supporting references, see
E.W. Fudge, *The Fire That Consumes: The Biblical Case for Conditional Immortality,*
pp. 11–20.

Anglican, David L. Edwards. The dialogue involved a discussion of eschatology, in which Stott leaned towards conditionalism while finally declaring himself to be 'tentative' about whether it should replace the traditional view.[58] Stott's arguments echoed those that had been put forward by Guillebaud and Atkinson, but especially resonated with the stance that had been taken fourteen years previously by another Anglican evangelical, John Wenham. In his 1974 study *The Goodness of God*, Wenham had offered careful arguments that gained a respectful hearing and prompted some lively responses.[59] Not least, he inspired the American scholar Edward William Fudge to produce a full-length survey of the biblical material that rapidly became the standard reference work on evangelical conditionalism.[60] Subsequently, at a major conference on hell in 1992, Wenham expounded his position in a paper entitled 'The Case for Conditional Immortality'.[61] In fact, the book based on this conference represented just one in a stream of works on hell produced by evangelicals in the period after Stott had made his views known. Respected evangelical leaders like Philip Hughes, Michael Green, Nigel Wright, Earle Ellis, Clark Pinnock and Robert Brow were just some of those who 'went public' as conditionalists at this time.[62] Predictably,

---

58 J. Stott & D.L. Edwards, *Essentials: A Liberal-Evangelical Dialogue* (London: Hodder & Stoughton, 1988), p.320.

59 J. Wenham, *The Goodness of God*.

60 Fudge, *Fire That Consumes*, pp.9-10.

61 In N.M. de S. Cameron, (ed.), *Universalism and the Doctrine of Hell* (Carlisle: Paternoster Press, 1992), pp.161-90. For Wenham's personal reflections on this debate, and on its antecedents, see *Facing Hell: An Autobiography 1913-1996* (Carlisle: Paternoster Press, 1998), pp.229-57.

62 J. Wenham, 'The Case for Conditional Immortality', in Cameron (ed.) *Universalism and the Doctrine of Hell*, 1992, pp.161-91; also *Facing Hell*. Fudge, *Fire That Consumes*; M. Green, *Evangelism Through the Local Church* (London: Hodder & Stoughton, 1990), pp.69f.; C.H. Pinnock & R.C. Brow, *Unbounded Love: A Good News Theology for the 21*[st] *Century* (Carlisle: Paternoster Press, 1994), pp.87-95; E. Ellis, 'New Testament Teaching on Hell', in K.E. Brower & M.W. Elliott, (eds), *The Reader Must Understand: Eschatology in Bible and Theology*; N. Wright, *The Radical Evangelical: Seeking a Place to Stand* (Leicester: Apollos, 1997), pp.87-102.

their pronouncements in turn spurred more traditionalist evangelicals, such as J.I. Packer, Ajith Fernando, David Pawson, John Blanchard, Donald Carson and Robert Peterson, to reiterate the doctrine of eternal conscious punishment.[63]

The debate that was now developing led ACUTE to appoint a working group on hell in early 1998. As well as Hilborn, this included Philip Johnston (the Wycliffe Hall Old Testament lecturer), Tony Lane (the London Bible College historical theologian), Tony Gray (of the Universities and Colleges Christian Fellowship), Faith Forster and Robert Amess. As the group began their work, they were aware that a theological survey conducted a few months earlier had shown 14% of Alliance member churches inclining towards annihilationism, with 80% holding to the traditional view on hell.[64] The next year they duly presented their report to the Alliance Council. The Council spent a morning debating it, and then commended it to the membership for 'study, reflection and constructive response'. Shortly afterwards, the report was published by Paternoster Press as *The Nature of Hell*.[65]

Stressing that hell represents one side of the church's response to the universal human concern about what happens when we die, the working group began by outlining the traditional Christian understanding of it as eternal conscious torment for the unredeemed. They then contrasted this understanding with conditionalism, and also with universalism – the view that all will eventually be saved. Having stressed that universalism has never been accepted by any more than a tiny proportion of evangelicals, and having rejected arguments for

---

63 J.I. Packer, *The Problem of Eternal Punishment* (Disley: Orthos, 1990); A. Fernando, *Crucial Questions About Hell* (Eastbourne: Kingsway, 1991); D. Pawson, *The Road to Hell* (London: Hodder and Stoughton, 1992); Blanchard, *Whatever Happened to Hell?* (Darlington: Evangelical Press, 1993); Peterson, *Hell on Trial* (Phillipsburg: P. and R, 1995); D.A. Carson, *The Gagging of God: Christianity Confronts Pluralism* (Leicester: Apollos, 1996), pp.515–36.
64 EA Member Churches: The 1998 Opinion Survey, Question 7, 6; *Ear*, Spring 1999, p.1.
65 ACUTE, *The Nature of Hell*.

it, for purgatory and for so-called 'post-mortem' or 'second chance' conversion, the report focused on the respective merits and demerits of everlasting punishment and conditional immortality/annihilation. In doing so, it emphasised that despite their obvious divergence on significant points, traditionalist and conditionalist evangelicals could still each affirm a number of crucial beliefs in respect of the 'last things'. They both characteristically assented to the finality of death, the general resurrection, the reality of final judgement and its consequence in either heavenly redemption or irreversible condemnation, the prospect of divine punishment for the reprobate, the uniqueness of Christ for salvation, justification by grace through faith in him, the promise of a renewed cosmos, and the priority of evangelism in the face of all this.[66] These, it suggested, were sufficiently important in themselves to oblige church leaders, theological colleges and religious educators to present hell as an intrinsic feature of Christian faith and history. They also demanded serious and sensitive treatment in the pastoral context.[67]

Despite these areas of consensus, however, the report acknowledged that evangelicals had come increasingly to disagree on whether the 'eternity' of hell was an eternity of *duration* or *effect* – that is, 'whether an individual's punishment in hell will literally go on "for ever", as a ceaseless conscious experience, or whether it will end in a destruction which will be "forever" in the sense of being final and irreversible'. In addition, it recognised that although the Bible often pictured hell in terms of destruction as well as suffering, 'evangelicals diverge on whether this destruction applies to the actual *existence* of individual sinners (eventual annihilation) or to the *quality of their relationship with God* (eternal conscious punishment)'.[68] *The Nature of Hell* accepted that both traditionalism and conditionalism had their 'signature texts' – Mark 9:48,

66  Ibid., pp.130–32.

67  Ibid., pp.110–21, 133–4.

68  Ibid., p.132.

Matthew 25:46 and Revelation 20:10 for traditionalists, and Matthew 10:28, John 3:16 and Romans 6:23 for conditionalists/ annihilationists. It interrogated these and other references in great detail, as well as surveying arguments from ancient and modern theologians in relation to each view. On the basis of this work, it reached four key conclusions.

First, ACUTE deemed the interpretation of hell as eternal conscious punishment to be 'the classic, mainstream evangelical position', and the one most widely attested by the church in its historic understanding of Scripture. Second, however, it formally recognised conditional immortality as representing a 'significant minority evangelical view'. Third, it declared that the debate on these two positions 'should be regarded as a secondary rather than a primary issue for evangelical theology', and that the holding of either one of them against the other was 'neither essential in respect of Christian doctrine, nor finally definitive of what it means to be an evangelical Christian'. Fourth, it affirmed that in contrast with the original 1846 Basis of Faith, the current Evangelical Alliance Statement of Faith would 'allow both traditionalist and conditionalist interpretations of hell'.[69]

Insofar as *The Nature of Hell* affirmed the credentials of conditionalism, it did so cautiously. The burden of proof, it suggested, still rested with this view, since the weight of historic theological witness and *de facto* evangelical understanding was against it, and since biblical arguments for it were hardly straightforward over against traditionalism. In any case, the authors also suggested, biblical references such as 2 Thessalonians 1:8-9, coupled with new insights from cosmology, might eventually reveal the truth to lie not in one view alone, but in an as yet unresolvable fusion of both.[70]

Although it was longer and more patently 'academic' than *Faith, Hope and Homosexuality, The Nature of Hell* attracted a surprisingly comparable level of media interest. Hilborn was

---

69  Ibid., pp.134-5.
70  Ibid., p.125.

interviewed about it on Radio 4's *Today* and *Sunday* programmes, and recorded half-hour features on it for the World Service, BBC Wales and BBC Ulster. Jonathan Petre in the *Sunday Telegraph* contrasted its robustness with a more equivocal statement on the same issue made by the Church of England's Doctrine Commission; the *Independent on Sunday* followed suit, and there was extensive coverage in the British Christian press. Perhaps most notably of all, it was accorded the distinction of an eight-page cover feature in the leading American magazine *Christianity Today*, where Professor Robert Peterson called it an 'outstanding resource' and 'a model of how evangelicals can study together constructively, even when they must agree to disagree'.[71] By this point, *The Nature of Hell* had already sold out its first print run. Clive Calver's hopes for ACUTE were becoming a reality.

## Conclusion

For all its success in the 1980s, the Alliance under Clive Calver's leadership came to realise that the reassertion of its historic pragmatism must be married with, and checked by, responsible theological and ethical reflection. This realisation was due in no small part to the rise of certain critical debates during this period – on evangelical identity, the Toronto Blessing, human sexuality, and hell. Although it had previously convened theological committees and conferences to deal with specific concerns, the Alliance now adopted a more programmatic approach, through the formation of ACUTE and the Policy Commission. As they developed, the work of these two bodies did much to confirm the Alliance as a distinctive contributor to evangelical thought, as well as to evangelical action.

As we write, further ACUTE projects in process include studies of generationally based mission and church planting,

---

71 R.A. Peterson, 'Undying Worm; Unquenchable Fire', *Christianity Today*, 23 October 2000, pp.30-37.

evangelical ecclesiology and a Reader in evangelical theology. The Policy Commission is preparing to publish a document on genetically modified foods, and is planning to convene a special 'commission of inquiry' on issues of church and state. Here, as before, the emphasis will be on thorough research presented in a clear style for thinking evangelicals. As we shall see in the final chapter, it is an approach intended to reflect a growing commitment within the Alliance to speak with authority on issues of concern not only to the church itself, but also to the whole of society.

# 14

# A Movement for Change

*Shaping the Alliance for the Twenty-First Century*

## A New General Director

As Clive Calver departed for the USA in May 1997 he made it
known that if the new General Director was to be appointed
internally, his preferred successor would be Joel Edwards. In
this, he echoed the sentiments of his senior collegues. Edwards
had worked with Calver since 1992 as UK Director, having
served for four years prior to that as General Director of the
African Caribbean Evangelical Alliance (ACEA). In the event,
the Council noted Calver and his team's wishes, but insisted
that the appointment process should be open and above board.
The job was duly advertised, resulting in a short-list of three
candidates.[1] As it turned out, the interview group were unanimous in offering Edwards the position, and he accepted.[2] Just
four years on, Adrian Hastings, the renowned British church
historian, would be describing him as 'perhaps, all in all, the
most significant ecclesiastical figure of the 1990s'.[3]

As he would later recount in his part-autobiographical book
*Lord, Make Us One – But Not All the Same!,* Joel Edwards came
to Britain from Jamaica at the age of seven, in 1960.[4] Brought

1 *idea*, September/October 1997, p.21.
2 *idea*, November/December 1997, p.15.
3 Hastings, *English Christianity 1920–2000*, p.xlvi.
4 Edwards, *Lord, Make Us One*, pp.1–19.

here by a mother fleeing a bad marriage, he grew up in the north London district of Kentish Town. As one of the first wave of West Indian immigrants to the UK, he told *idea* magazine, shortly after becoming General Director, that on settling in the capital he felt 'suddenly confronted with being a very different person'. In the face of culture shock and racial tensions, his local New Testament Church of God became a solace – 'the place where you were kept alive … your social centre'. It was in this Pentecostal setting that Edwards was converted at the age of eleven. Around the same time, however, he was caught stealing sweets from Woolworth's and was put on probation. With hindsight, this would prove ironic: a bright student at school, Edwards would go on to study theology at London Bible College, after which he decided to become a probation officer instead of entering into full-time ministry immediately. By 1988 when he left the probation service to work for ACEA, Edwards had begun to pastor part-time at the New Testament Assembly in Leyton, east London. Despite the demands of his subsequent roles for the Alliance, he has maintained links with this church, and continues to relate influentially to the Pentecostal community, both nationally and internationally.[5]

## Redoubled Activism

Under the banner of 'New Leadership for a New Era', Edwards' Directorship was launched in October 1997 at special 'induction services' in London and Manchester – respectively the same cities that had hosted the inaugural meetings of the World's Alliance and the British Organisation in 1846.[6] These events were followed up early the next year with 'Seizing the Moment' – a 28-town tour in which Edwards and a team of evangelical leaders introduced Alliance members to a new 'Manifesto'. The thirty-three 'pledges'

---

5  *idea*, September/October 1997, pp.21-2.
6  *idea*, November/December 1997, p.15.

contained in this document covered a wide spectrum of concerns, from more effective evangelism and preaching to the promotion of biblical morality and appropriate local co-operation with other churches. There was also a strong undertaking to harness rapidly advancing computer technologies – an undertaking borne out by the launch of an Alliance internet website. However, if there was a distinctive theme running through the 'Seizing the Moment' Manifesto, it was a serious re-commitment to social transformation. With his background, Edwards was able to bring authority and authenticity to this commitment, and it would soon become a defining feature of his portfolio as General Director. A commentary on the pledges emphasised that the Alliance had 'gained credibility over the years not by standing on soapboxes, but by regularly engaging with public debates'. As part of intensifying this process, there would, it added, be a redoubled effort 'to influence Government policies from a Christian perspective, as well as to generate greater respect and co-operation from local authorities and Government'.[7]

The Alliance pursued this fresh social and political commitment on a number of fronts. In November 1997 Sir Fred Catherwood, its President, launched a major report entitled *Surveying the Roots of Social Breakdown*. This was the fruit of research done by Catherwood and an Alliance-based team over five years, in which they had surveyed 70 church projects providing care for some 44,000 people affected by problems like homelessness, poverty and addiction. By highlighting what evangelicals on the ground were already accomplishing, the report sought to urge Alliance congregations to participate further in 'Christian Action Networks' (CANS). These networks would, according to the report, 'encourage the sharing of expertise and good practice, and ... help identify gaps in social provision and potential resources from within the Christian community to fill those gaps'.[8] The report also committed

---

7 Ibid., pp.16-7.
8 Evangelical Alliance, *Surveying the Roots of Social Breakdown*, p.6.

the Alliance to 'approach the British Government and local authorities to press for more funding, recognition and partnership with the voluntary and church sectors'.[9] Specifically, it demonstrated chronic problems arising from family dysfunction, unemployment, loss of community, drug and alcohol abuse, and crime. Yet it held out the hope that more active co-operation between government and church could significantly ameliorate such problems.[10] As the work of CANS developed over the next four years, the Alliance would come to see all the major political parties approach the 2001 General Election seriously addressing the issue of 'faith-based welfare' and government support for church social projects.[11]

If the CANS initiative recalled the evangelical social activism of the Victorian Alliance, another project the following year echoed its historic co-ordination of national prayer. From modest beginnings, an Alliance initiative called 'Amen – A Day to Pray' caught the imagination of evangelical churches and a wide range of Christian communities. On 7 June 1998 some 6,000 congregations were duly mobilised to intercede for the well being of their communities, for evangelisation, for parliament and for revival. A rally was held in Westminster, and a special service was broadcast on BBC Radio 4.[12] The Alliance's head of prayer, Jane Holloway, was particularly pleased when George Carey, the Archbishop of Canterbury, warmly endorsed the project.

After the 'Amen Day', the Alliance sought to maintain the momentum it was gaining in the public arena. Its Disability Network launched a 'Churches for All' scheme designed to raise issues of access;[13] its Youth and Children's Unit hosted a

9  *idea*, November/December 1997, p.26.

10 Evangelical Alliance, *Surveying*, 22-3; 'Opening a CAN of Works', *idea*, April/May 2000, p.5.

11 'Window of Opportunity?', *idea*, May/June 2001, pp.20-25.

12 *idea* April/May 1998, p.3; *idea*, April/May 1998, p.30; *idea*, April/May 1998, pp.30, 34.

13 *idea*, September/October 1998, pp.27-8; *idea,* November/December 1998, pp.26-7.

high-profile conference on social exclusion;[14] a new consultancy called Whitefield Associates was developed to enable
more effective lobbying of government; and an 'Anno Domini'
office was created to promote missionary opportunities presented by the approaching millennium.[15]

Also in 1998 the Good Friday Agreement was ratified by
the people of Northern Ireland and the Republic of Ireland.
The major constitutional and social changes promised by this
new accord were addressed by the Alliance, most particularly
by David McCarthy in its Belfast office; he worked hard to
maintain dialogue between evangelicals who had divided over
the issue.[16] David Porter, an Alliance Executive Member, also
regularly briefed Council members on developments from his
perspective as Director of ECONI – the Evangelical Contribution on Northern Ireland. Moreover, as devolution was realised through the Scottish Parliament, the Welsh Assembly and
the Greater London Assembly, the Alliance's expanding Public
Affairs department worked closely with its national offices to
ensure that the evangelical voice was heard in each forum.
Martyn Eden, the Public Affairs Director, and Shona Wallace,
the Parliamentary Officer, co-ordinated major reports on
evangelical-political engagement and the proposed Greater
London Assembly; David Anderson, the Scottish General
Director, worked with Jeremy Balfour, Parliamentary Officer,
to win the confidence of new MSPs, and in Wales Aarfon
Jones, Elfed Gooding and Daniel Boucher developed *Gweini*
(meaning 'to serve') to help voluntary organisations make
their presence felt in Cardiff.[17]

As campaigns like these raised public awareness of the Alliance's work, so the media opportunities for which Clive
Calver and others had pressed so hard began to increase. Along
with Martyn Eden, David Hilborn and Paul Harris (Evange-

14 *idea*, April/May 1998, p.8.
15 *idea*, June/July/August 1999, p.13.
16 *idea,* June/July/August 1998, pp.22-3; *idea,* September/October 1998, pp.30-31.
17 *idea*, April/May 2000, pp.22-5.

lism Secretary), Joel Edwards found himself appearing with greater regularity in the press, and on radio and television. One clear sign of the respect he was winning came in the form of a 1998 London Weekend Television interview requested by Melvyn Bragg, the prominent cultural affairs presenter. As part of a series that also featured the Archbishop of Canterbury, the Archbishop of Westminster and the Chief Rabbi, Edwards spoke at length to Bragg about his Pentecostal background and the history and work of the Alliance.[18] Shortly afterwards, Edwards became a regular contributor to 'Pause for Thought' on BBC Radio 2, and then began to appear in the prestigious 'Thought for the Day' slot on Radio 4. He also featured on the same station in *Any Questions* and *The Moral Maze*, and formed part of the panel on BBC 1's *Question Time*.

While the Alliance made these considerable strides forward on the wider social stage, it was careful not to neglect its core work of resourcing and networking local churches. In early 1999 John Smith was appointed as Church Life Director in succession to John Earwicker, who left the Alliance to return to local ministry. One of Smith's first tasks was to help lead a new Alliance tour. Entitled 'Shaping Tomorrow's Church', this covered fifteen regional centres and presented Alliance members with the latest thinking on church growth, evangelism and cultural engagement.[19] It also introduced those who attended to the 'Disciple Making Church' process pioneered by Bill Hull and Rick Warren of Saddleback Community Church in Orange County, California. Subsequently, the Alliance would invite Bill Hull to lead a series of day conferences, and would organise guided study visits to Saddleback.[20]

Also during this period, a special 'Evangelical Relationships Commitment' was drafted and agreed with the British Evangelical Council. This undertook to maintain good biblical practice in dealing with the media, and obliged parties in

---

18  *idea*, April/May 1998, p.6.
19  *idea*, January–March 1999, pp.4–5.
20  *idea*, November/December 1998, pp.22–3.

doctrinal and other disputes to consult and establish facts before issuing critical statements.[21] Within the Alliance Council, important steps were also taken to update the Alliance's constitution, with legal and fiduciary responsibilities being shifted to a new Executive Board. Alongside these changes, Robert Amess, recently retired from ministry at Duke Street Baptist Church, took over from Derek Copley as Chair of Council, while Fran Beckett (Shaftesbury Society Director) was appointed Vice-Chair.[22] Along, most notably, with Faith Forster of the Ichthus Fellowship, Beckett had already done much to model a more prominent leadership role for women than had hitherto been demonstrated within the Alliance.

In the autumn of 1999 the Alliance looked to build on the success of the 'Seizing the Moment' and 'Shaping Tomorrow's Church' tours by launching another. The theme this time was 'Truth on the Streets', and a team including Joel Edwards and Steve Chalke, the popular evangelical TV presenter, took the tour to fifteen venues. This time, the format was somewhat more radical than had been attempted before. The backbone of each evening's presentation was a sequence of playlets scripted by Nick Page and performed by Rob Lacey. Lacey portrayed various characters, each of whom, in different ways, starkly illustrated the challenges facing the evangelical church in contemporary culture – a fashion designer called Justin raised pertinent questions about gay people and artistic expression; Graham was a Christian, but so obsessed by work that his lifestyle undermined the faith he professed; eco-warrior Moonstick was on a spiritual quest whose destination might depend on his treatment by evangelicals; and a bumbling vicar personified common public perceptions of the Church. All were portrayed as they attended the funeral of a mutual Christian friend, Jay, who had committed suicide after struggling with a desire to change his sex. The aim was to provoke debate, and the Alliance received substantial feedback, most of which

---

21  *idea*, June/July/August 1999, p.4.
22  *idea*, January–March 1999, p.4.

was constructive. Indeed, so enthusiastic was the response that the 'Truth on the Streets' presentation was subsequently recorded and marketed as a successful video resource.[23]

For all the progress that was being made, the Alliance was also confronted with some sobering realities. A new English church census showed regular attendance at services dipping to below 8% from 10% just a decade before, and while evangelical congregations had suffered less from this decline than others, the aggregate losses were still alarming.[24] When the Alliance sought to address this and other issues in August 2000 by co-sponsoring a new youth music festival called 'Junction 1', it had to cancel at the eleventh hour due to lack of interest, and lost a significant amount of money as a result.[25] These setbacks did not deter the Alliance from pressing ahead with its busy programme of activities, but in the latter part of 2000 it resolved to announce a more co-ordinated agenda to its members.

## Developing the Alliance as 'A Movement for Change'

In October 1998 Martyn Eden had suggested to his fellow managers that the Alliance had 'come to the end of a chapter in its existence' and that it needed to 'plan and prepare for a new one'. Too often, he wrote, the organisation had 'dissipated' its energies 'by majoring on minor issues'. Now, however, it needed to 'agree some strategic priorities'. Eden proposed that this should be done through reconfiguring the Alliance as a 'Movement for Change'. Specifically, he argued, this new movement would learn from the example of minority interest groups in other cultures who, despite their relatively small numbers, had exceeded expectations in terms of the impact

---

23  *idea*, January/February 2001, p.27.
24  P. Brierley, *The Tide is Running Out* (Eltham/London: Christian Research/Harper Collins, 2000).
25  *idea*, June/July/August 2000, p.9.

they had made. Citing Robert Bellah, the sociologist, Eden stressed that the quality of a culture could be changed when just 2% of its population caught a new vision. The vision that the Alliance needed to catch, he went on, was a vision of social transformation that would be 'holistic' and 'participatory'. In particular, he noted, this vision would need to be focused on 'the continual erosion of Christian values' within society, its 'relativist, pluralist, materialist and individualist' ethos and the 're-establishment' of the gospel as 'public truth in British society'. A useful picture of social change, he added, 'sees society as a marching column. Evangelicals are in the middle of that column, calling out to the other marchers that the front-markers are leading us towards a precipice, and urging them to wheel in a new direction or to break ranks before we reach the precipice.'[26]

Having tested and introduced it to staff and council through 1999, in September 2000 Joel Edwards launched the 'Movement for Change' initiative as a prophetic, long-term project that would 'work with what the Holy Spirit is already doing, and develop a corporate consciousness of actively working together for change within our respective ministries'. The Alliance may have achieved a great deal through the 1980s and '90s, but, added Edwards, it would need to build on these achievements by determining 'to unite for a cause greater than our unity'. Under the new banner of 'Uniting to Change Society', he told readers of *idea* magazine:

> If it is true that two per cent of a population can change a culture, what might a million evangelicals do as we bring our distinctive contribution to the wider Christian community and our society? Such a movement has all the potential under God to shape our values, restore families, and influence our media and politics. God is blowing a wind of change, and we want to offer our Alliance as a catalyst at the heart of a movement, bringing our personal members, churches and organisations together for this purpose ... It's true: one person can call for change, but one million people can become *a movement for change.*[27]

---

26  M. Eden, 'EA: The Next Chapter: Building a Movement for Change', Internal Alliance Paper, 10 August 1998.

27  *idea*, November/December 2000, p.4.

As we write, these aspirations have yet to be translated into a detailed plan of action, but the Alliance has undertaken to refine and deliver this plan through a major National Assembly at Cardiff in November 2001 and a wide-ranging mission campaign in 2002. By early 2001 the Assembly programme had been designed to offer 'Reasons for Hope in the 21$^{st}$ Century' and had promised four focal points: Society, Truth, Church and Discipleship. The 2002 project had been entitled 'Face Values', and had agreed a brief to be 'flexible' and locally-orientated as it operated with three main motives:

1   To stimulate thinking and action on the gospel and culture.
2   To mobilise a nationwide effort in evangelism.
3   To help churches 'identify ways in which they can serve their communities and ... direct them to additional help and support'.[28]

These plans were presented in February 2001 to a gathering of senior British evangelicals at the Temple Hall, London. The 100-strong guest list included government ministers, Lords, key business leaders and senior representatives from several churches, many of whom expressed high hopes for the Alliance's future.[29]

## Conclusion – and Postscript

Following Joel Edwards' appointment as General Director in 1997, the Alliance developed 'Movement for Change' as a conscious attempt to recover the *raison d'être* and cultural influence of its nineteenth-century founders. At a time of ecclesiastical division, these early Victorian pioneers had been justifiably glad to celebrate the fact of their unity, and had

---

28  *idea*, November/December 2000, p.6.
29  *idea*, May/June 2001, p.4.

announced it in the original slogan of the Alliance: 'We are One Body in Christ'. Yet, where some had argued then that the mere formation of the Alliance might be testimony enough to Christian catholicity, the Alliance itself moved beyond this in its earliest decades. Like the founders, Joel Edwards has been strongly committed to tangible expressions of unity. In this vein, he accepted the invitation to become an Honorary Canon of St Paul's Cathedral in July 2001 – a striking move for a Pentecostal. Around the same time, he also joined a special steering group charged with remodelling the World Evangelical Fellowship for the new century, as it prepared to change its name, appropriately enough, to 'The World Evangelical Alliance'. Yet over and above such expressions of unity, the Alliance's founders had also pursued an agenda of 'common action' at home and abroad, and now, some 155 years on, Edwards has set out to apply this legacy to a new chapter in the Alliance's life. Hence his recent reminder to Alliance members that while their unity was 'the envy of many evangelical bodies around the world', it could never be an end in itself. 'We are united for a mission', he declared: 'a mission to see a changed society.'[30]

30 *idea*, May/June 2001, p.3.

# Appendix 1

## The Provisional Doctrinal Basis of Faith of the World's Evangelical Alliance (1845)

1  The divine inspiration, authority and sufficiency of Holy Scripture.
2  The unity of the Godhead, and the Trinity of Persons therein.
3  The utter depravity of human nature in consequence of the fall.
4  The incarnation of the Son of God and His work of atonement for sinners of mankind.
5  The justification of the sinner by faith alone.
6  The work of the Holy Spirit in the conversion[1] and sanctification of the sinner.
7  The right and duty of private judgment in the interpretation of Holy Scripture.
8  The divine institution of the Christian ministry and the authority and perpetuity of the ordinances of Baptism and the Lord's Supper.

---

1  The text proposed to the Conference by R.S. Candlish's drafting sub-committee had 'regeneration' at this point, but the Conference agreed to amend it to 'conversion'.

# The Doctrinal Basis of Faith of the World's Evangelical Alliance (1846)

The parties composing the Alliance shall be such persons only as hold and maintain what are usually understood to be evangelical views, in regard to the matters of doctrine understated, namely:

1   The divine Inspiration, Authority and Sufficiency of the Holy Scriptures.
2   The Right and Duty of Private Judgment in the Interpretation of the Holy Scriptures.
3   The Unity of the Godhead, and the Trinity of Persons therein.
4   The utter Depravity of Human Nature, in consequence of the Fall.
5   The Incarnation of the Son of God, His work of Atonement for sinners of mankind, and His Mediatorial Intercession and Reign.
6   The Justification of the sinner by faith alone.
7   The work of the Holy Spirit in the Conversion and Sanctification of the sinner.
8   The Immortality of the Soul, the Resurrection of the Body, the Judgment of the World by our Lord Jesus Christ, with the Eternal Blessedness of the Righteous, and the Eternal Punishment of the wicked.
9   The divine Institution of the Christian Ministry, and the obligation and perpetuity of the Ordinances of Baptism and the Lord's Supper.

(i) It is, however, distinctly declared that this brief summary is not to be regarded, in any formal or ecclesiastical sense, as a creed or confession, nor the adoption of it as involving an assumption of the right authoritatively to define the limits of Christian brotherhood.

(ii) In this Alliance it is also distinctly declared that no compromise of the views of any member, or sanction of those of others on the points wherein they differ, is either required or expected; but that all are held free as before to maintain and advocate their religious convictions with due forbearance and brotherly love.

(iii) It is not contemplated that this Alliance should assume or aim at the character of a new ecclesiastical organization, claiming and exercising the functions of a Christian Church. Its simple and comprehensive object, it is strongly felt, may be successfully promoted without interfering with, or disturbing the order of, any branch of the Christian Church to which its members may respectively belong.

# Evangelical Alliance (UK) Basis of Faith
## (1970)

Evangelical Christians accept the revelation of the triune God given in the Scriptures of the Old and New Testaments and confess the historic faith of the Gospel therein set forth. They here assert doctrines which they regard as crucial to the understanding of the faith, and which should issue in mutual love, practical Christian service and evangelistic concern.

1  The sovereignty and grace of God the Father, God the Son and God the Holy Spirit in creation, providence, revelation, redemption and final judgement.
2  The divine inspiration of the Holy Scripture and its consequent entire trustworthiness and supreme authority in all matters of faith and conduct.
3  The universal sinfulness and guilt of fallen man, making him subject to God's wrath and condemnation.
4  The substitutionary sacrifice of the incarnate Son of God as the sole and all-sufficient ground of redemption from the guilt and power of sin, and from its eternal consequences.
5  The justification of the sinner solely by the grace of God through faith in Christ crucified and risen from the dead.
6  The illuminating, regenerating, indwelling and sanctifying work of God the Holy Spirit.
7  The priesthood of all believers, who form the universal Church, the Body of which Christ is the Head and which

is committed by his command to the proclamation of the gospel throughout the world.

8　The expectation of the personal, visible return of the Lord Jesus Christ in power and glory.

## Appendix 4

# Eight General Resolutions of the British Organization of the World's Evangelical Alliance (1846)

… the Members of the British Organization, fully concurring in the sentiments and recommendations expressed in a series of resolutions agreed upon by the London Conference of the Evangelical Alliance, and exhibited in the 'Abstract of the Proceedings and Final Resolutions', under the title of 'General Resolutions', in the following terms adopt them as their own:

1   That the Members of this Alliance earnestly and affectionately recommend to each other in their own conduct, and particularly in their use of the press, carefully to abstain from and put away all bitterness, and wrath, and anger, and clamour, and evil-speaking, with all malice; and, in all things in which they may yet differ from each other, to be kind, tender-hearted, forbearing one another in love, forgiving one another, even as God, for Christ's sake, hath forgiven them; in everything seeking to be followers of God, as dear children, and to walk in love, as Christ also hath loved them.

2   That, as the Christian Union which this Alliance desires to promote can only be obtained through the blessed energy of the Holy Spirit, it be recommended to the Members present, and absent brethren, to make this matter the subject of simultaneous weekly petition at the throne of grace, in their closets and families; and the forenoon of Monday is suggested as the time for

that purpose. And that it be further recommended, that the week beginning with the first Lord's day of January, in each year, be observed by the members and friends of the Alliance throughout the world, as a season for concert in prayer on behalf of the grand objects contemplated by the Alliance.

3   That, in seeking the correction of what the members of the Alliance believe to be wrong in others, they desire, in humble dependence on the grace of God, themselves to obey, and by their practice and influence to impress upon others, the command of Christ, to consider first the beam that is in their own eye: that they will, therefore, strive to promote each in his own communion, a spirit of repentance and humiliation for its peculiar sins; and to exercise a double measure of forbearance in reproving, where reproof is needful, the faults of those Christian Brethren who belong to other bodies than their own.

4   That, when required by conscience to assert or defend any views or principles wherein they differ from Christian Brethren who agree with them in vital truths; the members of this Alliance will aim earnestly, by the help of the Holy Spirit, to avoid all rash and groundless insinuations, personal imputations, or irritating allusions, and to maintain the meekness and gentleness of Christ, by speaking the truth only in love.

5   That, while they believe it highly desirable that Christians of different bodies, holding the Head, should own each other as Brethren by some such means as the Evangelical Alliance affords, the Members of the Alliance disclaim the thought, that those only who openly join this Society are sincere friends to the cause of Christian Union; that, on the contrary, they regard all those as its true friends who solemnly purpose in their hearts, and fulfil that purpose in their practice, to be more watchful in future against occasions of strife, more tender and charitable towards Christians from whom they differ, and more

constant in prayer for the union of all the true disciples of Christ.

6　That the members of this Alliance would therefore invite, humbly and earnestly, all ministers of the gospel, all conductors of religious publications, and others who have influence in various bodies of Christians, to watch more than ever against sins of the heart, or the tongue, or the pen, towards Christians of other denominations; and to promote more zealously than hitherto a spirit of peace, unity, and godly love, among all true believers in the Lord Jesus Christ.

7　That, since all the disciples of Christ are commanded by the Holy Spirit to add to brotherly kindness, love, and are bound to pray that all who profess and call themselves Christians should be led into the way of truth; it is earnestly recommended to the Members of the Evangelical Alliance, to offer special prayer for all merely nominal Christians, as well as for Jews and Gentiles throughout the world.

8　That the members of this Alliance, earnestly longing for the universal spread of Christ's kingdom, devoutly praise God for the grace whereby, in late years, evangelical Christians have been moved to manifold efforts to make the Saviour known to both Jew and Gentile, and faithful men have been raised up to undertake the toil. They would offer to all evangelical missionaries their most fraternal congratulations and sympathy; would hail the flocks they have been honoured to gather, as welcome and beloved members of the household of God; and above all, would implore the Head of the Church to shield his servants, to edify his rising churches, and by the outpouring of his Holy Spirit, to enlighten Israel with the knowledge of the true Messiah, and to bring the heathen out of darkness into light. They would also record their confident hope, that their beloved missionary brethren will strive more and more to manifest, before the Israelite and other classes who know not the Redeemer, that union in their blessed Lord, the spirit of which, the members of this Alliance would gratefully acknowledge, they have generally cherished.

# Practical Resolutions of the Evangelical Alliance (1996)

Our commitment as Christians should at all times reflect our commitment to Scripture.

The 1846 Assembly which launched the Alliance, as well as agreeing a Basis of Faith, passed eight resolutions to guide members in their relationships with each other and with other Christians.

Given the historic significance of these eight resolutions we have sought to maintain both the spirit and the original sentiments of the guidelines in the hope that members will apply it with modernity to our contemporary problems.

As fellow members of the Evangelical Alliance:

1   We encourage one another in making public comment to place the most charitable construction on the statements made by fellow Christians and particularly those who are members of the Alliance and, where expressions of disagreement are made, to do so with courtesy, humility, and graciousness (Eph. 4:31).
2   We seek to bring the purposes of the Alliance to God in regular prayer and especially during the annual week of prayer.
3   We call on each other, where issues of faith and practice divide us, to take care that when we offer correction that this is done with awareness of our own failings (whether as individuals or churches) and the possibility that we ourselves may be mistaken (Eph. 4:15).

4 We urge each other, at all times when matters of theology are in dispute, to avoid personal hostility and abuse, speaking in truth in love and gentleness (Eph. 4:15).

5 We recognise that not all who seek to know and serve Christ as Saviour and Lord, will wish to be members of the Alliance and that such persons are not, thereby, to be regarded as being out of Christian fellowship.

6 We urge all Christian leaders of trinitarian churches to promote peace, unity and fellowship within the Body of Christ.

7 We wish to encourage all Christians to commit themselves to biblical truth and, to that end, we pray that everyone including those of other or no religions may find in Christ true hope and salvation.

8 We rejoice in the spread of the Christian gospel across the world and thank God for its advance, also acknowledging the tensions which this has sometimes brought, and longing for the completion of Christ's kingdom of peace and justice, to the glory of the one God, Father, Son and Holy Spirit.

*Ephesians 4:3 'Make every effort to keep the unity of the spirit through the bond of peace.'*

# Appendix 6

# The World Evangelical Fellowship Basis of Faith (1951)

A condition of membership is adherence to the following evangelical statement of faith, adopted at the Woudschoten Convention:

1  The Holy Scriptures as originally given by God, divinely inspired, infallible, entirely trustworthy; and their supreme authority in all matters of faith and conduct.
2  One God, eternally existent in three persons, Father, Son and Holy Spirit.
3  Our Lord Jesus Christ, God manifest in the flesh. His virgin birth, his sinless human life, his divine miracles, his vicarious and atoning death, his bodily resurrection, his ascension, his mediatorial work, and his personal return in power and glory.
4  The salvation of lost and sinful men through the shed blood of the Lord Jesus Christ by faith apart from works, and regeneration by the Holy Spirit.
5  The Holy Spirit by whose indwelling the believer is enabled to live a holy life, to witness and work for the Lord Jesus Christ.
6  Unity in the Spirit of all true believers, the Church, the Body of Christ.
7  The resurrection of both the saved and the lost; they that are saved unto the resurrection of life, and they that are lost unto the resurrection of damnation.

# Bibliography

ACUTE, 'What is an Evangelical?' (London: Evangelical Alliance, 1996)

—, *Faith, Hope and Homosexuality* (Carlisle: Paternoster, 1998)

—, *The Nature of Hell* (Carlisle: Paternoster, 2000)

Adams, W., 'Address of Welcome', *Sixth General Conference of the Evangelical Alliance held in New York* (New York: Harper & Brothers, 1874)

Alton, D., 'Preface', in C. Colson & R. J. Neuhaus (eds.), *Evangelicals and Catholics Together: Working Towards a Common Mission* (London: Hodder & Stoughton, 1996), v–viii

Amess R., 'Evangelicals and the Ecumenical Movement' (unpublished M.Phil Thesis, Open University, 1998)

Bacon, E. W., *Spurgeon: Heir of the Puritans – A Biography* (London: Allen & Unwin, 1967)

Baird, H.M., *The Life of the Rev. Robert Baird* (New York: A.D.F. Randolph, 1866)

Baird, R., *Address on the History, Present State, and Prospects, of the Evangelical Alliance cause in the United States* (London, 1851)

Baker, F., *John Wesley and the Church of England* (London: Epworth, 1970)

Baptist Union of Great Britain, 'A Response to the Papal Encyclical *Ut Unum Sint* from the Faith and Unity Executive Committee of the Baptist Union of Great Britain', April 1997

Barclay, O., *Evangelicalism in Britain, 1935-1995: A Personal Sketch* (Leicester: IVP, 1997)

Bauckham, R.J., 'Universalism: A Historical Survey', *Themelios* 4.2 (January 1979), pp.48–54.

Bebbington, D.W., 'The Life of Baptist Noel', *Baptist Quarterly* 24 (1972), pp.389–411

—, 'The Persecution of George Jackson', in W.J. Sheils (ed.), *Persecution and Toleration* (Studies in Church History, Vol. 21; Oxford: Basil Blackwell, 1984)

—, 'The Advent Hope in British Evangelicalism since 1800', *Scottish Journal of Religious Studies*, 9.2 (1988), pp.103-14

—, *Evangelicalism in Modern Britain: A History from the 1730s to the 1980s* (London: Unwin Hyman, 1989)

—, 'Baptists and Fundamentalism in Inter-War Britain', in K. Robbins (ed.), *Protestant Evangelicalism: Britain, Ireland, Germany and America, c. 1750–c. 1950, Studies in Church History* (Subsidia 7; Oxford: Basil Blackwell, 1990), pp.316-20

—, 'Missionary Controversy and the Polarising Tendency in Twentieth-Century British Protestantism', *Anvil* 13.2 (1996), pp.141-57

—, *'Evangelism and Spirituality in Twentieth-Century Protestantism'* (unpublished paper, 2000)

—, *Holiness in Nineteenth-Century England* (Carlisle: Paternoster Press, 2000)

—, 'Evangelism and Spirituality in Twentieth-Century Protestant Nonconformity' (forthcoming)

Bennett, J., *Memoirs of the Life of the Revd David Bogue DD* (London, 1827)

Best, G., 'Evangelicalism and the Victorians', in A. Symondson (ed.), *The Victorian Crisis of Faith* (London: SPCK, 1970)

Bickersteth, E., *A Scripture Help, Designed to Assist in Reading the Bible Profitably* (17th edn; London, 1838)

—, *The Promised Glory of the Church of Christ* (London, 1844)

Binfield, C., *George Williams and the YMCA: A Study in Victorian Social Attitudes* (London: Heinemann, 1973)

Birks, T.R., *Memoir of the Rev. Edward Bickersteth* (2 Vols., London: Seeleys, 1850)

—, *The Victory of Divine Goodness* (London: Rivingtons, 1867)

—, 'The Rev. T.R. Birks to Rev. Dr. Blackwood', *Evangelical Christendom*, 1 March 1870, p.69

—, *Supernatural Revelation* (London 1879)

Blanchard, J., *Whatever Happened to Hell?* (Darlington: Evangelical Press, 1993)

Bloesch, D., *The Future of Evangelical Christianity: A Call for Unity Amid Diversity* (New York: Doubleday, 1983)

Bochenski, M.I. (ed.), *Evangelicals and Ecumenism: When Baptists Disagree* (Didcot: Baptist Union, 1993)

Bonnington, M., 'The Bible and Christian Organisations', A Report Presented to the Bible Society Comprising the Results of the Salt and Light Research Project, January 1997, summarised by Roy McCloughry, October, 1999

Bordeaux, M., *Protestant Opposition to Soviet Religious Policy* (Basingstoke: Macmillan, 1968)

—, *Gorbachev, Glasnost and the Gospel* (London: Hodder & Stoughton, 1990)

Bradley, I., *The Call to Seriousness* (London: Jonathan Cape, 1976)

Brady S. & H. Rowdon (ed.), *For Such a Time as This: Perspectives on Evangelicalism Past, Present and Future* (London/Milton Keynes: Evangelical Alliance/Scripture Union, 1996), pp.1–22

Bray, G., *Biblical Interpretation Past and Present* (Leicester: Apollos, 1996)

Brierley P. (ed.), *UK Christian Handbook: Religious Trends 2000-2001, No. 2* (Eltham/London: Christian Research/Harper Collins, 1999)

—, *Religious Trends 2000/2001 No.2* (London: Christian Research/Harper Collins, 1999)

Brierley, P., *The Tide is Running Out* (Eltham/London: Christian Research/Harper Collins, 2000)

Briggs, J.H.Y., *The English Baptists of the Nineteenth Century* (Didcot: The Baptist Historical Society, 1994)

—, 'F.A. Cox of Hackney: Nineteenth-Century Baptist Theologian, Historian, Controversialist and Apologist', *The Baptist Quarterly* 38.8 (2000), pp.392–411

Bromham, R., 'A More Charitable Christian Eschatology: Attempts from the Victorian Era to the Present Day to Mitigate the Problem of Eternal Punishment, with Particular Attention to the Teaching of T.R. Birks and Its Influence' (M.Phil., University of Wales, 2000)

Brown, C.G., *The Social History of Religion in Scotland since 1730* (London: Methuen, 1987)

—, *The Death of Christian Britain* (London: Routledge, 2001)

Buchanan, C.O., E.L. Mascall, J.I. Packer, & The Bishop of Willesden, *Growing into Union: Proposals for Forming a United Church in England* (London, SPCK, 1970)

—, *Is the Church of England Biblical?* (London: Darton, Longman & Todd, 1998)

Calver, C., 'The Jerusalem Paper', Evangelical Alliance archive, London, dated 28 November 1992

—, 'The Rise and Fall of the Evangelical Alliance, 1835-1905', in S. Brady & H. Rowdon (eds), *For Such a Time as This: Perspectives on*

*Evangelicalism, Past, Present and Future* (London/Milton Keynes: Evangelical Alliance/Scripture Union, 1996), pp.148-62

Cameron, N.M. de S. (ed.), *Universalism and the Doctrine of Hell* (Carlisle: Paternoster Press, 1992)

Campbell, R.J., *The New Theology* (London: Chapman & Hall, 1907)

Carlyle G. (ed), *Proceedings of the Geneva Conference of the Evangelical Alliance* (London: Hamilton, Adams & Co, 1862)

Carson, D.A., *The Gagging of God: Christianity Confronts Pluralism* (Leicester: Apollos, 1996)

Carwardine, R., *Transatlantic Revivalism: Popular Evangelicalism in Britain and America, 1790-1865* (Westport: Greenwoood, 1978)

Catherwood, F., *At the Cutting Edge* (London: Hodder & Stoughton, 1995)

Centre for Contemporary Ministry, *Charismatic Crossroads* (Bawtry: PWM Team Ministries, 1995)

Chadwick, O., *The Victorian Church*, Part 1 (London: A. & C. Black, 1966)

Chalmers, T., *On the Evangelical Alliance; its Design, its Difficulties, its Proceedings and its Prospects: with Practical Suggestions* (Edinburgh, 1846)

Chalmers, T., Balmer, R., Candlish, R.S., James, J.A., King, D., Wardlaw, R., Struthers, G. and Symington, A., *Essays on Christian Union* (London: Hamilton, Adams & Co., 1845)

Chester, T., *Awakening to a World of Need* (Leicester: Inter-Varsity Press, 1993)

Chevreau, G., *Catch the Fire* (London: Marshall Pickering, 1994)

Christian Research Association, *Prospects for the Nineties* (London, 1991)

'Christian Union', *The Eclectic Review,* June 1845

Clements, K.W., *Lovers of Discord: Twentieth-Century Theological Controversies in England* (London: SPCK, 1988)

—, *Faith on the Frontier: A Life of J. H. Oldham* (Edinburgh/Geneva: T. & T. Clark/WCC Publications, 1999)

Colquhoun, F., *Harringay Story* (London: Hodder & Stoughton, 1955)

Community Religions Research Project, *A Report on Afro-Caribbean Christianity in Britain* (Leeds: Community Religions Project Research Papers, No. 4, 1987)

Cosner, W.H., *Church and Confession: Conservative Theologians in Germany, England and America, 1815-1866* (Macon: Mercer University Press, 1984)

Cox, J., *The English Churches in a Secular Society: Lambeth, 1870-1930* (New York: Oxford University Press, 1977)

Currie, R., A.D. Gilbert & L. Horsley, *Churches and Churchgoers: Patterns of Church Growth in the British Isles since 1700* (Oxford: Clarendon Press, 1977)

Dale, R.W., *The Life and Letters of J.A. James* (London, 1861)

Densil Morgan, D., *The Span of the Cross: Christian Religion and Society in Wales, 1914-2000* (Cardiff: University of Wales Press, 1999)

Dixon, P., *Signs of Revival* (Eastbourne: Kingsway, 1994)

Drummond, L., *Spurgeon: Prince of Preachers* (Grand Rapids: Kregel, 1992)

Dudley-Smith, T., *John Stott: The Making of a Leader* (Leicester: Inter-Varsity Press, 1999)

'EA Member Churches: 1998 Opinion Survey', Question 11, p. 7 (London: Evangelical Alliance, 1998)

Eden, M., 'EA: The Next Chapter: Building a Movement for Change', Internal Alliance Paper, 10 August 1998

Edwards, Joel, *Lord, Make us One – But Not All the Same!* (London, Hodder & Stoughton, 1999)

—, *Cradle, Cross and Empty Tomb: A Faith We Can Be Proud to Proclaim* (London: Hodder & Stoughton, 2000)

Edwards, Jonathan, *The Religious Affections* (1746) (Edinburgh: Banner of Truth Trust, 1961)

—, *The Distinguishing Marks of the Spirit of God* (1741), in J. Edwards, *Jonathan Edwards on Revival* (Edinburgh: Banner of Truth Trust, 1965)

Ellis, C.J., *Together on the Way: A Theology of Ecumenism* (London: British Council of Churches, 1990)

Ellis, E., 'New Testament Teaching on Hell', in K.E. Brower & M.W. Elliott (eds), *The Reader Must Understand: Eschatology in Bible and Theology* (Leicester: Apollos, 1997), pp.199-219

Evangelical Alliance, *Conference on Christian Union; Being a Narrative of the Proceedings of the Meeting held in Liverpool, October 1845* (London, 1845)

—, *Report of the Proceedings of the Conference Held at Freemasons' Hall, London, 1846* (London, 1847)

—, *Conference on Missions Held in 1860 at Liverpool* (London: James Nisbet & Co., 1860)

—, Proceedings of the Amsterdam Conference of the Evangelical Alliance (London, 1868)

—, *Deputation to the American Branch of the Evangelical Alliance* (London, 1870)

—, *History, Essays, Orations and other documents of the Sixth General Conference of the Evangelical Alliance held in New York, October 2-12 1873* (New York, 1874)

—, *The Jubilee of the Evangelical Alliance* (London, 1896)

—, *Maintaining the Unity: Report of the Eleventh International Conference of the Evangelical Alliance* (London, 1907)

—, *Report of the Commission on Church Unity to the National Assembly of Evangelicals* (London, 1966)

—, *Unity in Diversity: Evangelicals, the Church and the World* (London: Evangelical Alliance, 1967)

—, *On the Other Side: The Report of the Evangelical Alliance's Commission on Evangelism* (London: Scripture Union, 1968)

—, *Surveying the Roots of Social Breakdown* (London: Evangelical Alliance, 1997)

—, *EA Member Churches: The 1998 Opinion Survey* (London: The Evangelical Alliance, 1998)

Evangelical Alliance Policy Commission, *Transsexuality* (Carlisle: Paternoster Press, 2000)

Ewing, J.W., *Goodly Fellowship: A Centenary Tribute to the Life and Work of the World's Evangelical Alliance* (London/Edinburgh: Marshall, Morgan & Scott, 1946)

Fearon, M., *A Breath of Fresh Air* (Guildford: Eagle, 1984)

Fernando, A., *Crucial Questions About Hell* (Eastbourne: Kingsway, 1991)

Finlayson, G.B.A.M., *The Seventh Earl of Shaftesbury, 1801-1885* (London: Eyre Methuen, 1981)

Fletcher, C., 'Hell in the New Testament and Church History' (unpublished M.Phil., University of Sheffield, 1997)

Francis, L.J., M. Robbins & W.K. Kay, 'Pastoral Care: Practice, Problems and Priorities in Churches Today: An Interim Report from the Major Survey Conducted for CWR and the Evangelical Alliance by the Centre for Ministry Studies, University of Wales, Bangor' (Presented to Evangelical Alliance Council, September 2000)

Fudge, E.W., *The Fire that Consumes: The Biblical Case for Conditional Immortality* (Carlisle: Paternoster, 1992 [1984])

Fuller, W.H., *People of the Mandate: The Story of the World Evangelical Fellowship* (WEF; Grand Rapids/Carlisle: Baker Book House/Paternoster Press, 1996)

Gibson, A., *Holding Hands in the Dark* (St Albans, 1988)

Gilley, S. & W.J. Sheils (eds), *A History of Religion in Britain* (Oxford: Blackwell, 1994)

Gilley, S., *Newman and his Age* (London: Darton, Longman & Todd, 1996)

Gledhill, R., 'Spread of Hysteria Fad Worries Church', *The Times*, 18 June 1994

Gooch, H.M., *William Fuller Gooch: A tribute and testimony* (London: World's Evangelical Alliance, 1929)

Goodall, N., *The Ecumenical Movement* (London: Oxford University Press, 1964)

Grady, J.L., 'Classical Pentecostals Wary of the 'Toronto Blessing', *Charisma* (November 1995), pp.41–2

Graham, B., *The Work of an Evangelist* (World's Evangelical Alliance: London, 1953)

Graham, S.R., *Cosmos in the Chaos: Philip Schaff's Interpretation of Nineteenth-Century American Religion* (Grand Rapids: Eerdmans, 1995)

Grant, R.M. & D. Tracy, *A Short History of the Interpretation of the Bible* (London: SCM, 1984)

Green, M., *Evangelism Through the Local Church* (London: Hodder & Stoughton, 1990)

Guinness, O., *Fit Bodies: Fat Minds: Why Evangelicals Don't Think and What to Do About It* (London: Hodder & Stoughton, 1995)

Hancock, C.D., 'Birks, Thomas Rawson', in D.M. Lewis (ed.), *Dictionary of Evangelical Biography*, Vol.1 (Oxford: Blackwell, 1995), pp.101–110

Harrison, J.F.C., *The Second Coming: Popular Millenarianism, 1780-1850* (London: Routledge, 1979)

Hastings, A., *A History of English Christianity, 1920-2000* (London: SCM, 2001)

Heasman, K., *Evangelicals in Action* (London: Geoffrey Bles, 1961)

Hennell, M., *Sons of the Prophets* (London: SPCK, 1979)

Hilborn, D., *Picking Up the Pieces: Can Evangelicals Adapt to Contemporary Culture?* (London: Hodder & Stoughton, 1997)

Hilborn, D. (ed.), *Toronto in Perspective: Papers on the New Charismatic Wave of the Mid-1990s* (Carlisle: Paternoster Press, 2001)

Hocken, P., *Streams of Renewal: The Origins and Early Development of the Charismatic Movement in Great Britain* (rev'd edn; Carlisle: Paternoster Press, 1997 [1986])

Hogg, W.R., *Ecumenical Foundations* (New York, Harper & Brothers, 1952)

Hopkins, C.H., *John R Mott, 1865-1955: A Biography* (Grand Rapids: Eerdmans, 1979)

Hopkins, M.T.E., 'Spurgeon's Opponents in the Downgrade Controversy', *The Baptist Quarterly*, Vol. 32, April 1988, No. 6, pp.274-94

Howard, D.M., *The Dream That Would Not Die: The Birth and Growth of the World Evangelical Fellowship, 1846-96* (Wheaton/Exeter: World Evangelical Fellowship/Paternoster Press, 1986)

Hylson-Smith, K., *Evangelicals in the Church of England* (Edinburgh: T. & T. Clark, 1988)

—, *High Churchmanship in the Church of England* (Edinburgh: T. & T. Clark, 1993)

—, 'Roots of Pan-Evangelicalism, 1735-1835', in S. Brady & H. Rowdon (eds), *For Such a Time as This: Perspectives on Evangelicalism, Past, Present and Future* (London/Milton Keynes: Evangelical Alliance/Scripture Union, 1996), pp.137-47

Interserve/Middle East Media, *Turning Over a New Leaf: Protestant Missions and the Orthodox Churches of the Middle East* (London, Lynnwood, 1992)

Jasper, R.C.D., *George Bell: Bishop of Chichester* (London: Oxford University Press, 1967)

Jeremy, D.J., 'Businessmen in Interdenominational Activity: Birmingham Youth for Christ, 1940s-1950s, *The Baptist Quarterly* 33.7 (1990), pp.336-43

—, *Capitalists and Christians: Business Leaders and the Churches in Britain, 1900-1960* (Oxford: Clarendon, 1990)

Johnson, J. (ed.), *Report of the Centenary Conference on the Protestant Missions of the World, held in Exeter Hall (June 9th-19th), London, 1888* (2 Vols.; London: James Nisbet & Co., 1888)

Jones, B.P., *The King's Champions* (Cwmbran, Gwent: Christian Literature Press, 1986)

—, *An Instrument of Revival: The Complete Life of Evan Roberts* (South Plainfield: Bridge Publishing, 1995)

Jones, H.R., 'The Doctor and the British Evangelical Council', in H.R. Jones (ed.), *D. Martyn Lloyd-Jones: Unity in Truth* (Darlington: Evangelical Press, 1991), pp.7-19

Jordan, E.K.H., *Free Church Unity: History of the Free Church Council Movement, 1896-1941* (London: Lutterworth Press, 1956)

Jordan, P.D., *The Evangelical Alliance for the United States of America, 1847-1900: Ecumenism, Identity and the Religion of the Republic* (New York & Toronto: Edwin Mullen, 1982)

Kay, W.K., *Pentecostals in Britain* (Carlisle: Paternoster Press, 2000)

Kaye, E., *Mansfield College, Oxford: Its Origin, History and Significance* (Oxford: Oxford University Press, 1996)

Kent, J., *The Age of Disunity* (London: Epworth Press, 1966)

—, *Holding the Fort: Studies in Victorian Revivalism* (London: Epworth Press, 1978)

Kessler, J.B.A., *A Study of the Evangelical Alliance in Great Britain* (Goes, Netherlands: Oosterbaan & Le Cointre, 1968)

King D. (ed.), *Essays on Christian Union* (London 1845)

Kirby, G.W., 'The Post-War Years', *The Evangelical Alliance Broadsheet*, Summer 1962, pp.1-3

—, 'In All Things – Charity', *The Evangelical Alliance Broadsheet*, Winter 1963, p.2

Kruppa, P.S., *Charles Haddon Spurgeon: A Preacher's Progress* (New York: Garland, 1982)

Larsen, T., *Friends of Religious Equality: Nonconformist Politics in Mid-Victorian England* (Woodbridge: The Boydell Press, 1999)

Lawrence, J., *The Hard Facts of Unity: A Layman Looks at the Ecumenical Movement* (Naperville: SCM Book Club, 1961)

Lewis, D.M., *Lighten Their Darkness: The Evangelical Mission to Working-Class London, 1828-1860* (Carlisle: Paternoster Press, 2001)

Lewis, P., 'Renewal, Recovery and Growth: 1966 Onwards', in S. Brady & H. Rowdon (eds), *For Such a Time as This: Perspectives on Evangelicalism, Past, Present and Future* (London/Milton Keynes: Evangelical Alliance/Scripture Union, 1996), pp.178-91

Little, D., 'Reformed Faith and Religious Liberty', *Church and Society* (May/June 1986, pp.6-28

Livingstone, D.N., *Darwin's Forgotten Defenders: The Encounter Between Evangelical Theology and Evolutionary Thought* (Grand Rapids/Edinburgh: Eerdmans/Scottish Academic Press, 1987)

—, *Evangelicals and Science in Historical Perspective* (Oxford: Oxford University Press, 1999)

Lovett, R., *The History of the London Missionary Society, 1795-1895* (2 Vols; London: Henry Frowde, 1899)

MacConnachie, J., *The Significance of Karl Barth* (London: Hodder & Stoughton, 1931)

—, *The Barthian Theology* (London: Hodder & Stoughton, 1933)

MacDonald, H.D., *Theories of Revelation* (London: George Allen & Unwin, 1963)

Machin, G.I.T., *Politics and the Churches in Great Britain, 1832-1868* (Oxford: The Clarendon Press, 1977)

—, 'Reservation under Pressure: Ritual in the Prayer Book Crisis', in R.N. Swanson (ed.), *Continuity and Change in Christian Worship* (Studies in Church History, Vol. 35; Woodbridge, Suffolk: Boydell & Brewer, 1999), pp.447-52

Mackintosh, W.H., *Disestablishment and Liberation* (London: Epworth, 1972)

Marsden, G.M., 'Fundamentalism as an American Phenomenon: A Comparison with English Evangelicalism, *Church History* 46.2 (1977), pp.215-32

—, *Fundamentalism and American Culture: The Shaping of Twentieth-Century Evangelicalism, 1870-1925* (New York: Oxford University Press, 1980)

Martin, R.H., *Evangelicals United: Ecumenical Stirrings in Pre-Victorian Britain, 1795-1830* (Metuchen & London: The Scarecrow Press, 1983)

Martin, W., *The Billy Graham Story: A Prophet with Honour* (London: Hutchinson, 1992)

Marty, M., *Modern American Religion: The Noise of Conflict, 1919-1941* (Chicago: University of Chicago Press, 1991)

Massie, J.W., *The Evangelical Alliance: its Origin and Development* (London, 1847)

Maurice, F.D., *Theological Essays* (Cambridge/London, 1853)

McBain, D., *Charismatic Christianity* (Basingstoke: Macmillan, 1997)

—, *Fire Over the Waters: Renewal among the Baptists and Others from the 1960s to the 1990s* (London: Darton, Longman & Todd, 1997)

McCosh, J., *Christianity and Positivism: A Series of Lectures to the Times on Natural Theology and Christian Apologetics* (London: Macmillan, 1871)

—, 'Religious Aspects of the Doctrine of Development', in P. Schaff & S. Irenaeus Prime (ed.), *History, Essays, Orations and Other Documents of the Sixth General Conference of the Evangelical Alliance* (New York: Harper & Brothers, 1874), pp.264-71

—, *The Religious Aspect of Evolution* (New York: Scribner's, 1890)

Mews, S., 'Spiritual Mobilization in the First World War', *Theology* (June 1971), pp.258-64

—, 'The Sword of the Spirit: A Catholic Cultural Crusade of 1940', in W. J. Sheils (ed.), *The Church and War* (Studies in Church History, Vol 20 Oxford: Basil Blackwell, 1983), pp.409-30

Moberg, D., *The Great Reversal: Evangelism versus Social Concern* (London: Scripture Union, 1973)

Monod, A., 'Intervention of the Evangelical Alliance on Behalf of Persecuted Brethren', *Evangelical Christendom,* Vol. V (1851)

Moore, J.R., *The Post-Darwinian Controversies* (Cambridge, 1979)

Morrison, A., *We All Fall Down* (Crich: Diakrisis, 1994)

Mumford, E., 'Spreading Like Wildfire', in W. Boulton (ed.), *The Impact of Toronto* (Crowborough: Monarch, 1995), pp.17-9

Murray, I.H., *The Forgotten Spurgeon* (Edinburgh: Banner of Truth Trust, 1973)

—, *D. Martyn Lloyd-Jones: The Fight of Faith, 1939-1981* (Edinburgh: Banner of Truth Trust, 1990)

—, *Revival and Revivalism, the Making and Marring of American Evangelicalism, 1750-1858* (Edinburgh: Banner of Truth Trust, 1994)

—, *Evangelicalism Divided: A Record of Crucial Change in the Years 1950 to 2000* (Edinburgh: Banner of Truth Trust, 2000)

National Anglican Evangelical Congress, *Keele '67, The National Evangelical Anglican Congress Statement* (London 1967)

Newsome, D., *The Parting of Friends* (London: John Murray, 1966)

Nicholls, M., *C.H. Spurgeon: The Pastor Evangelist* (Didcot: Baptist Historical Society, 1992)

Nockles, P.B., *The Oxford Movement in Context: Anglican High Churchmanship, 1760-1857* (Oxford: Clarendon Press, 1994)

Noel, B.W., *The Unity of the Church, Another Tract for the Times, Addressed Particularly to Members of the Establishment* (London, 1837)

Norman, E.R., *Anti-Catholicism in Victorian England* (London: George Allen & Unwin, 1968)

Oropeza, W.J., *A Time to Laugh: The Holy Laughter Phenomenon Examined* (Peabody: Hendrickson, 1995)

Orr, E., *The Second Evangelical Awakening* (London & Edinburgh: Marshall, Morgan & Scott, 1955)

Packer, J.I., *The Problem of Eternal Punishment* (Disley: Orthos, 1990)

Palmer, D., *Strangers No Longer* (London: Hodder & Stoughton, 1990)

Pawson, D., *The Road to Hell* (London: Hodder & Stoughton, 1992)

Payne, E., *The Baptist Union: A Short History* (London: Baptist Union, 1958)

Peterson, R.A., *Hell on Trial: The Case for Eternal Punishment* (Phillipsburg: P&R Publishing, 1995)

—, 'Undying Worm; Unquenchable Fire', *Christianity Today*, 23 October 2000, pp.30-37

Pickering, W.S.F., *Anglo-Catholicism* (London: Routledge, 1989)

Pietersen L. (ed.), *Mark of the Spirit? A Charismatic Critique of the Toronto Blessing* (Carlisle: Paternoster Press, 1998)

Pinnock C.H. & R.C. Brow, *Unbounded Love: A Good News Theology for the 21st Century* (Carlisle: Paternoster Press, 1994)

Podmore, C.J., *The Moravian Church in England, 1728-1760* (Oxford: Clarendon Press, 1998)

Pollock, J.C., *The Keswick Story* (London: Hodder & Stoughton, 1964)

Powys, D., 'The Nineteenth and Twentieth Century Debates about Hell and Universalism', in N.M. de S. Cameron (ed.), *Universalism and the Doctrine of Hell* (Carlisle: Paternoster Press, 1992), pp.93-138

Price C. & I. M. Randall, *Transforming Keswick* (Carlisle: OM, 2000)

Rack, H.D., *Reasonable Enthusiast: John Wesley and the Rise of Methodism* (London: Epworth, 1989)

Rae, J., *Conscience and Politics* (London: Oxford University Press, 1970)

Railton, N.M., *No North Sea: The Anglo-German Evangelical Network in the Middle of the Nineteenth Century* (Leiden: Brill, 2000)

Ramm, B., *The Evangelical Heritage: A Study in Historical Theology* (Grand Rapids: Baker Book House, 1981 [1973])

Randall, I.M., 'Mere Denominationalism: F. B. Meyer and Baptist Life', *The Baptist Quarterly* 35.1 (1993), pp.19-34

—, 'Incarnating the Gospel: Melbourne Hall, Leicester, in the 1880s as a model for holistic ministry', *The Baptist Quarterly* 35.8 (1994), pp.394-5

—, *Quest, Crusade and Fellowship: The Spiritual Formation of the Fellowship of the Kingdom* (Horsham: Fellowship of the Kingdom, 1995)

—, 'Southport and Swanwick: Contrasting Movements of Methodist Spirituality in Inter-War England', *Proceedings of the Wesley Historical Society* 50, Part 1 (1995)

—, 'Schism and Unity: 1905-1966', in S. Brady & H. Rowdon (ed.), *For Such a Time as This: Perspectives on Evangelicalism, Past, Present and Future* (London/Milton Keynes: Evangelical Alliance/Scripture Union, 1996), pp.163-77

—, 'The Role of Conscientious Objectors: British Evangelicals and the First World War', *Anabaptism Today*, Issue 11 (1996)

—, 'Capturing Keswick', *The Baptist Quarterly* 36.7 (1996), pp.331-48

—, '"We All Need Constant Change": The Oxford Group and Mission in Europe in the 1930s', *European Journal of Theology* 9.2 (2000), pp.171-85

—, *Evangelical Experiences: A Study in the Spirituality of English Evangelicalism, 1918-1939* (Carlisle: Paternoster Press, 1999)

—, *Educating Evangelicalism: The Origins, Development and Impact of London Bible College* (Carlisle: Paternoster Press, 2000)

Reardon, B., *Religion in the Age of Romanticism* (Cambridge: Cambridge University Press, 1985)

Robbins, K., 'The Spiritual Pilgrimage of the Rev. R. J. Campbell', *Journal of Ecclesiastical History*, Vol. 30, No. 2 (1979)

Roberts, D., *The 'Toronto' Blessing* (Eastbourne: Kingsway, 1994)

Robertson, M., 'A Power Encounter Worth Laughing About', in K. Springer (ed.), *Power Encounters Among Christians in the Western World* (San Fransisco: Harper & Row, 1988), pp.149-57

Rogers, J., 'John Scopes and the Debate over Evolution', in R.C. White, L. Weeks & G. Rosell, *American Christianity: A Case Approach* (Grand Rapids: Eerdmans, 1986)

Roseveare, H., *On Track: The Story of the Girl Crusaders' Union* (St Albans: Girl Crusaders' Union, 1990)

Rouse R. & S.C. Neill (eds), *A History of the Ecumenical Movement 1517-1948* (2nd edn; London: SPCK, 1967 [1954])

Rowell, G., *Hell and The Victorians* (Oxford: Clarendon Press, 1974)

Rowlandson, M., *Life with Billy: An Autobiography* (London: Hodder & Stoughton, 1992)

Sandeen, E.R., *The Roots of Fundamentalism: British and American Millenarianism, 1800-1930* (Chicago: University Press of Chicago, 1970)

—, 'The Distinctiveness of American Denominationalism: A Case Study of the 1846 Evangelical Alliance', *Church History* 45.2 (1976), pp.222-34

Saward, M., *The Anglican Church Today: Evangelicals on the Move* (Oxford: Mowbray, 1987)

Schaff P. & S.I. Prime (eds), *History, Essays, Orations and Other Documents of the Sixth General Conference of the Evangelical Alliance* (New York: Harper Row, 1874)

Schmucker, S.S., *Fraternal Appeal to the American Churches* (1838)

Scorgie, G.C., *A Call for Continuity: The Theological Contribution of James Orr* (Macon: Mercer University Press, 1988)

Scotland, N., *John Bird Sumner: Evangelical Archbishop* (Leominster: Gracewing, 1995)

—, *Charismatics and the New Millennium* (2nd edn; Guildford: Eagle, 2000)

Sell, A.P.F., *Defending and Declaring the Faith: Some Scottish Examples, 1860-1920* (Exeter: Paternoster Press, 1987)

Shea, G.B., *Then Sings My Soul* (Old Tappan/London: Hodder & Stoughton, 1968)

Slack, K., *Despatch from New Delhi: The Story of the World Council of Churches, Third Assembly, New Delhi, 18 Nov.–5 Dec. 1961* (London: SCM Press, 1962)

Smith, A.E., *Another Anglican Angle: The History of the AEGM* (Oxford: Amate, 1991)

Smith, R.P., 'Christian Union Consistent with Denominational Distinctives', *Sixth General Conference of the Evangelical Alliance held in New York* (London: Harper & Brothers, 1874), pp.145–9

Smith, T.L., *Revivalism and Social Reform: American Protestants on the Eve of the Civil War* (New York: Harper & Row, 1965)

Stanley, B. *The History of the Baptist Missionary Society, 1792-1992* (Edinburgh: T. & T. Clark, 1992)

Steane, E. (ed.), *The Religious Condition of Christendom: A Series of Papers Read at the fifth annual Conference Held at Freemasons' Hall, London August 20th to September 3rd 1851* (London: James Nisbet & Co., 1852)

—, *The Religious Condition of Christendom: The Conference Held in Berlin, 1857* (London, 1857)

Stott J. & D.L. Edwards, *Essentials: A Liberal-Evangelical Dialogue* (London: Hodder & Stoughton, 1988)

Stott, J. (ed.), *Making Christ Known: Historic Mission Documents from the Lausanne Movement, 1974-1989* (Carlisle: Paternoster Press, 1996)

Stout, H.S., *The Divine Dramatist: George Whitefield and the Rise of Modern Evangelicalism* (Grand Rapids: Eerdmans, 1991)

Stunt, T.C.F, *From Awakening to Secession* (Edinburgh: T. & T. Clark, 2000)

Symondson, A. (ed.), *The Victorian Crisis of Faith* (London: SPCK, 1970)

Thomas, G., 'Then and Now: 1966–1996', *Foundations* (1996), pp.30–34.

Thompson, D.M., 'The Liberation Society, 1844-1868', in P. Hollis (ed.), *Pressure from Without* (London: Edward Arnold, 1974)

Thomson, A. 'On the Extent to Which Religious Liberty is Enjoyed by Protestants or Denied to Them in Foreign Countries', *Evangelical Christendom*, Vol. V, 1851

*Thy Word is Truth: A Report of the Meetings for the Testimony to the Integrity of God's Word, Held in King's Hall, Holborn* (London, 1906)

Tidball, D., *Who Are the Evangelicals?* (London: Marshall Pickering, 1994)

Tillin, T., *Looking Beyond Toronto: The Source and Goal of Pentecost* (Banner Ministries, 1994)

Trevor, M., *Newman: The Pillar of Cloud* (London: Macmillan, 1962)

Vasey, M., *Strangers and Friends: A New Exploration of Homosexuality and the Bible* (London: Hodder & Stoughton, 1995)

Venn, H., 'The Fifteen Articles of the Countess of Huntingdon's Connexion', in E. Welch (ed.), *Two Calvinistic Methodist Chapels, 1743-1811* (Leicester: London Record Society, 1975)

—, *The Complete Duty of Man* (3rd edn; London, 1779)

Virgo, T., *A People Prepared* (Eastbourne: Kingsway, 1996)

Wagner, P.C., 'Third Wave', in S.M. Burgess, G.B. McGee & P.H. Alexander (eds), *Dictionary of Pentecostal and Charismatic Movements* (Grand Rapids: Zondervan, 1988), pp.843-4

Walker, A., *Restoring the Kingdom: The Radical Christianity of the House Church Movement* (Guildford: Eagle, 1998)

Ward, W.R., *Religion and Society in England* (London: Batsford, 1972)

Warner, R., *Prepare for Revival* (London: Hodder & Stoughton, 1995)

Watford, J., *Yesterday and Today: A History of Crusaders* (St Albans: Crusaders' Union, 1995)

Watts, M., *The Dissenters: Volume II: The Expansion of Evangelical Nonconformity, 1791-1859* (Oxford: Clarendon Press, 1995)

Weber, T.P., *Living in the Shadow of the Second Coming: American Premillennialism, 1875-1982* (Chicago: University of Chicago Press, 1987)

Welch E. (ed.), *Two Calvinistic Methodist Chapels, 1743-1811* (Leicester: London Record Society, 1975)

Wells, D.F., *God in the Wasteland: The Reality of Truth in a World of Fading Dreams.* (Leicester: IVP, 1994)

Wenham, J.W., *The Goodness of God* (Leicester: IVP, 1974). Later reprinted as *The Enigma of Evil,* 1985

—, 'The Case for Conditional Immortality', in N.M. de S. Cameron (ed.), *Universalism and the Doctrine of Hell* (Carlisle: Paternoster Press, 1992), pp.161-91

—, *Facing Hell: An Autobiography 1913-1996* (Carlisle: Paternoster Press, 1998)

Wigley, J., *The Rise and Fall of the Victorian Sunday* (Manchester: Manchester University Press, 1980)

Wilkinson, A., *Dissent or Conform?: War, Peace and the English Churches, 1900-1945* (London: SCM Press, 1986)

—, *The Church of England and the First World War* (London: SCM Press, 1996)

Wolffe, J., 'The Evangelical Alliance in the 1840s: An attempt to institutionalise Christian Unity', in W. Sheils & D. Wood (eds), *Voluntary Religion* (Studies in Church History, Vol. 23; Oxford: Blackwell, 1986), pp.333-46

—, *The Protestant Crusade in Britain, 1829-1860* (Oxford: Clarendon Press, 1991)

—, *God and Greater Britain: Religion and National Life in Britain and Ireland 1843-1945* (London: Routledge, 1994)

Wolffe, J. (ed.), *Evangelical Faith and Public Zeal: Evangelicals and Society in Britain, 1780-1980* (London: SPCK, 1995)

Wolffe, J., 'Unity in Diversity? North Atlantic Evangelical Thought in the mid-nineteenth century', in R.N. Swansson (ed.), *Unity in Diversity in the Church: Studies in Church History*, 32 (1996), (Oxford: Blackwell/ EHS, pp. 363–75).

Wood, F.P. & M.S. Wood, *Youth Advancing* (London: National Young Life Campaign, 1961)

Wright, N., *The Radical Evangelical: Seeking a Place to Stand* (London: SPCK, 1996)

Wright, R.C., 'The German Protestant Church and the Nazi Party in the Period of the Seizure of Power, 1932-3', in D. Baker (ed.), *Renaissance and Renewal in Christian History* (Studies in Church History, Vol. 14; Oxford: Blackwell, 1977), pp.393-418

# KEY PERIODICALS AND NEWSPAPERS

*Alpha*
*The Baptist Magazine*
*The Baptist Times*
*The Baptist Quarterly*
*The British Weekly*
*The Christian*
*Christian Century*
*Christianity*
*Christianity Today*
*The Christian Witness*
*The Christian World*
*Church Family Newspaper*
*Church History*
*Church Times*
*Crusade*
*Daily Telegraph*

*Decision*
*Evangelical Alliance Quarterly*
*Evangelical Broadsheet*
*Evangelical Christendom*
*The Evangelical Magazine*
*Evangelical Times*
*Journal of the Wesley Bible Union*
*Joy*
*Joyful News*
*The Life of Faith*
*The Nonconformist*
*The Record*
*Restoration*
*The Sword and the Trowel*
*The Times*
*Western Mail*

# Index